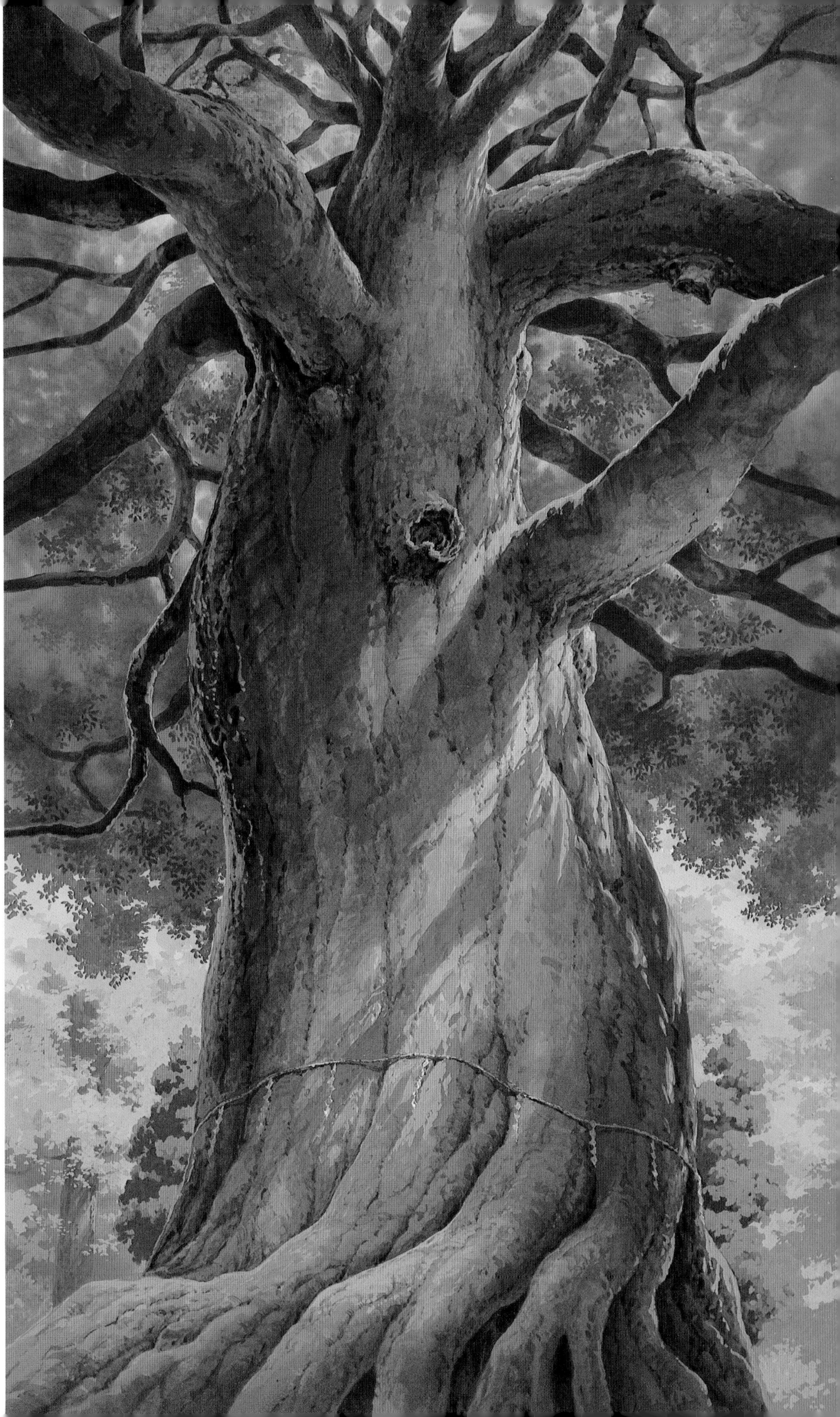

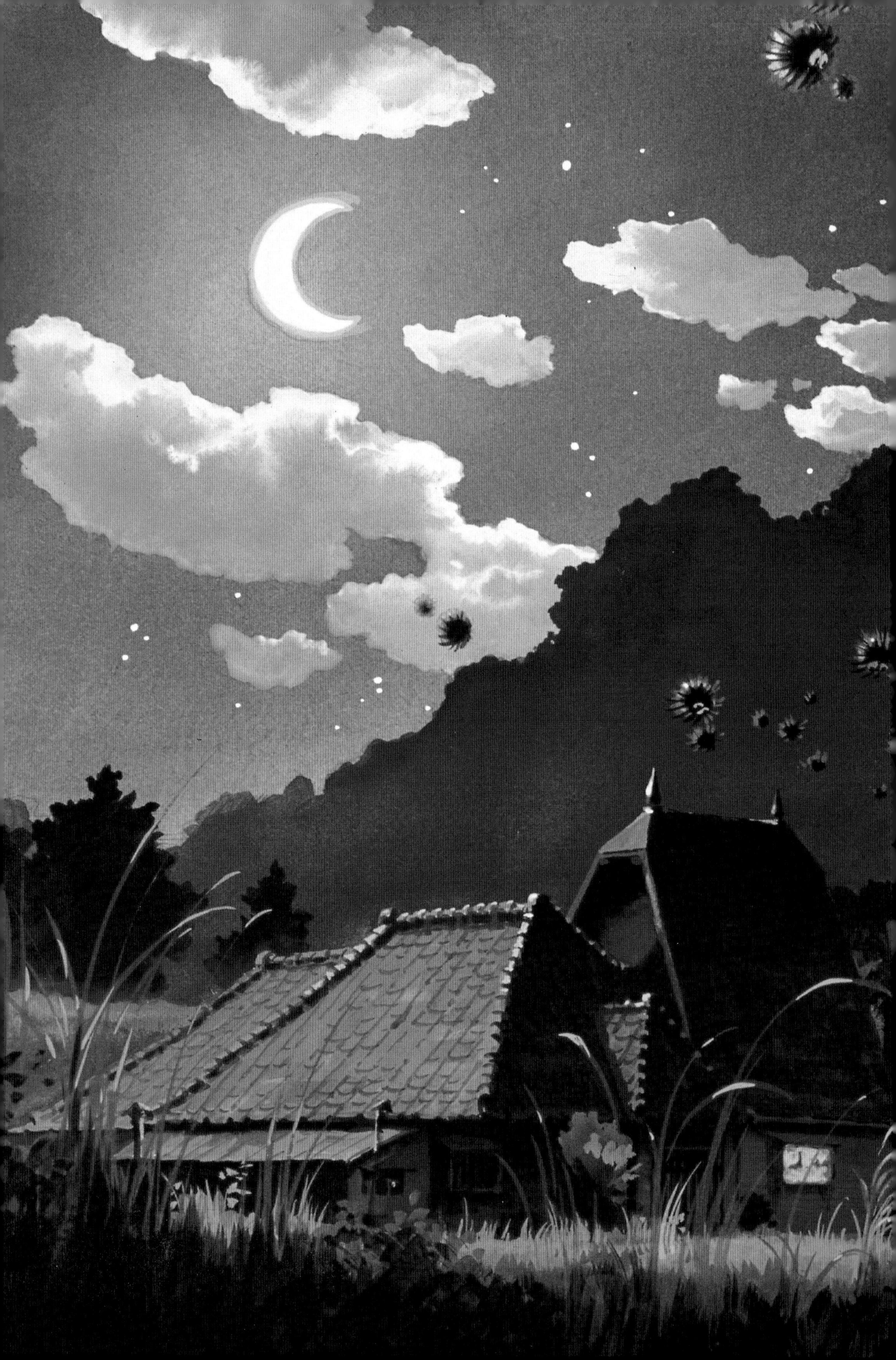

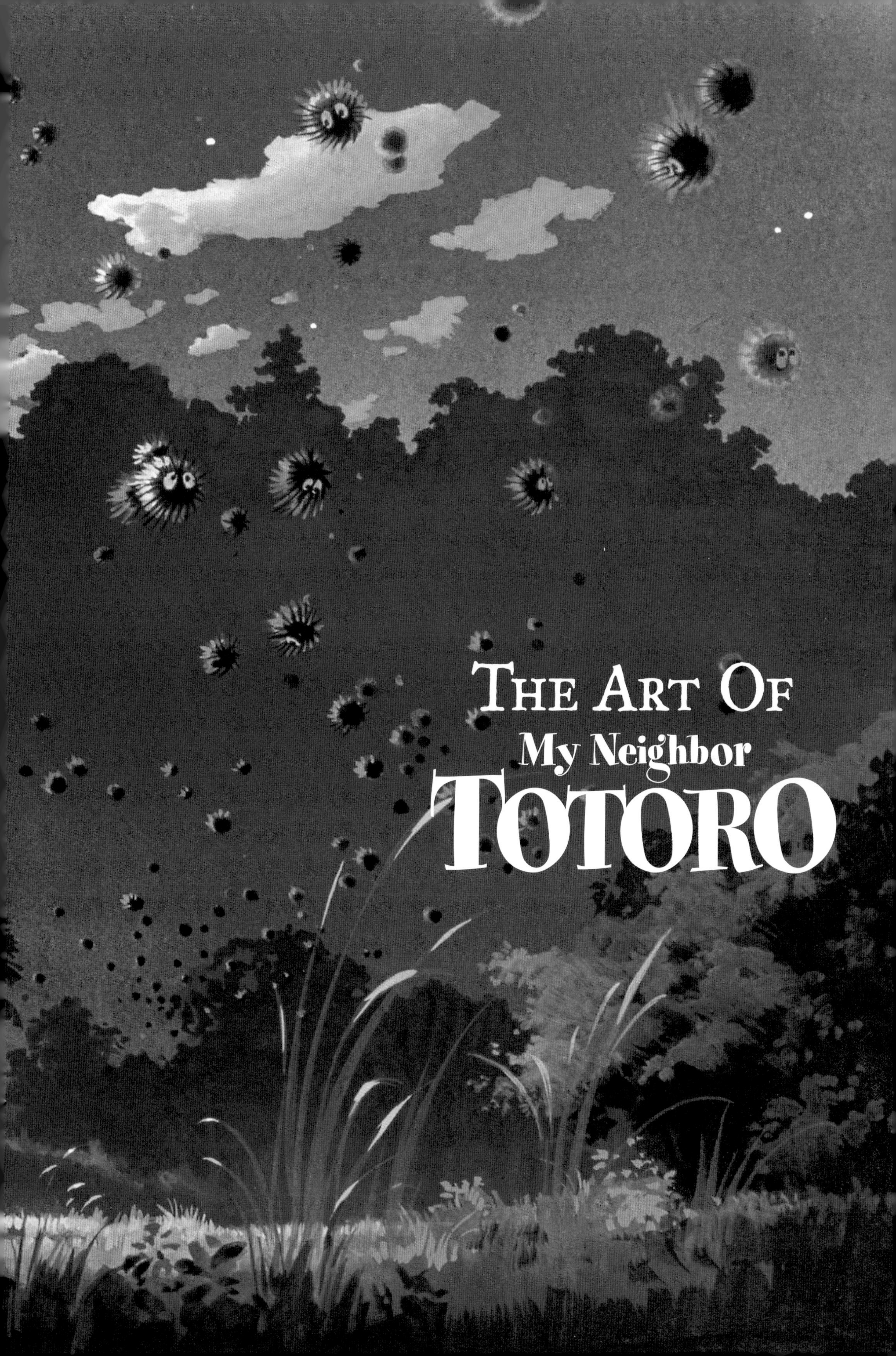
THE ART OF
My Neighbor
TOTORO

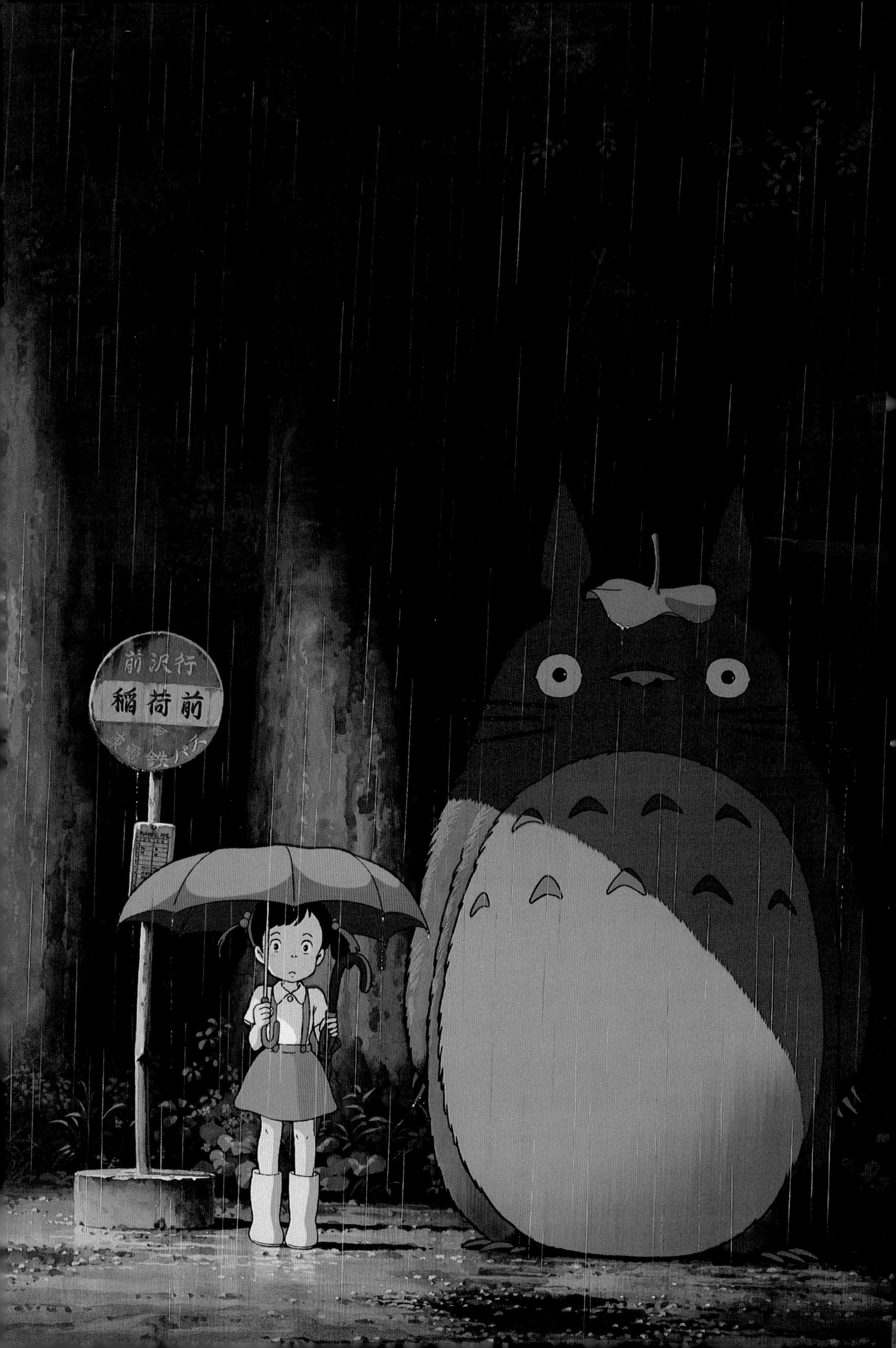
前沢行
稲荷前

# My Neighbor TOTORO

## I wanted to make a delightful, wonderful film set in Japan.

### Original Story/Screenplay/Directed by Hayao Miyazaki

I wanted *My Neighbor Totoro* to be a heartwarming feature film that would not only entertain and touch its viewers, but stay with them long after they have left the theaters. I wanted the spirit of the film to endear lovers to each other, inspire parents to fondly recall their childhood, and encourage kids to roam around temple grounds or climb trees.

What can Japan be proud of? Until recently, parents and kids have been able to easily answer, "nature and the seasonal beauty," but no one can say that anymore. Those of us who live in Japan—and who are indeed Japanese—shun [the reality of] our country, where animation is a form of escapism. Is this country that awful, so devoid of hope now?

Even in this global age, it's the most local things that can have a worldwide effect. Yet why doesn't anyone make a delightful and wonderful film set in Japan?

We need a new method and sense of discovery to be up to the task. Rather than be sentimental, the film must be a joyful, entertaining film.

> The forgotten.
> The ignored.
> Those that are considered lost.

Yet I made *My Neighbor Totoro* with the firm belief that these things still exist.


## What is Totoro?

It is the name that our protagonist, the four-year-old Mei, gives these creatures. No one knows what their real name is.

They dwelled in the forests here a long, long time ago, when the country was nearly uninhabited. Apparently they live over a thousand years. The large Totoro is over two meters tall. Big and furry, not unlike a big owl, beast, or bear, this animal might be considered a monster, but it never attacks people. These serene, carefree creatures have dwelled in forest caves or old tree holes, away from humans, but somehow the sisters Satsuki and Mei manage to find them.

The Totoros don't want any commotion, and although this is their first contact with humans, they've opened up to Satsuki and Mei.

Hayao Miyazaki is one of Japan's most beloved animation directors. In September 2005 he was awarded the Venice International Film Festival's Golden Lion Award for Lifetime Achievement, and his Studio Ghibli received the Festival's Osella Award for overall achievement in 2004. Miyazaki's films include *Spirited Away*, winner of the 2002 Academy Award® for Best Animated Feature Film, as well as *Kiki's Delivery Service*, *Princess Mononoke*, and *Howl's Moving Castle*, all of which have received great acclaim in the U.S. Miyazaki's other achievements include the highly regarded *Nausicaä of the Valley of the Wind*, which is published in English by VIZ Media and now available on DVD.

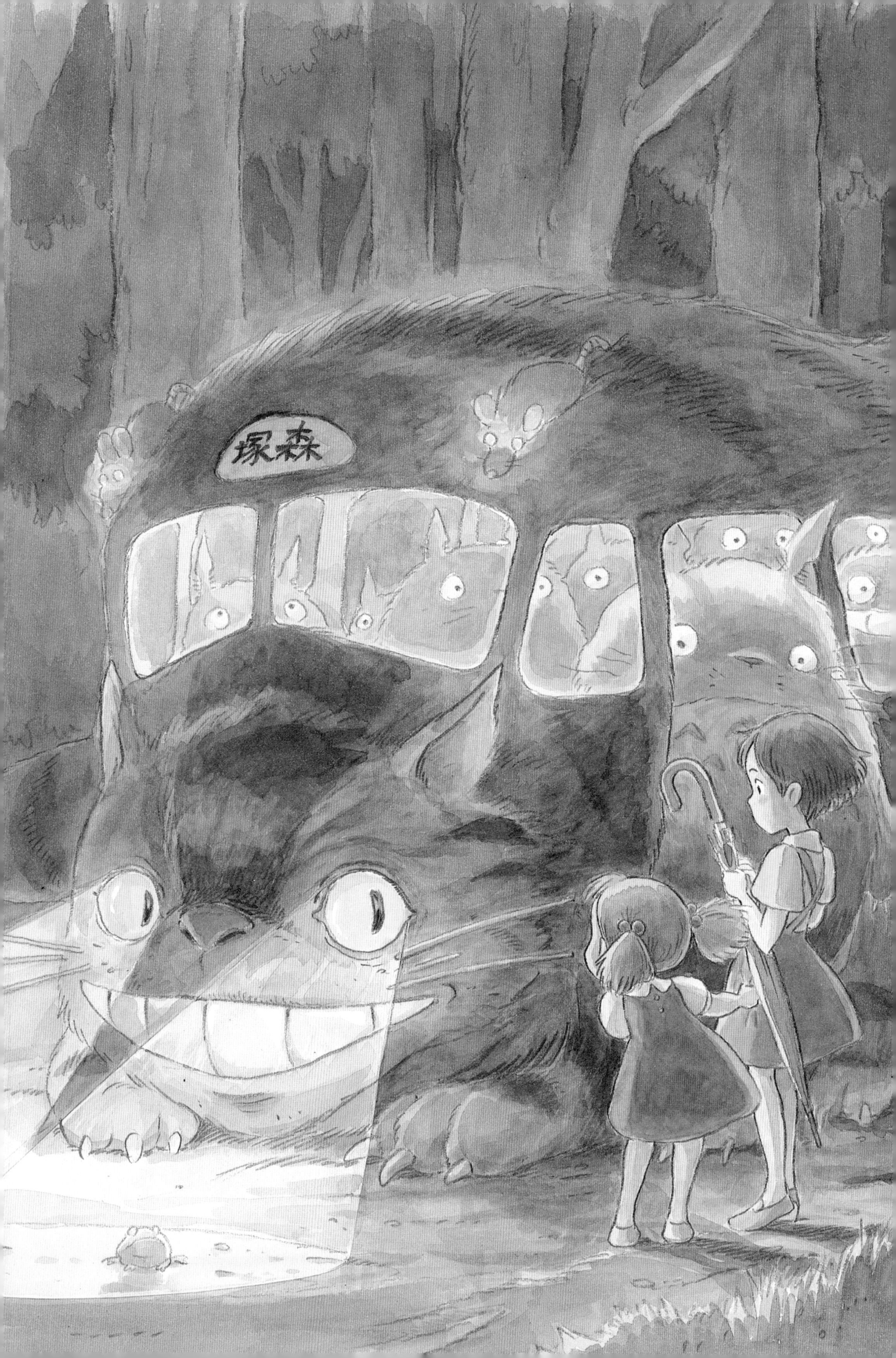
森塚

# My Neighbor
# TOTORO
## *Initial Concept Sketches*

The film *My Neighbor Totoro* was based on a children's book Miyazaki conceptualized while working on the TV series *3000 Miles in Search of Mother* (1976). Some of these initial concept sketches for the children's book ended up in the film, while others were left out. These images provide us a glimpse of the "other" *My Neighbor Totoro* Miyazaki had envisioned.

30才　　　5才　　　　　　　　1302才　　　　　679才

おおとうさん　　　とうさん
ミミンズク　　　　ズク

1-4　Concept sketches from when the big Totoro,
　　　medium-sized Totoro, and small Totoro were called
　　　Miminzuku, Zuku, and Mimin, respectively.  The ages
　　　assigned to each character and the initial designs for
　　　the soot sprites are noteworthy.

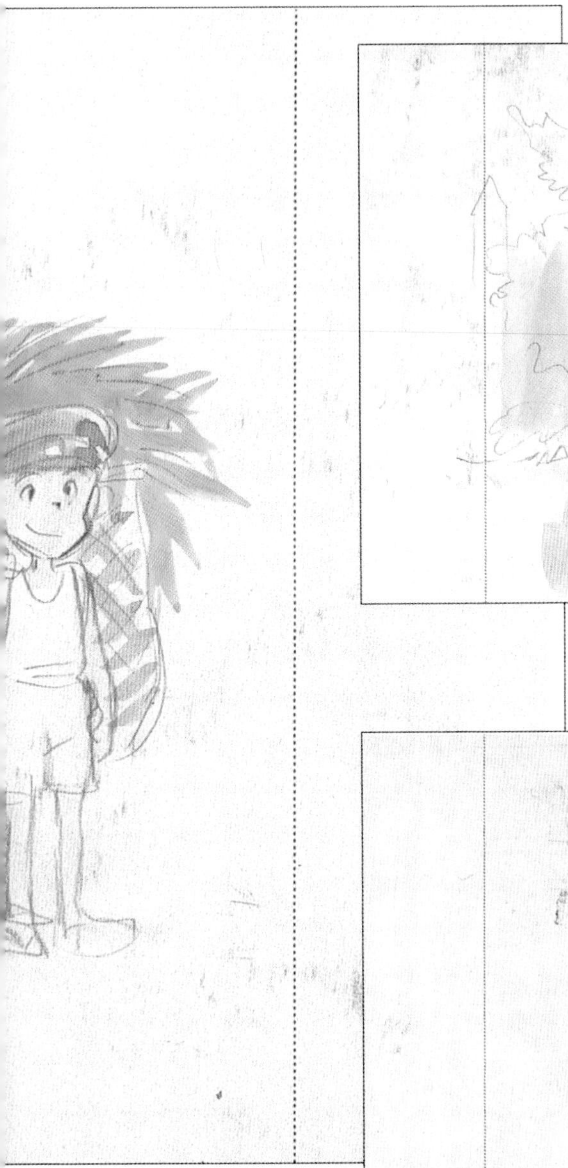

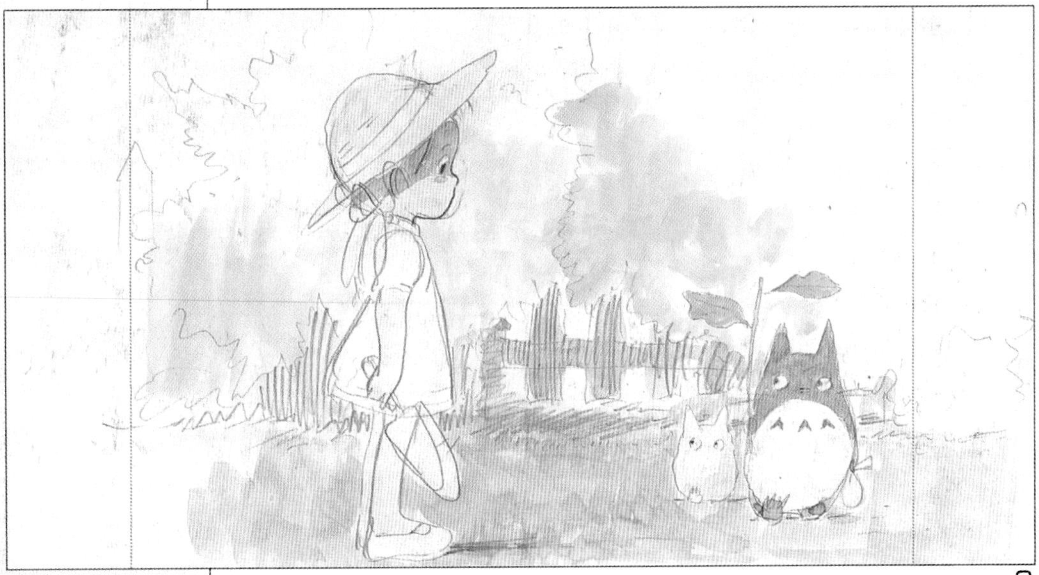

2

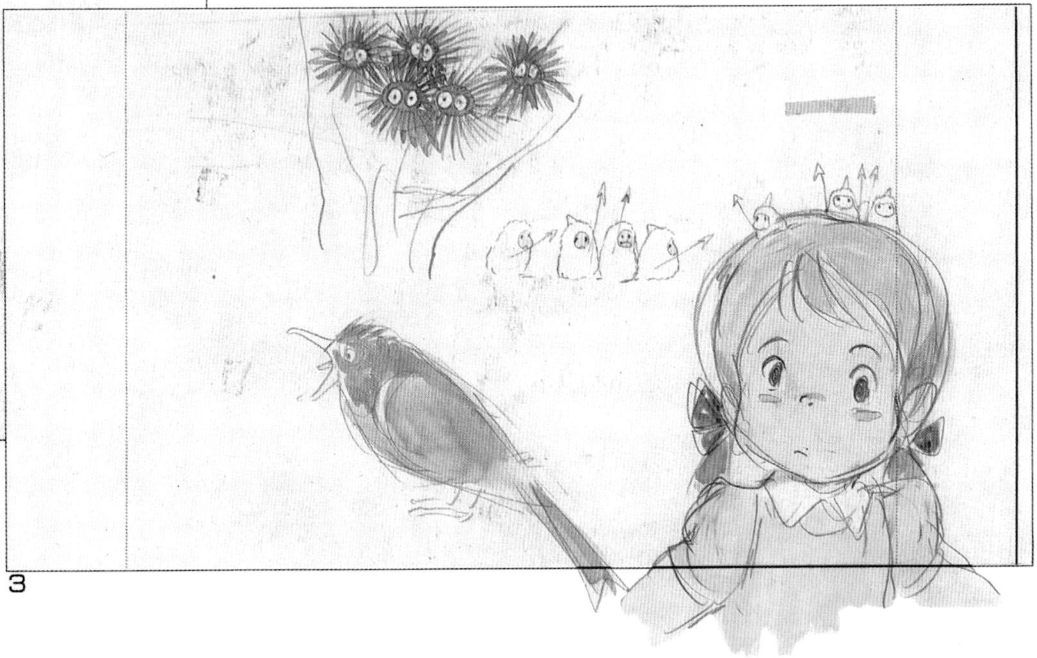

3

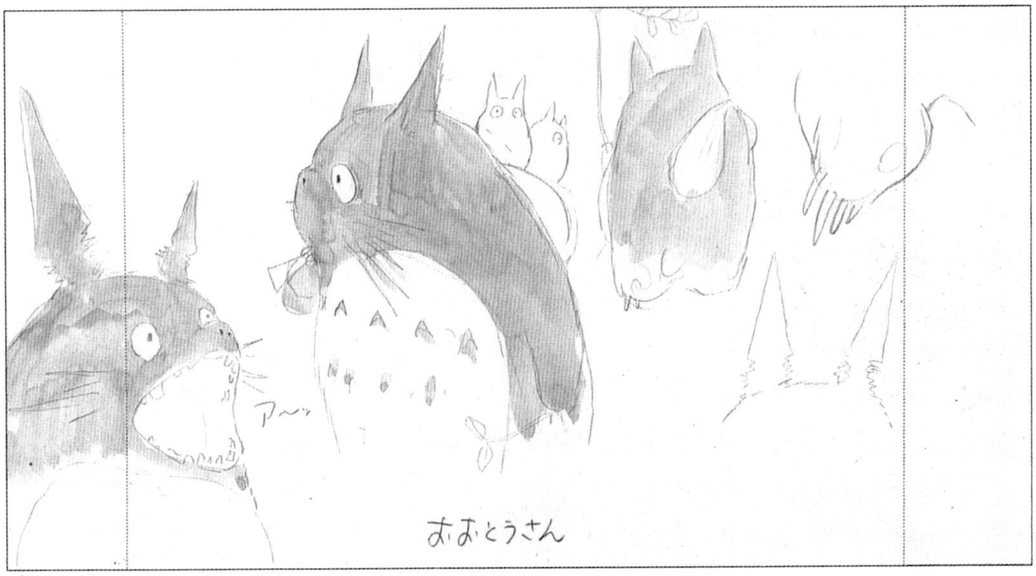
ア～ッ
おおとうさん

4

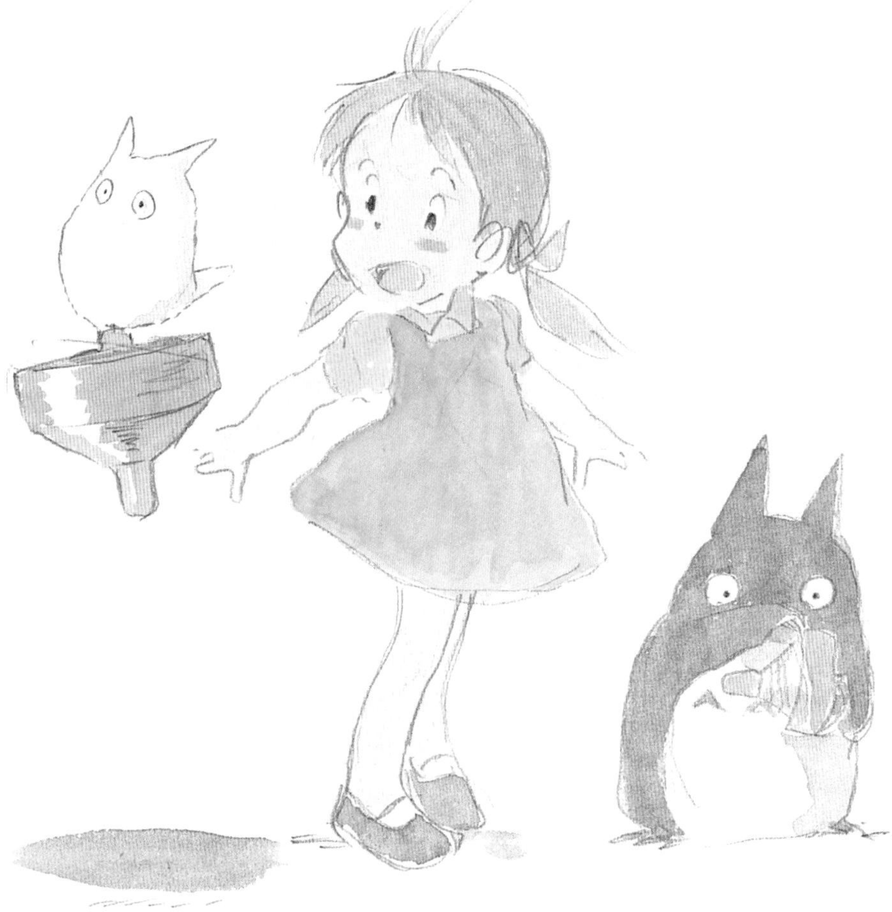

1

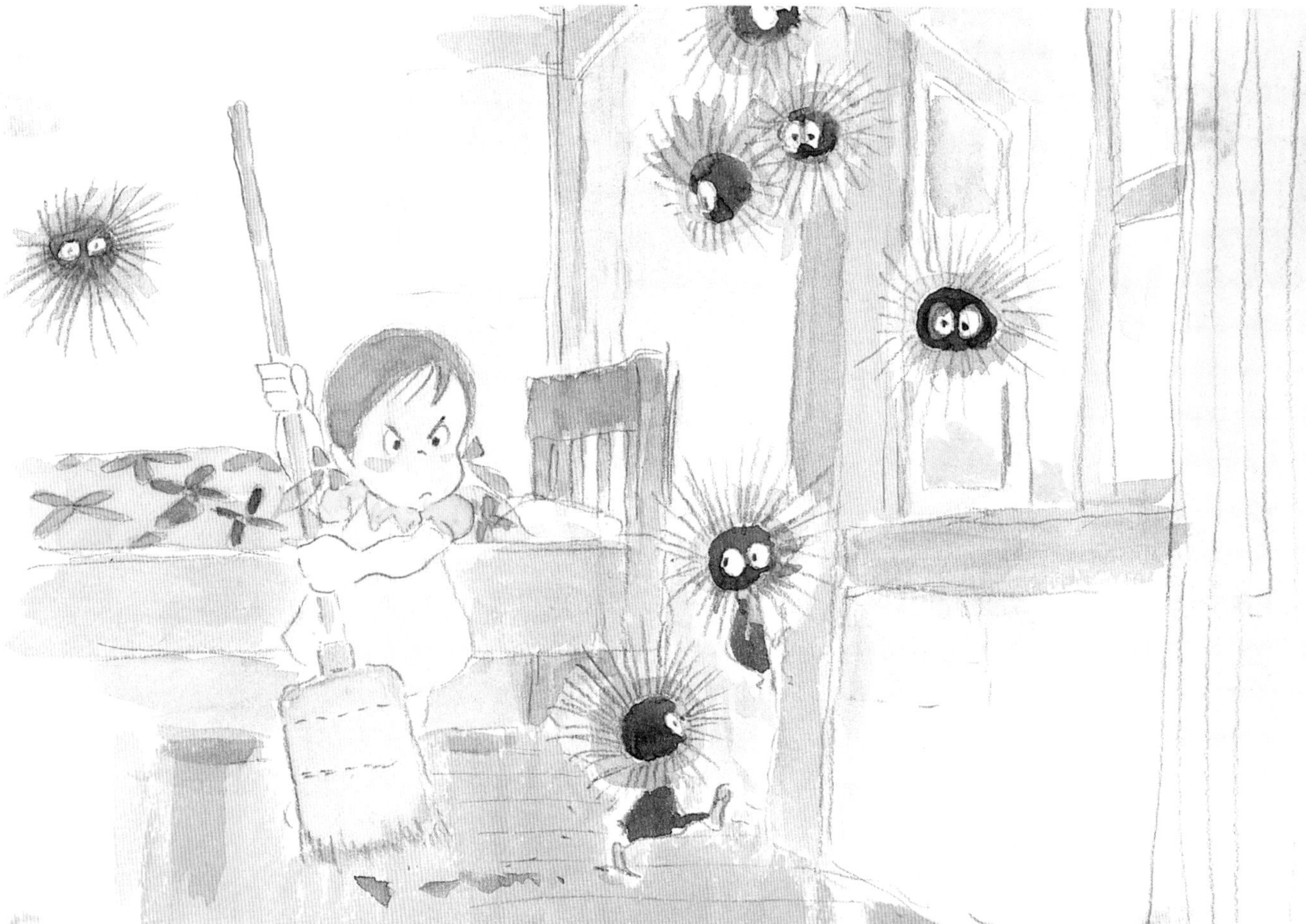

2

3

1-3 Mei encounters Totoro and the soot sprites. The first sketch depicts a girl encountering Totoro at a bus stop on a rainy day, but after completing *Lupin III: Castle of Cagliostro* (1979), Miyazaki drew another sketch depicting her encounter with little Totoro and medium-sized Totoro in broad daylight.

"If she was a little girl who plays around in the yard, she wouldn't be meeting her father at a bus stop, so we had to come up with two girls instead. And that was difficult. Her first encounter (with Totoro) at the bus stop seemed so perfect. At the same time, there's something appealing about a girl gazing at something really strange in the middle of a sunny field." (*Miyazaki. Interview excerpt from* My Neighbor Totoro: Storyboard Collection)

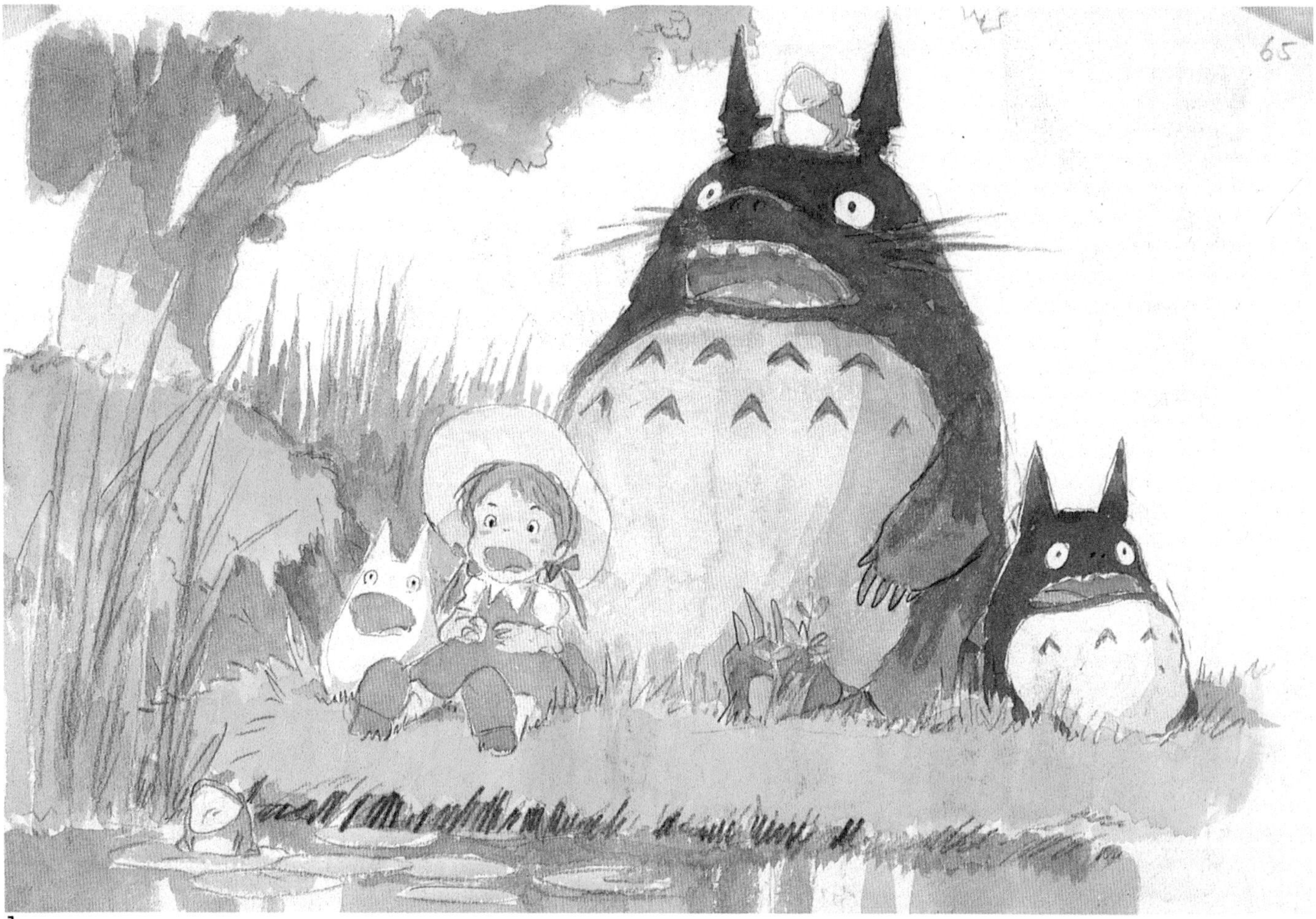
65
1

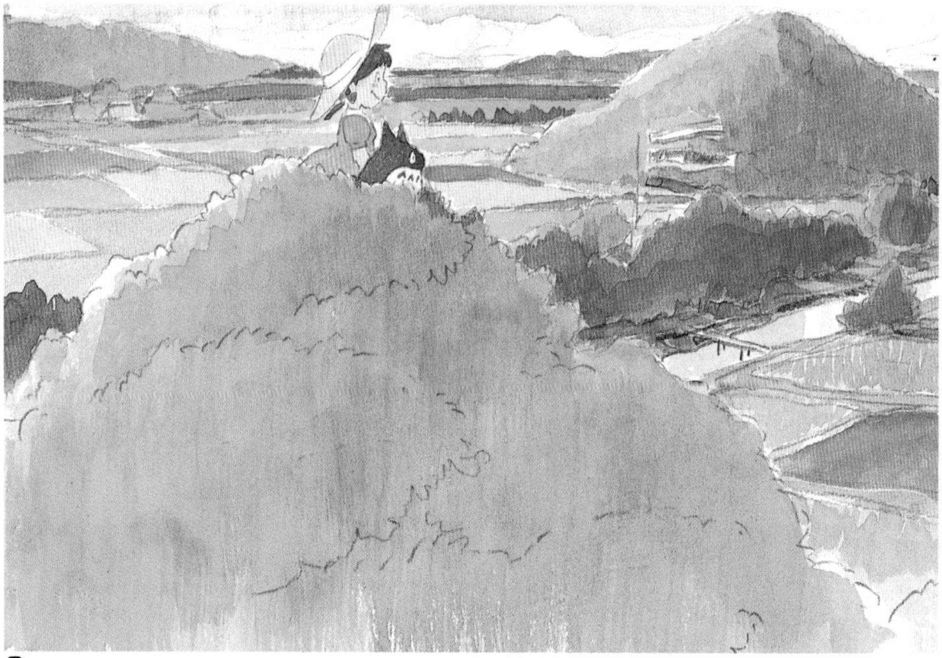
2

1-4 Concept sketches for the girl playing with the three Totoros following her encounter.

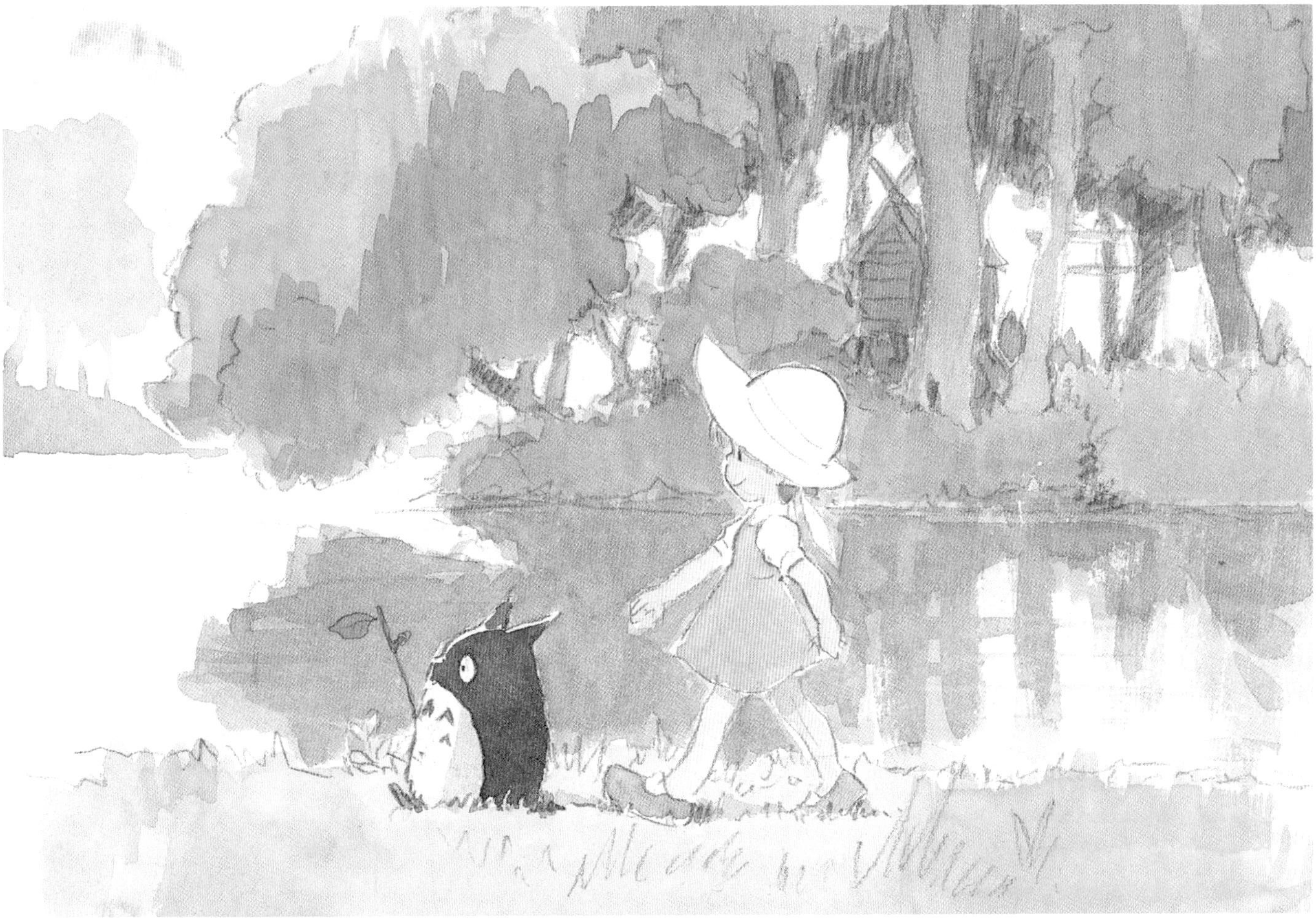

3

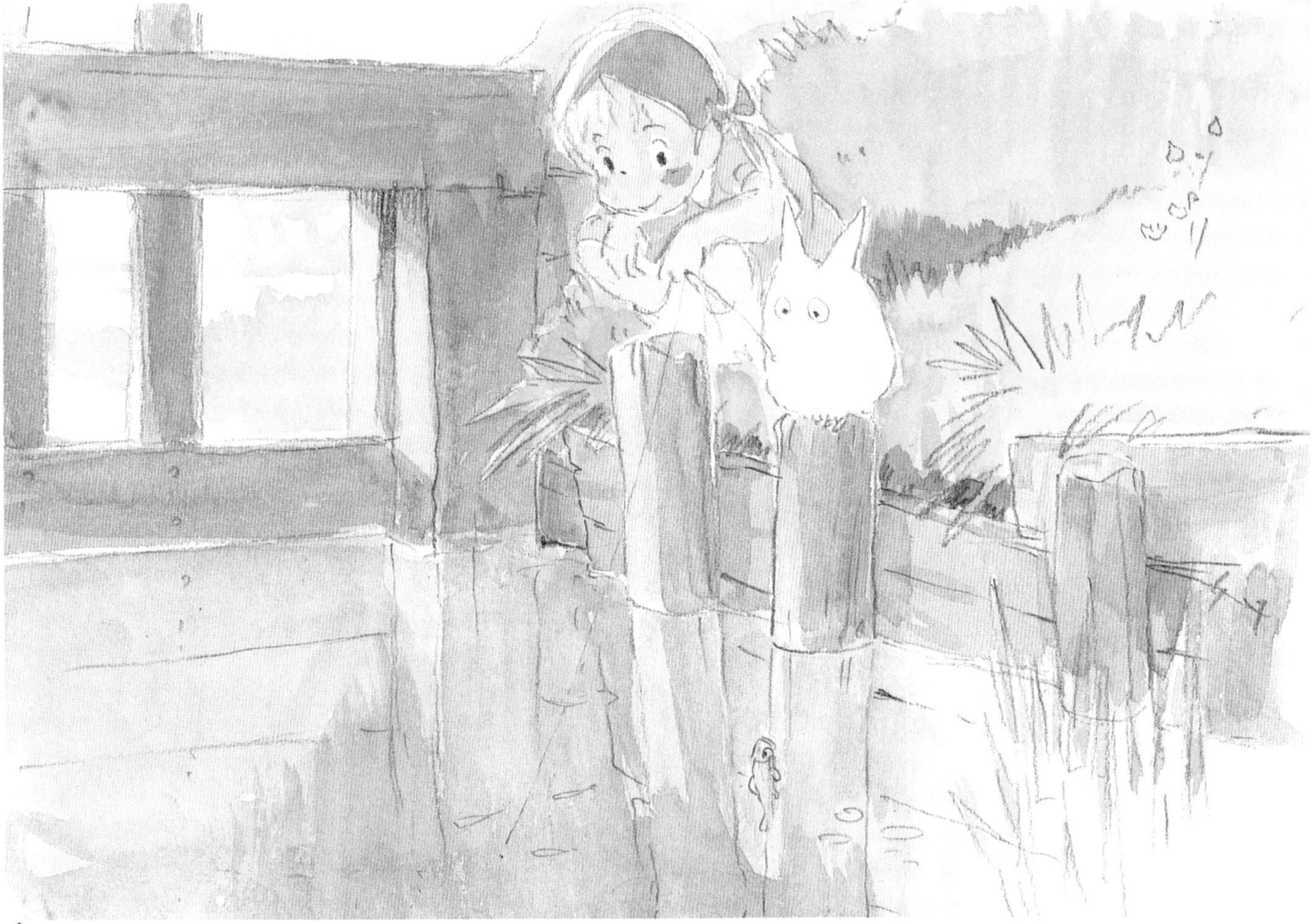

4

1

3

2 　　　　　　　　内のひかれに生けて 庭へ

1

新しい家へ.

5

6

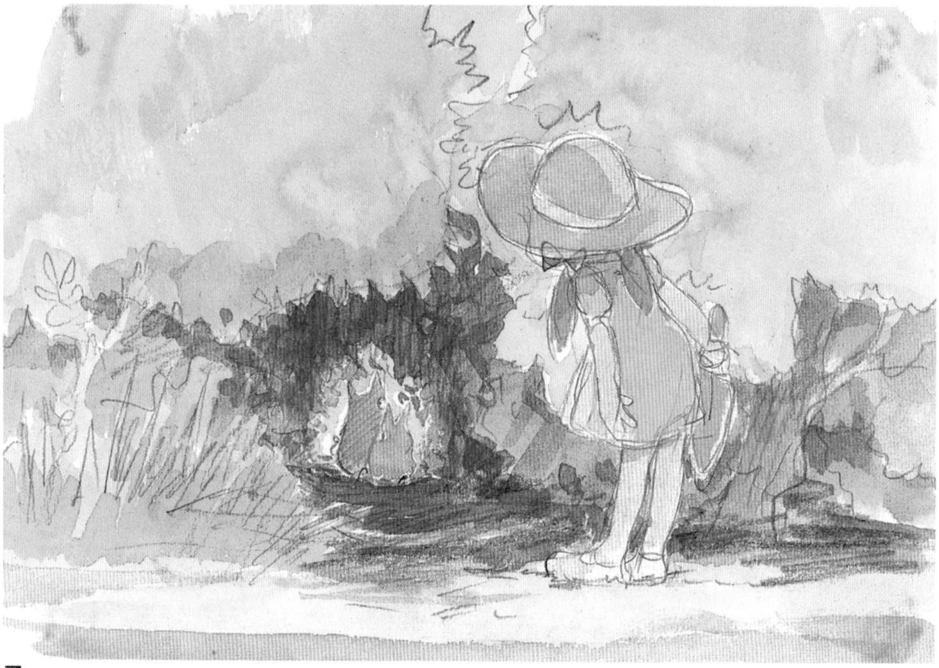
7

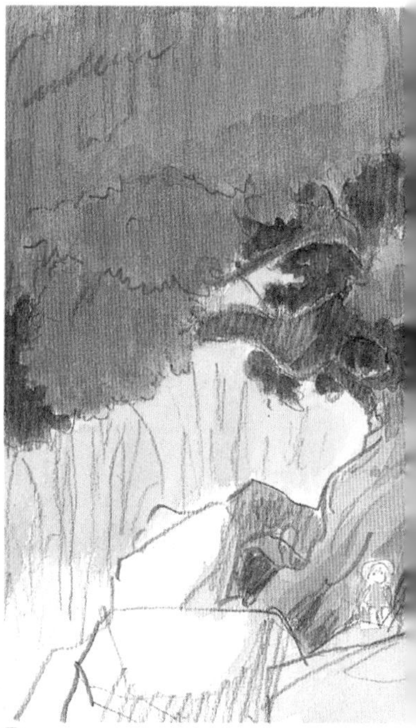
9

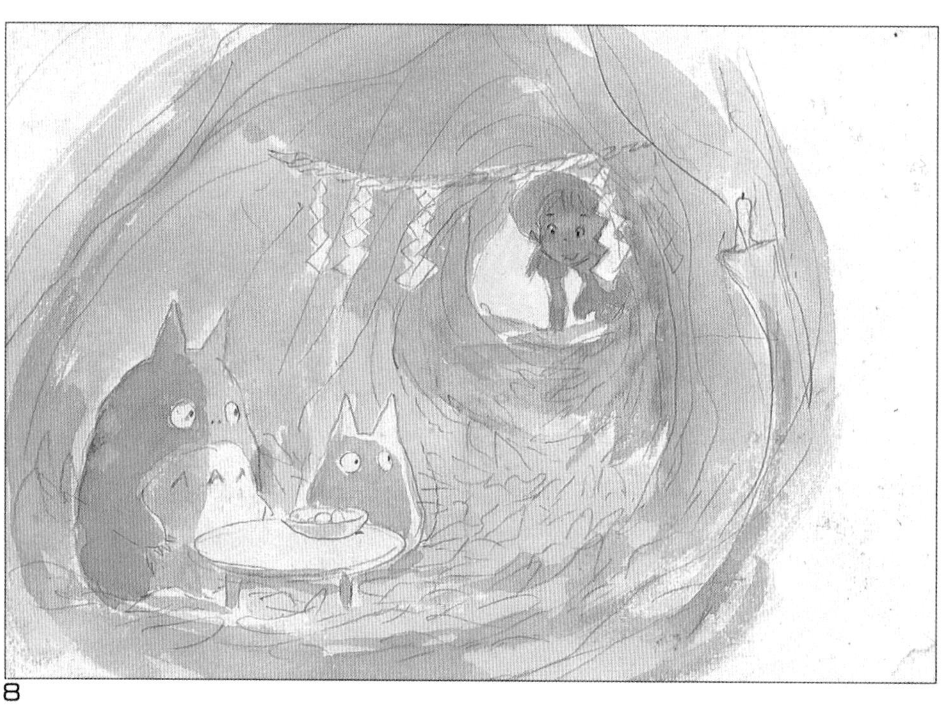
8

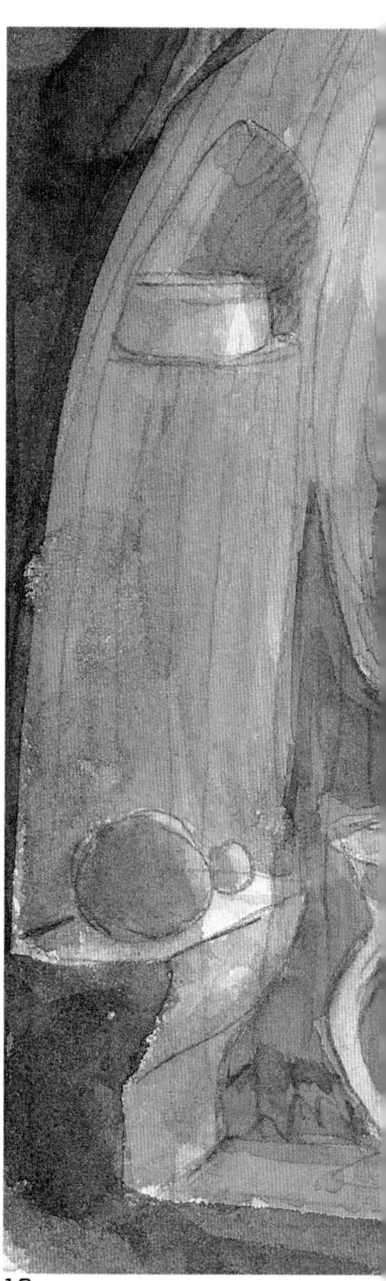
10

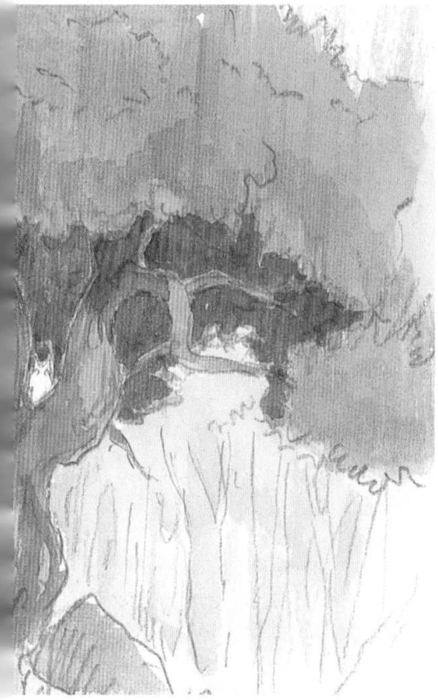

1-10 Initial storyboards depicting the girl's encounter with the Totoros.

"[Although the additional girl presented problems] I managed to come up with a proposal for *My Neighbor Totoro*. I made a scrapbook out of these sketches and submitted them to Tokyo Movie, telling them I'd come up with a story, if they could bring it to the screen. Several parties got involved, pitching it as a TV special, but it never got off the ground. The scrapbook was returned to me, and even after I left Telecom, it remained shelved." *(Miyazaki)*

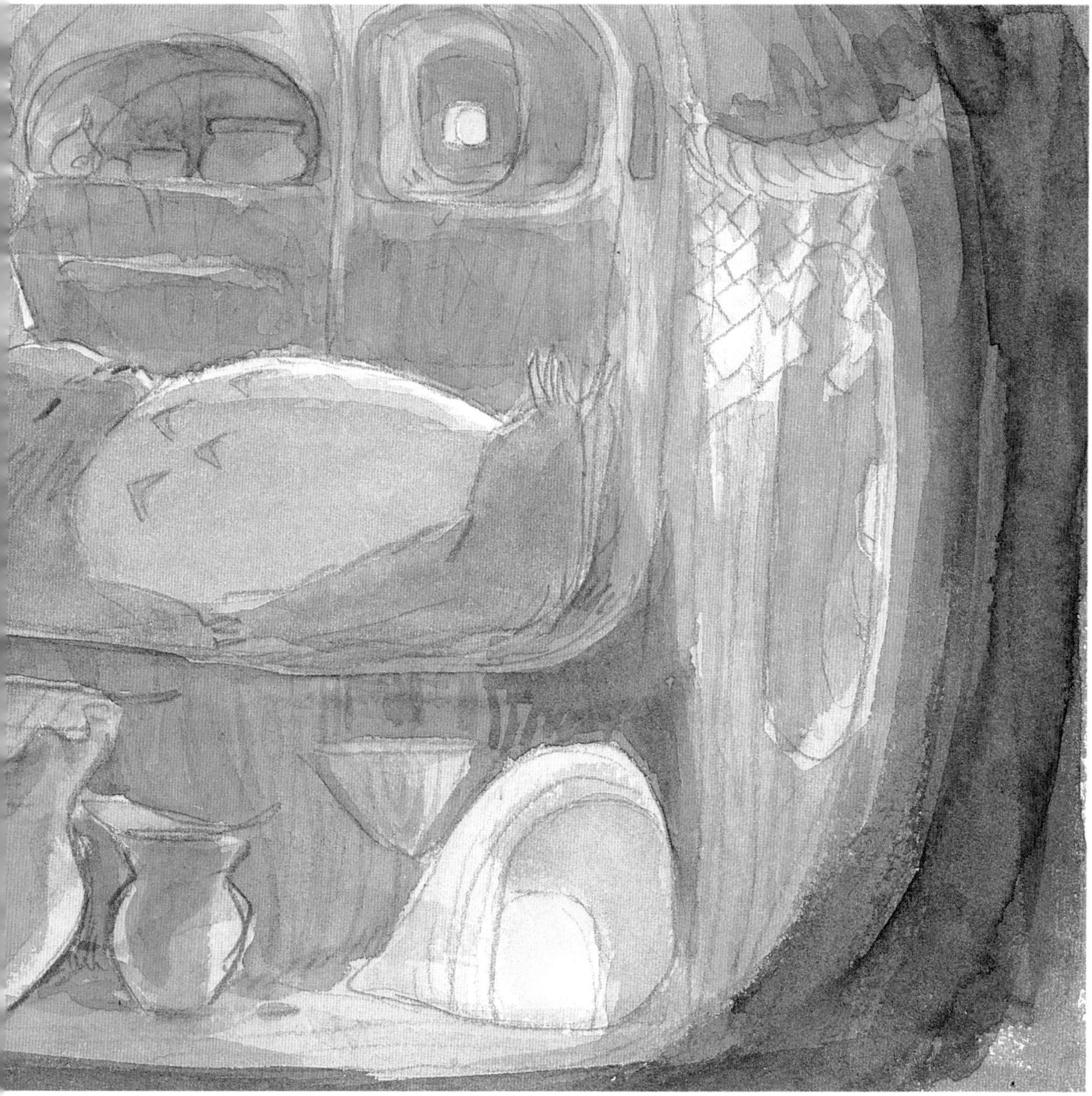

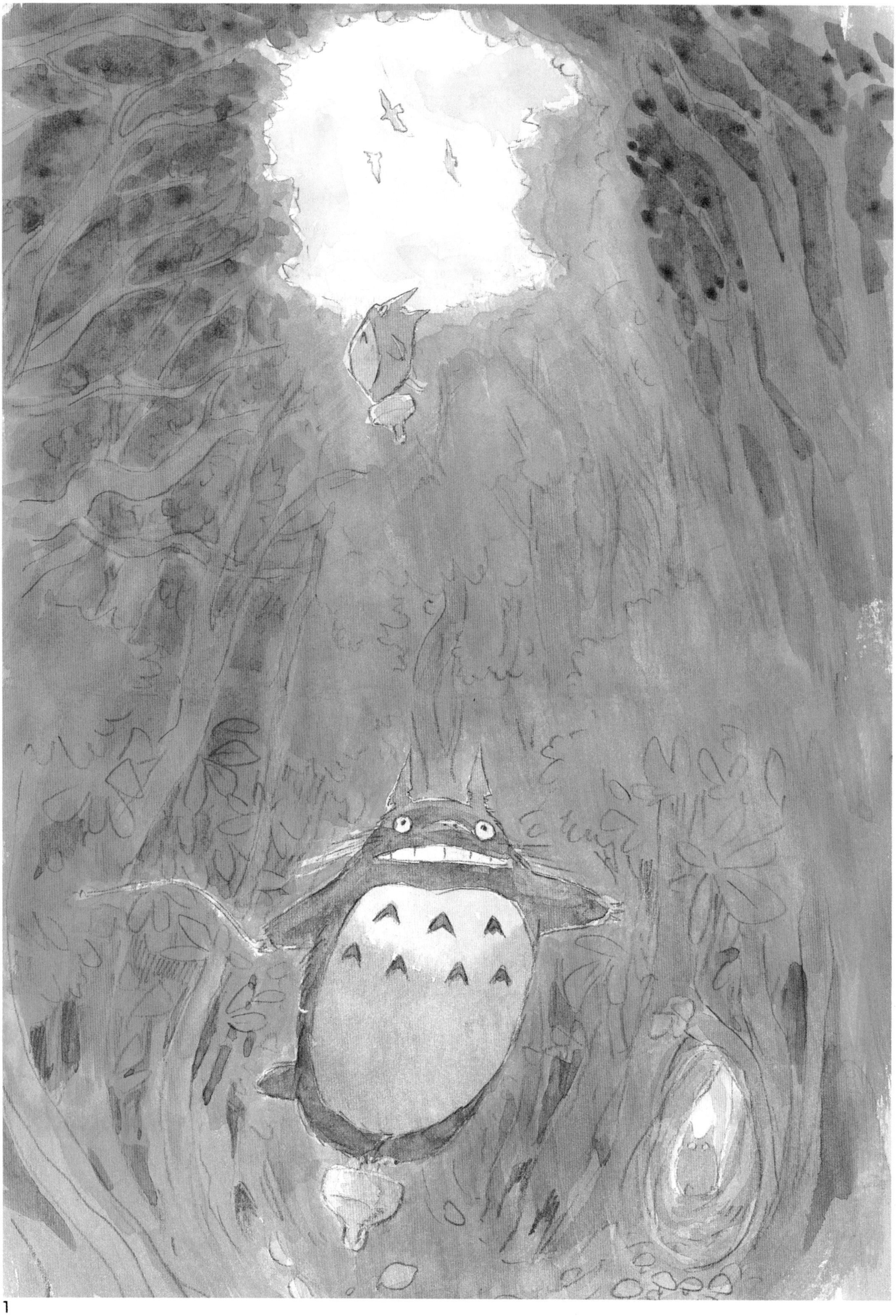

1

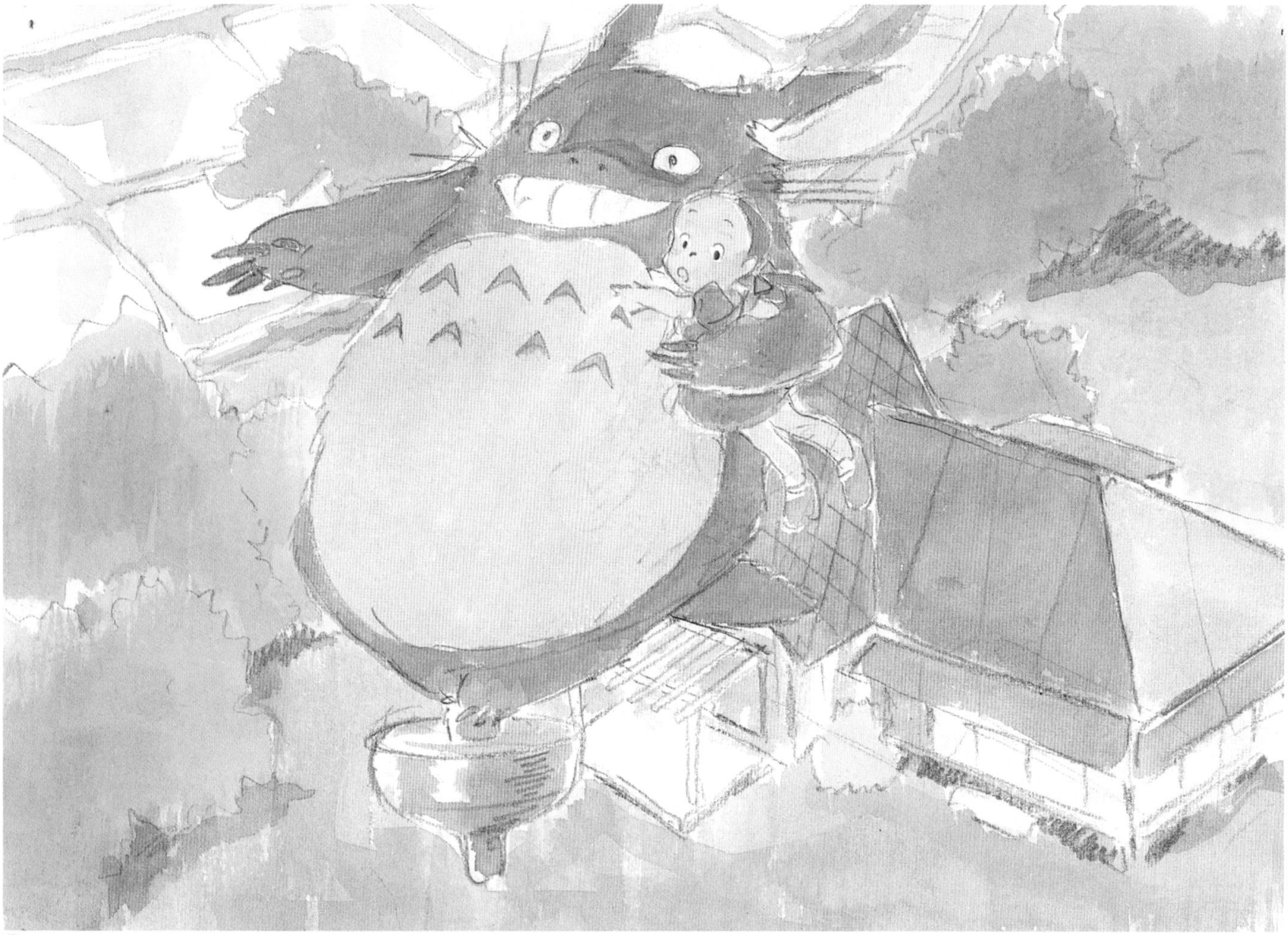

2

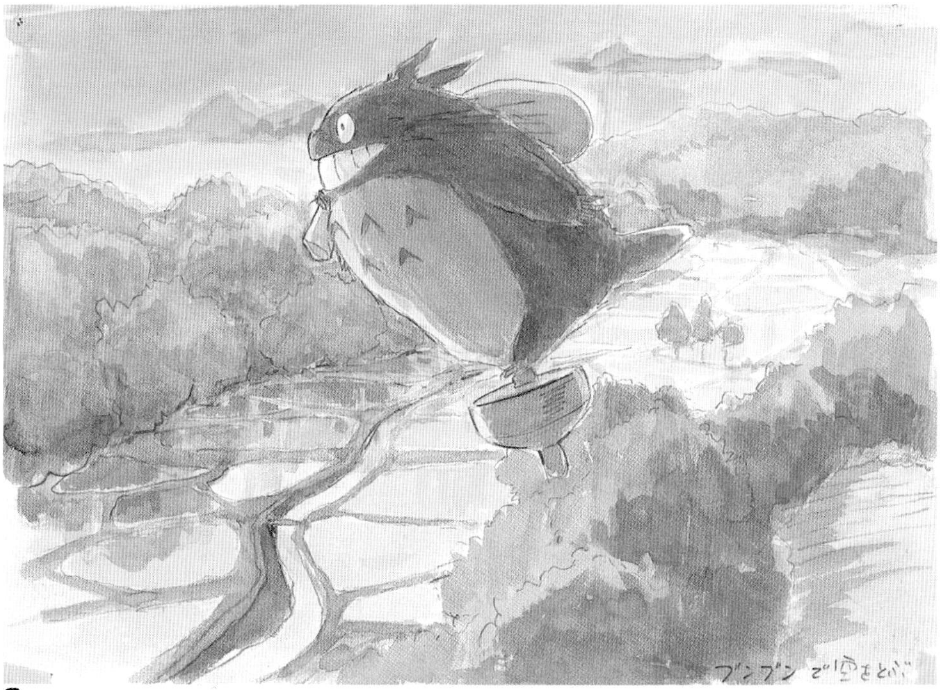
ブンブンで空をとぶ

3

1-3 Concept sketch and storyboard for Totoro flying on a top. The top is called "Bunbun."

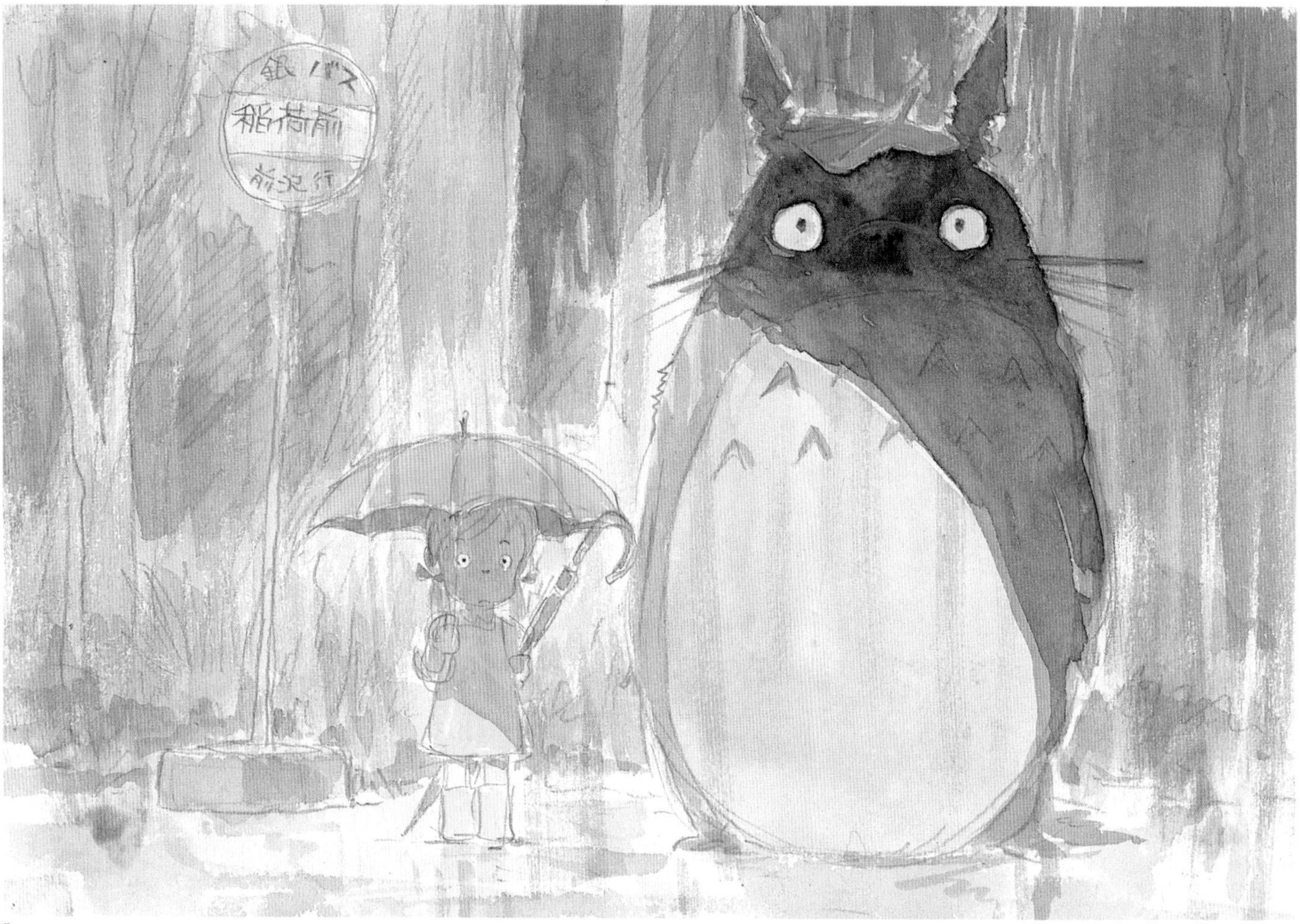
銀バス
稲荷前
前沢行

1

1-3 Concept sketch of the story's thematic "Rainy Day Encounter."

"It starts to rain, so the girl opens her umbrella as she walks up the trail to greet her father. She waits a long time at the corner bus stop, where there's an Inari stone statue. The bus never comes and darkness falls. Then something emerges from the dark. The creature is not wearing any shoes, its nails are long, and it isn't underneath an umbrella. They stand together for a while, but then the girl slowly offers her other umbrella to the creature and demonstrates how to use it. As they wait for the bus, one arrives, but it is a whimsical "Cat Bus." At the time, the idea was to have Totoro return the umbrella and give the girl a wrapped present. Then the bus containing the girl's father arrives. When they get home, the girl unwraps the present and finds acorns. The granny tells the children at the veranda how "...it grows into a tree in the yard." I wanted to tell a story set in a part of town where the only trees in the area grew near this house." *(Miyazaki)*

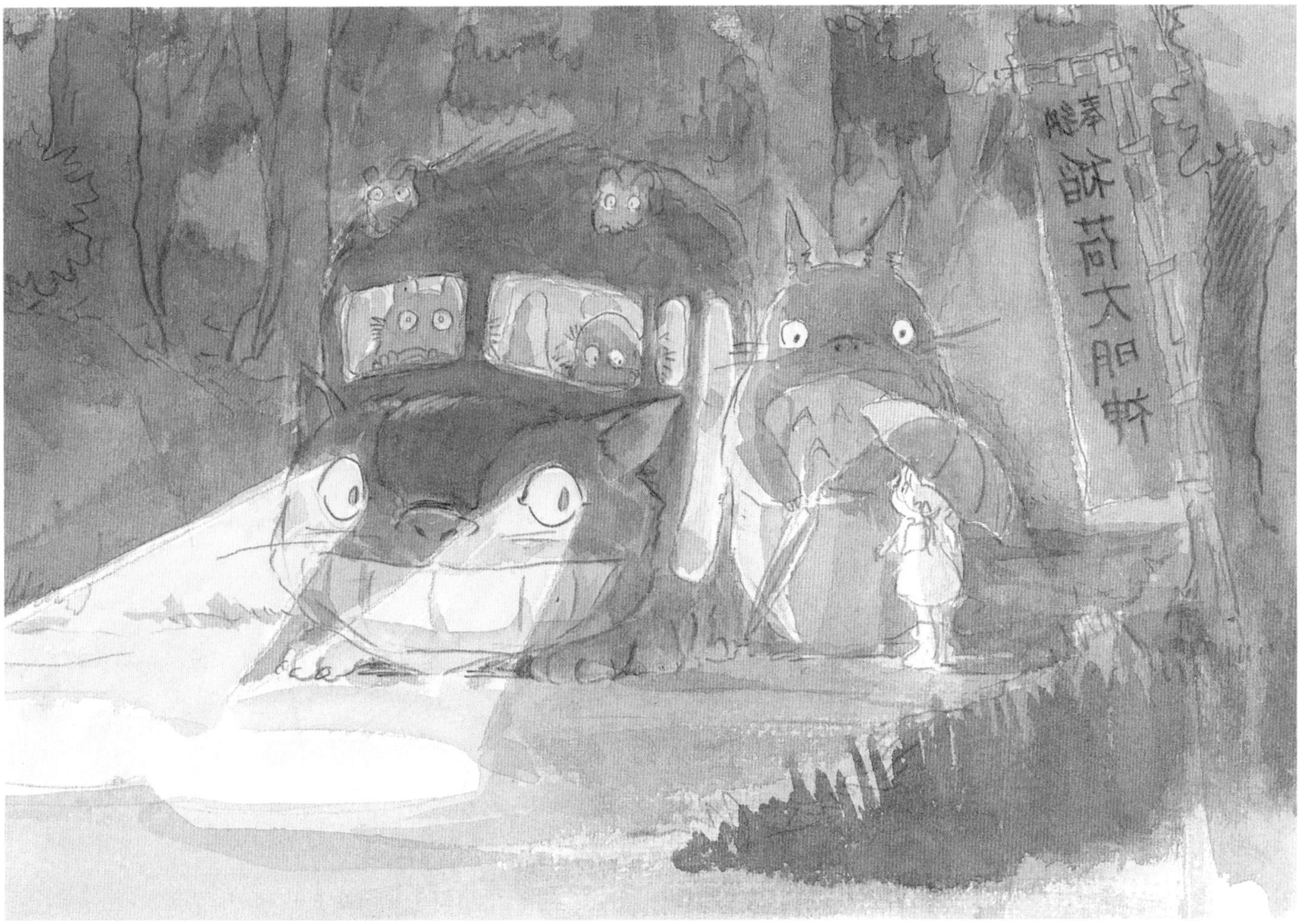
奉納
稲荷大明神

2

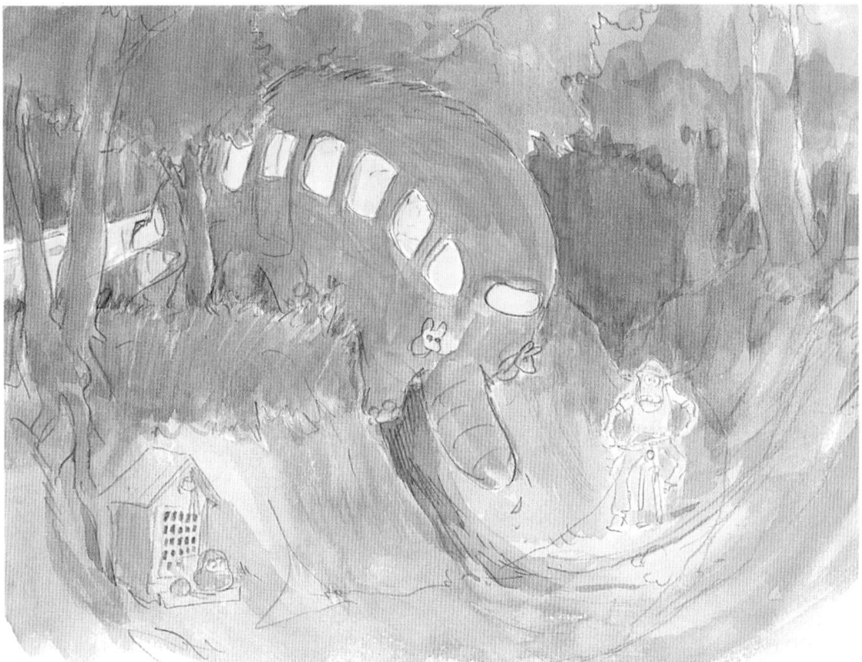
ネコバスはいく

3

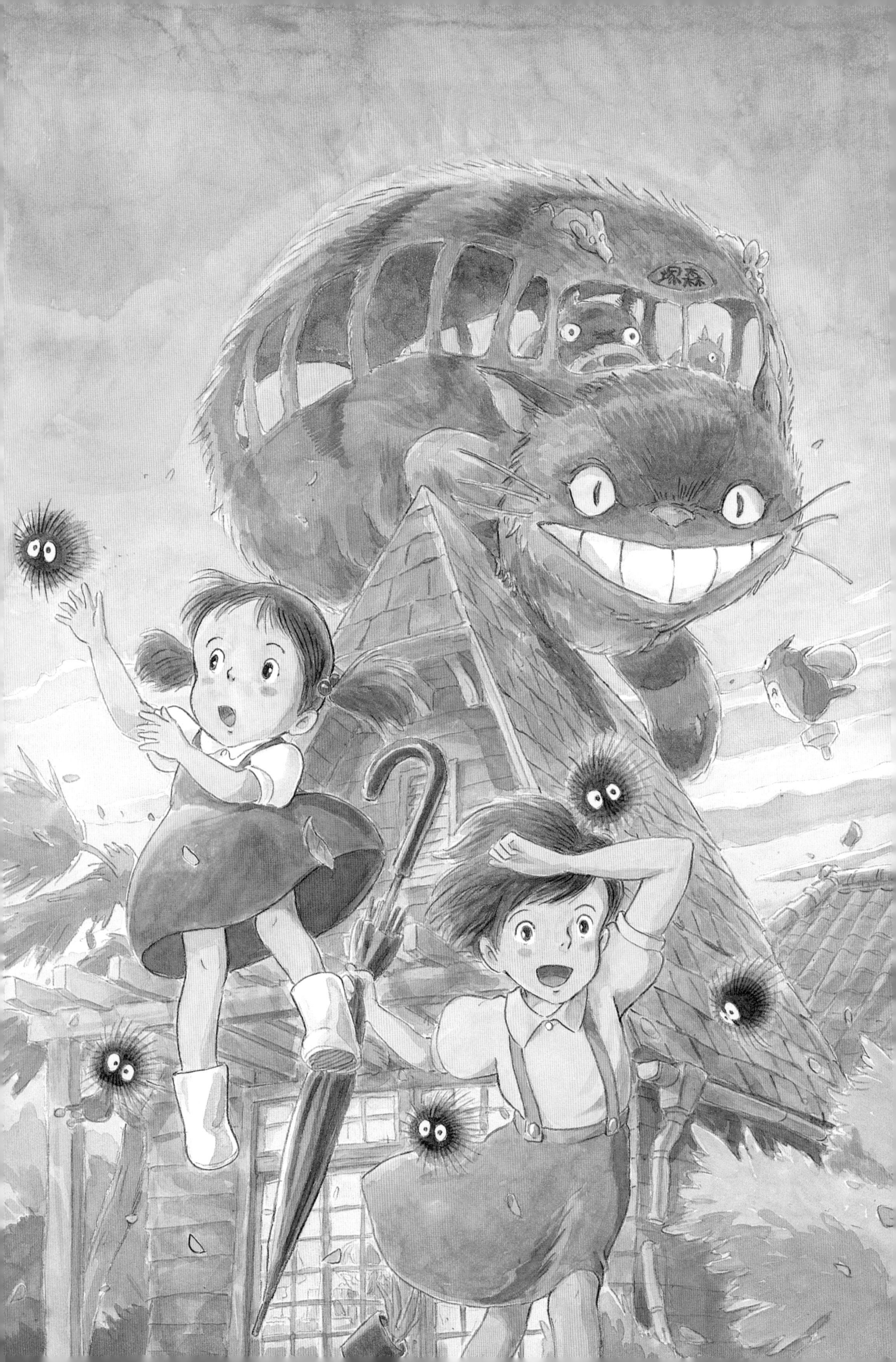
塚森

# My Neighbor TOTORO

## The Art of Animated Films

This is a collection of concept sketches, storyboards, concept art, cel art, and film images that tell the story of *My Neighbor Totoro*, an animated film conceived, scripted, and directed by Hayao Miyazaki. All concept sketches and storyboards are by Hayao Miyazaki. Concept art is by the art direction supervisor, Kazuo Oga. The commentary has been excerpted from interviews conducted with Hayao Miyazaki and Kazuo Oga published in *Romance Album* and *Storyboard Collection*.

Note: Unprocessed cel art may deviate from corresponding animation shots.

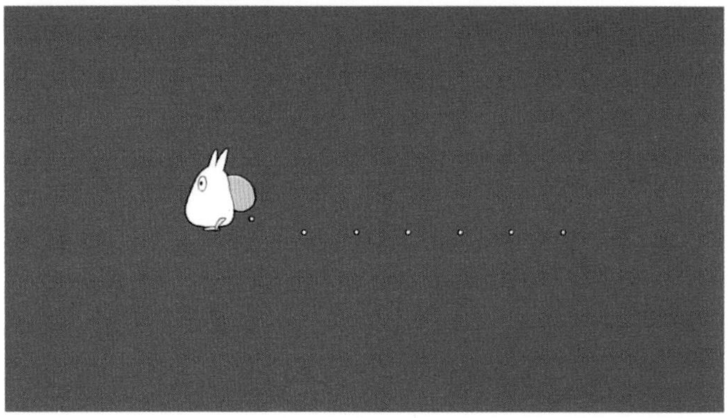
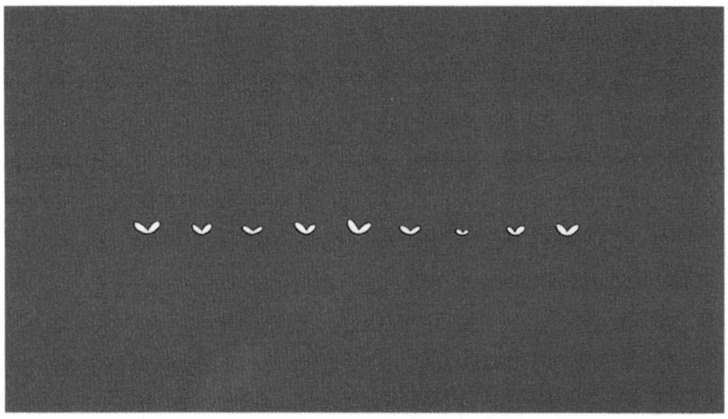
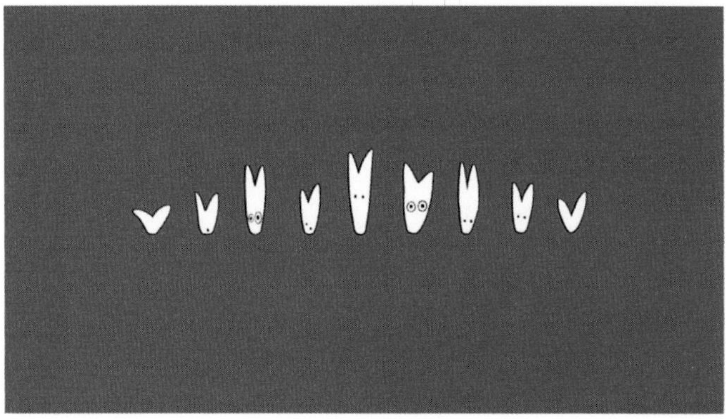
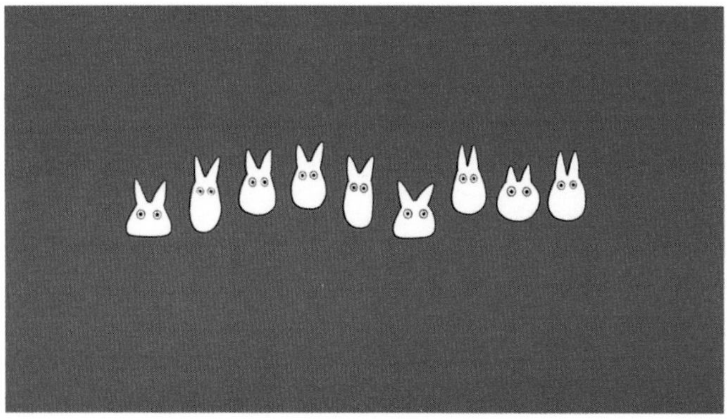
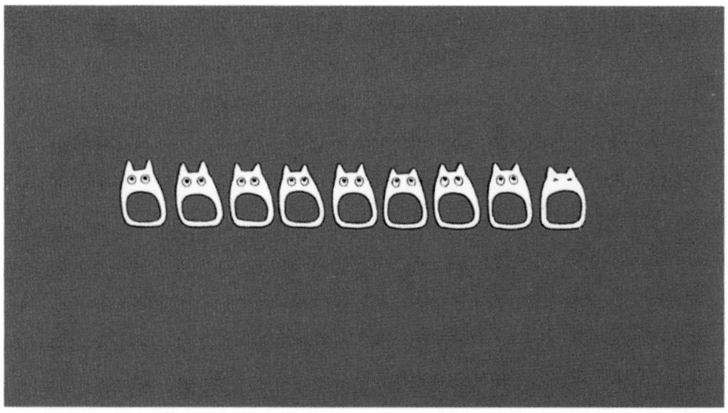
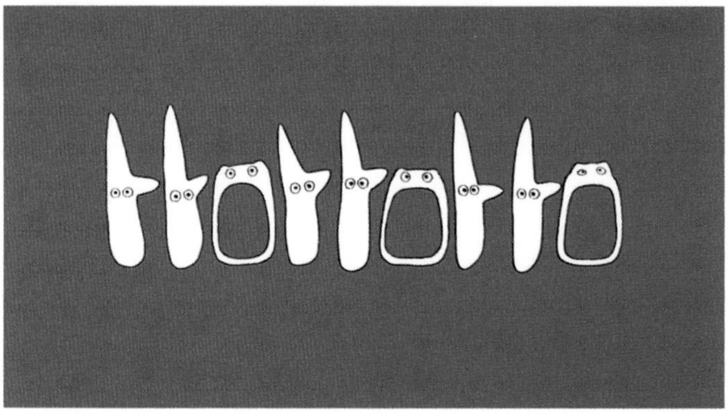
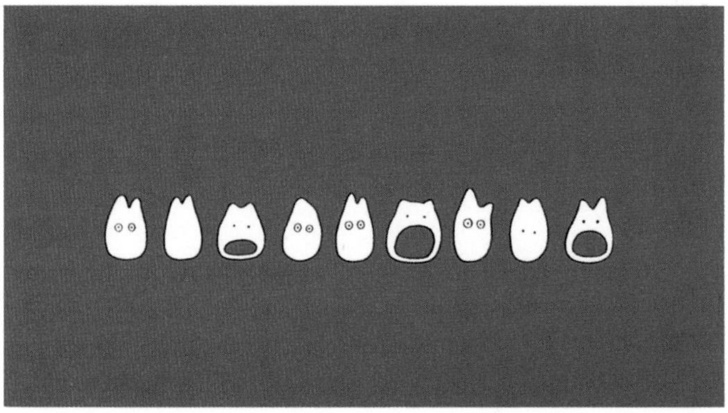
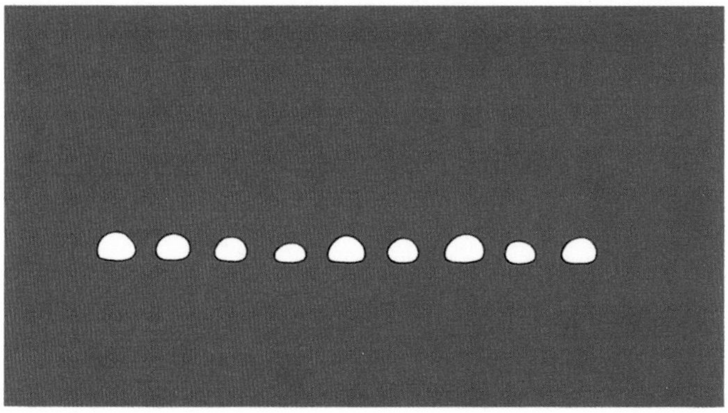
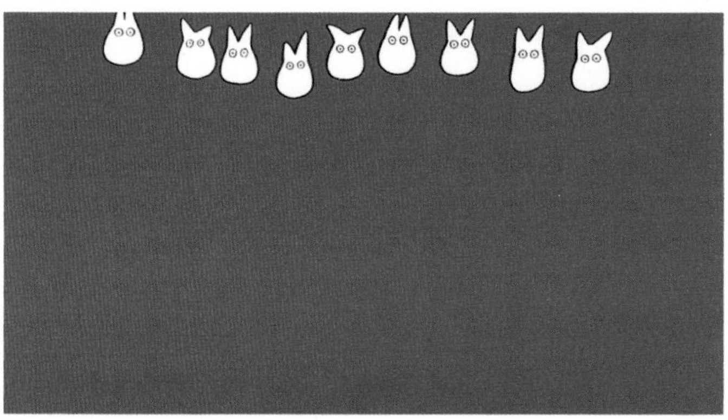

となりのトトロ

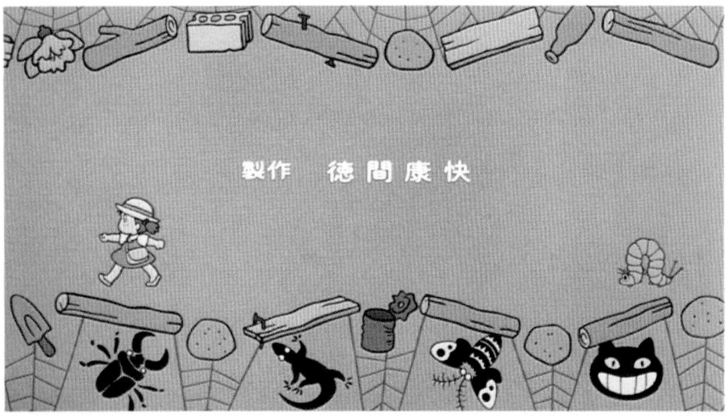
製作　徳間康快
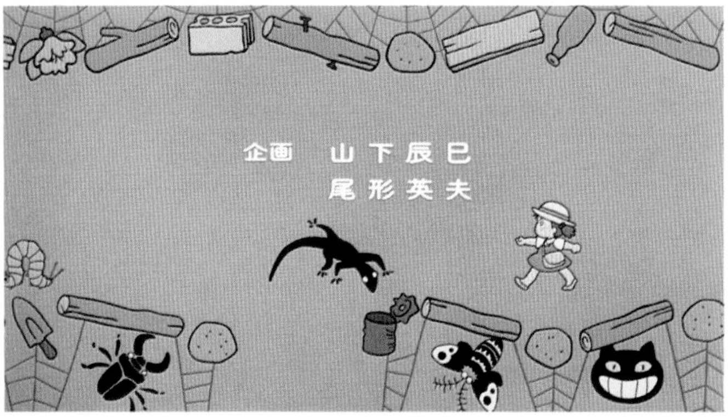
企画　山下辰巳
尾形英夫
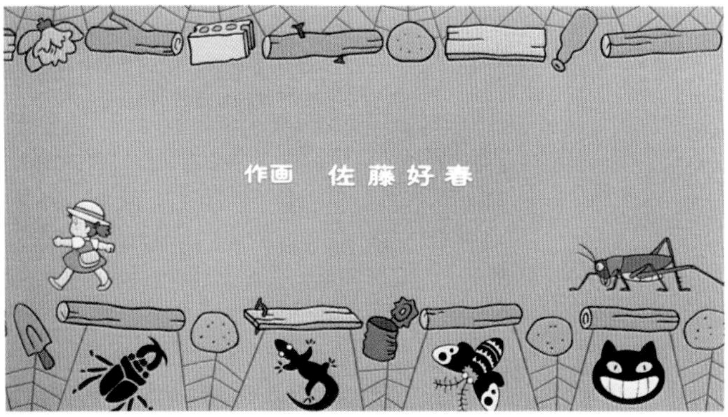
作画　佐藤好春
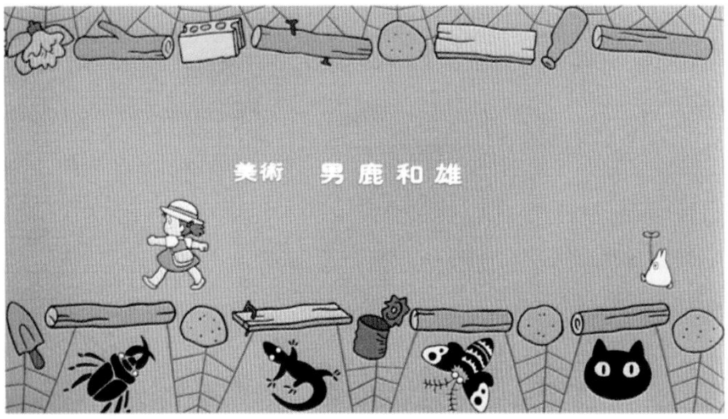
美術　男鹿和雄
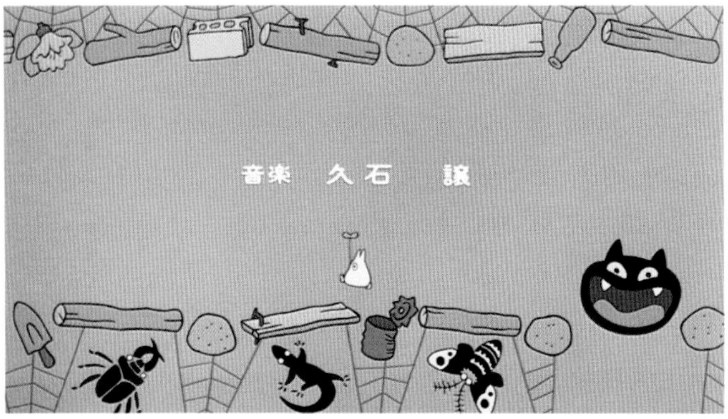
音楽　久石　譲
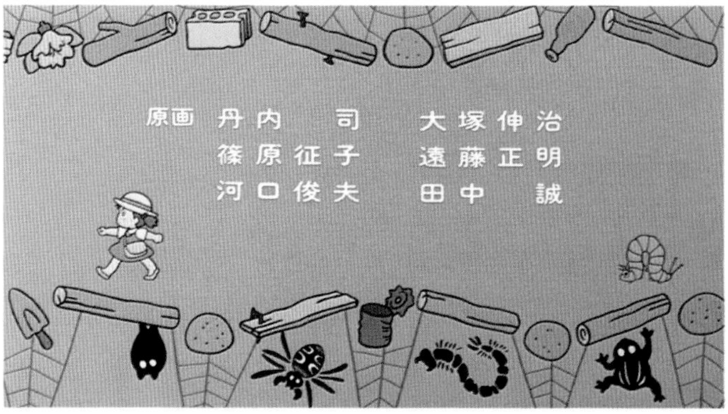
原画　丹内　司　大塚伸治
篠原征子　遠藤正明
河口俊夫　田中　誠
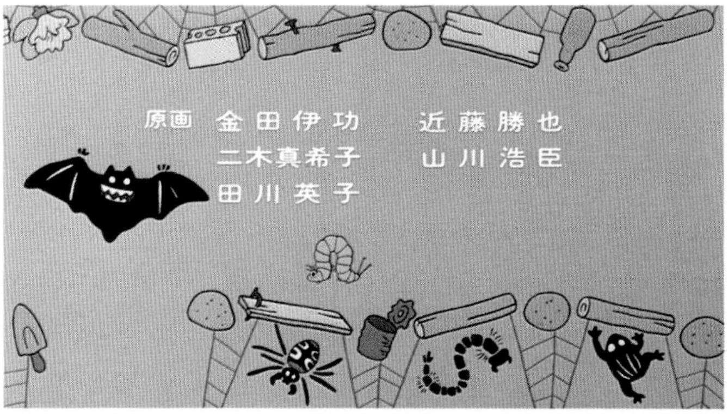
原画　金田伊功　近藤勝也
二木真希子　山川浩臣
田川英子
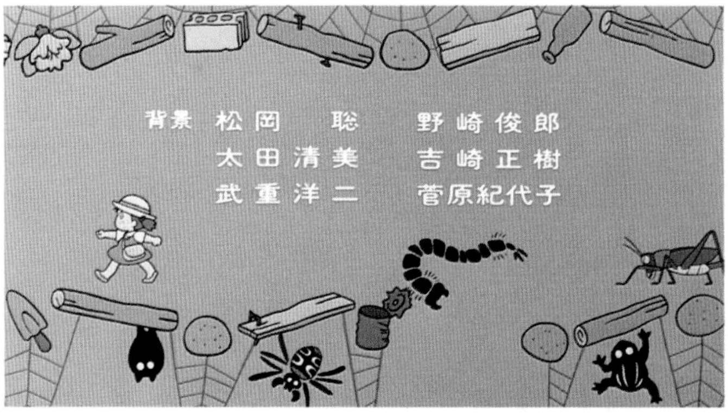
背景　松岡　聡　野崎俊郎
太田清美　吉崎正樹
武重洋二　菅原紀代子
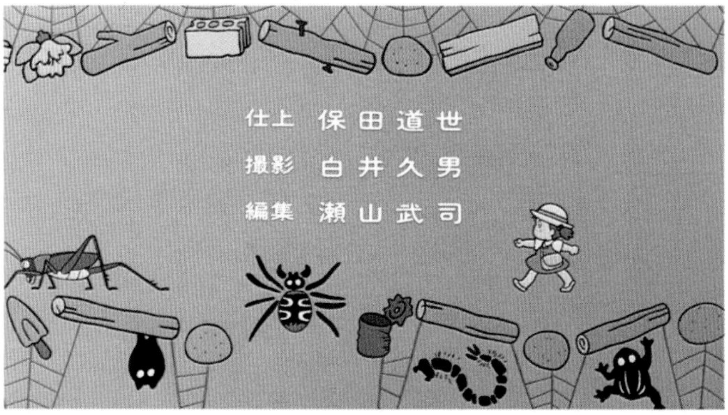
仕上　保田道世
撮影　白井久男
編集　瀬山武司
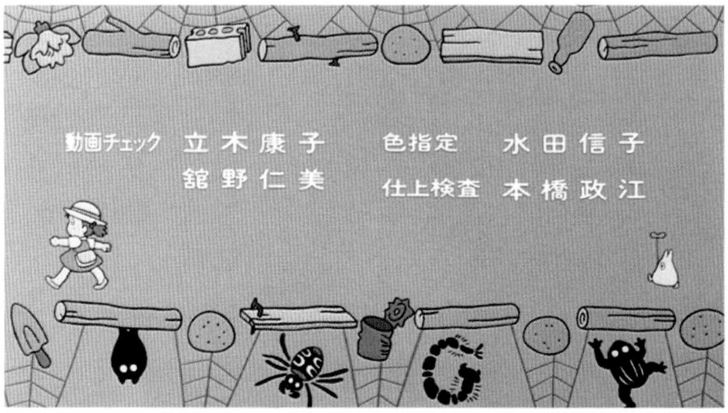
動画チェック　立木康子　色指定　水田信子
舘野仁美　仕上検査　本橋政江

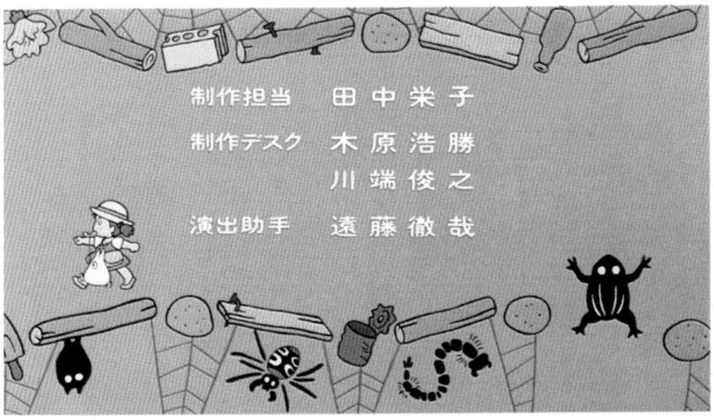
制作担当 田中栄子
制作デスク 木原浩勝
川端俊之
演出助手 遠藤徹哉

The storyboards for the opening sequence of *My Neighbor Totoro* don't really follow the form of "storyboards."

"I spoke to the animator Otsuka, describing the rough layout of the storyboards here. The sequence was determined through permutations and combinations determined by the time sheets. Each element was made individually and then combined in the time sheets, so there are no storyboards for this segment." *(Miyazaki)*

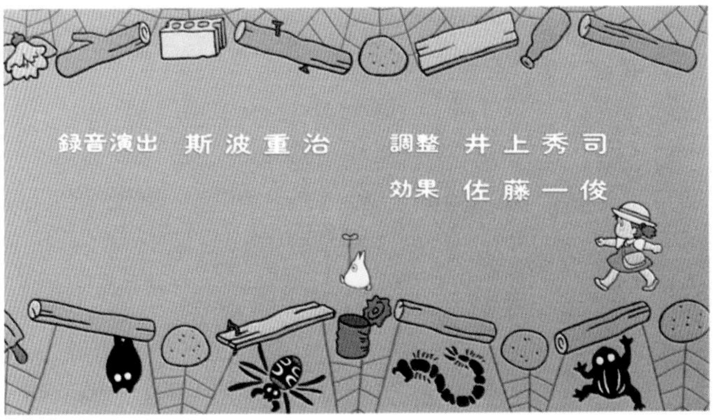
録音演出 斯波重治
調整 井上秀司
効果 佐藤一俊

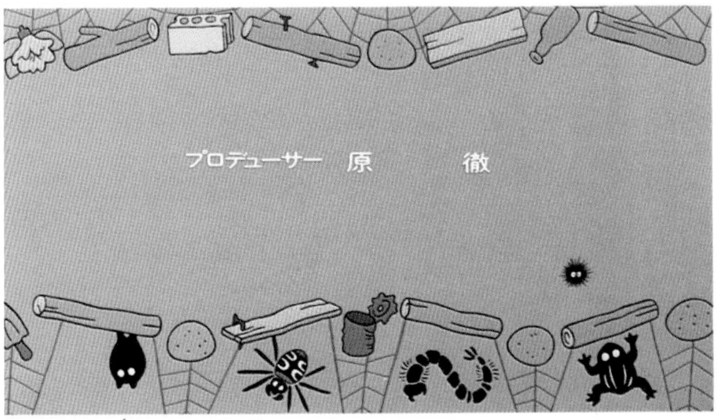
プロデューサー 原 徹

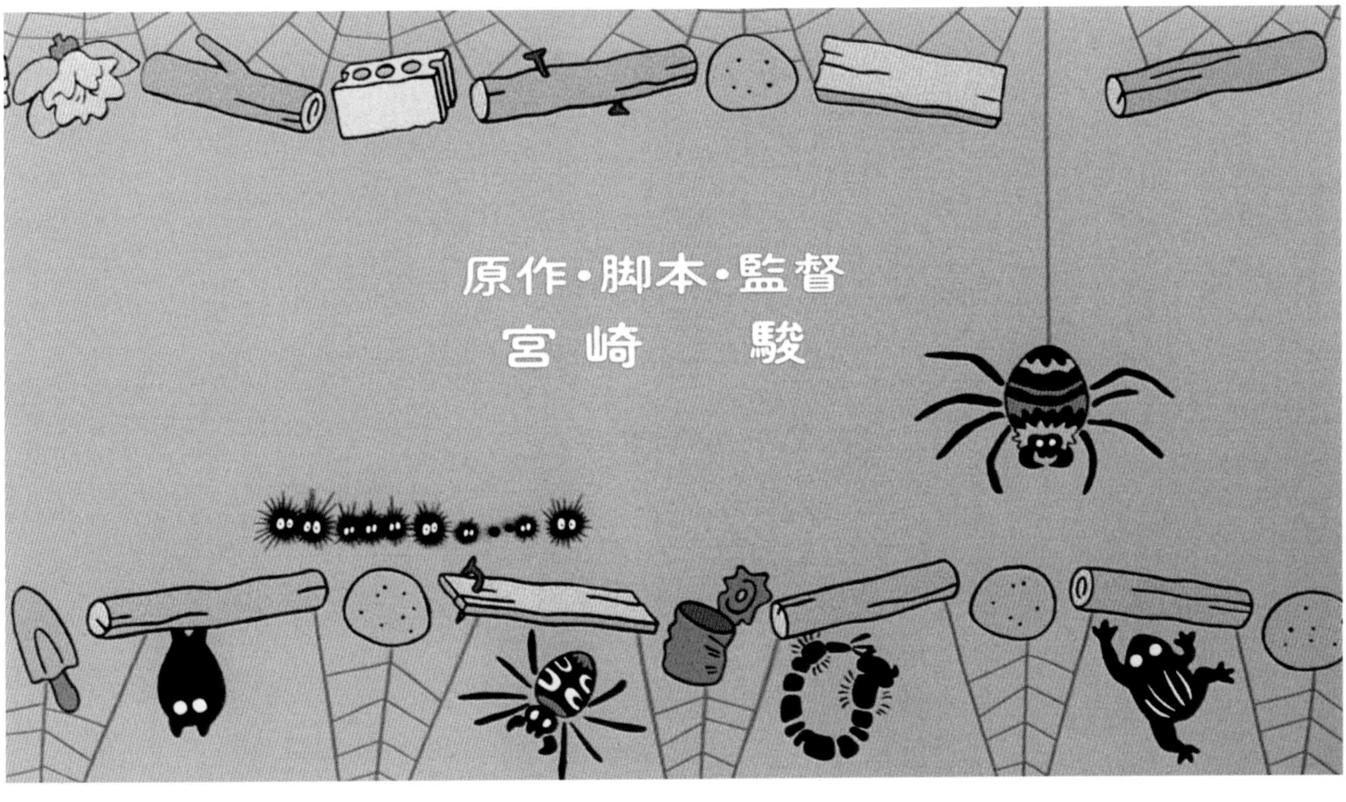
原作・脚本・監督
宮崎 駿

1

1 Three-wheeler truck passing through the wheat fields. *(cel art)*

2 Town with rows of apartment buildings. *(storyboard)*

3 The film opens on "A beautiful, clear day in May. A three-wheeler truck packed to the brim slowly passes through the middle of a wheat field." *(From storyboard)*. The first version of the storyboards was still influenced by the sketchbook.

"At the beginning there was only going to be one house surrounded by trees where the landscape would suddenly change. The trees there became smaller, and the main road became a trail. The residential area gave way to paddy fields, and sidewalks turned into waterways. The trees around the house really shrunk in size. That's where Satsuki's house would appear. The story would begin with the three-wheeler rumbling over there and end with the girls returning to their world. The kids who hear the story from a granny then ask, "Do the Totoros still exist, Granny?" The granny replies, "I wonder." Then we find the Totoros singing "Hoh Hoh" in the forest in the neon-lit city. Their voices may be drowned out by the city noise, but I was going to have the film end with them blowing on their ocarinas." *(Miyazaki)*

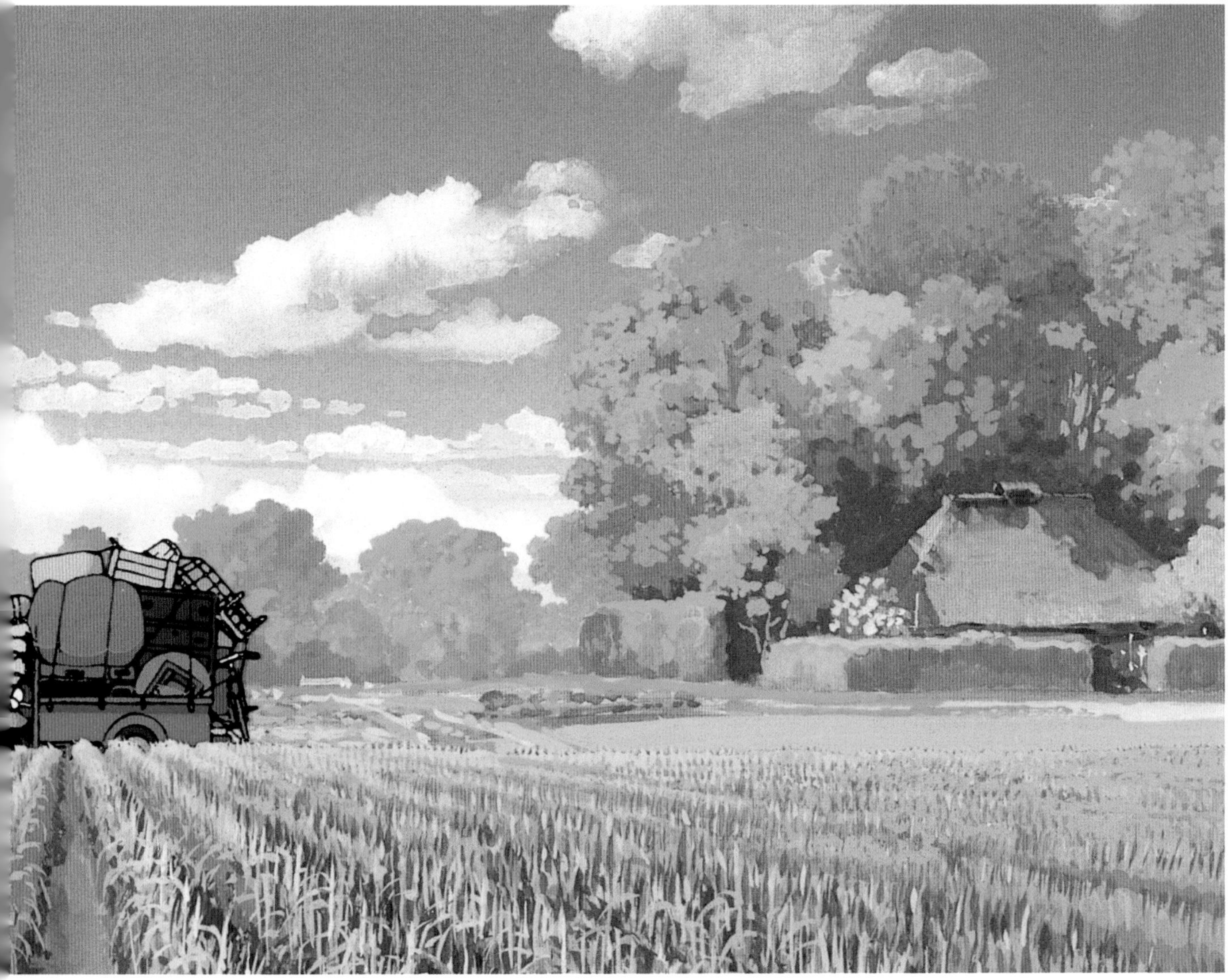

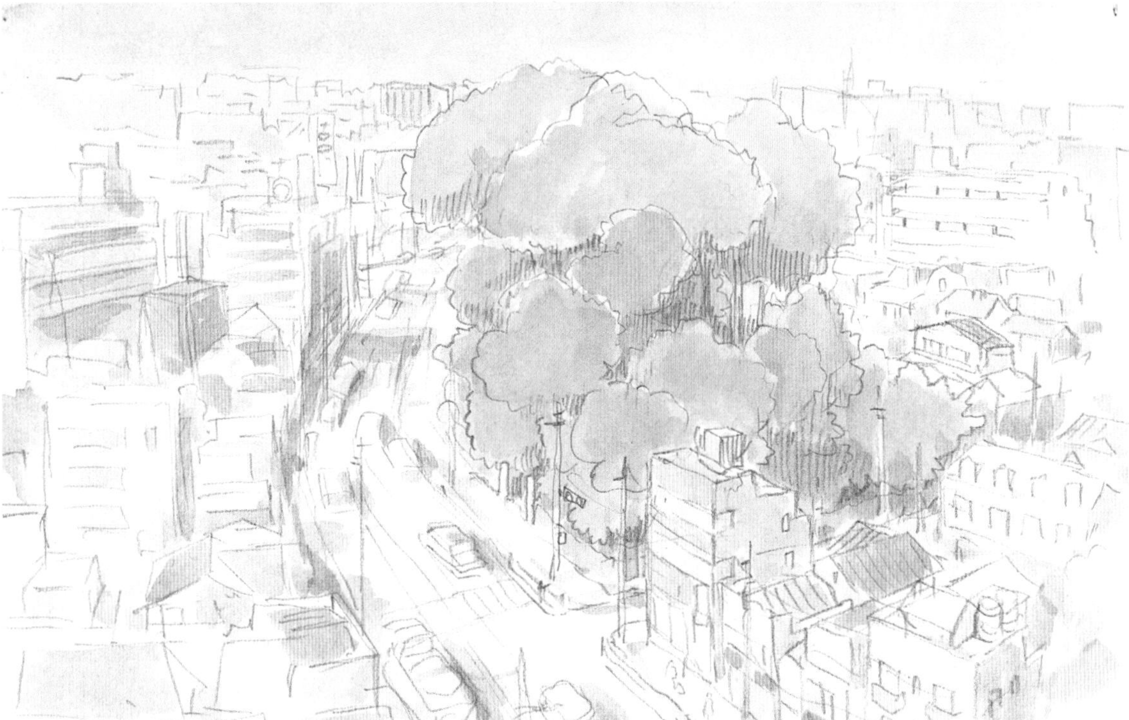

2

1

Ⓧ まだァ ╱×印は
Ⓜ だから トラックのうしろに
　すればよかったのに
Ⓧ ヤダヤ

引越し荷物の中の二人.

2

アメを少しずつ
すわせて

3

4

5

6

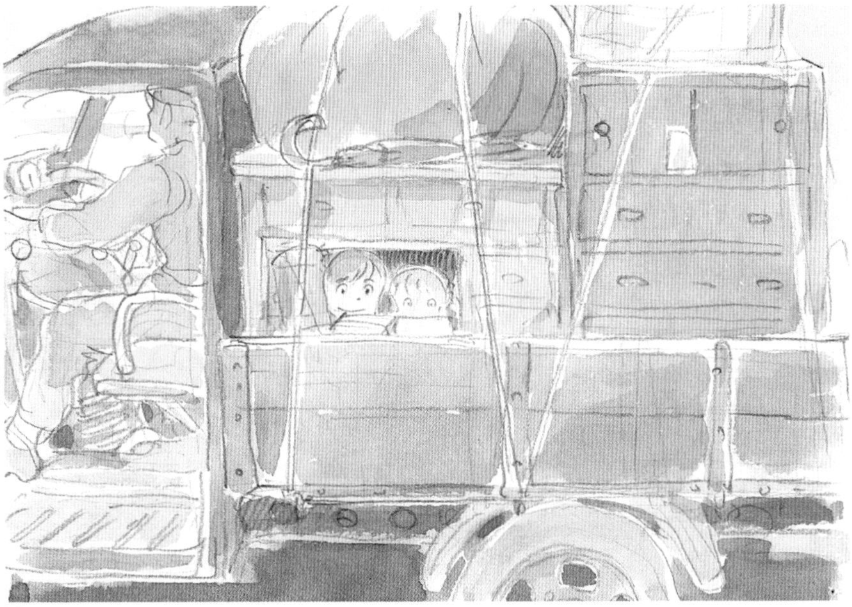
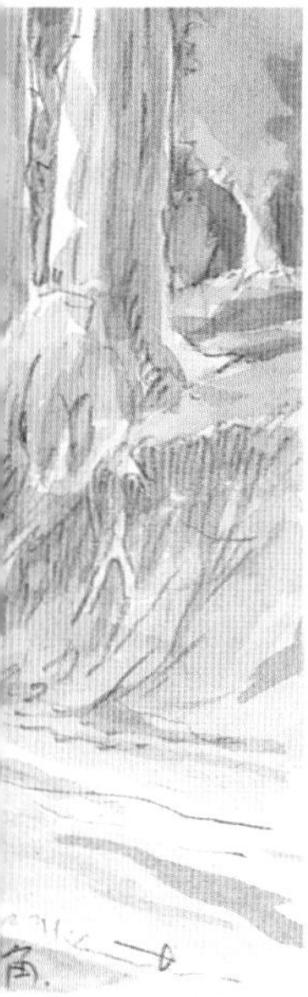

7

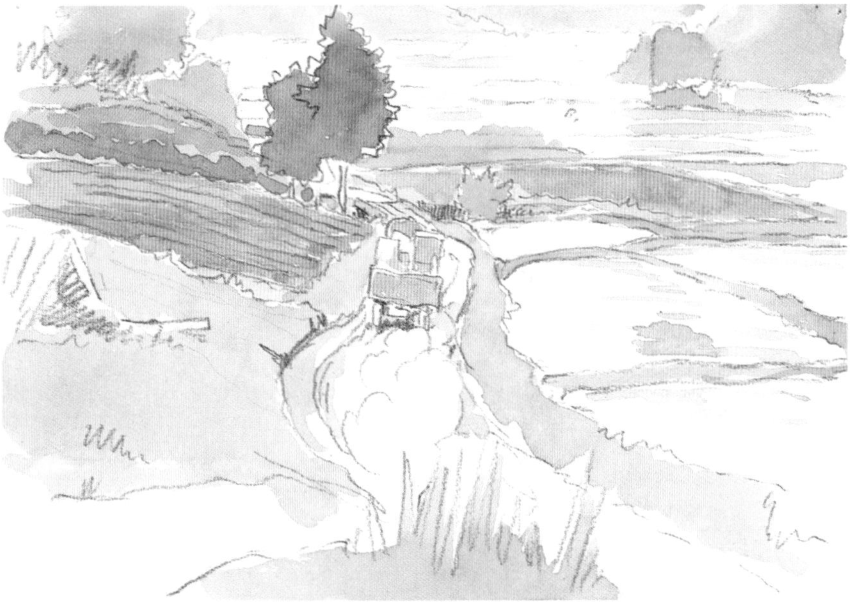
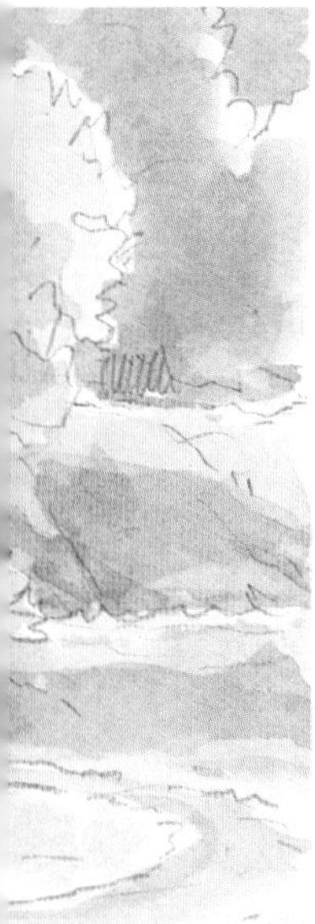

8

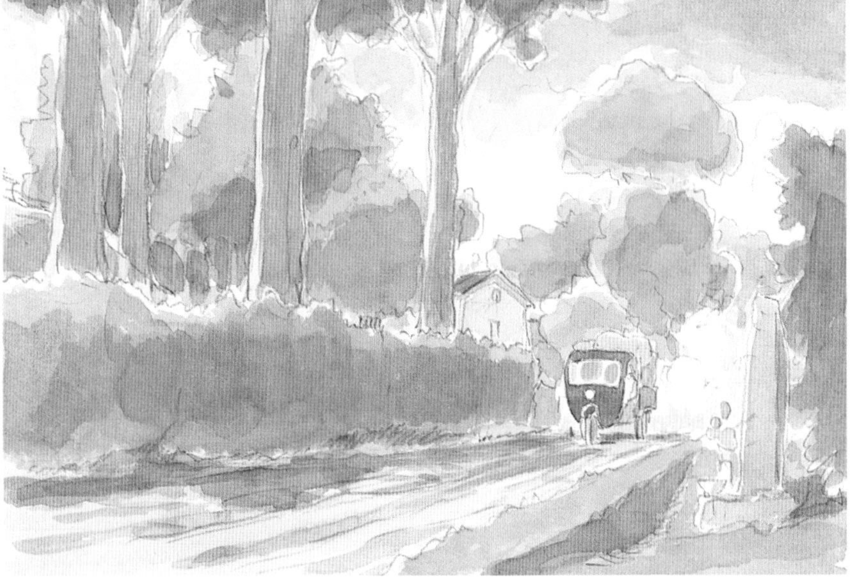
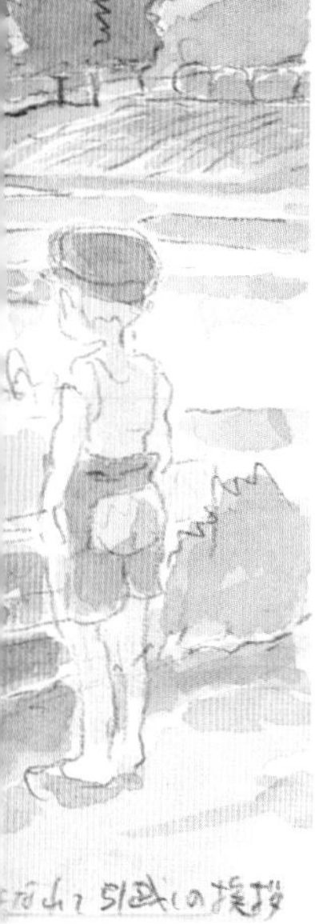

9

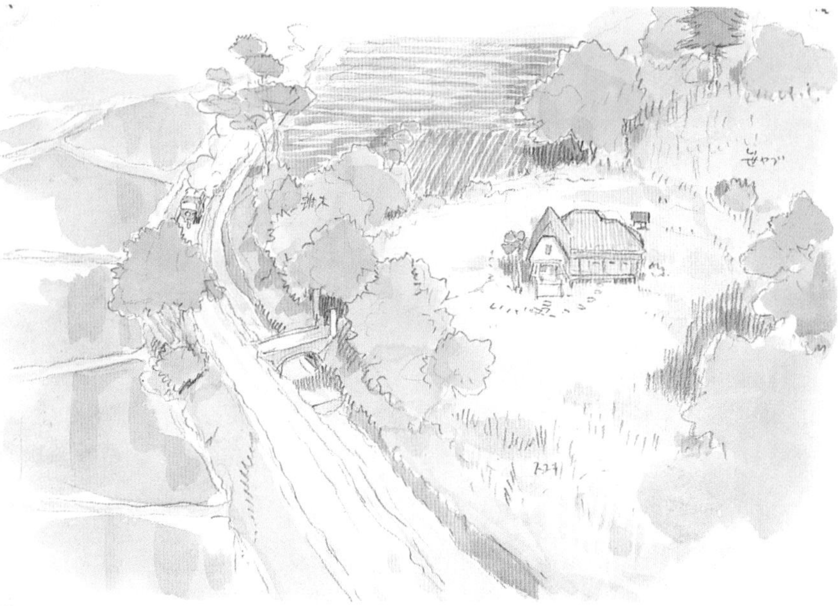

10

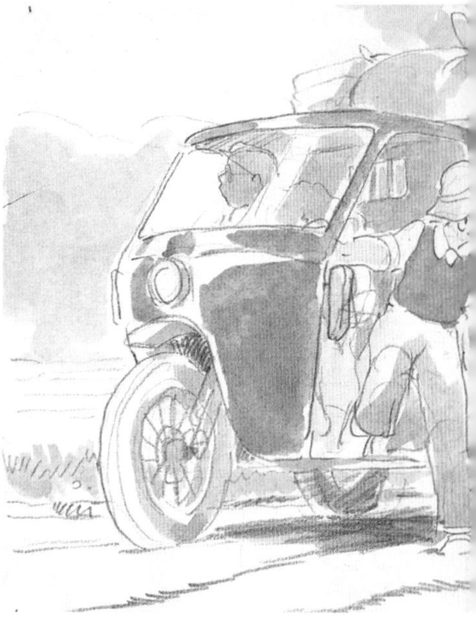

11

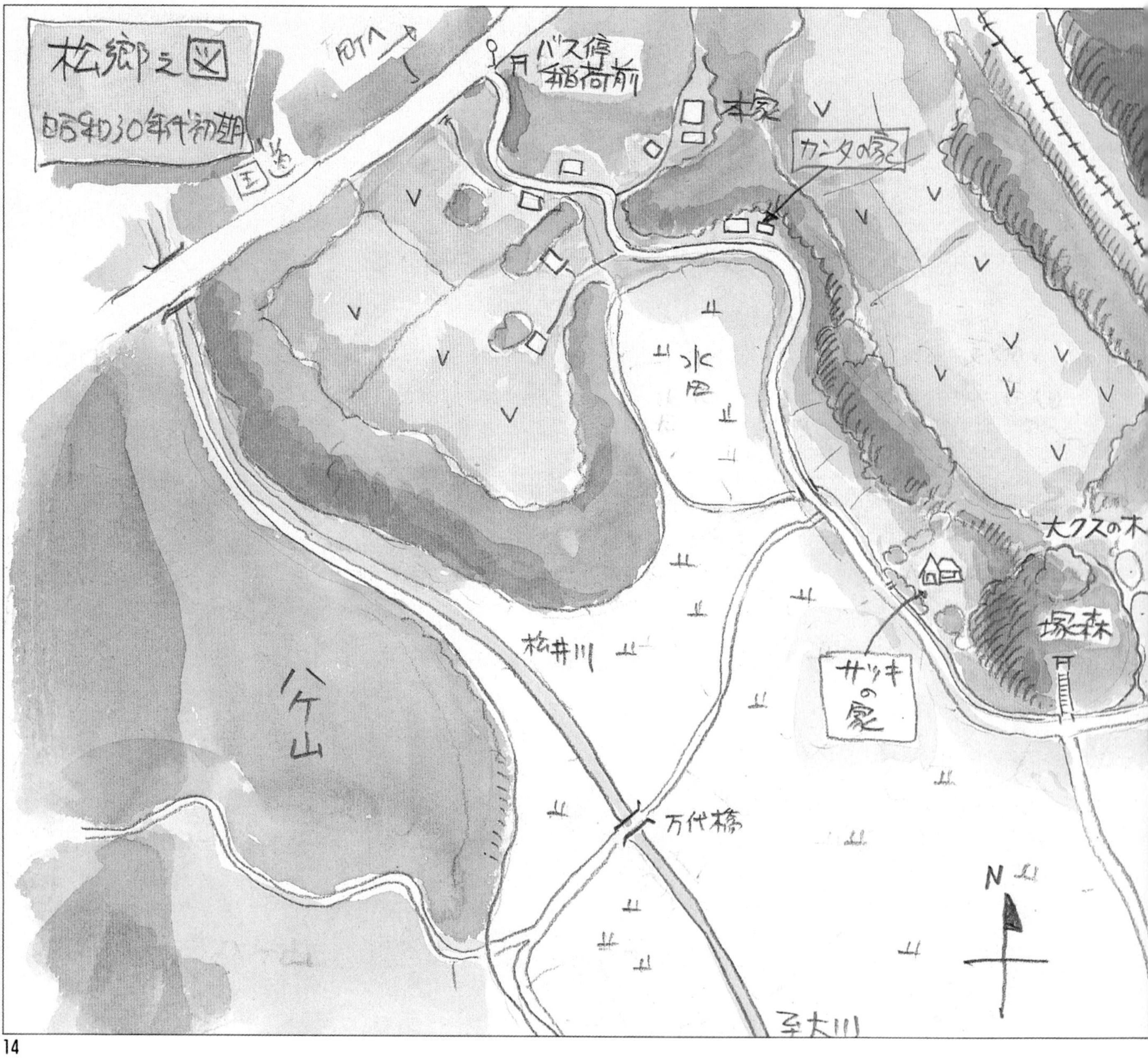
松郷之図
昭和30年代初期
町へ
国道
バス停
稲荷前
本家
カンタの家
水田
大クスの木
塚森
サツキの家
松井川
八ケ山
万代橋
至大川
N

14

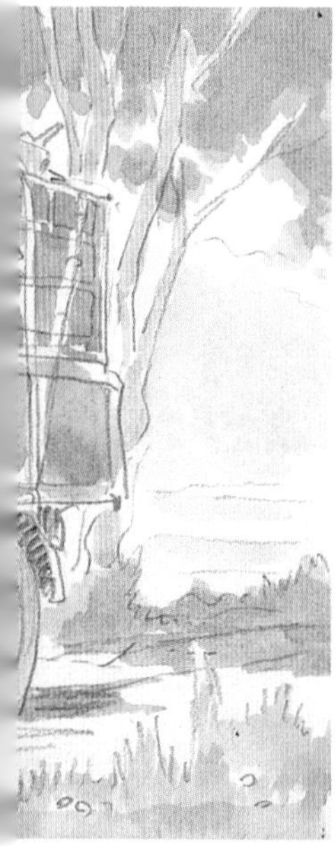

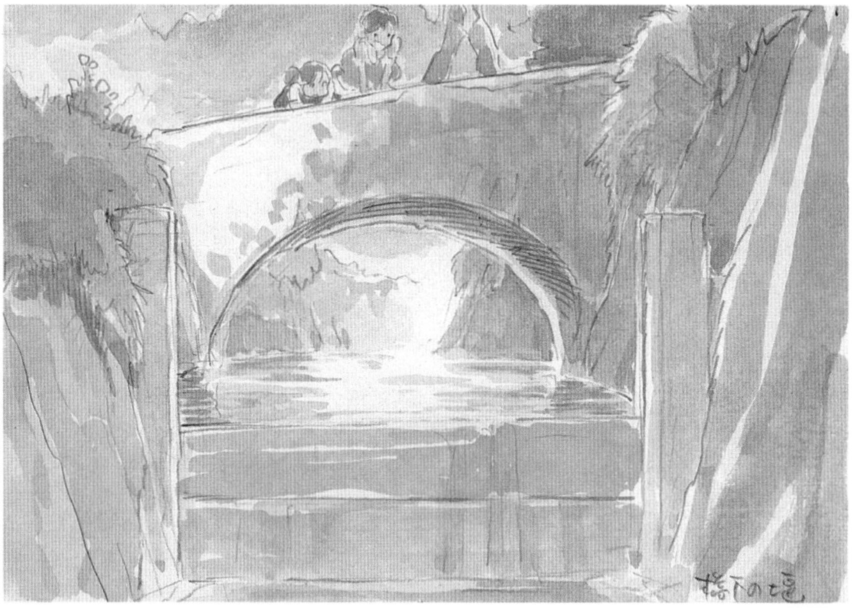

12

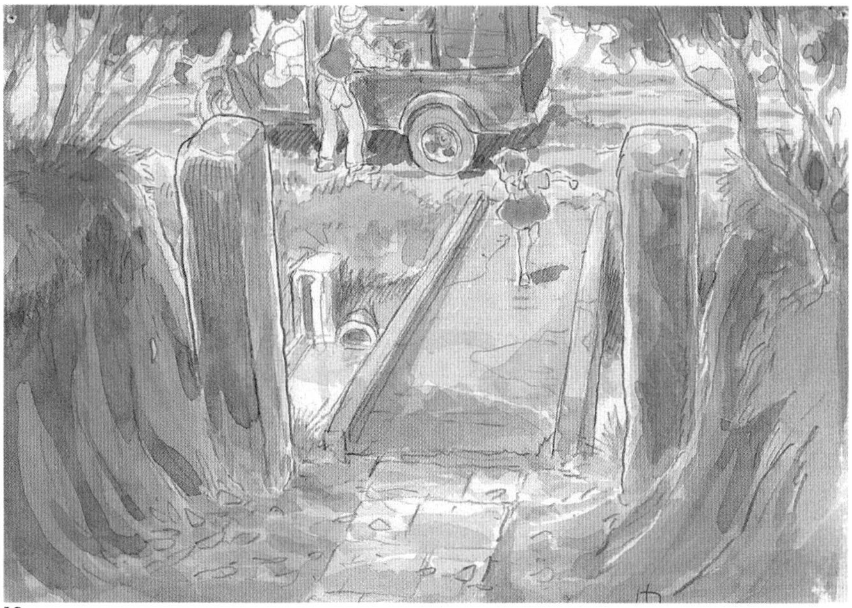

13

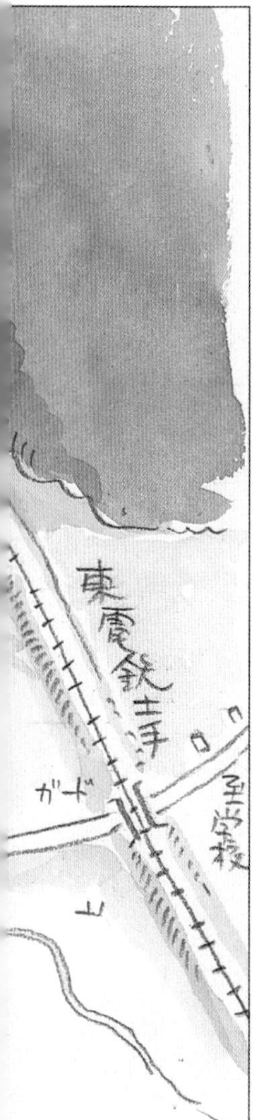
東電鉄土手
ガード
至小学校

1-13 Storyboards depicting Satsuki's family on their way to their new house by the forest.

14 A map of the story's setting. Matsugo, late 1950s.

"It's supposed to be 1955, but we weren't terribly thorough in our research. What we had in mind was `a recent past´ that everyone can relate to." *(Miyazaki)*

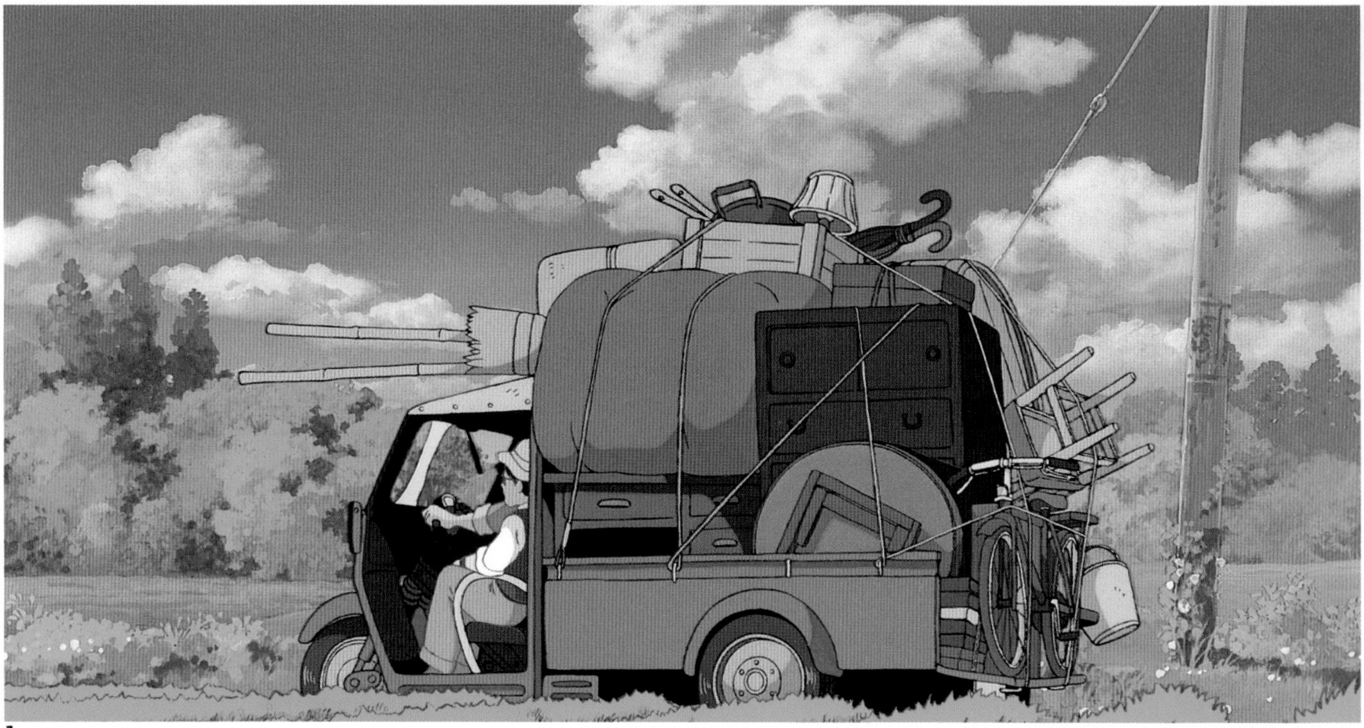

1

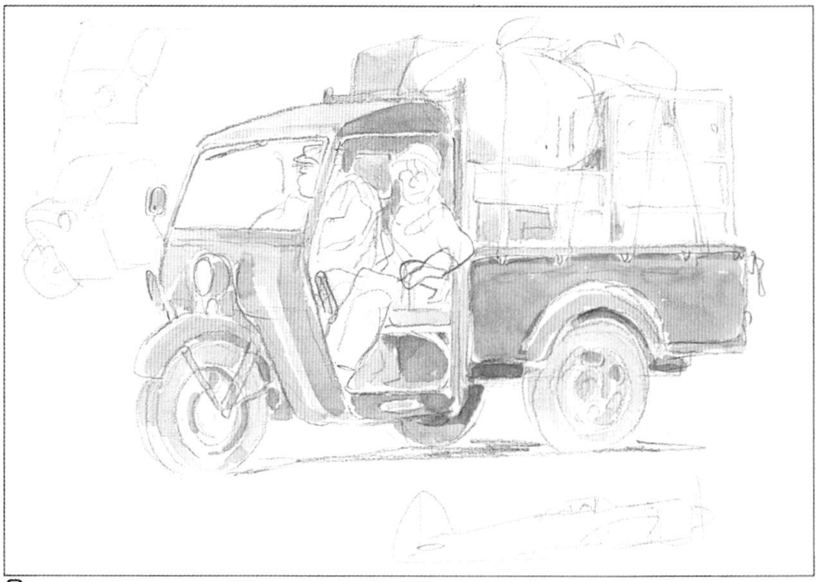

2

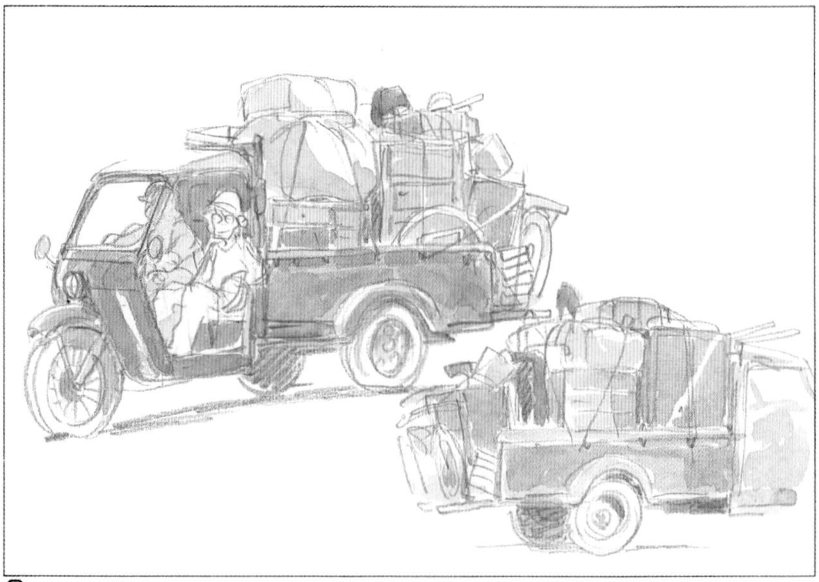

3

1 Three-wheeler truck. *(cel art)*

2, 3 Three-wheeler truck. *(concept art)*

4 Three-wheeler truck rumbling by on the trail between the farms and paddies. *(cel art)*

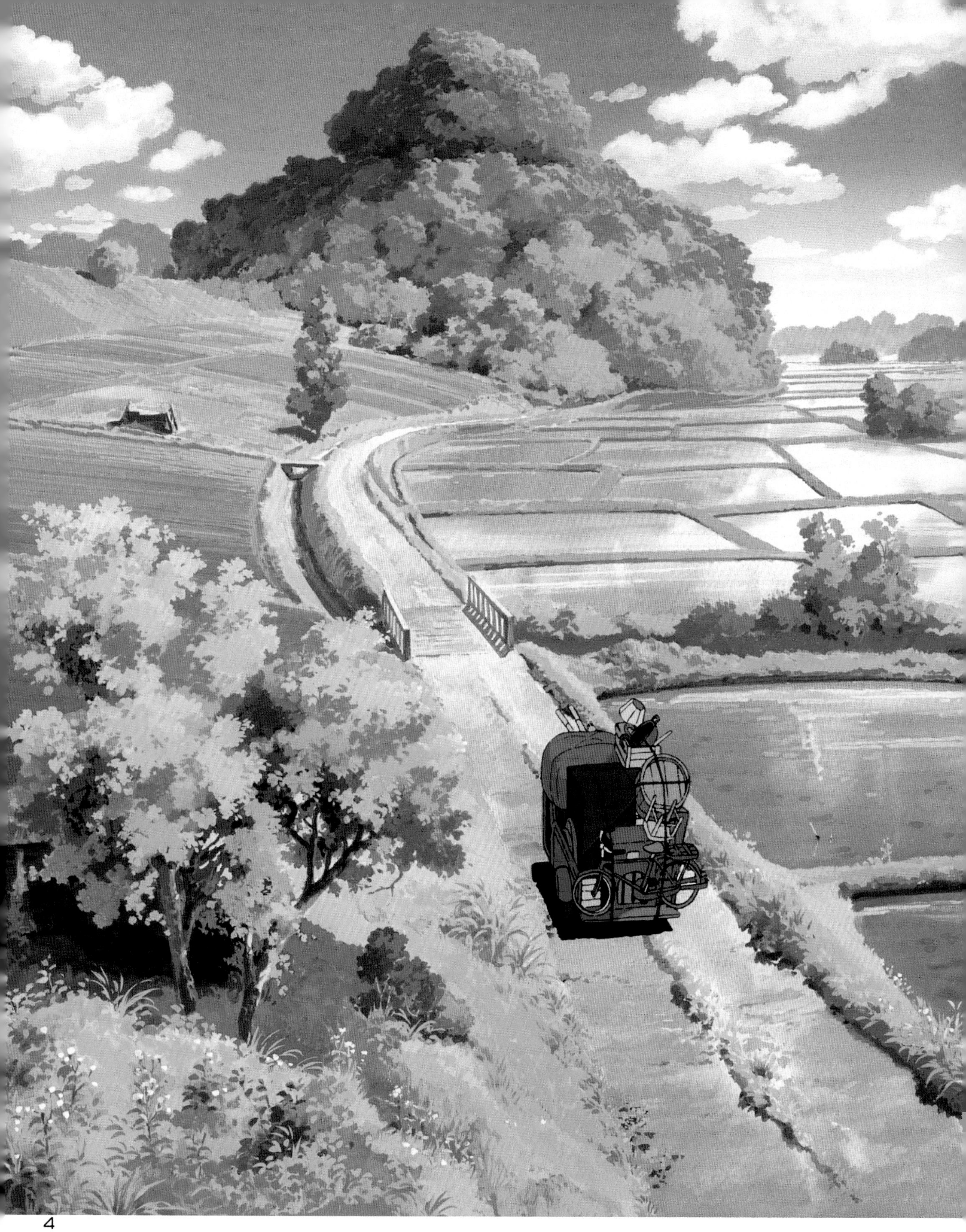
4

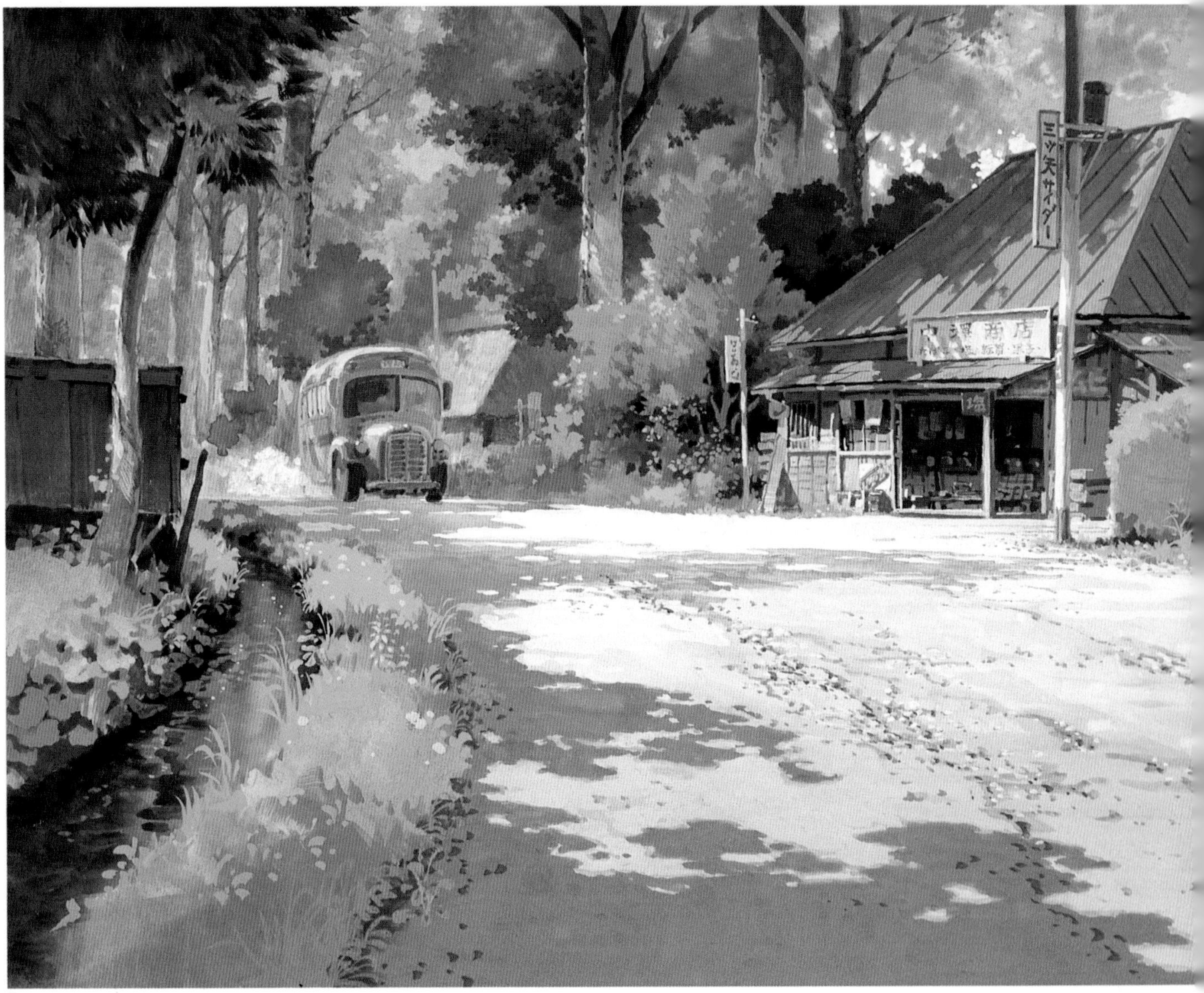
三ツ矢サイダー
1

1 Keyaki tree-lined street. *(concept art)*

2 Corner bus stop with Inari stone statue. *(background)*

3 Flowing stream. *(concept art)*

"Previously the darker patches of trees and weeds had a blue tint, which would give a cold tone to the dark areas. So we added a lot of warmer colors like green and brown to the dark areas, which gave a lustrous tone to both bright and dark areas." *(Kazuo Oga)*

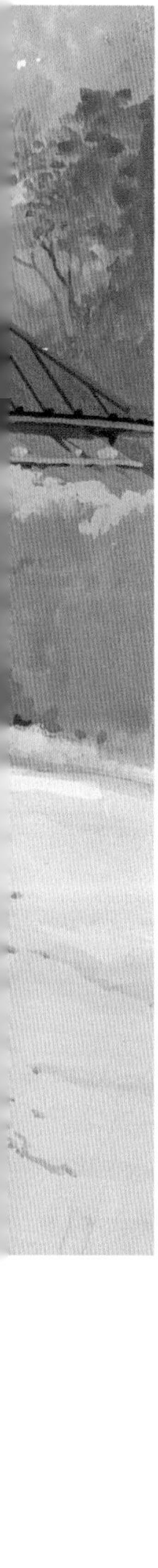

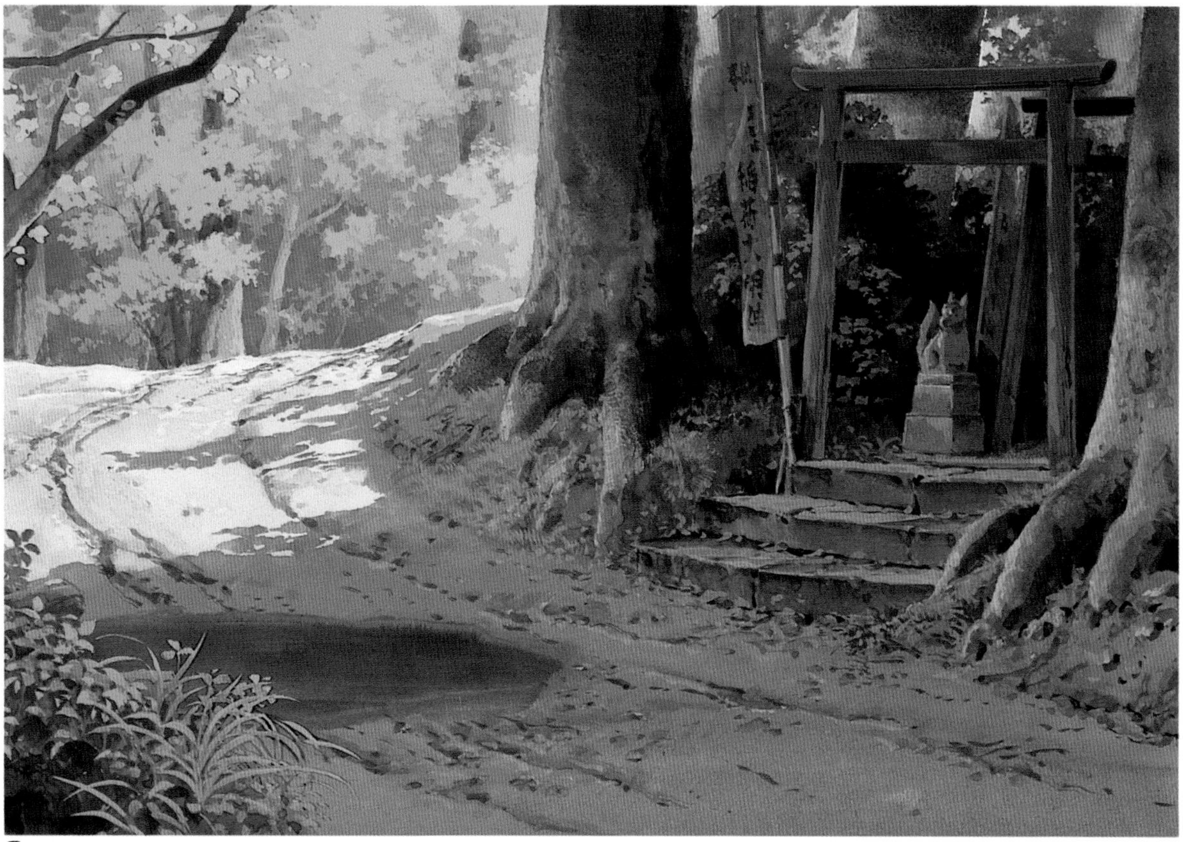

2

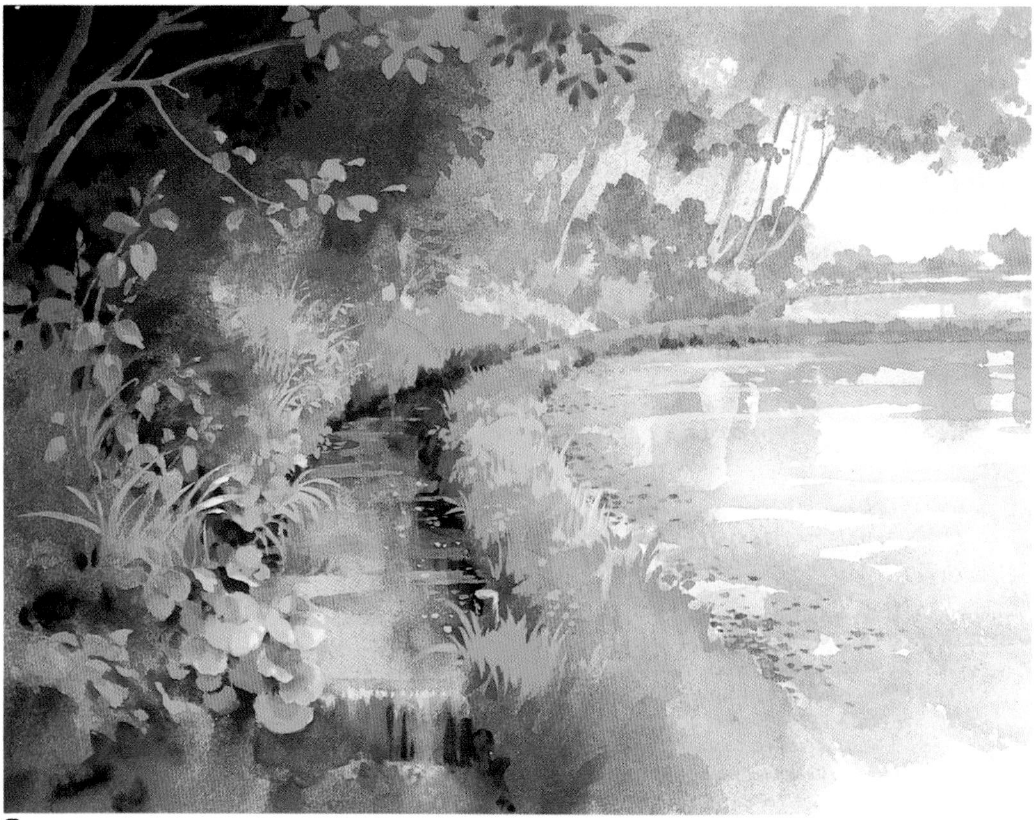

3

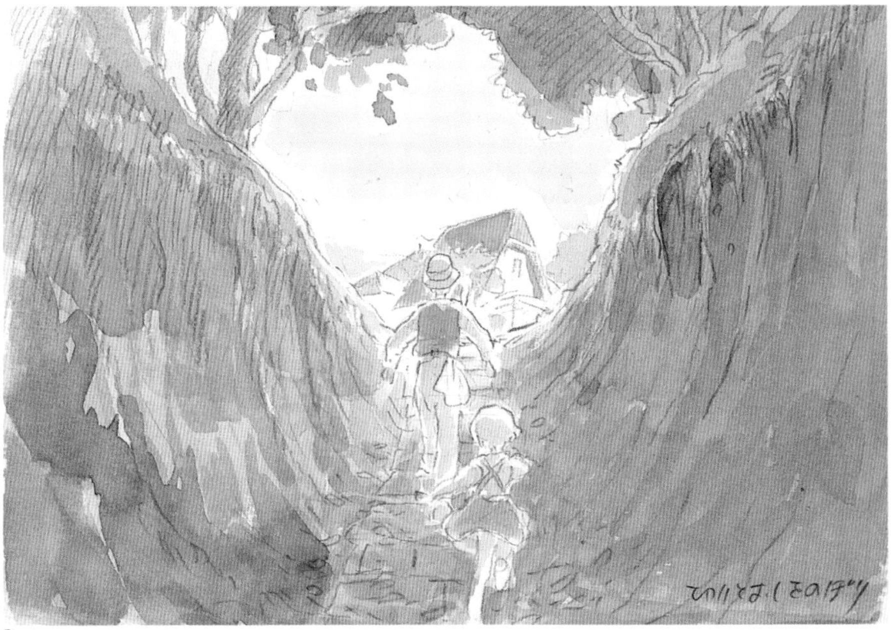

1

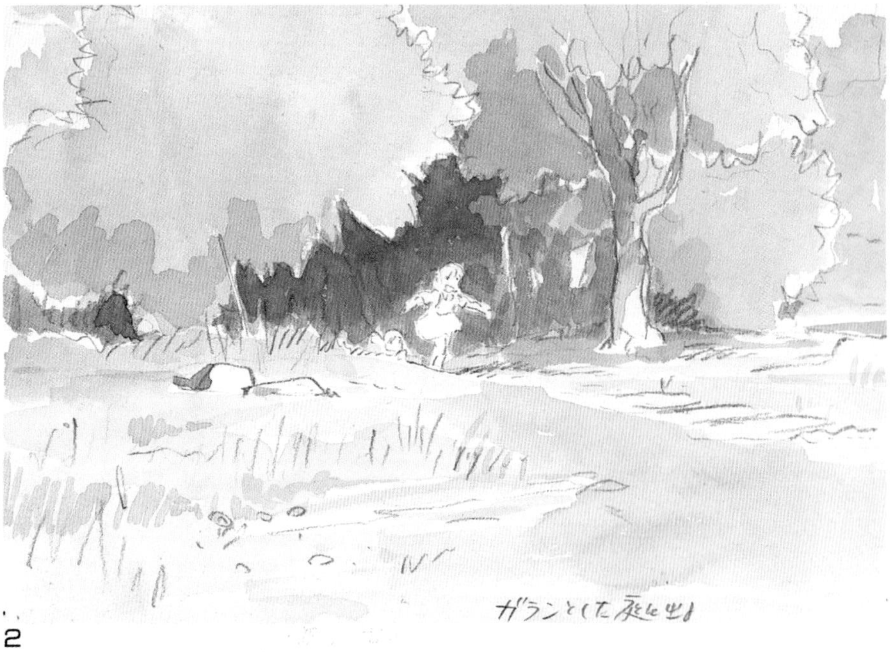

2

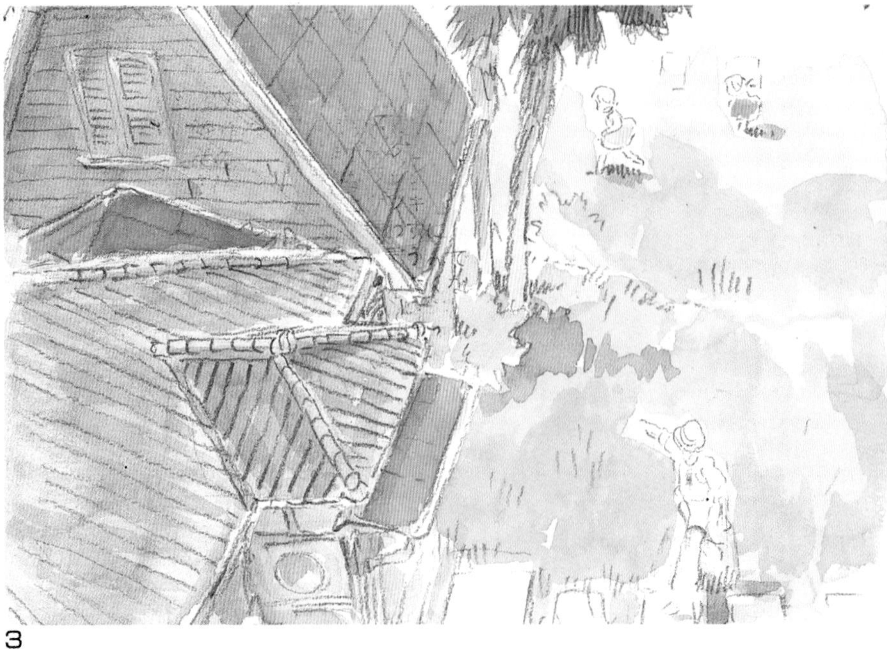

3

1-3 Climbing up the secret passageway, Satsuki's family find their new home. *(storyboard)*

4-5 Single house standing in the middle of a weed-ridden field. *(concept art)*

"We first imagined what an ideal house would look like. The staff came up with the idea, and then everyone looked at the rushes. Instead of being impressed by Satsuki and Mei's movements, they all said, `I want to live there.' Without wanting to lower their standard of living, they wanted to live in that kind of house." *(Miyazaki)*

4

その見た目．金星

5

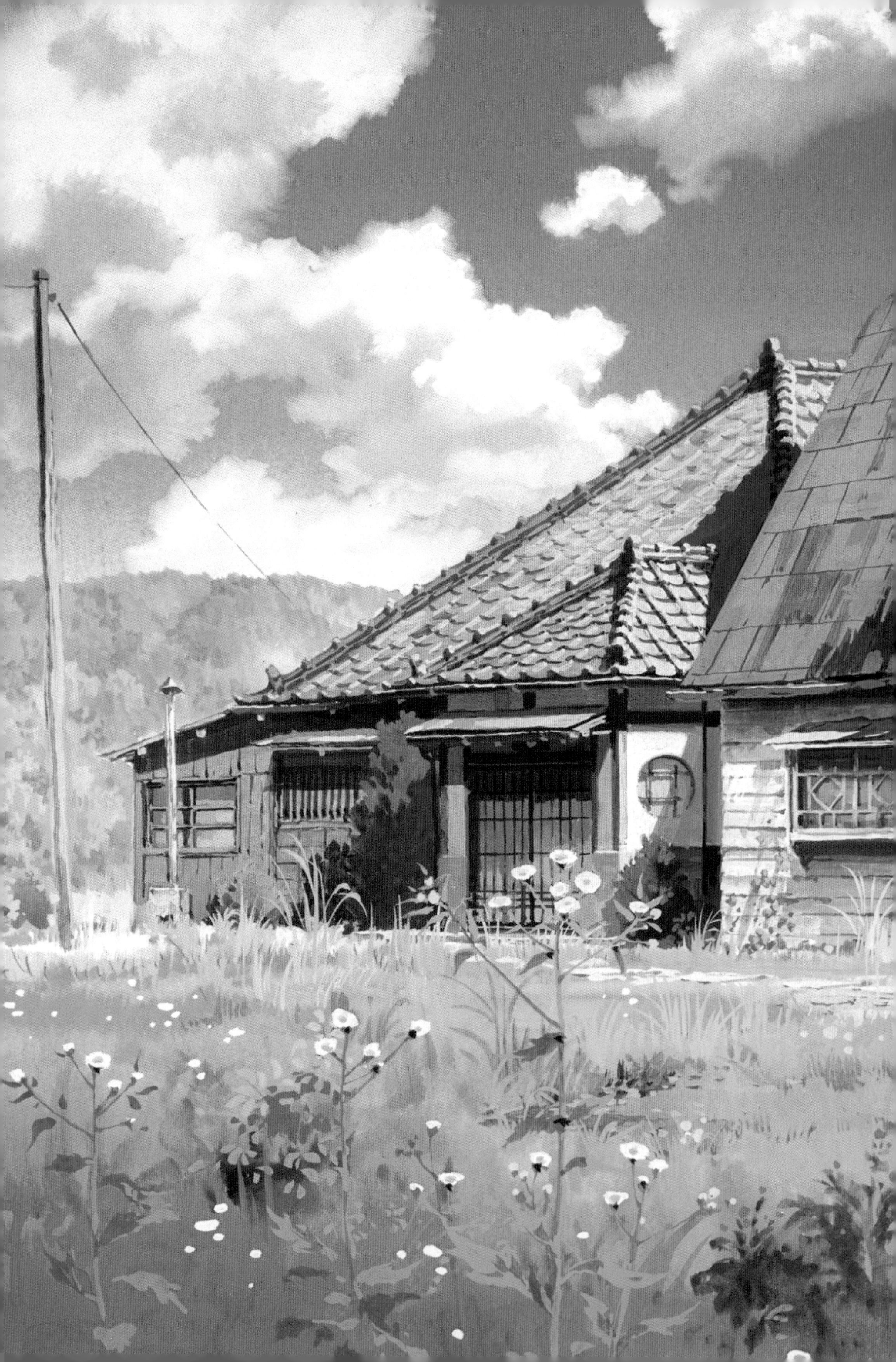

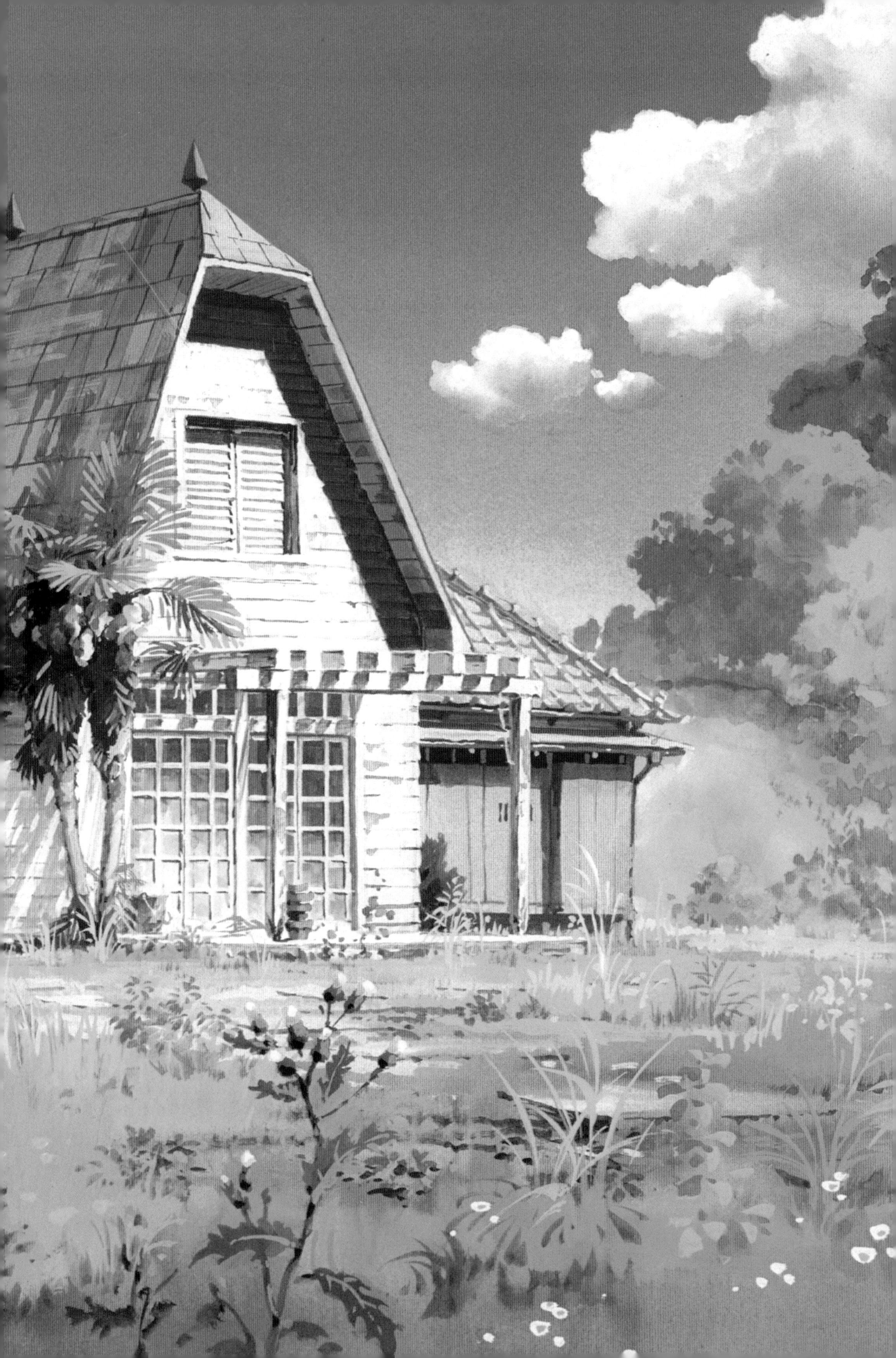

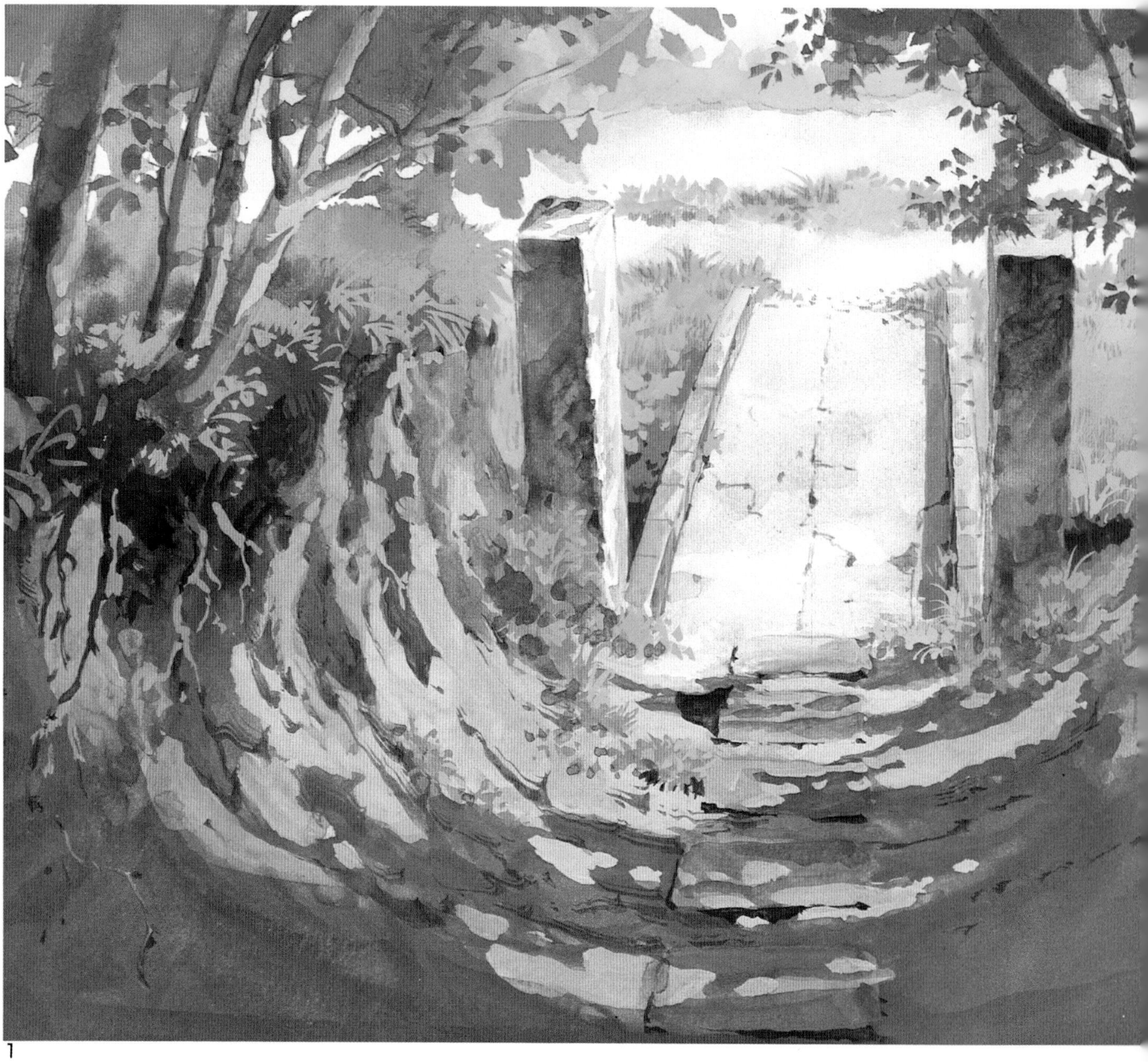
1

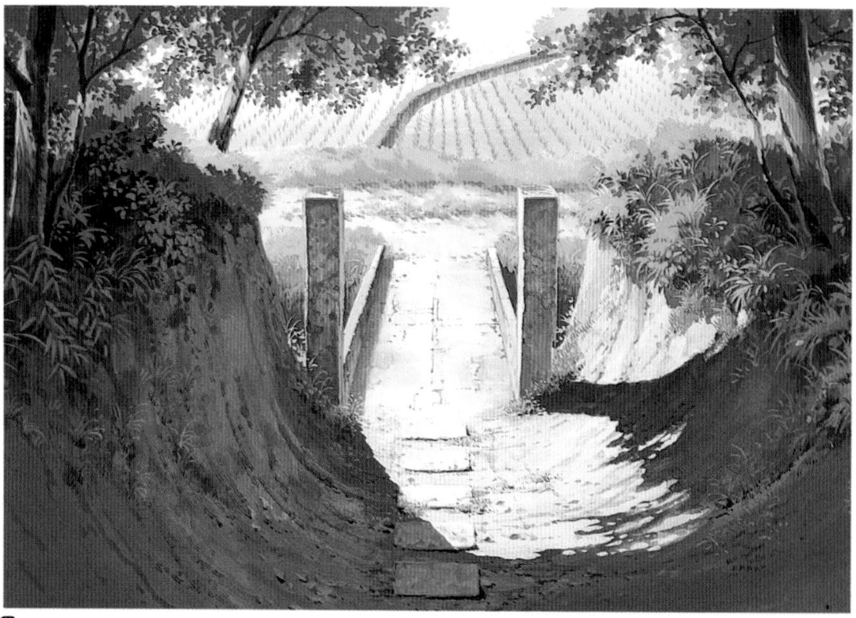
2

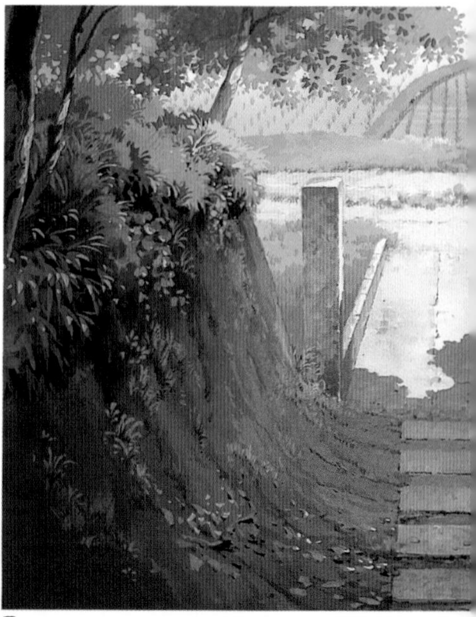
3

4

1     Gate to secret passageway. *(concept art)*

2     Gate to secret passageway in morning light. *(background)*

3     Gate to secret passageway at noon. *(background)*

Backgrounds for the same secret passageway gate are drawn with every shift in lighting, length of shade, and color.

4     The gate to the secret passageway as seen from the road. *(concept art)*

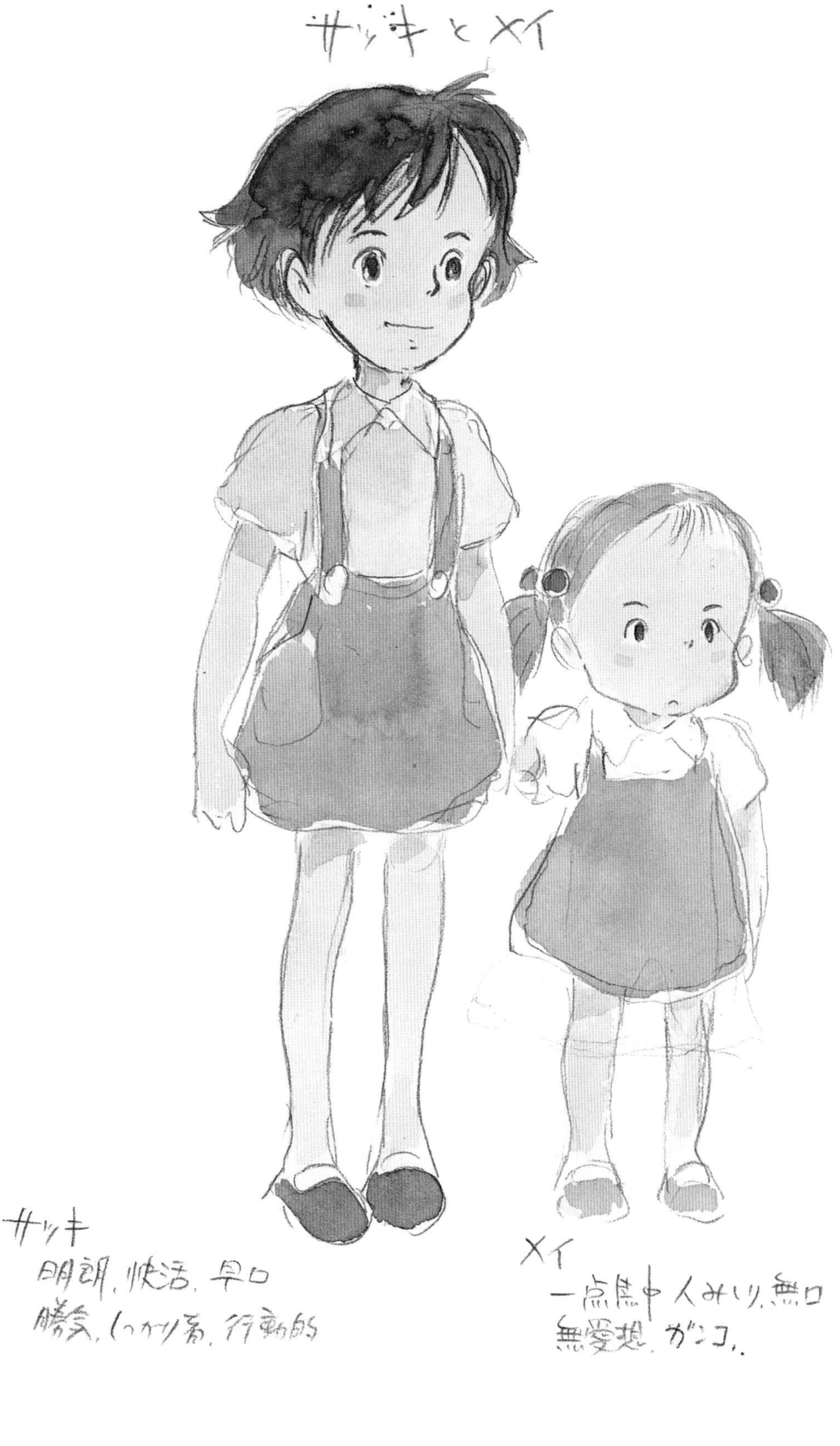
サツキとメイ
サツキ
明朗、快活、早口
勝気、しっかり者、行動的
メイ
一点集中 人みしり、無口
無愛想、ガンコ、、

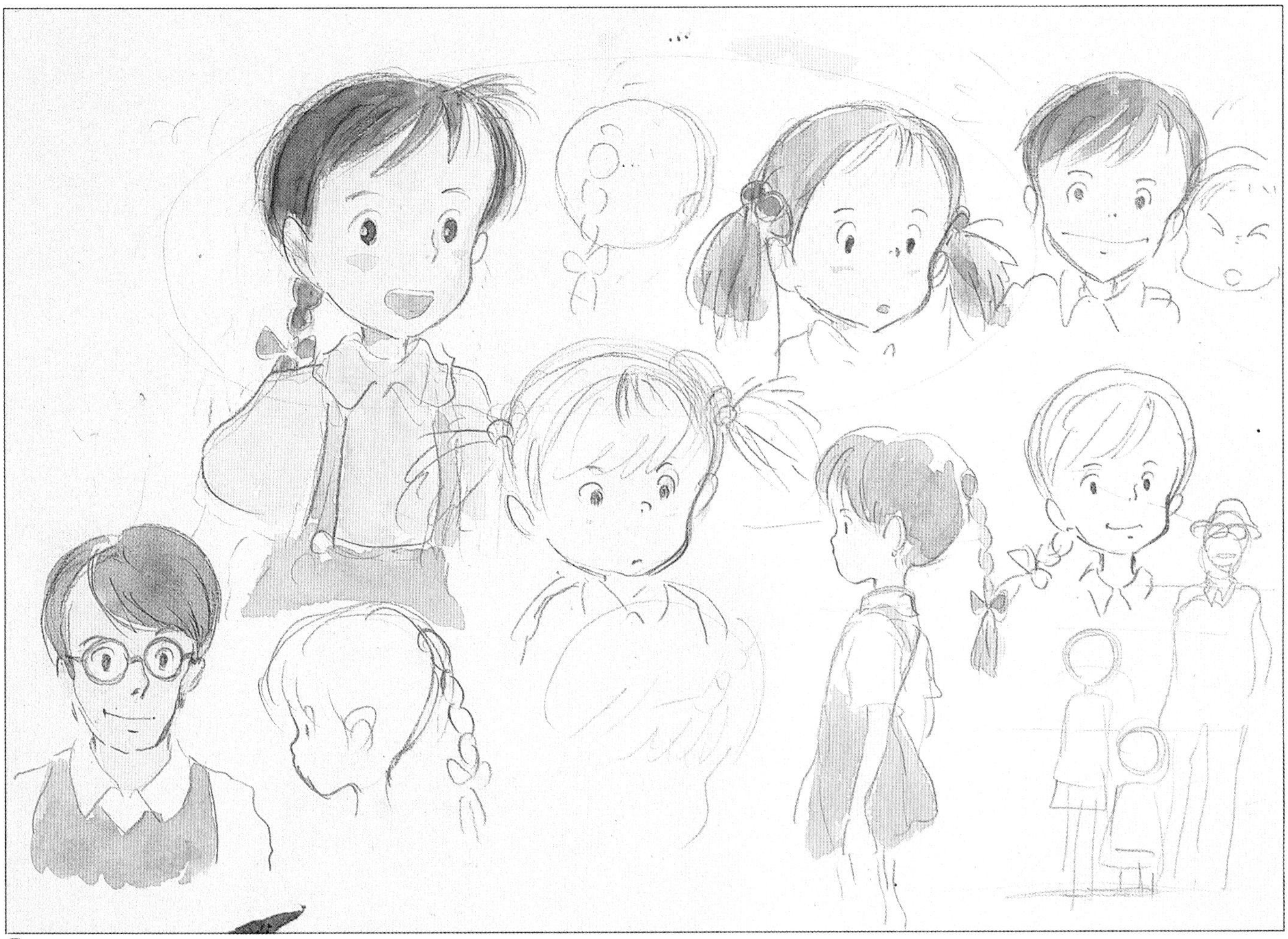

2

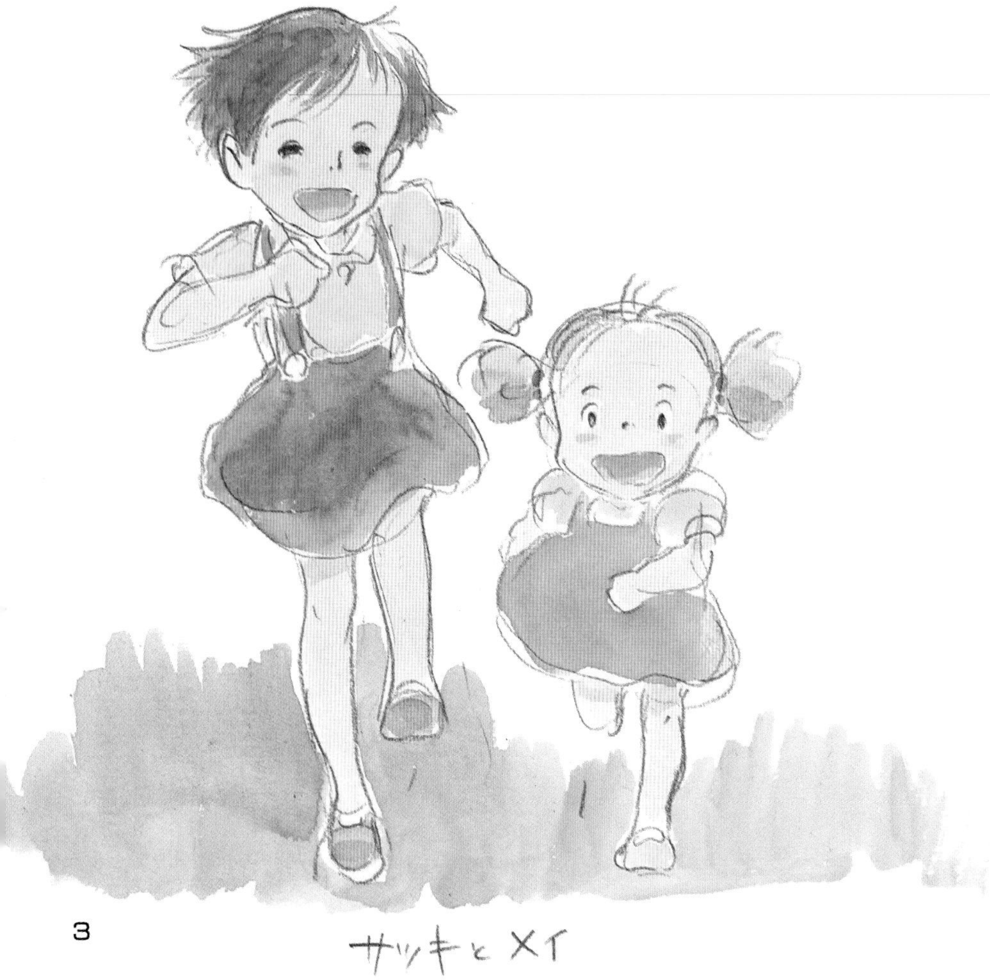
サツキとメイ

3

1 Satsuki and Mei. *(character design)*

2 Satsuki, Mei, and their father. *(character design)*

3 Satsuki and Mei frolicking around.*(concept sketch)*

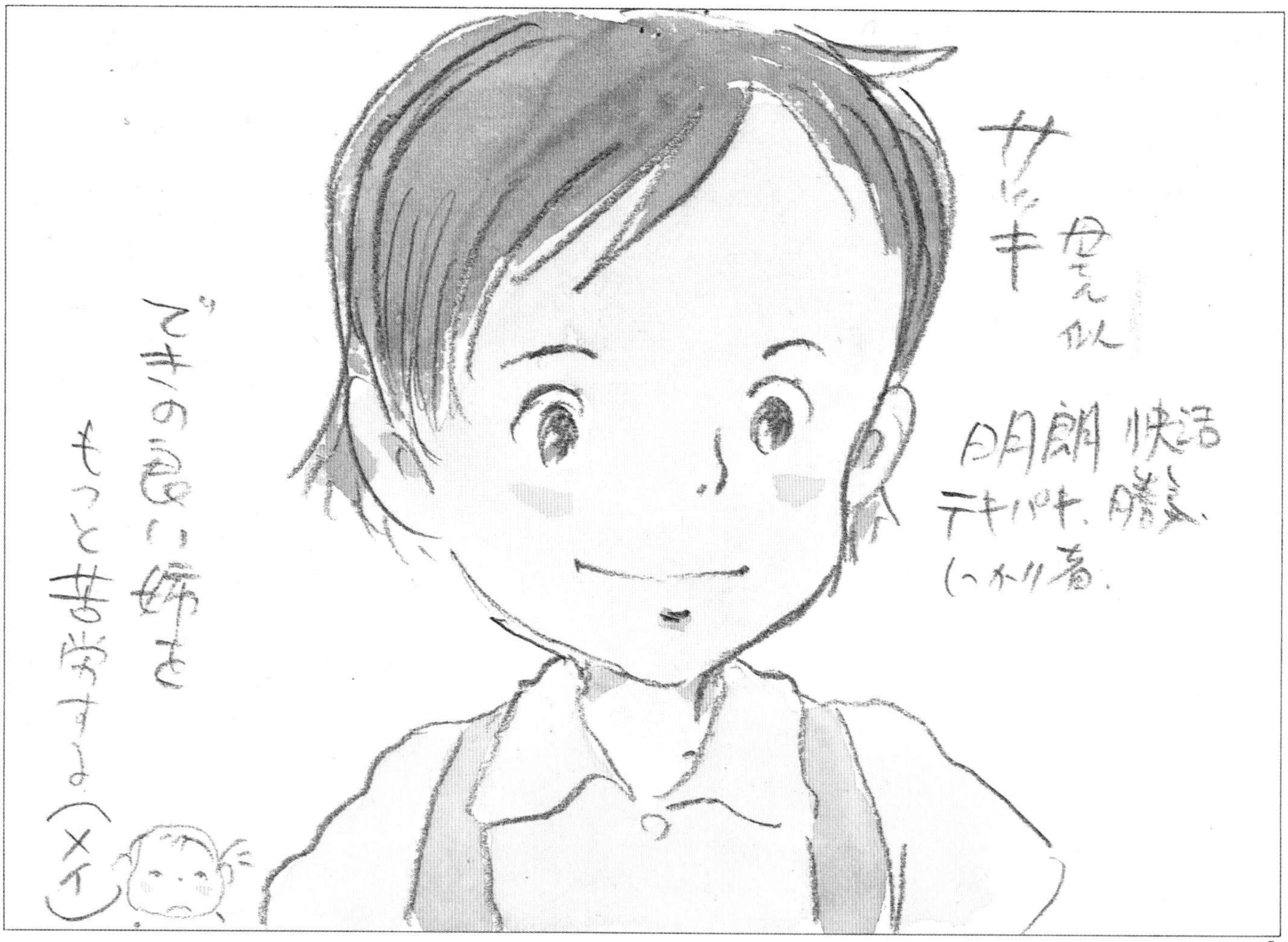
サツキ
母さん似
明朗快活
テキパキ、勝気
しっかり者
できの良い姉をもつと苦労するよ(メイ)

1

1-4 Satsuki, who takes after her mother. *(character design)*

5 Satsuki is athletic (good at the horizontal bars). *(film)*

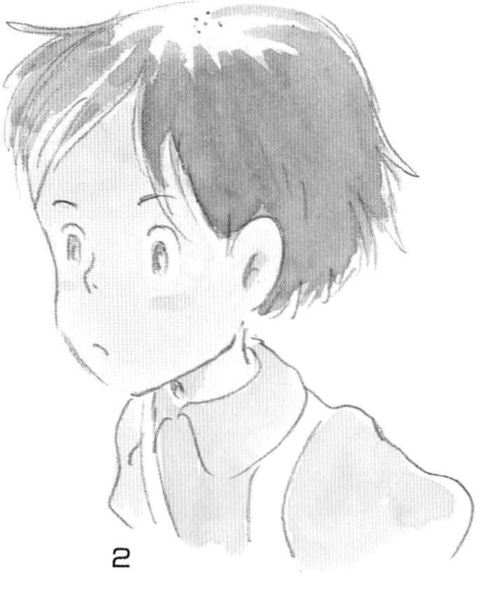

2

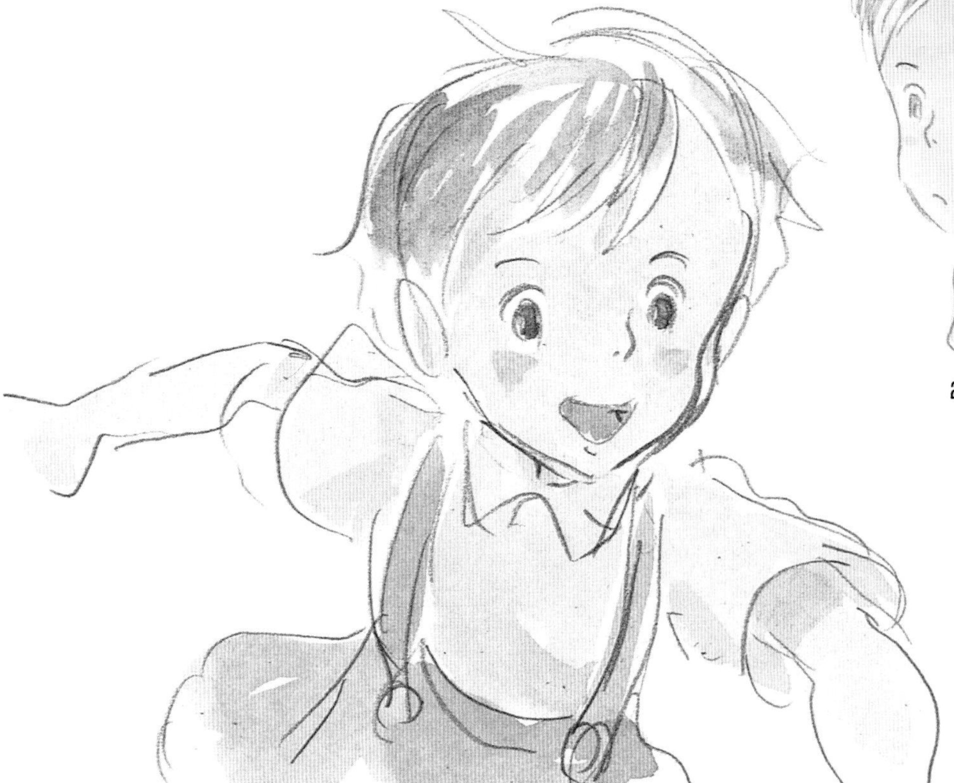

3

4

5

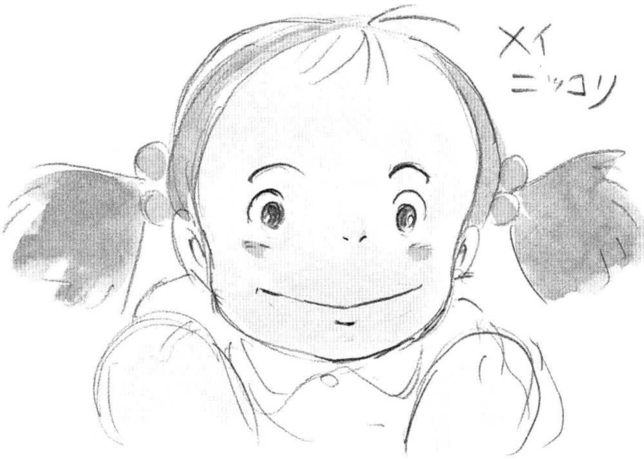
メイ
ニッコリ

1

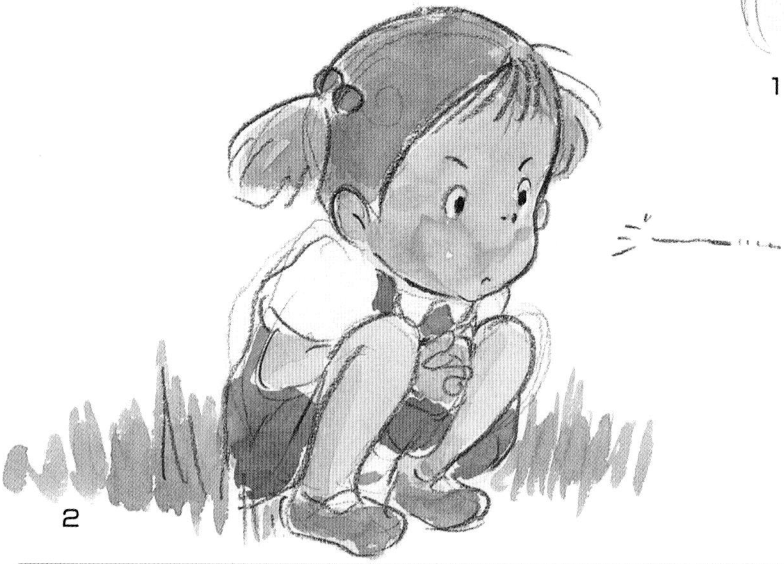
ジー……

2

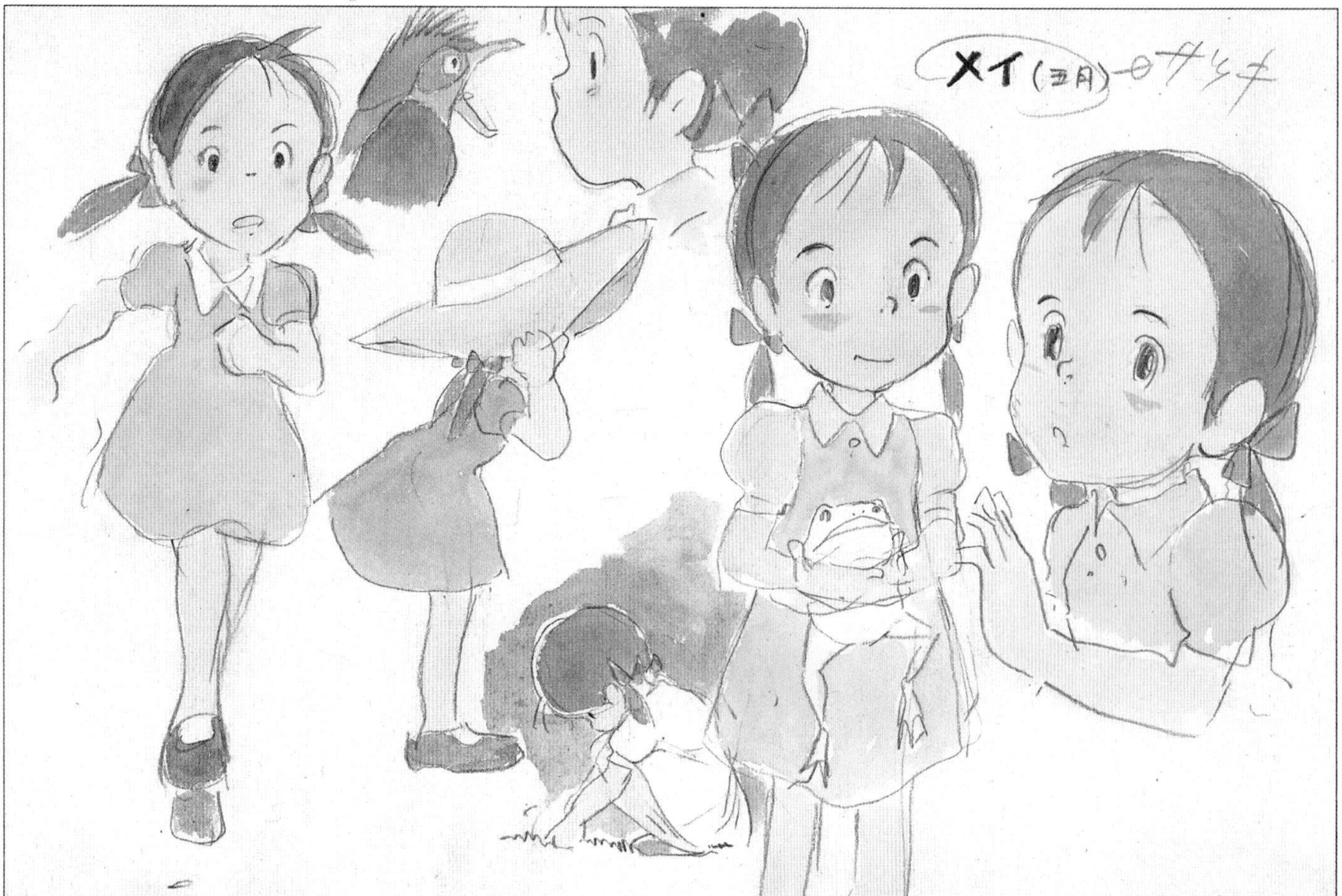
メイ(5月)
サツキ
一寸大きすぎ

3

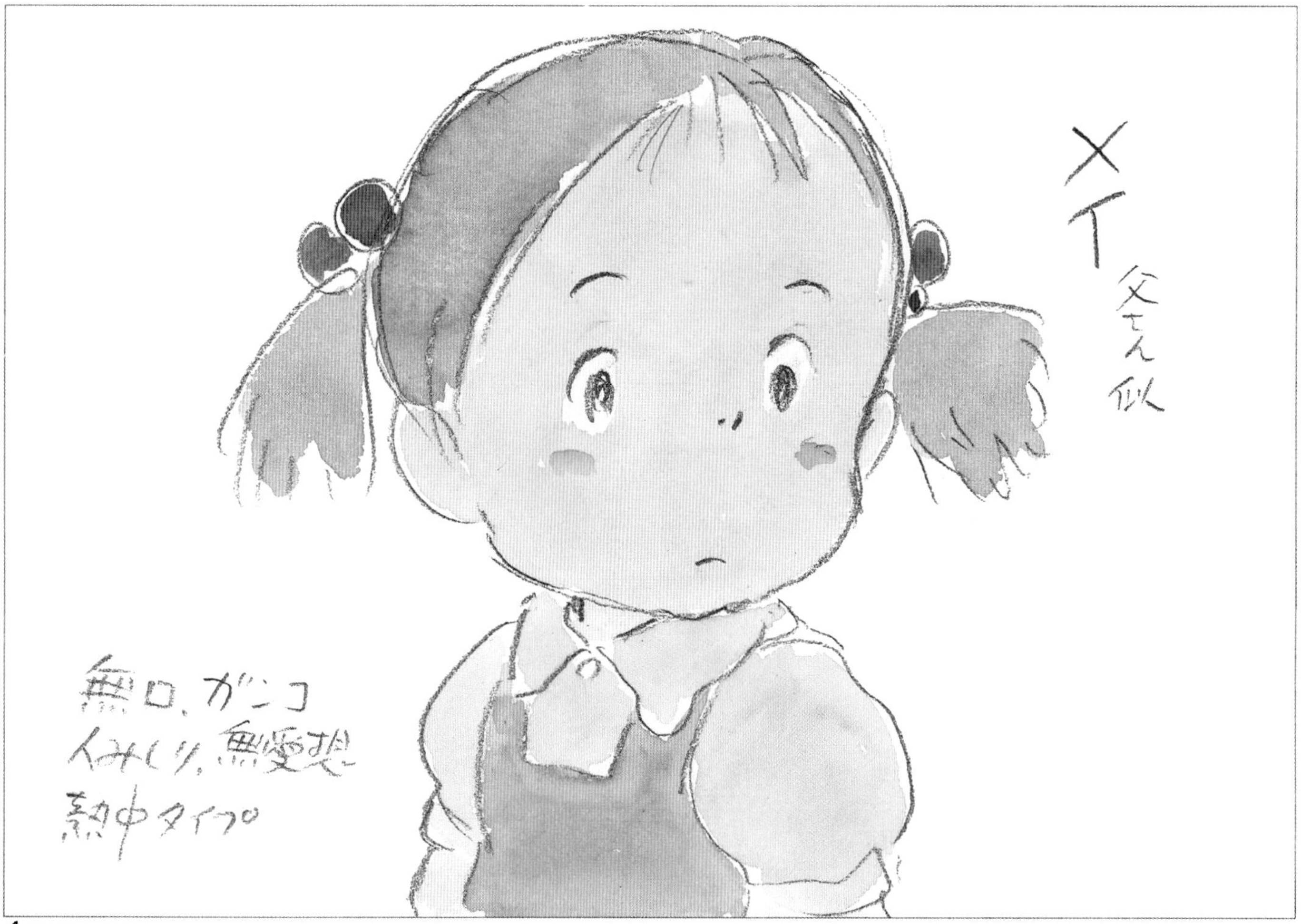
メイ
父さん似
無口、ガンコ
人みしり、無愛想
熱中タイプ

4

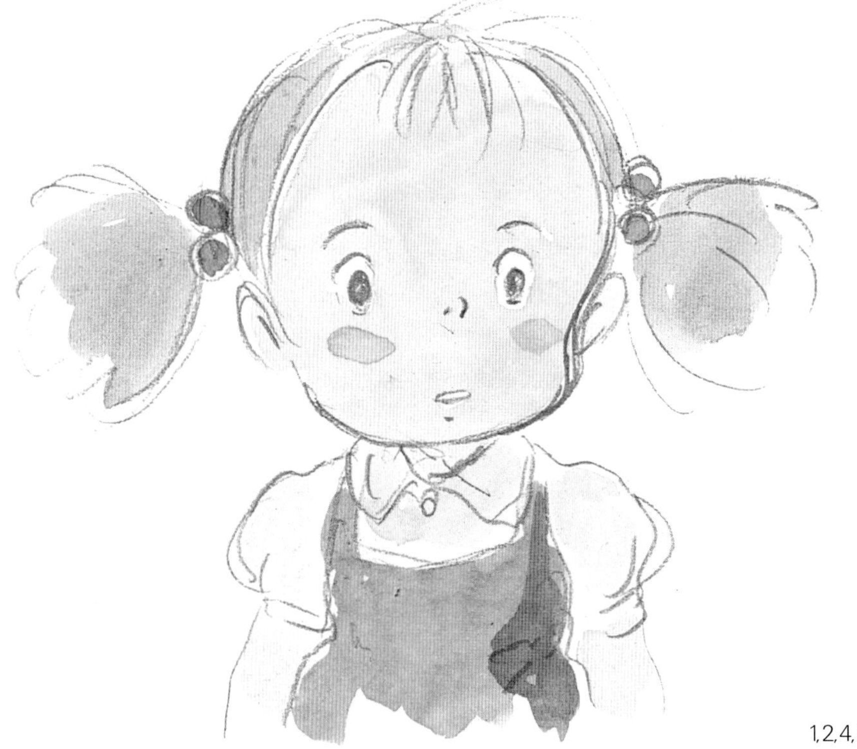

5

1,2,4,5 Mei, who takes after her father. *(character design)*

3 Initial concept sketch for Mei, who turned into the original intended character for Satsuki.

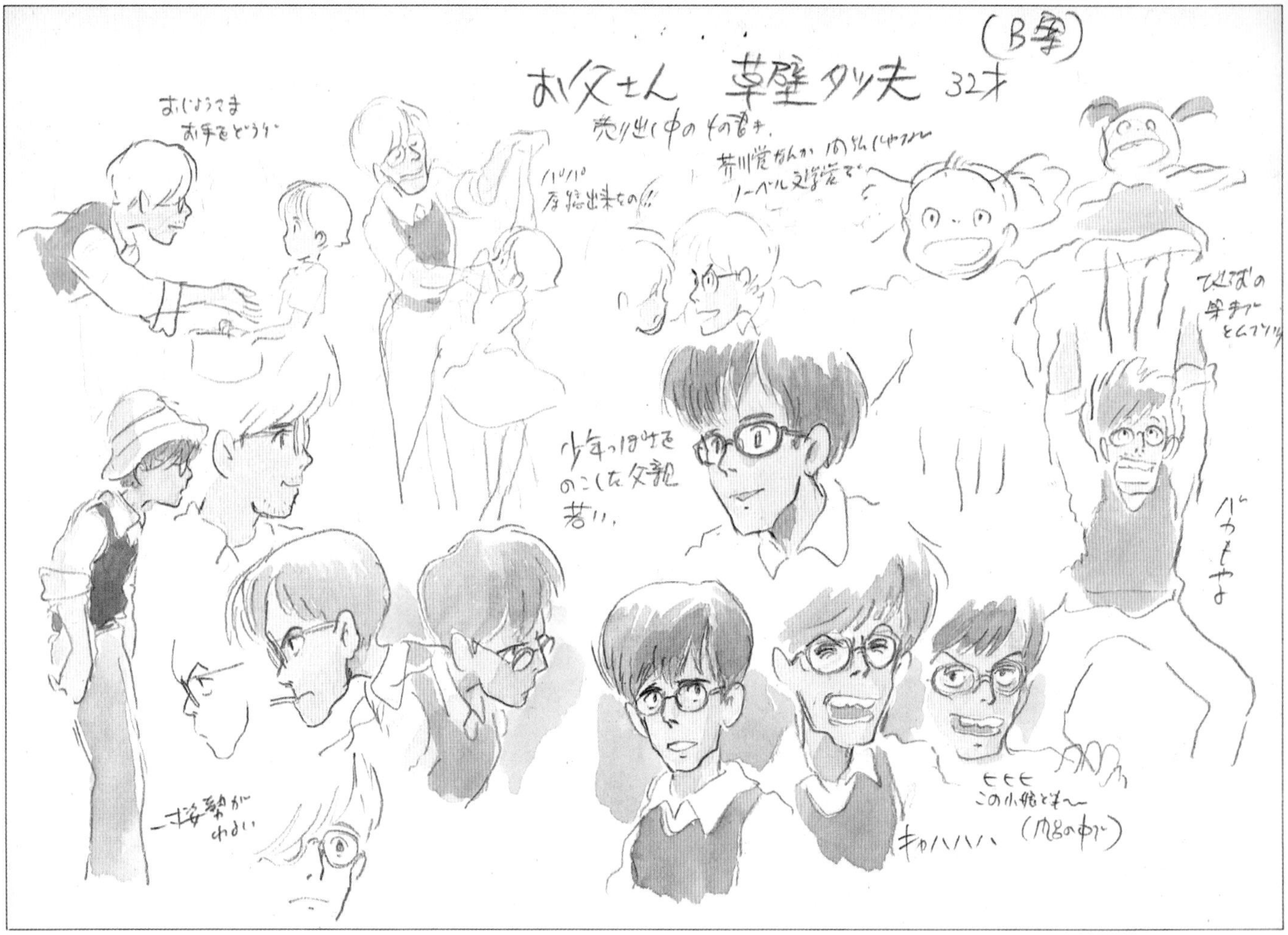
(B案)
お父さん 草壁タツ夫 32才
売り出し中のもの書キ
芥川賞なんか 問題じゃない
ノーベル文学賞で
パパ
キャハハハ

1

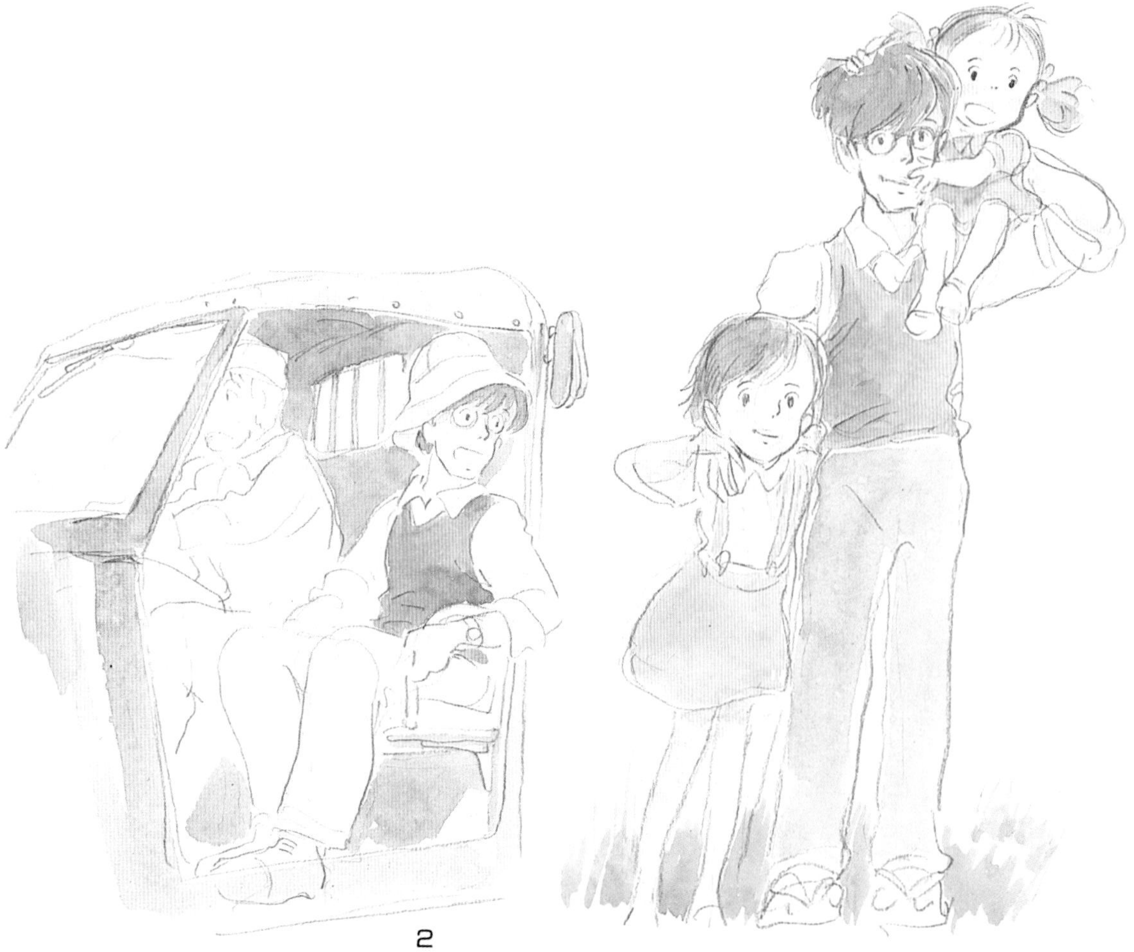

2

1 Satsuki and Mei's father, (Tatsuo Kusakabe) Idea B. *(character design)*

2 Final version of father. *(concept sketch)*

3 Father. *(initial design)*

4 Father, Idea A. *(character design)*

5 Father, Ideas C-F. *(character designs)*

6 Father. *(character design)*

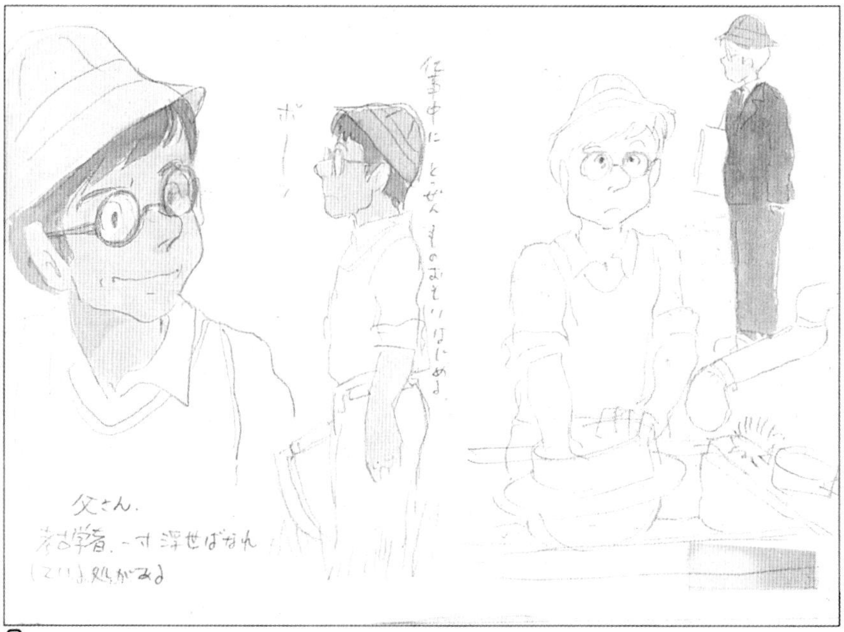
父さん.

3

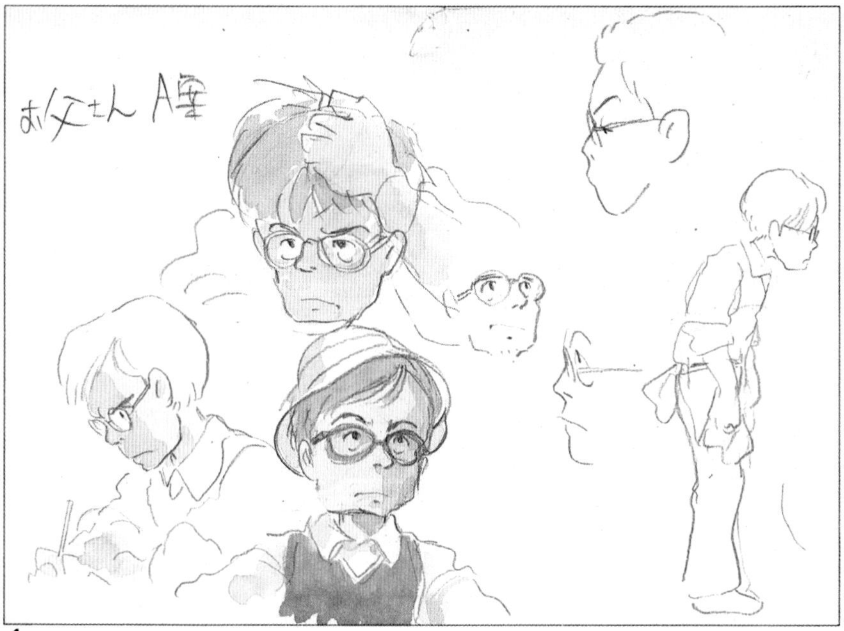
お父さん A案

4

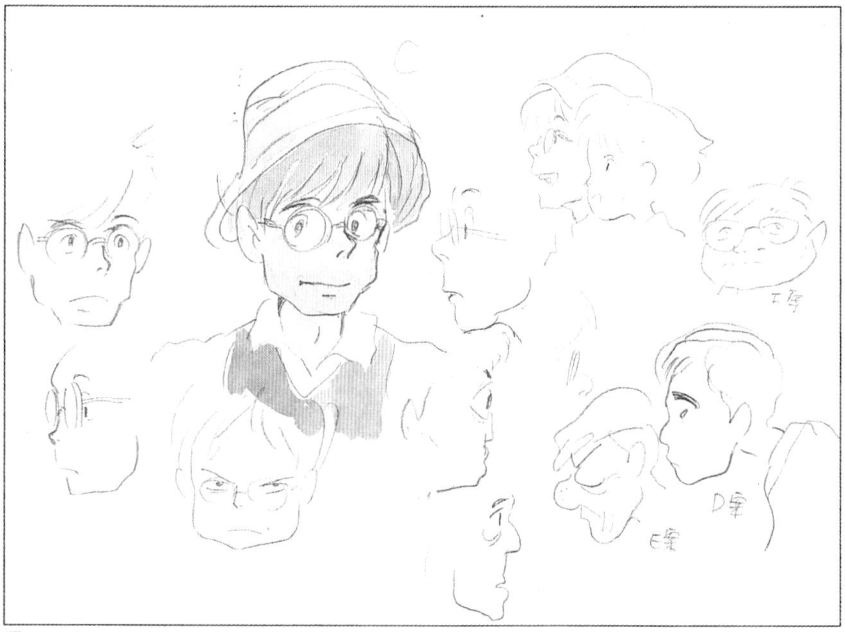
D案
E案

5

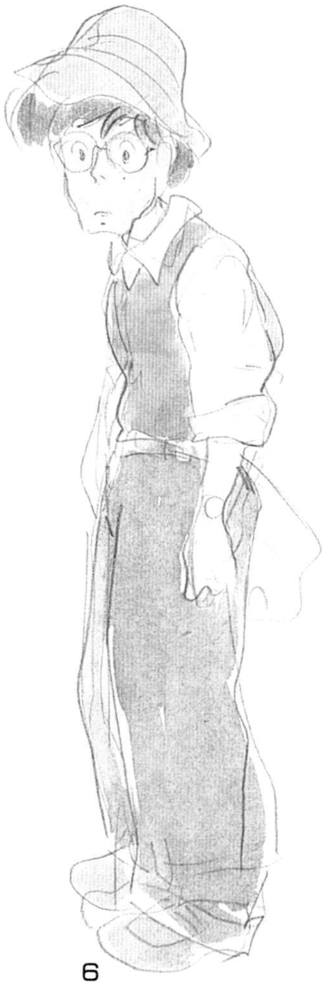

6

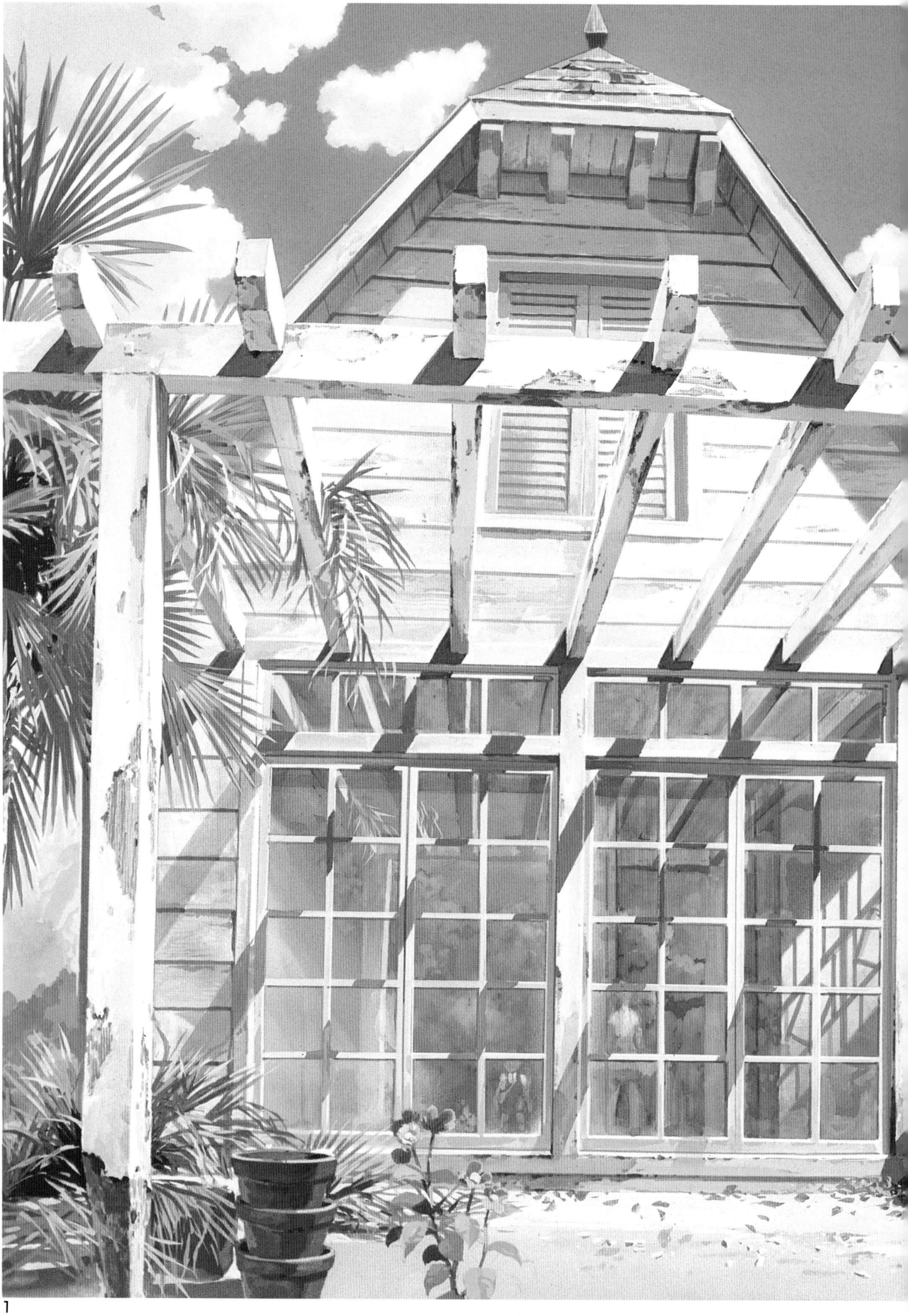

1

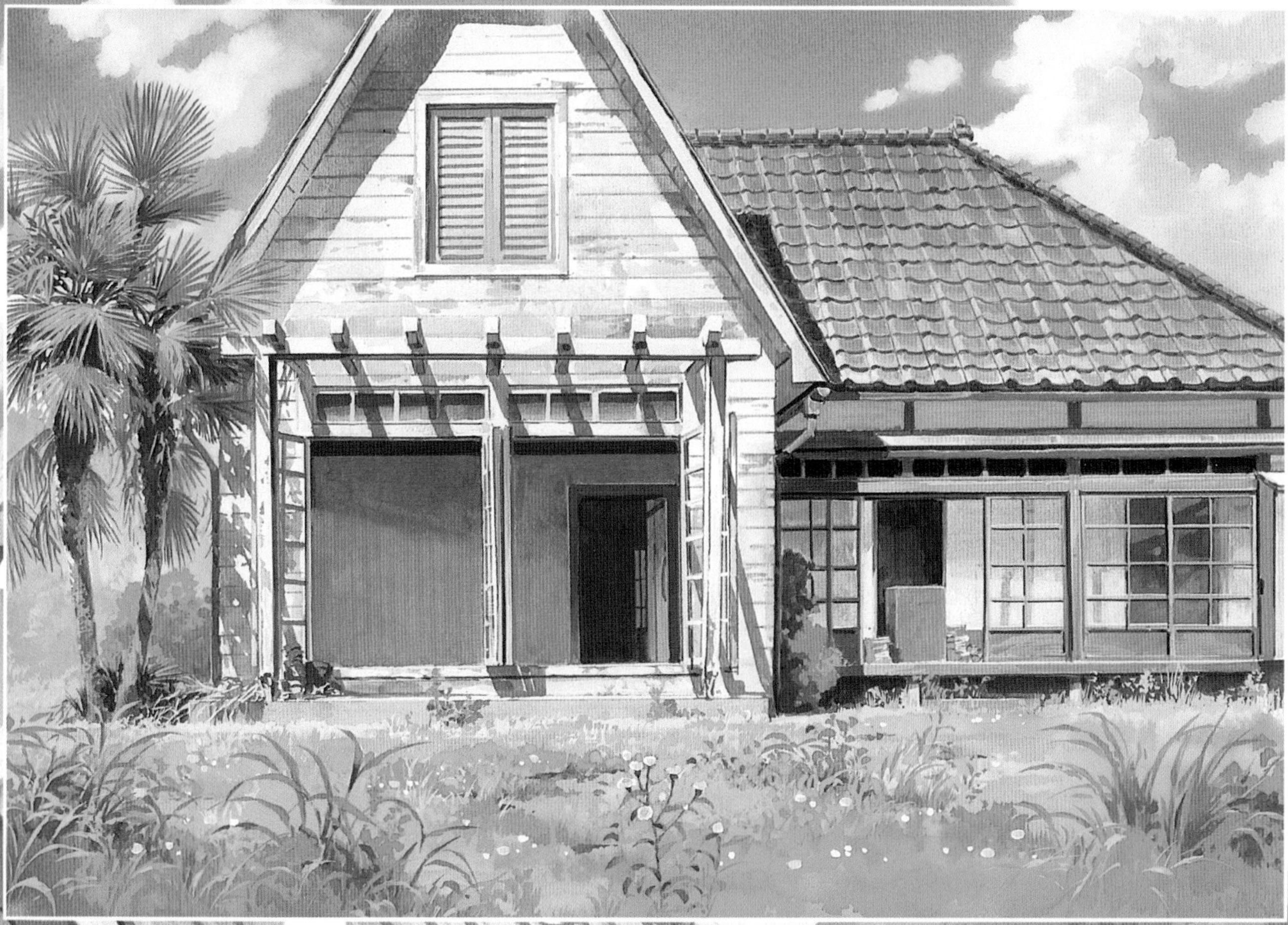

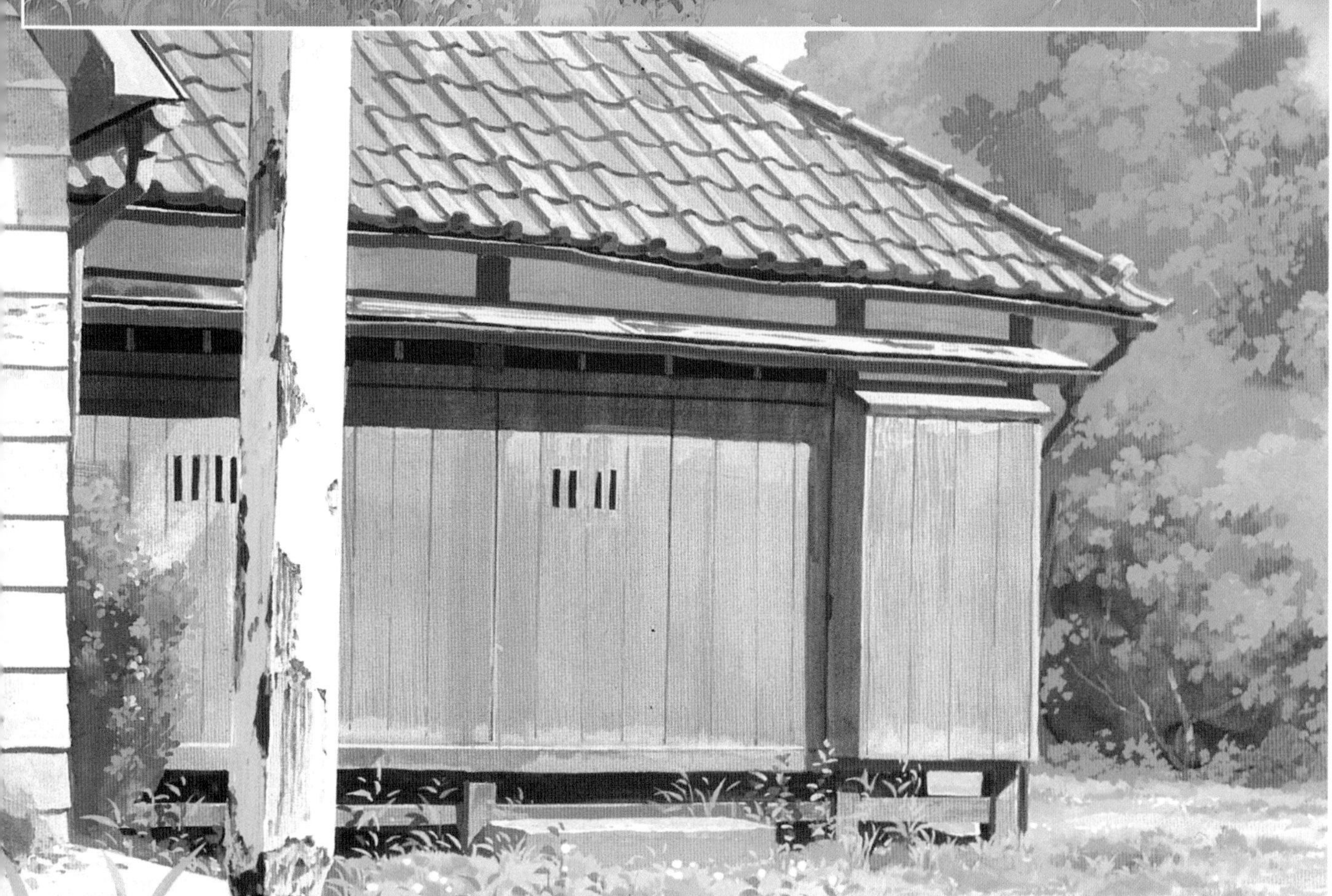

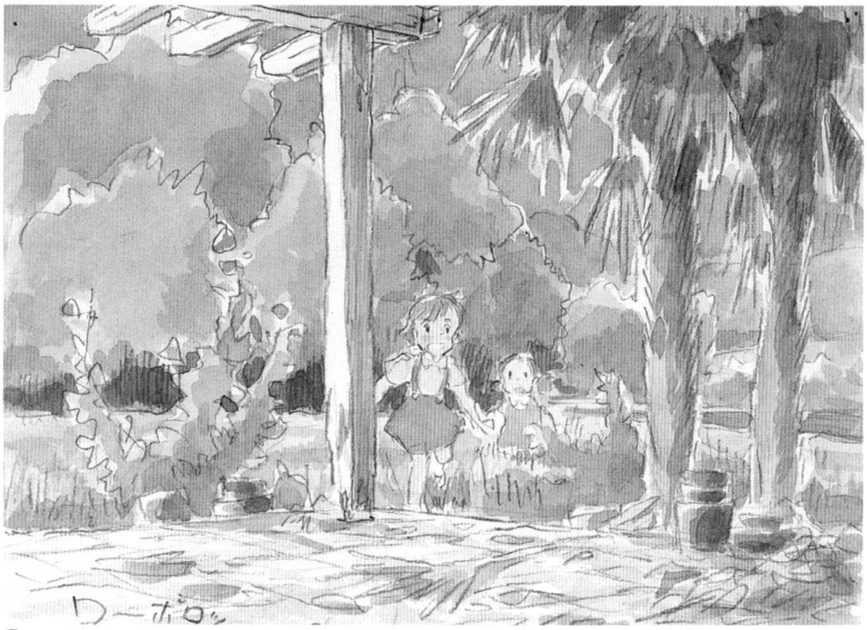
ワーボロッ

2

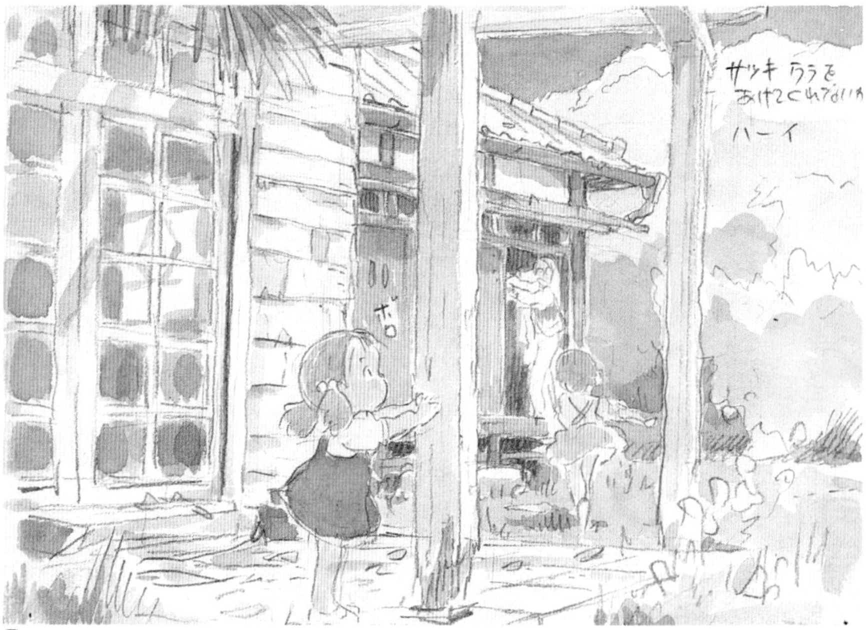
あけてくれないか
ハーイ

3

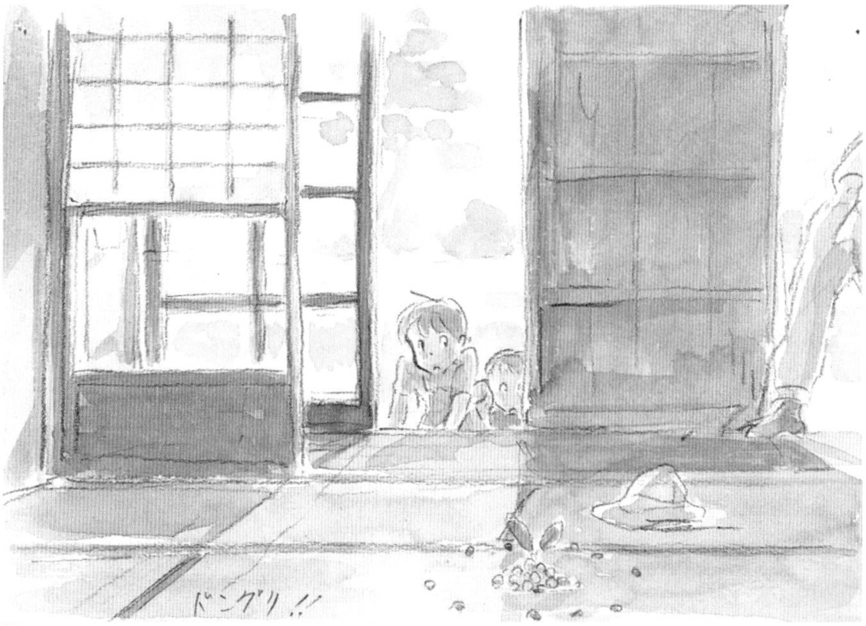
ドングリ!!

5

1 Kusakabe residence. *(background)*

2-6 "Wow, it's creepy!" Satsuki and Mei scream with delight. They're delighted to find acorns in the room. *(storyboard)*

"I didn't expect the film to be this long. Originally I thought it would be an hour or so, but by the time the proposal was finalized, it became 90 minutes [*laughs*]. The film had to be that long because it turned into a slice-of-life comic story. After all, the story begins with their move. At first, I had in mind children playing in the fields, where there wasn't much social context, but once it became a film, social factors such as the father's occupation and their reasons for moving had to be addressed. Incorporating all those elements expanded the scale of the film." *(Miyazaki)*

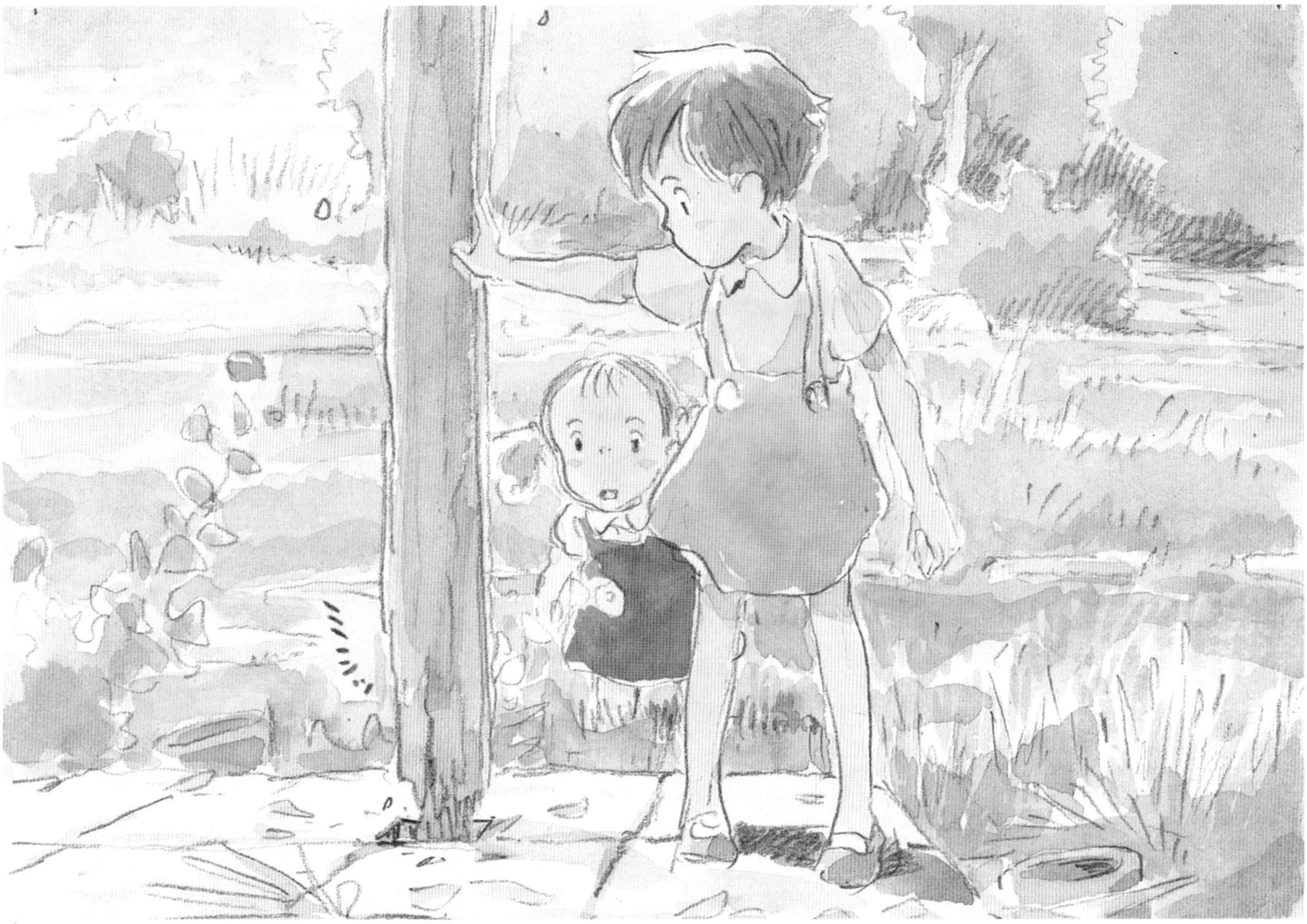

4

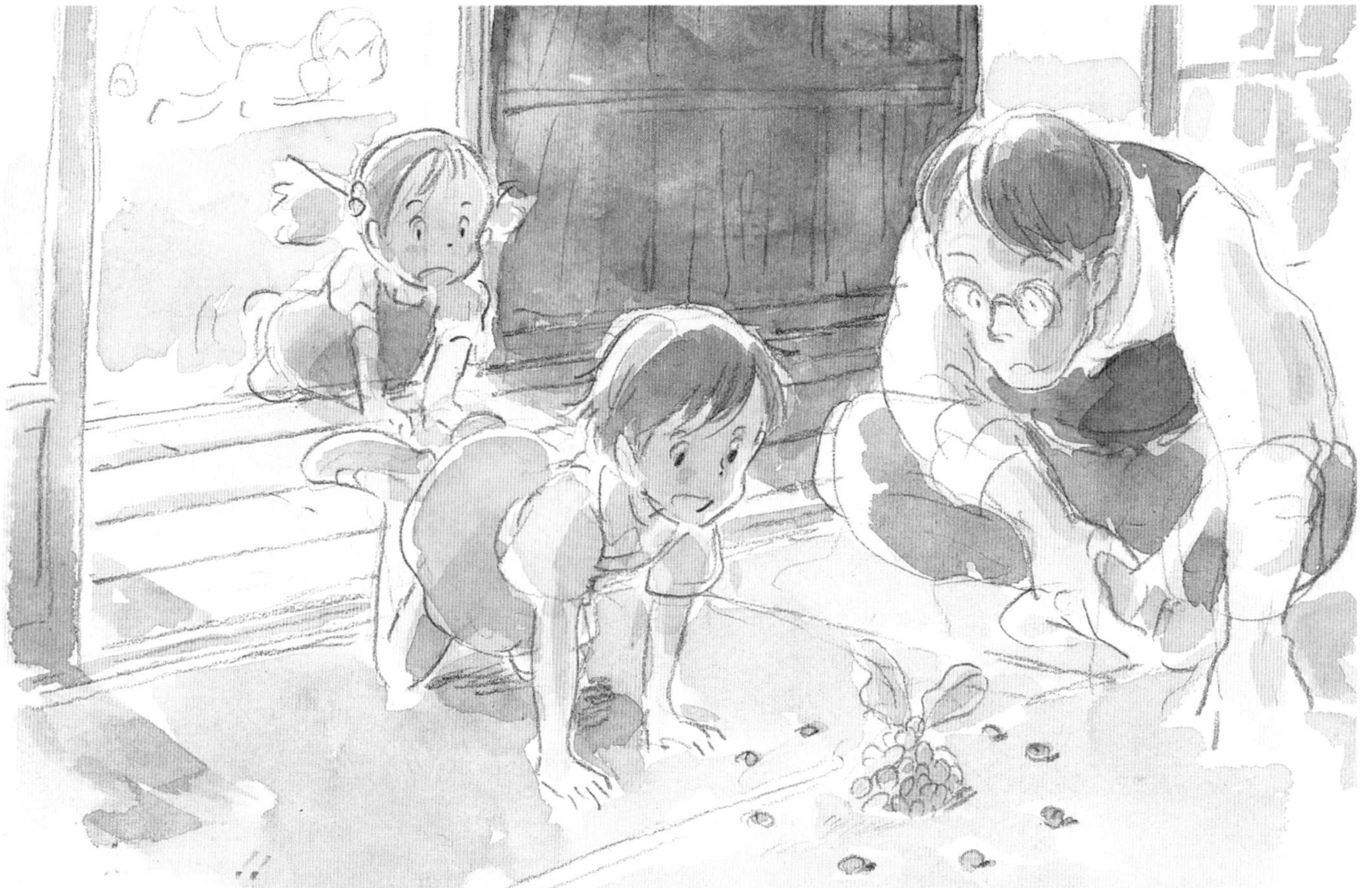
環状列石と同じ形状　カンジョウレッセキ?

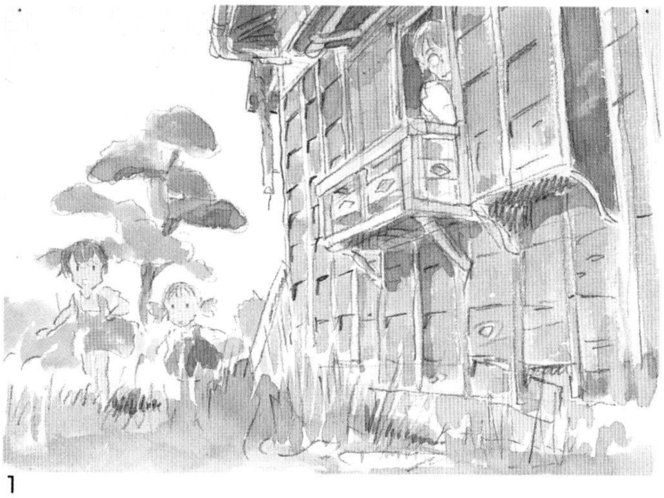

1

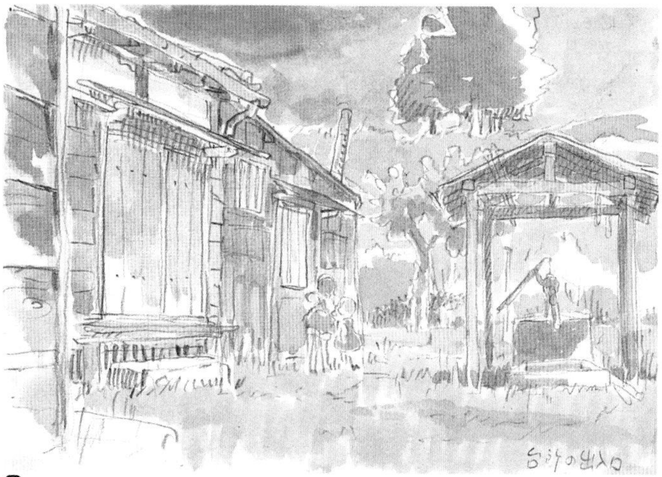
台所の出入口

2

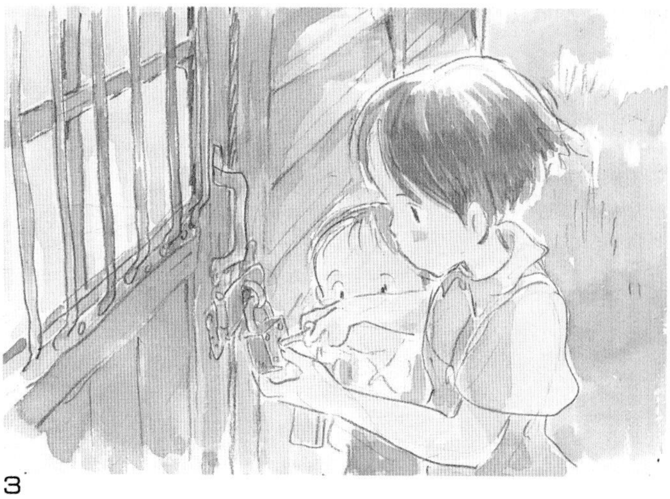

3

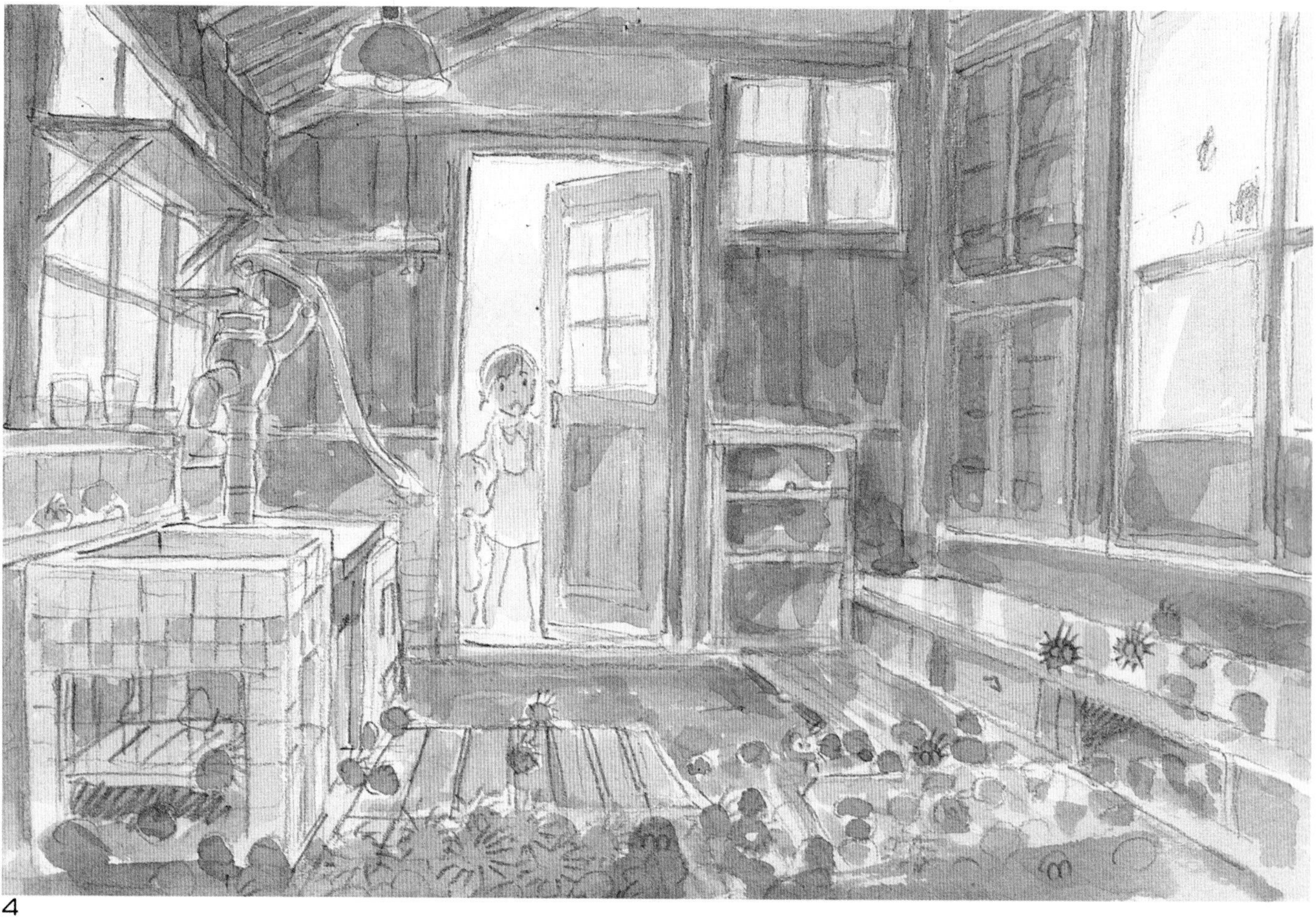

4

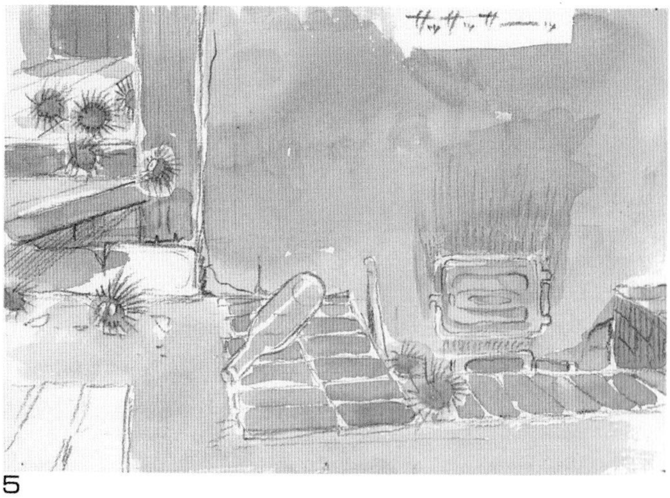
サッサッサーッ

5

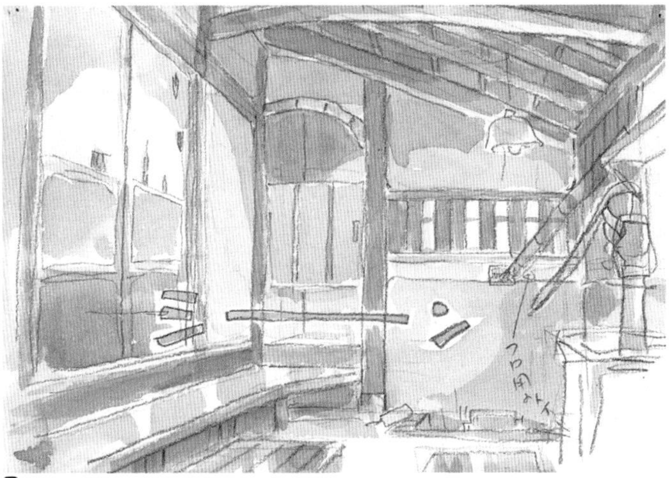

6

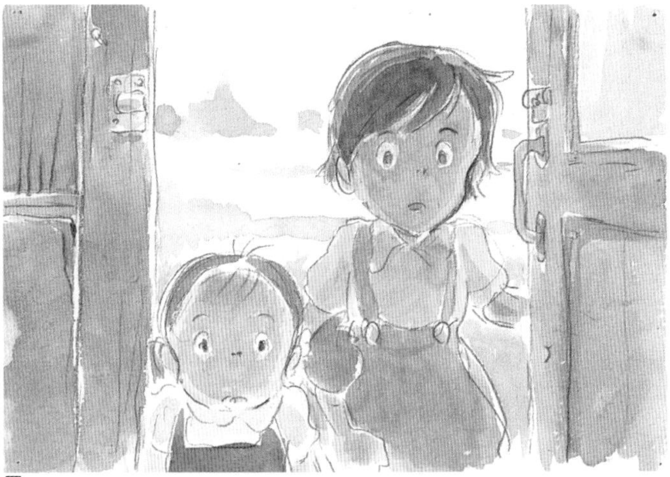

7

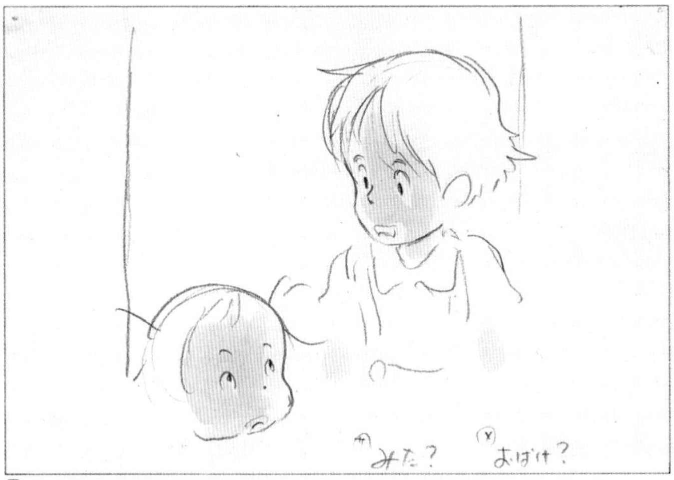
みた？
おばけ？

8

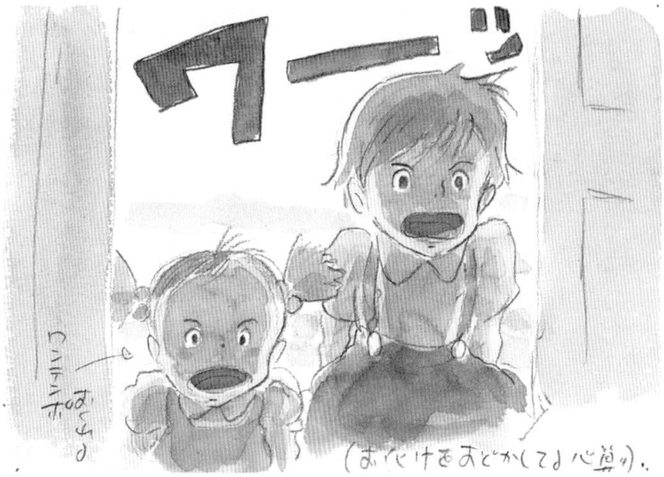
ワーッ

9

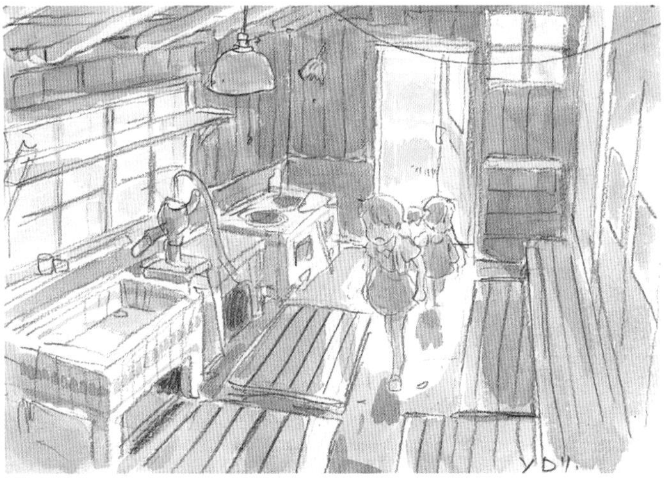

10

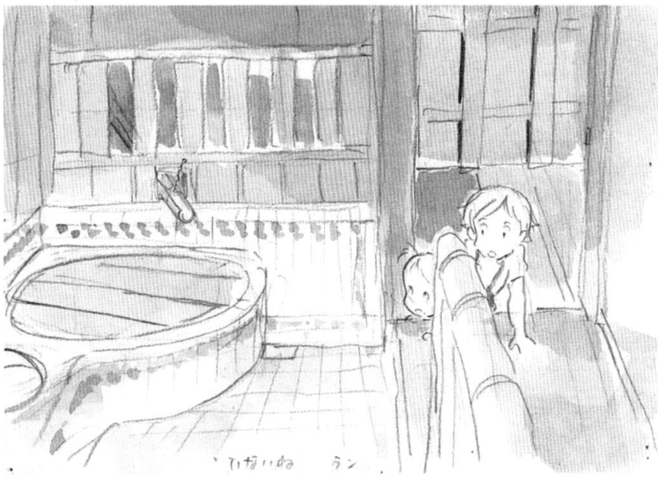

11

1-11 Satsuki and Mei go around the east side of the house and enter through the side entrance. The soot sprites disperse as the girls chase after them. *(storyboard)*

"It would be pointless to explain how the 'soot sprites' are born or where they reside. We present them just as soot sprites. They just suddenly vanish, and that's enough. It's pointless to elaborate any further than that." *(Miyazaki)*

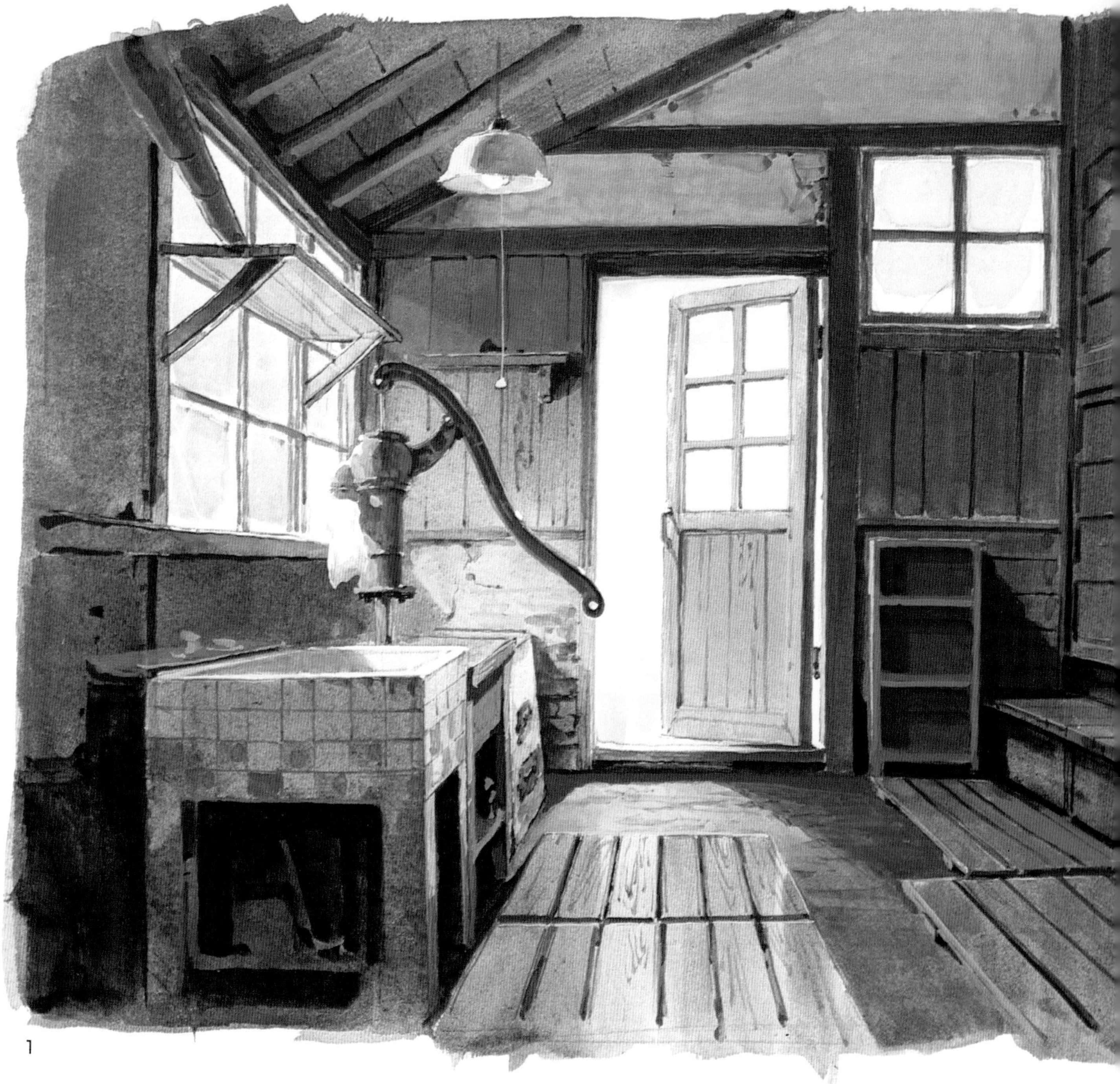

1

1 Kitchen. *(concept art)*

2 Backyard of the house with well. *(background)*

3 Kitchen from the side entrance angle. *(background)*

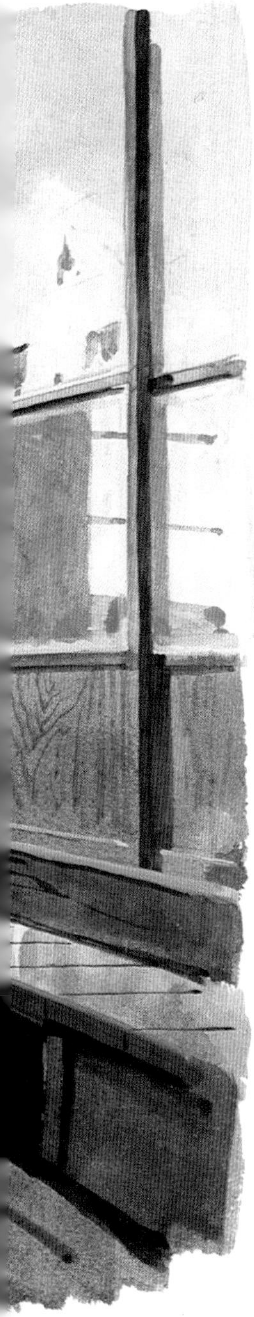

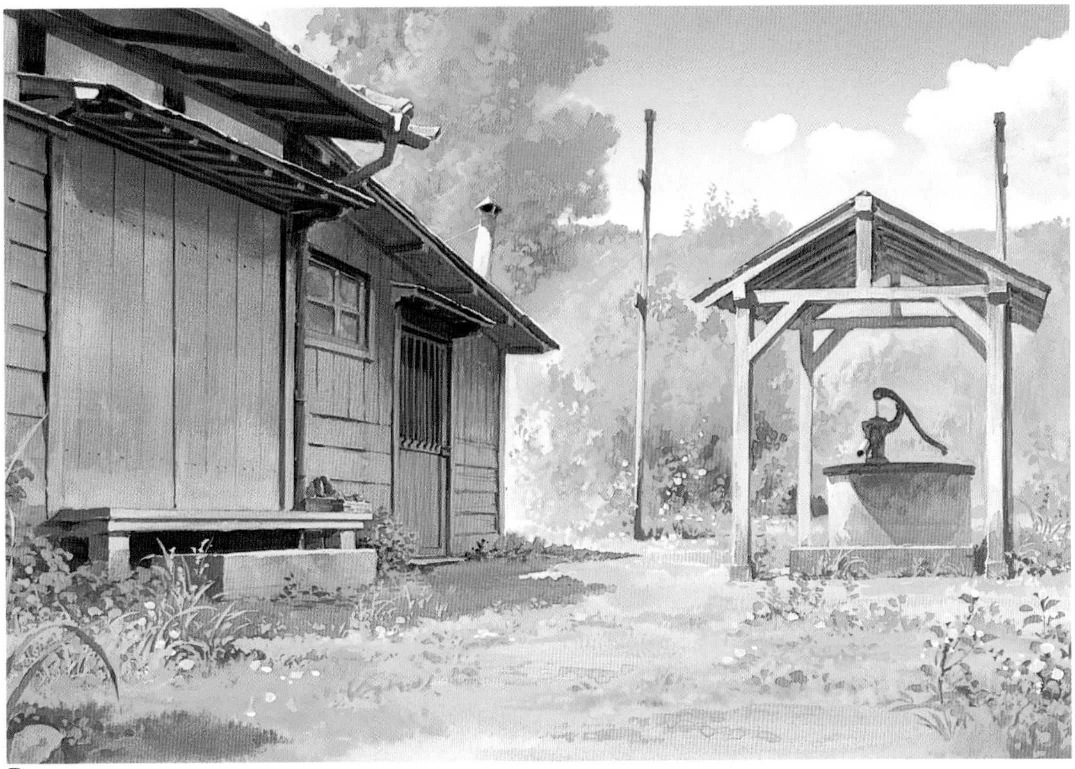

2

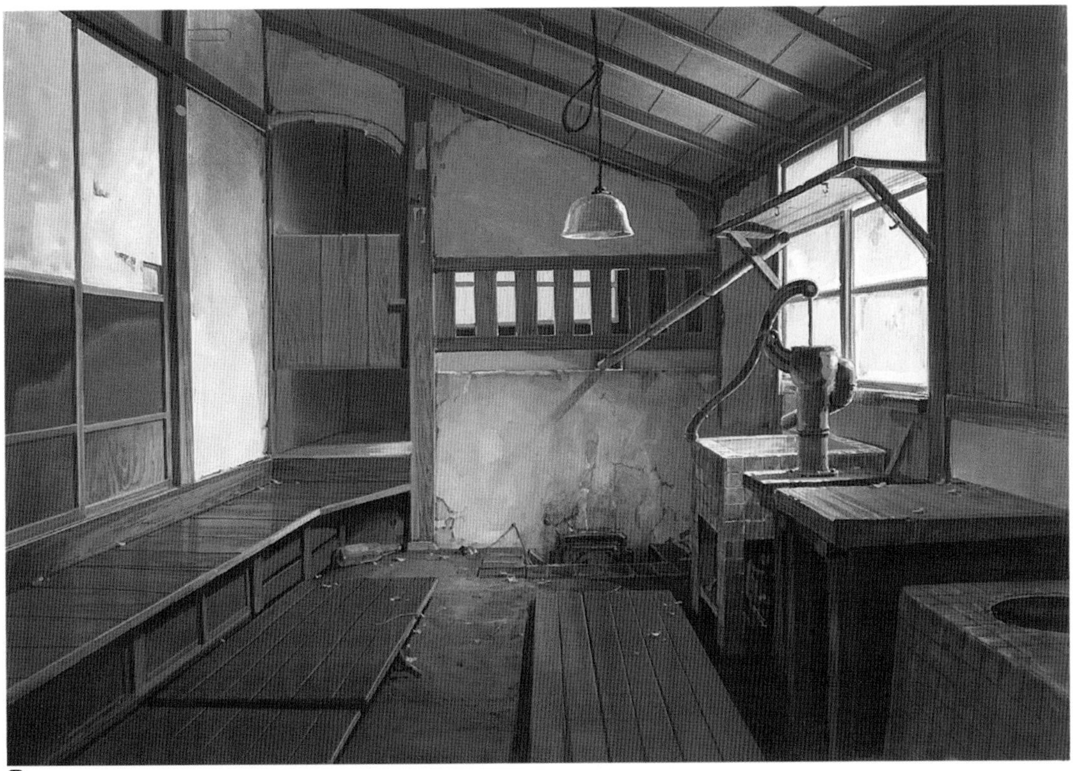

3

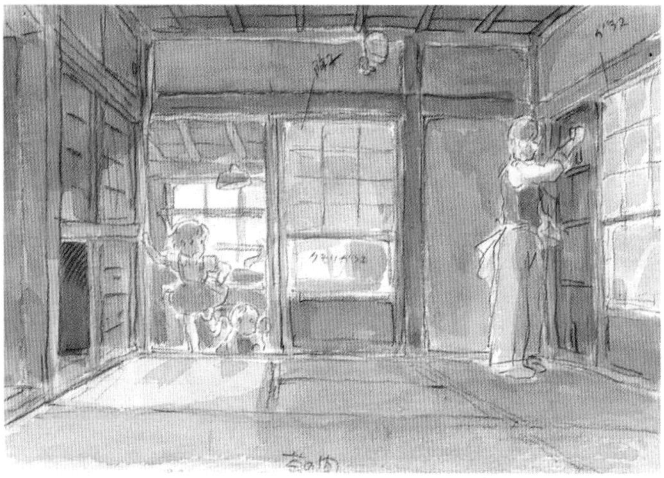

1

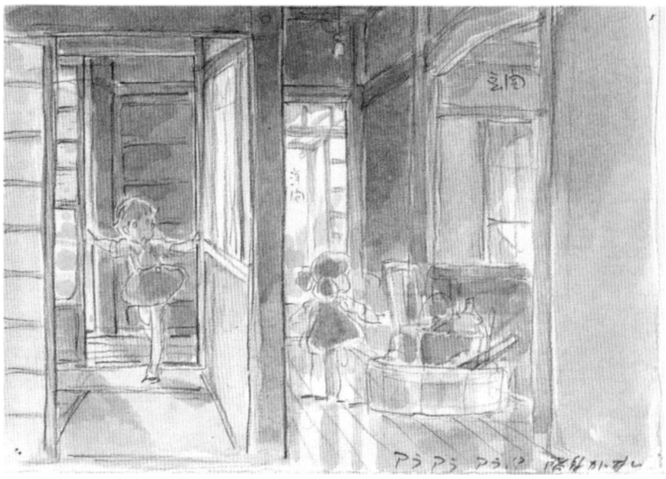

2

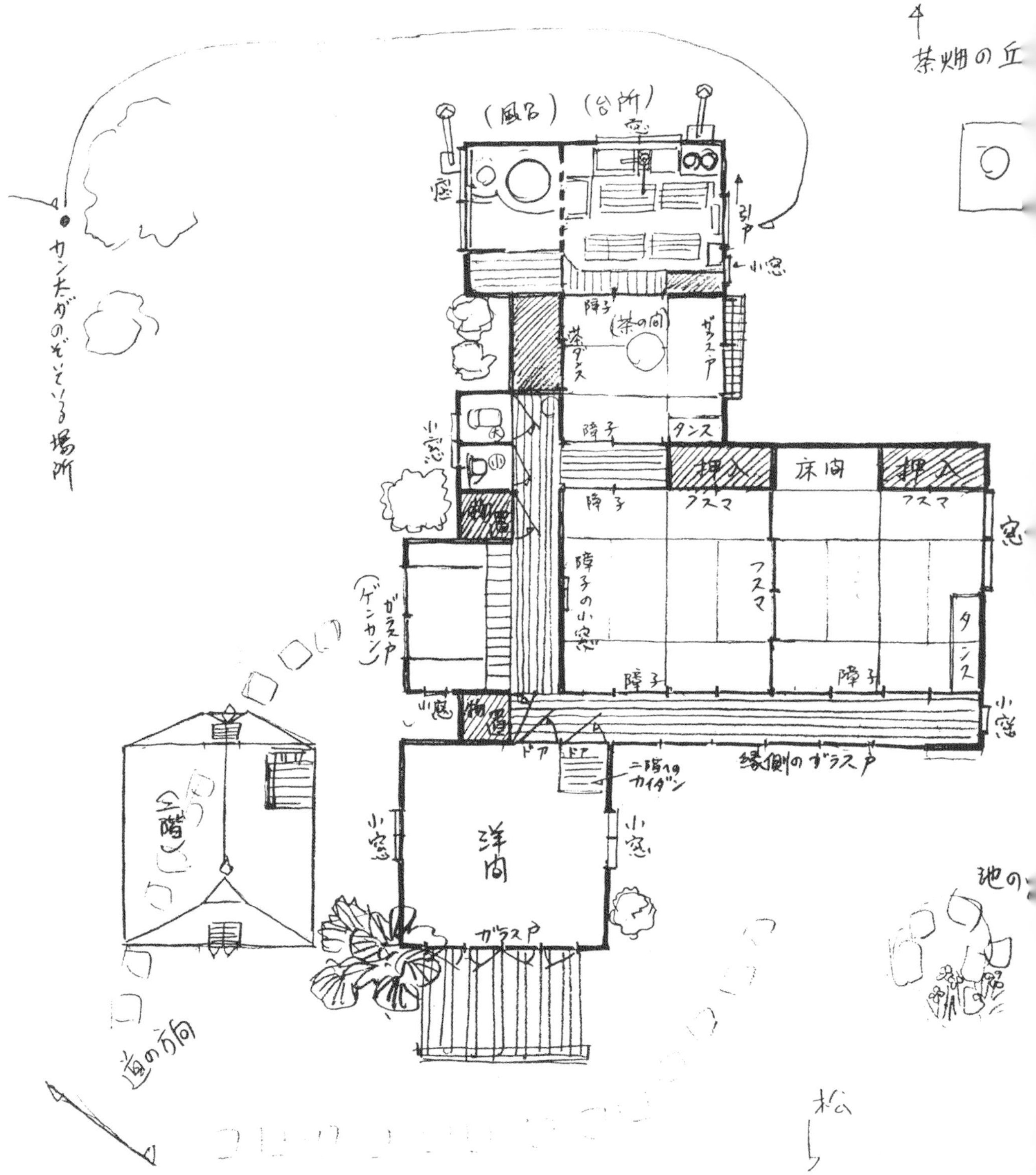
茶畑の丘
(風呂)
(台所)
窓
引戸
小窓
障子
(茶の間)
茶ダンス
ガラス戸
障子
タンス
押入
床の間
押入
フスマ
フスマ
窓
障子
障子の小窓
フスマ
タンス
障子
障子
(ゲンカン)
ガラス戸
小窓
物置
物置
小窓
ドア
ドア
二階へのカイダン
縁側のガラス戸
小窓
洋間
小窓
小窓
ガラス戸
二階
カン太がのぞいてる場所
池の
道の方向
松

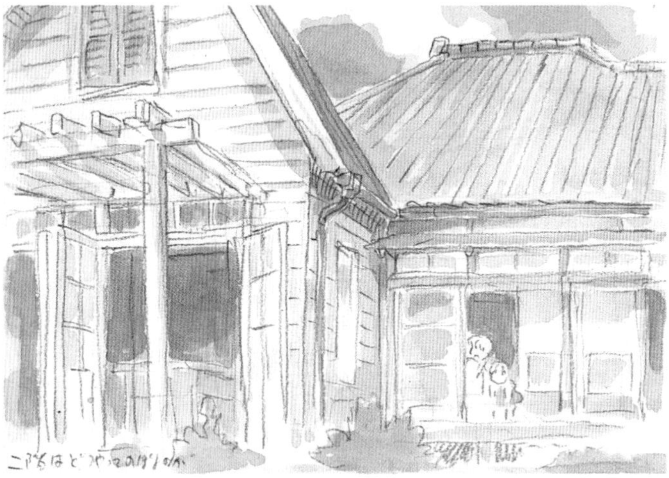

3

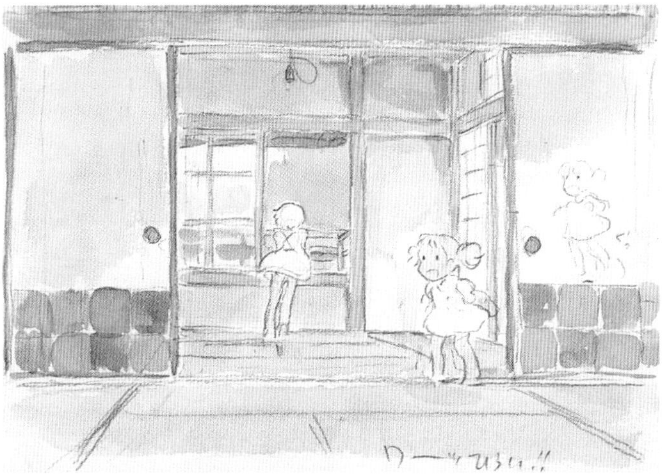
ワーッひろい!!

4

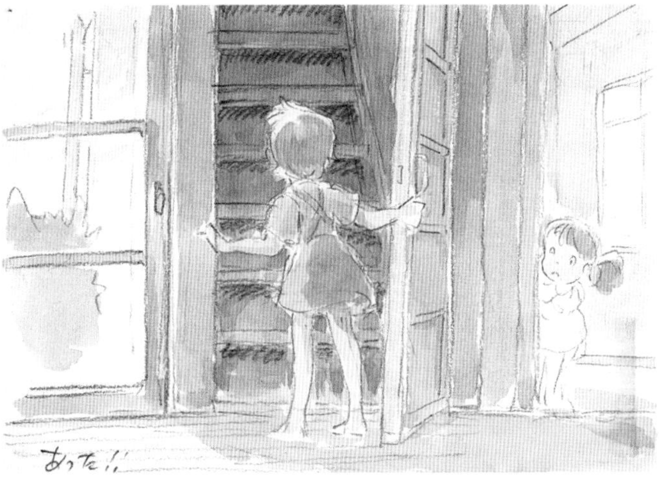
あった!!

5

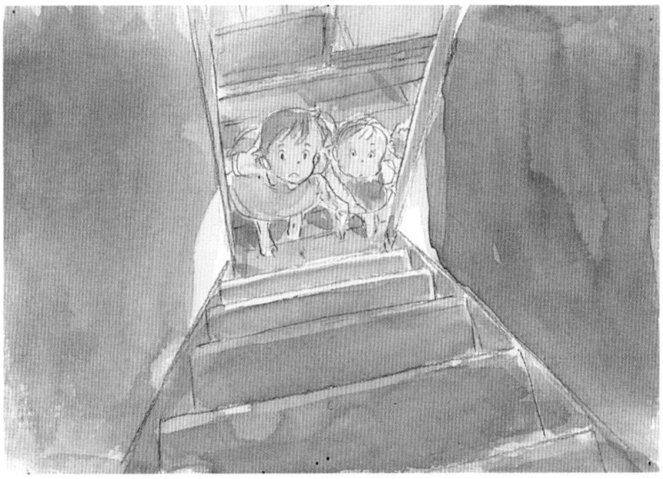

6

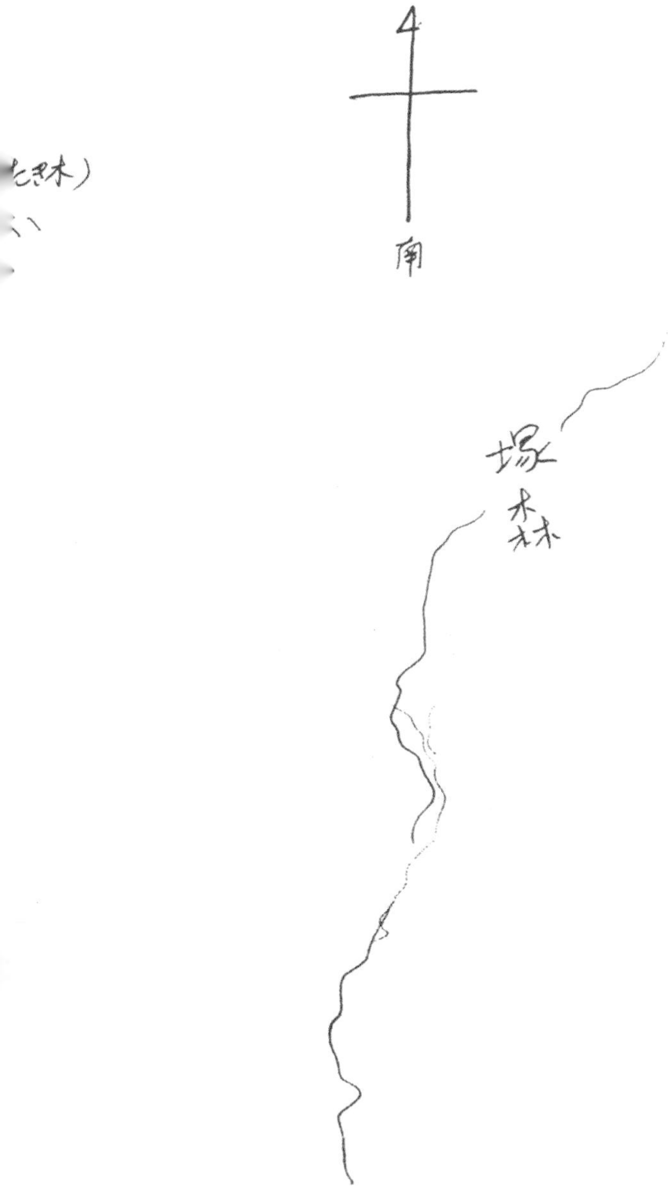
4
南
塚
森

1-6 Satsuki and Mei entering and running around the house. *(storyboards)*

7 Layout for the Kusakabe residence. *(design by Kazuo Oga)*

"They'd be running around, opening one door, exclaiming, `Nothing here!´ or `The bathroom!´ You run around and start giggling from excitement—that's what kids are like. But to be honest, it can be pretty noisy [*laughs*]." *(Miyazaki)*

1 Satsuki and Mei peek into the attic. *(storyboard)*

2 Looking up at the open window in the attic. *(background)*

3, 4 Attic. *(cel art)*

5 Veranda with baggage. *(concept art)*

(At the far end is a storage closet, on the left a door to the living room, and next to it, the door to the attic staircase.)

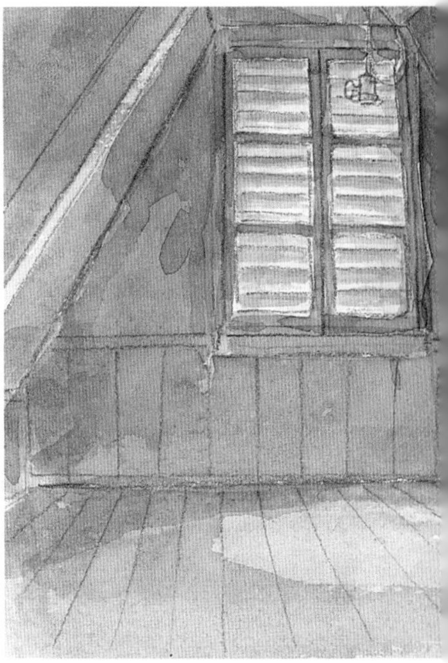

1

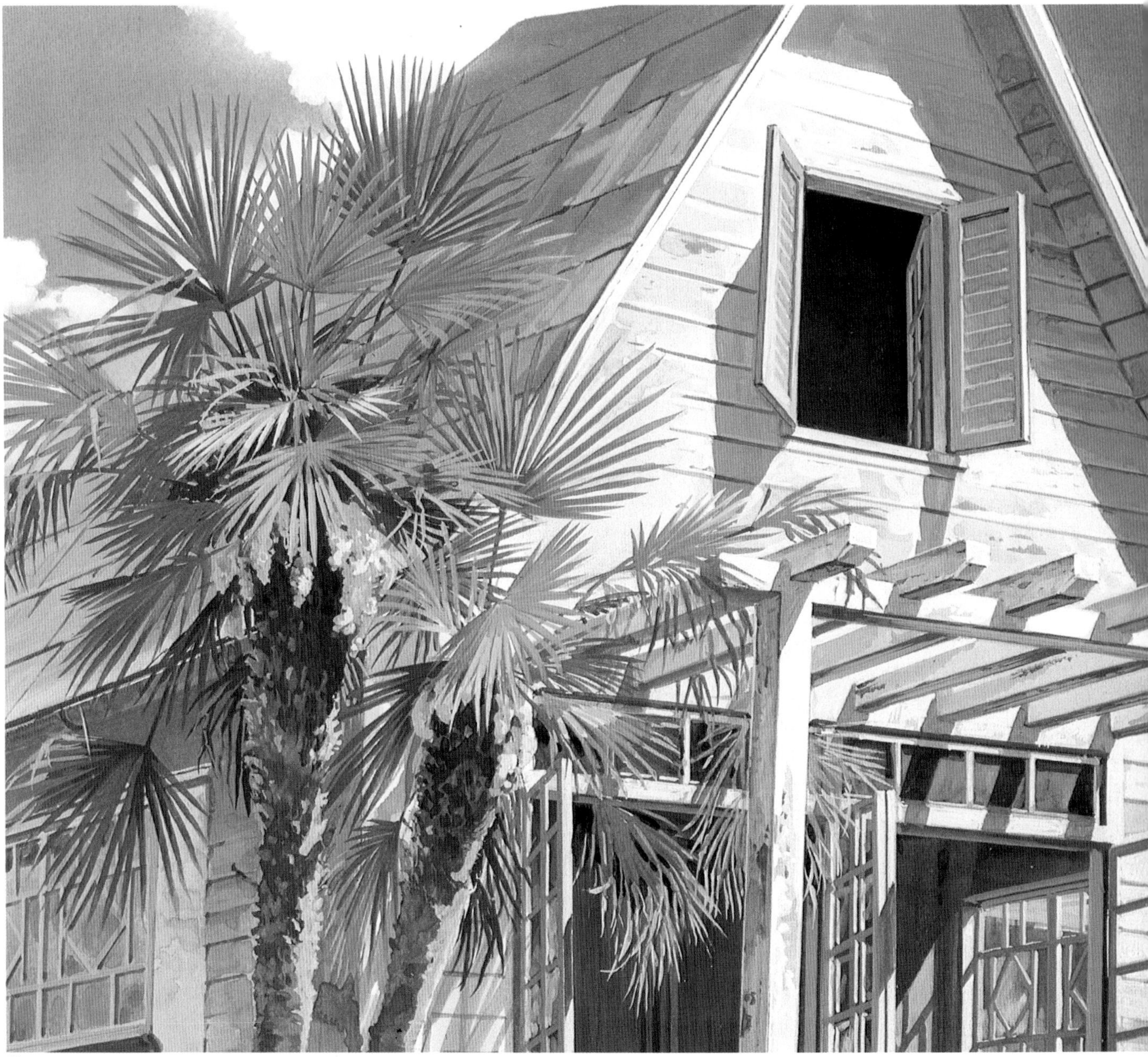

2

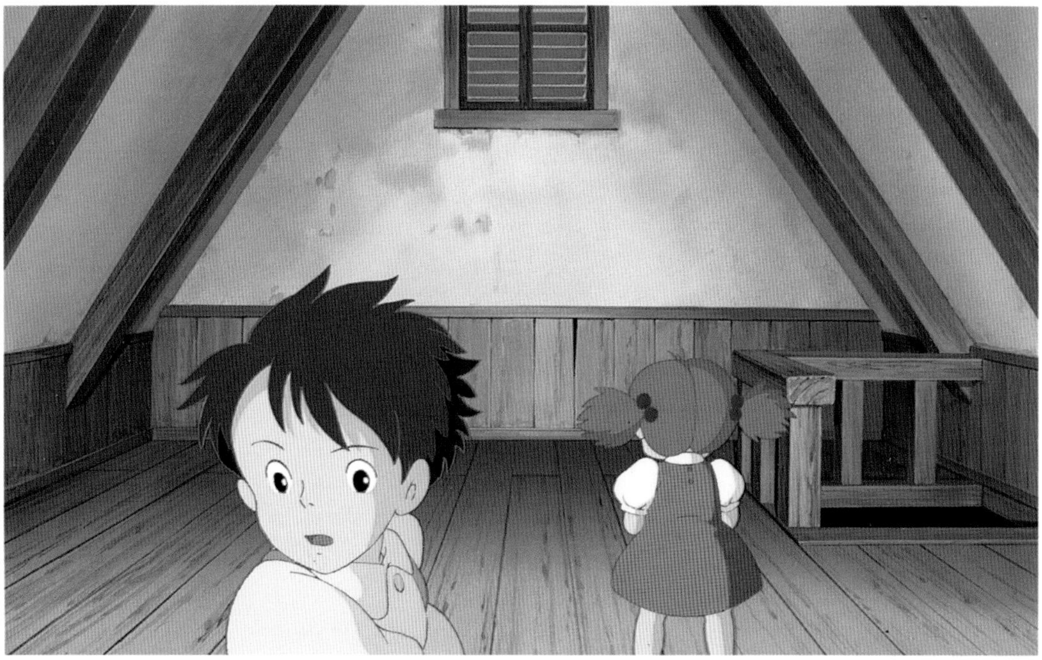
3
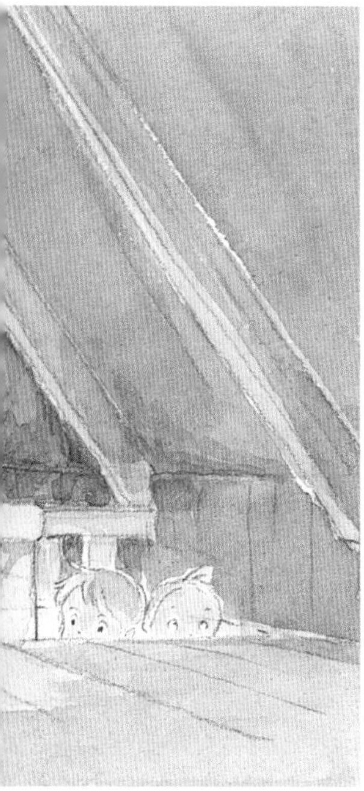
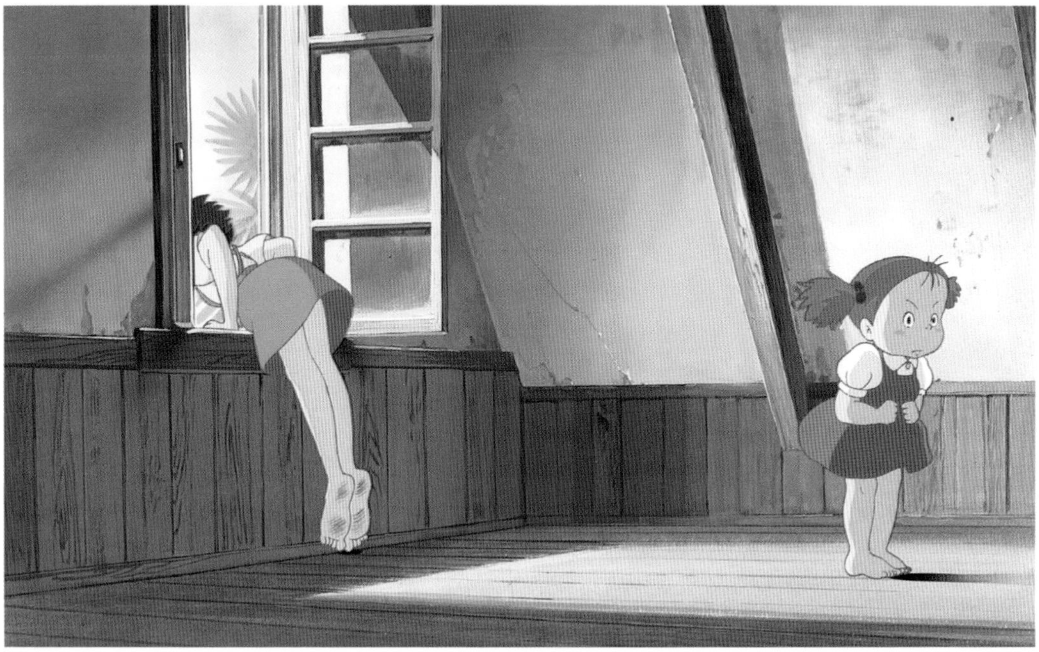
4
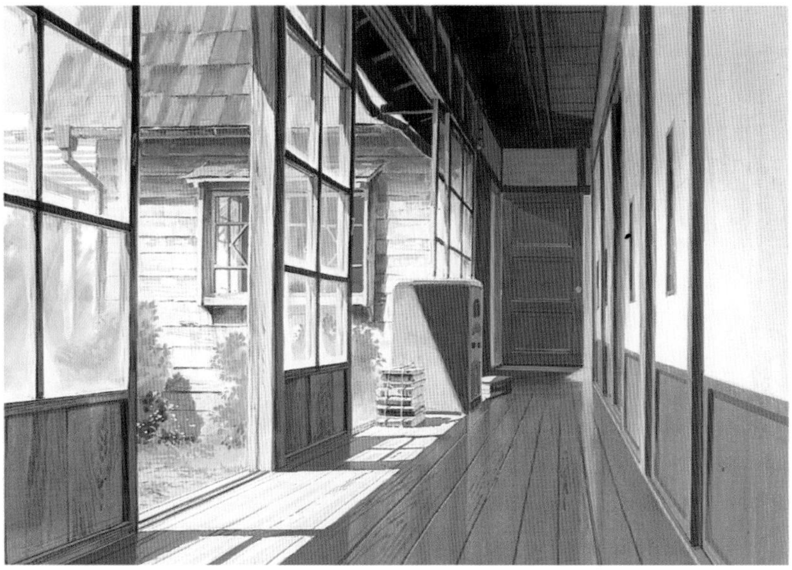
5
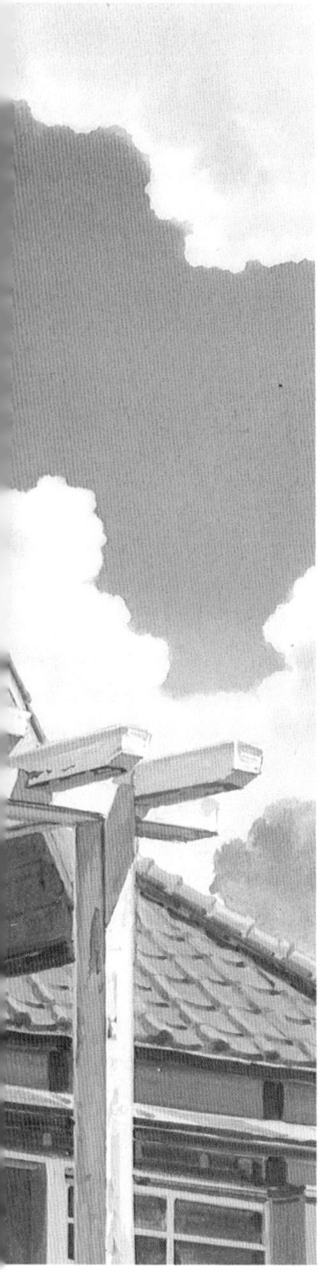

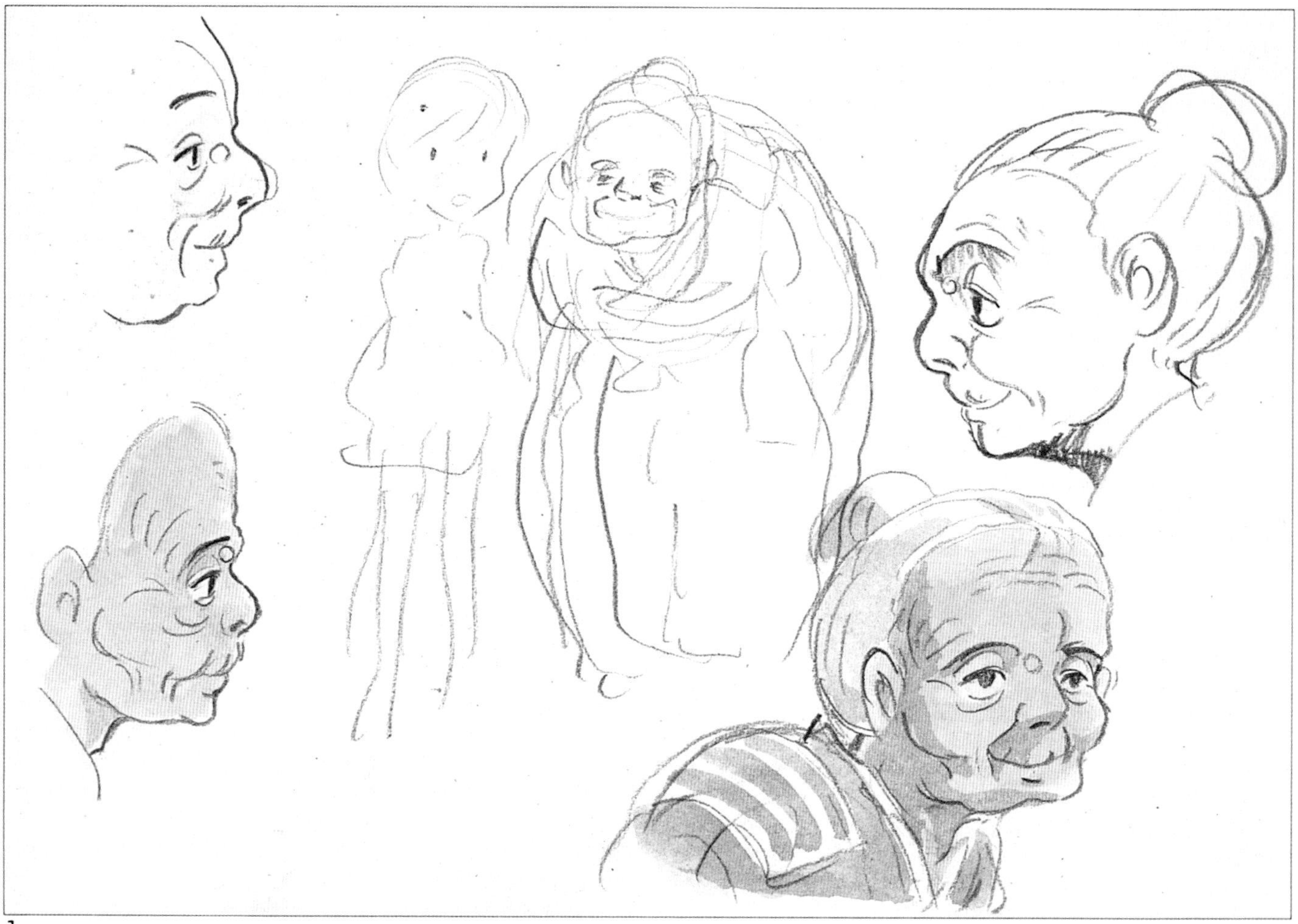

1

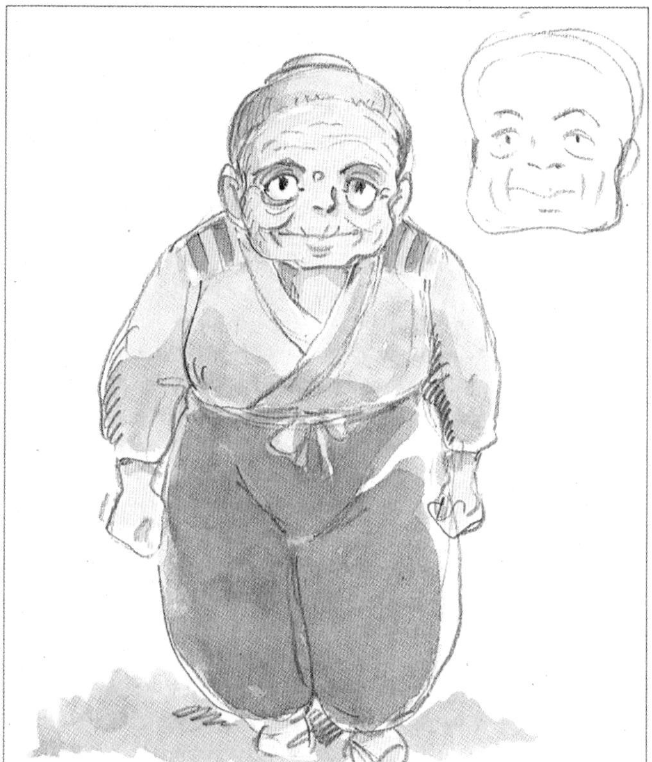

2

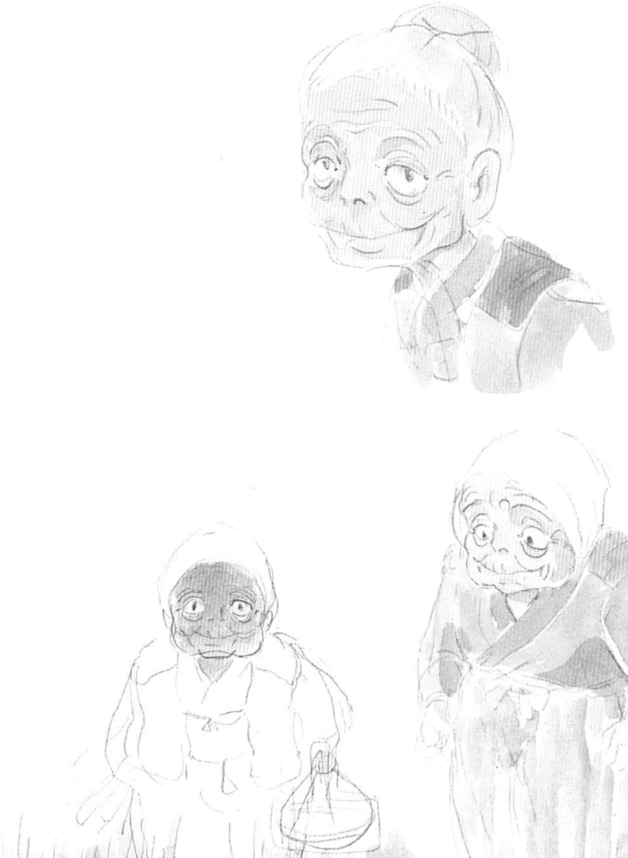

3

1-3 Kanta's grandmother. *(character design)*

4 Kanta. *(concept sketch)*

5 Kanta when he was first called Kanpei. *(initial concept sketch)*

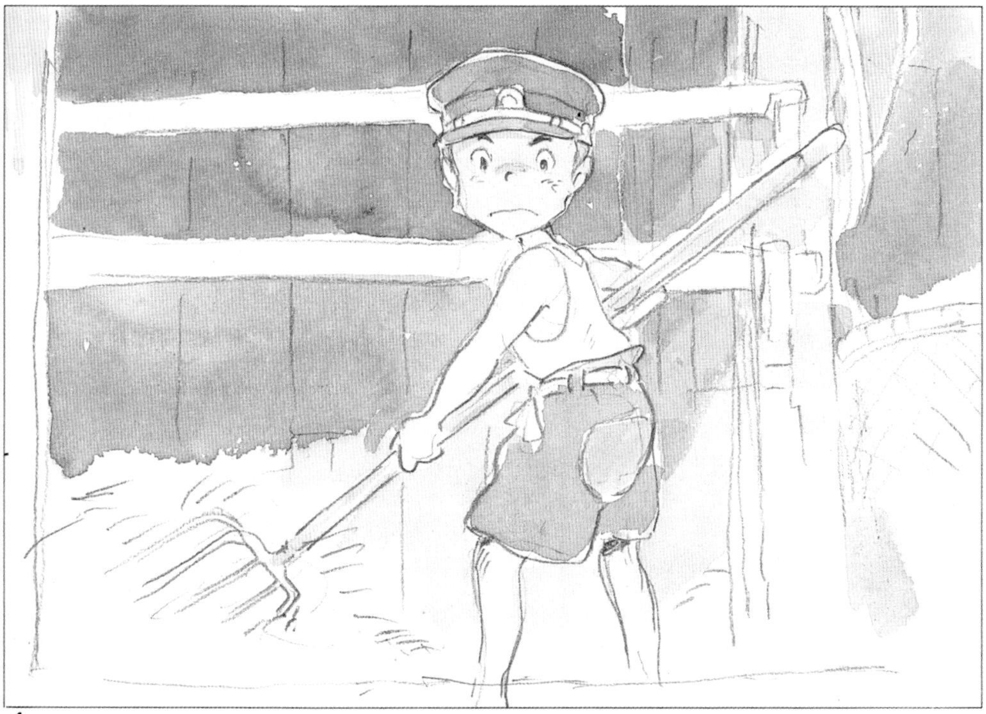

4

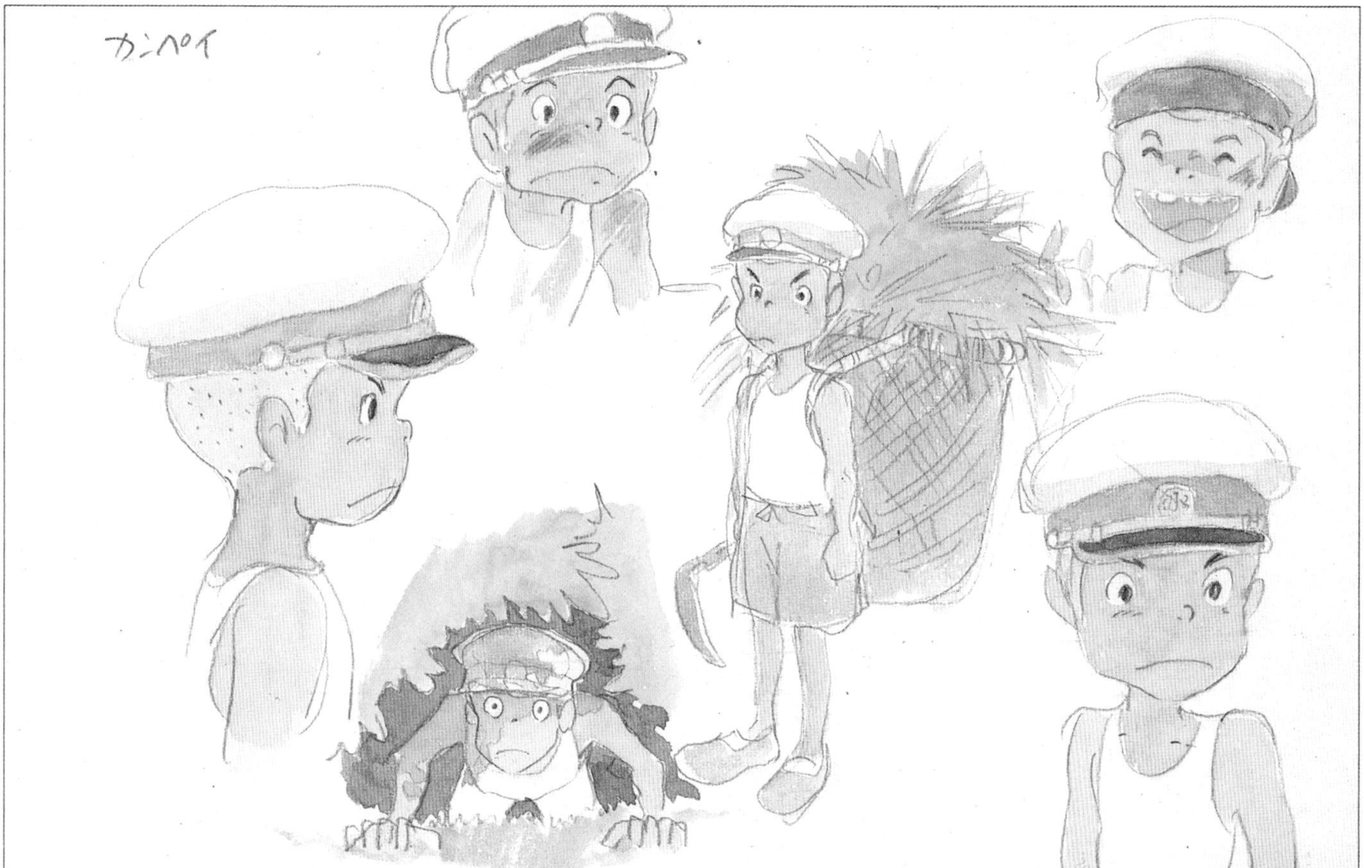
カンペイ

5

1, 2, 4 Satsuki and Mei scoop water from the river to pump-prime the well. *(cel art)*

3 Satsuki pumps the well. *(storyboard)*

5 Three-wheeler truck driver. *(character design)*

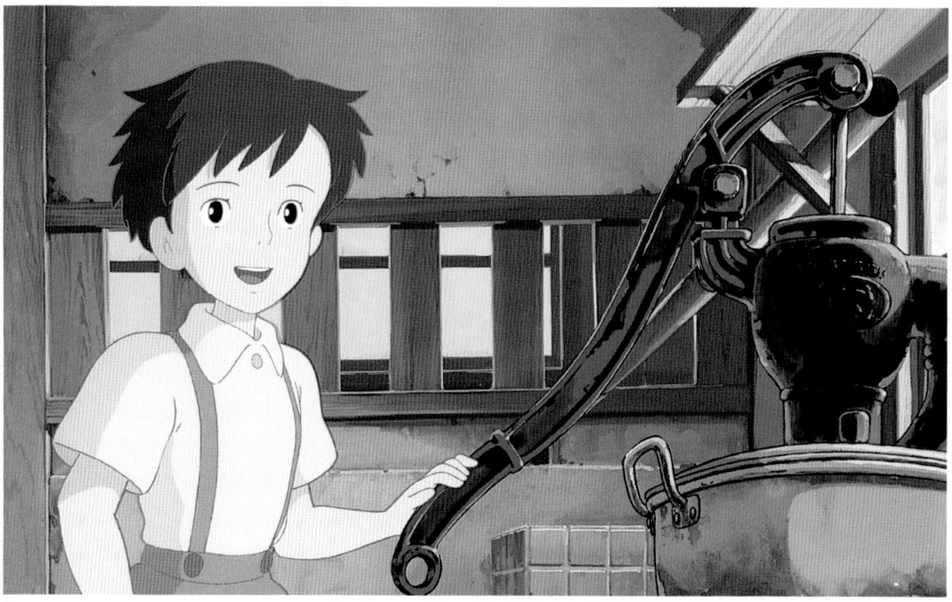

1

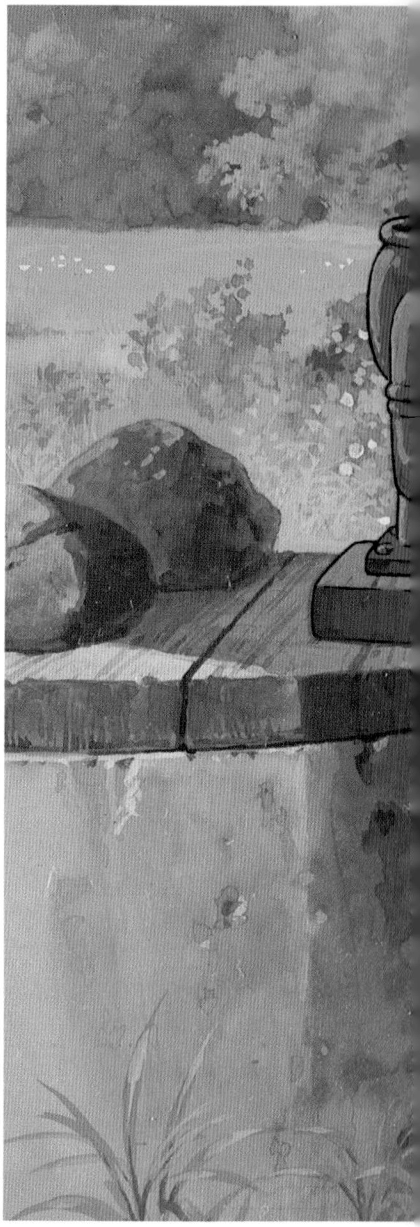

2

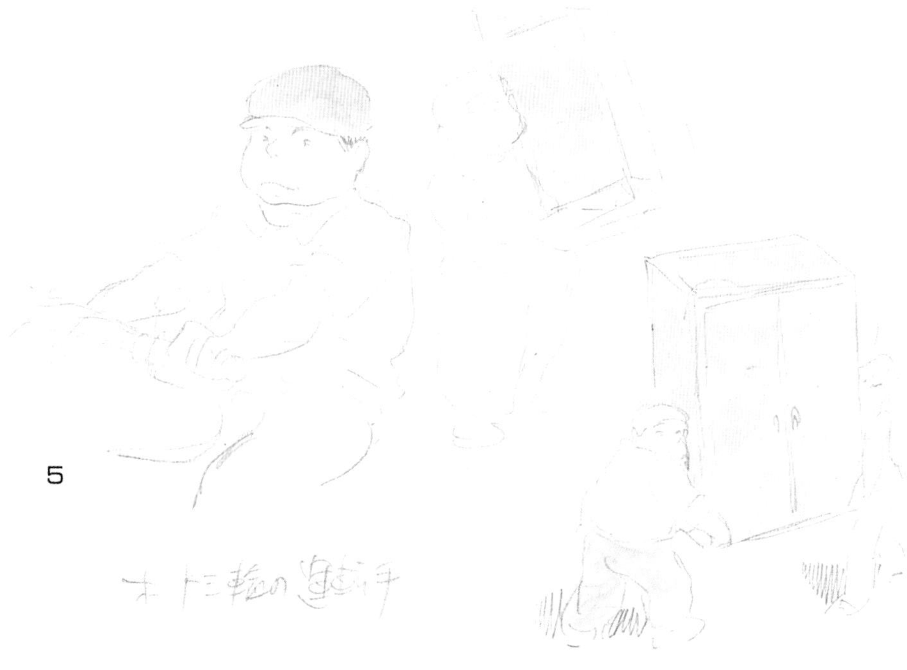
オート三輪の運転手

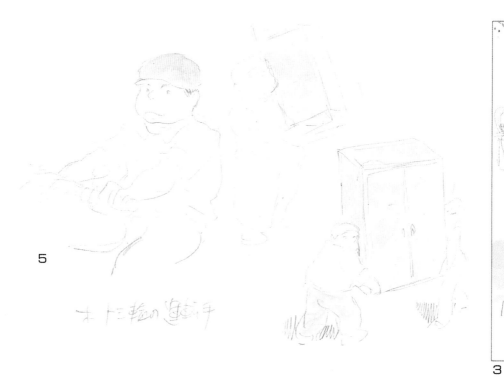

5

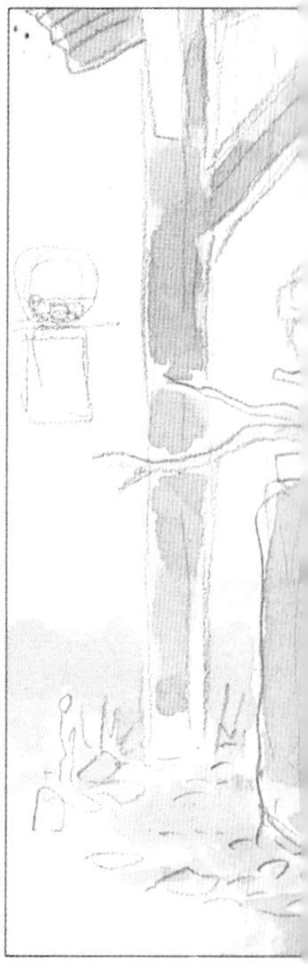

3

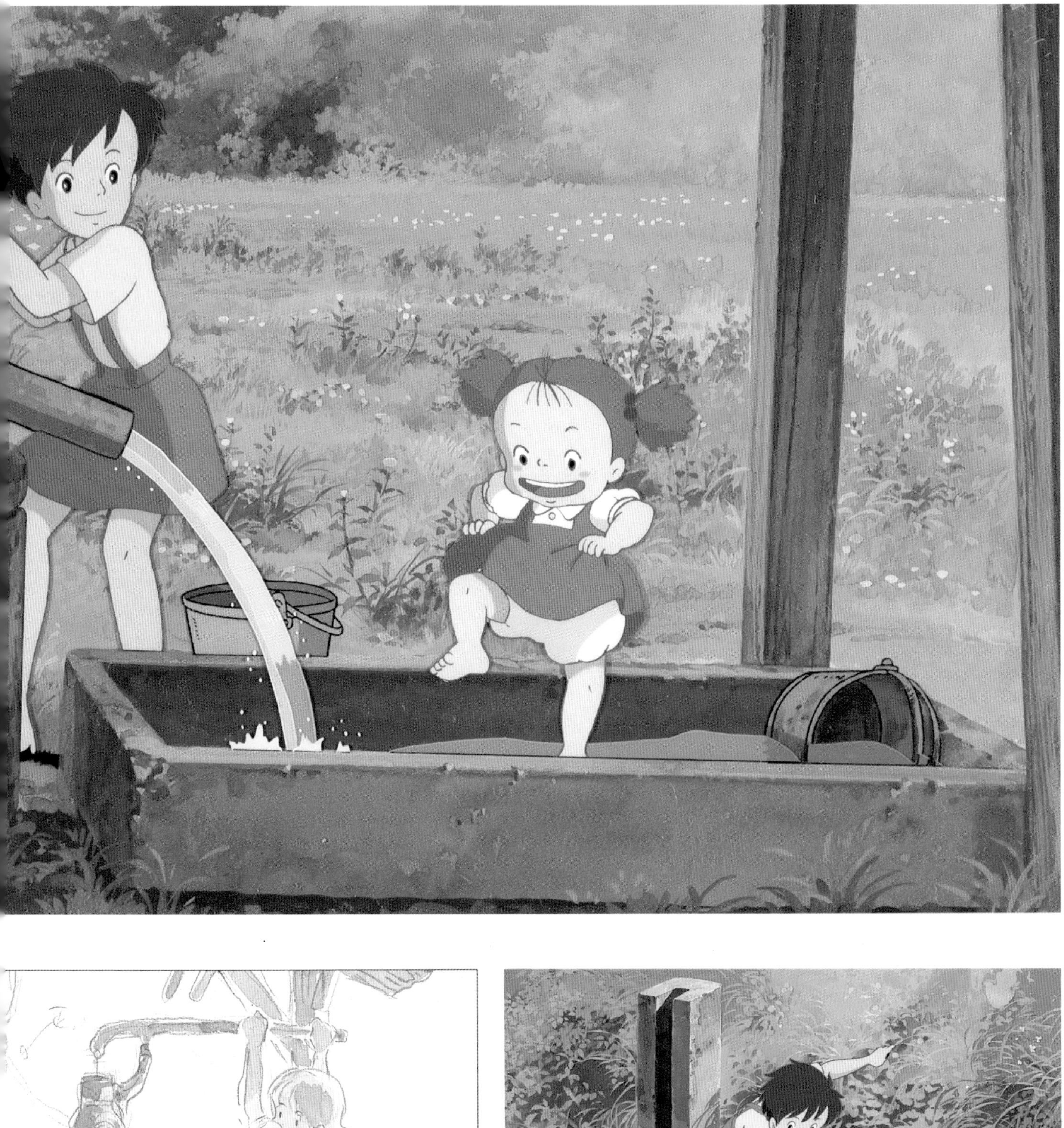

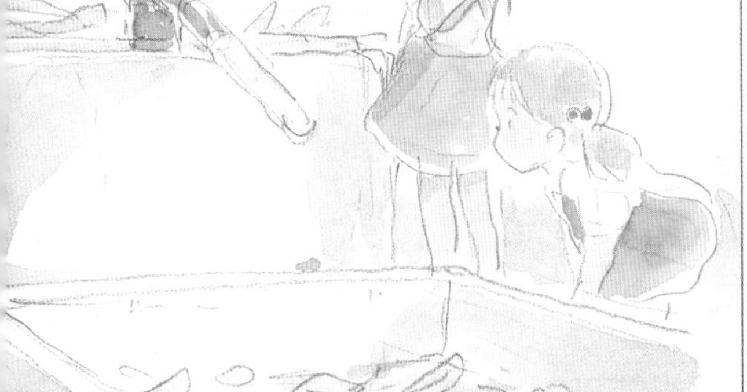

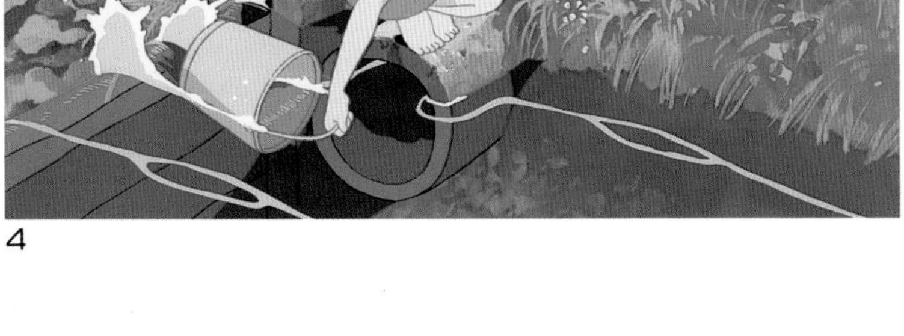

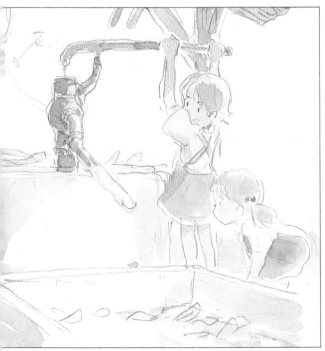

4

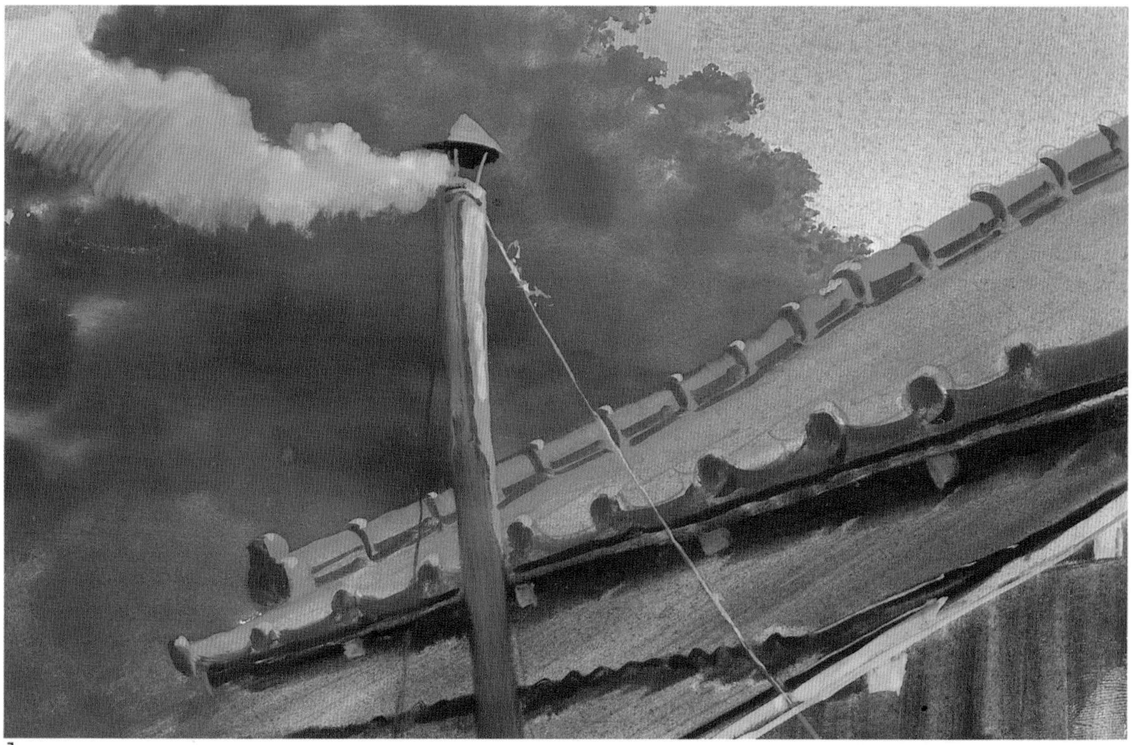

1

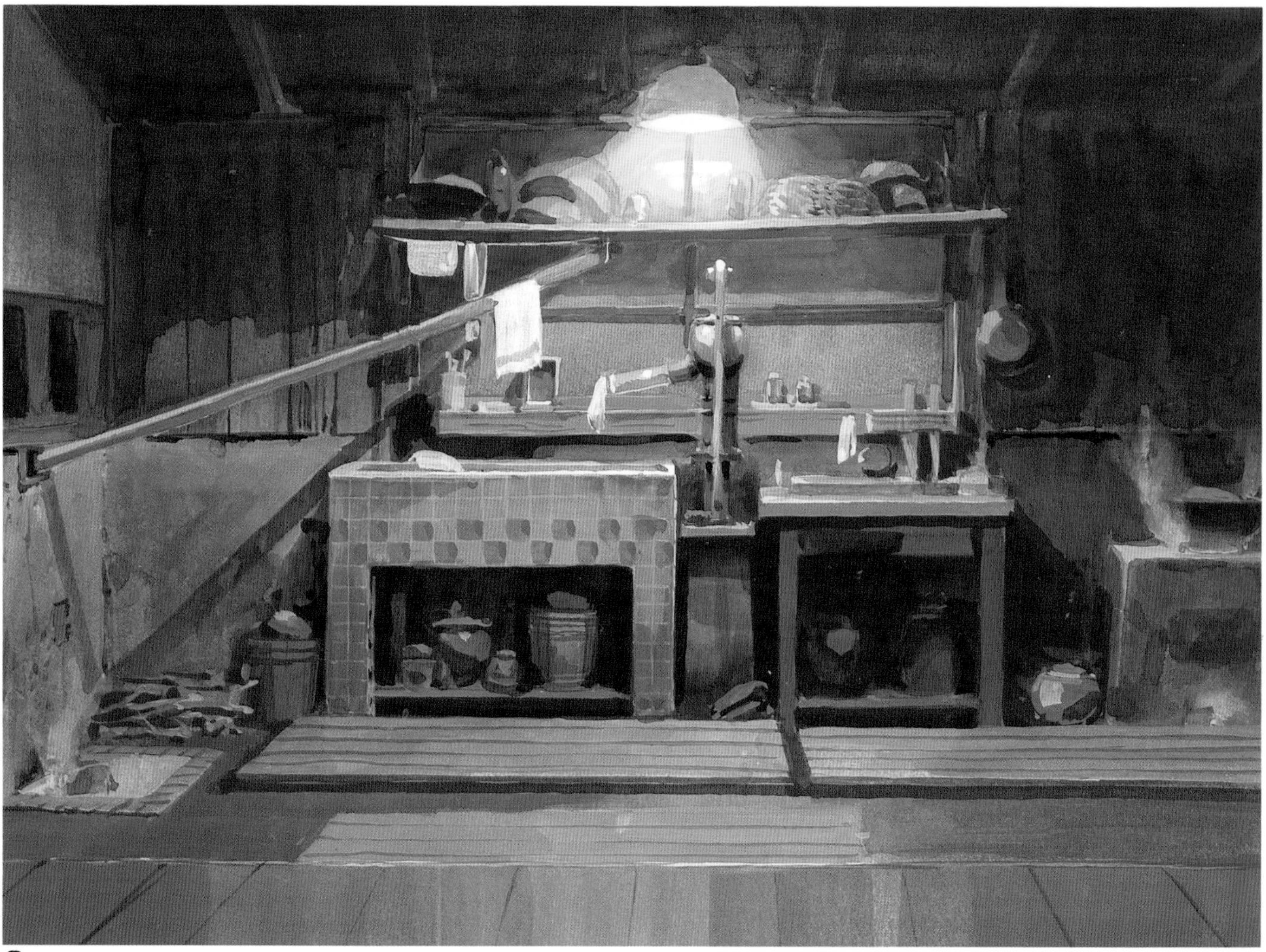

2

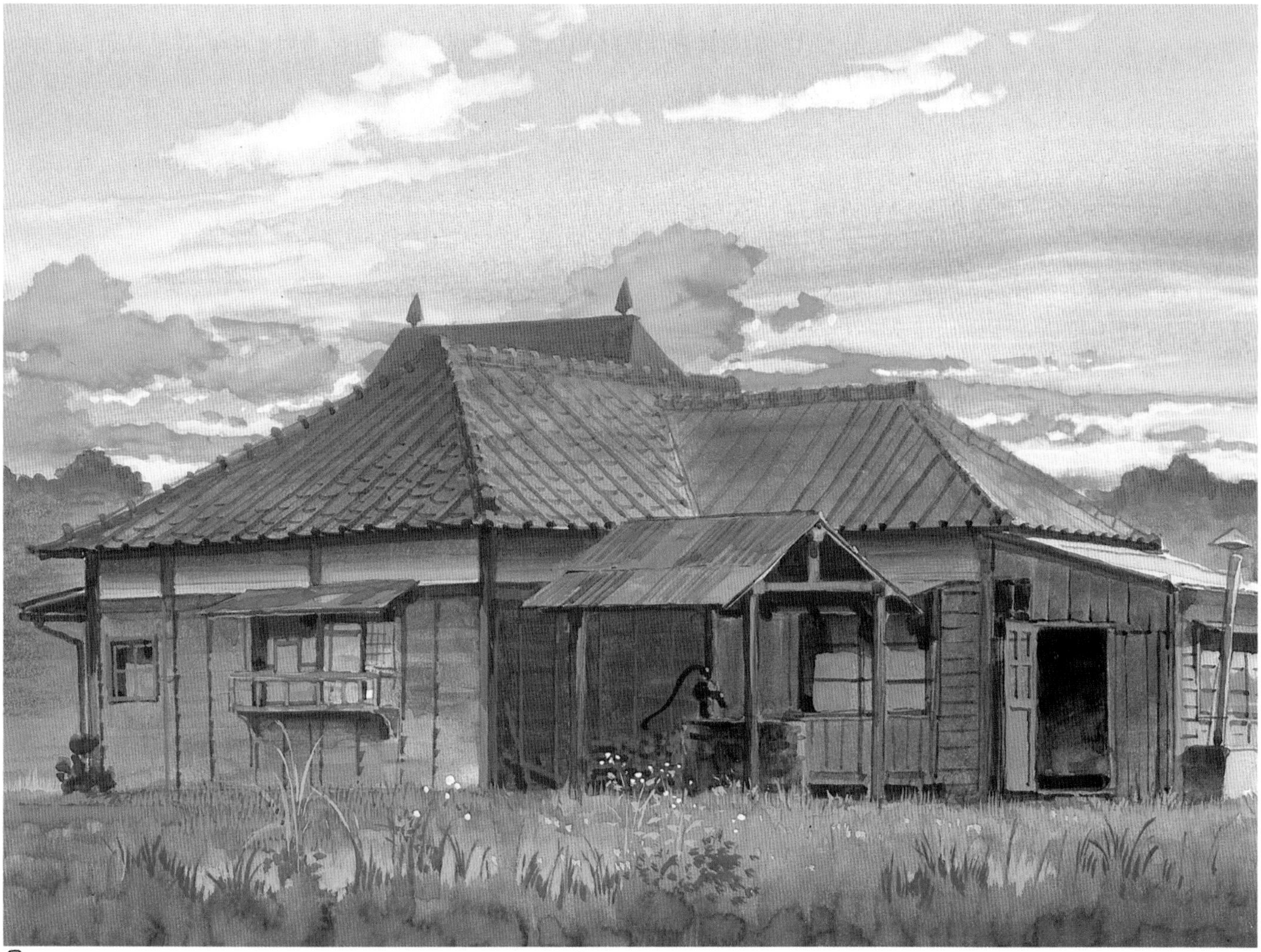

3

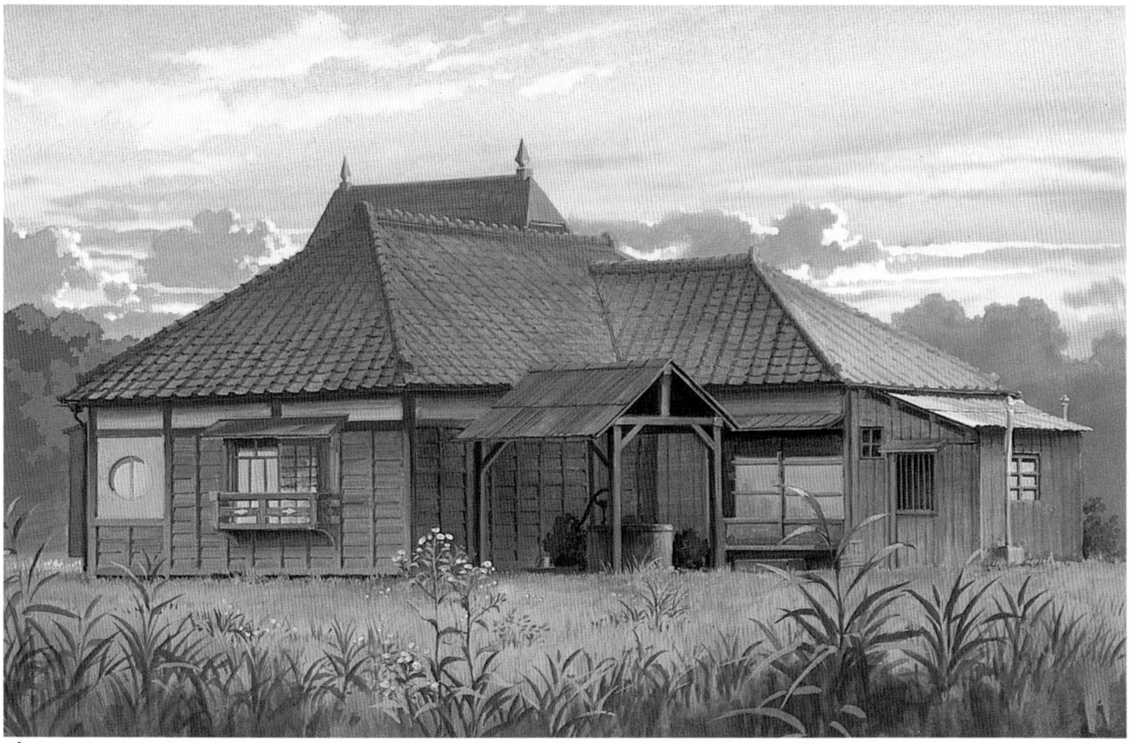

4

1 Smoking chimney *(concept art)*

2 Dim rays enter the kitchen lit from inside. *(concept art)*

3 Kusakabe residence at sunset. *(concept art)*

4 Background for 3.

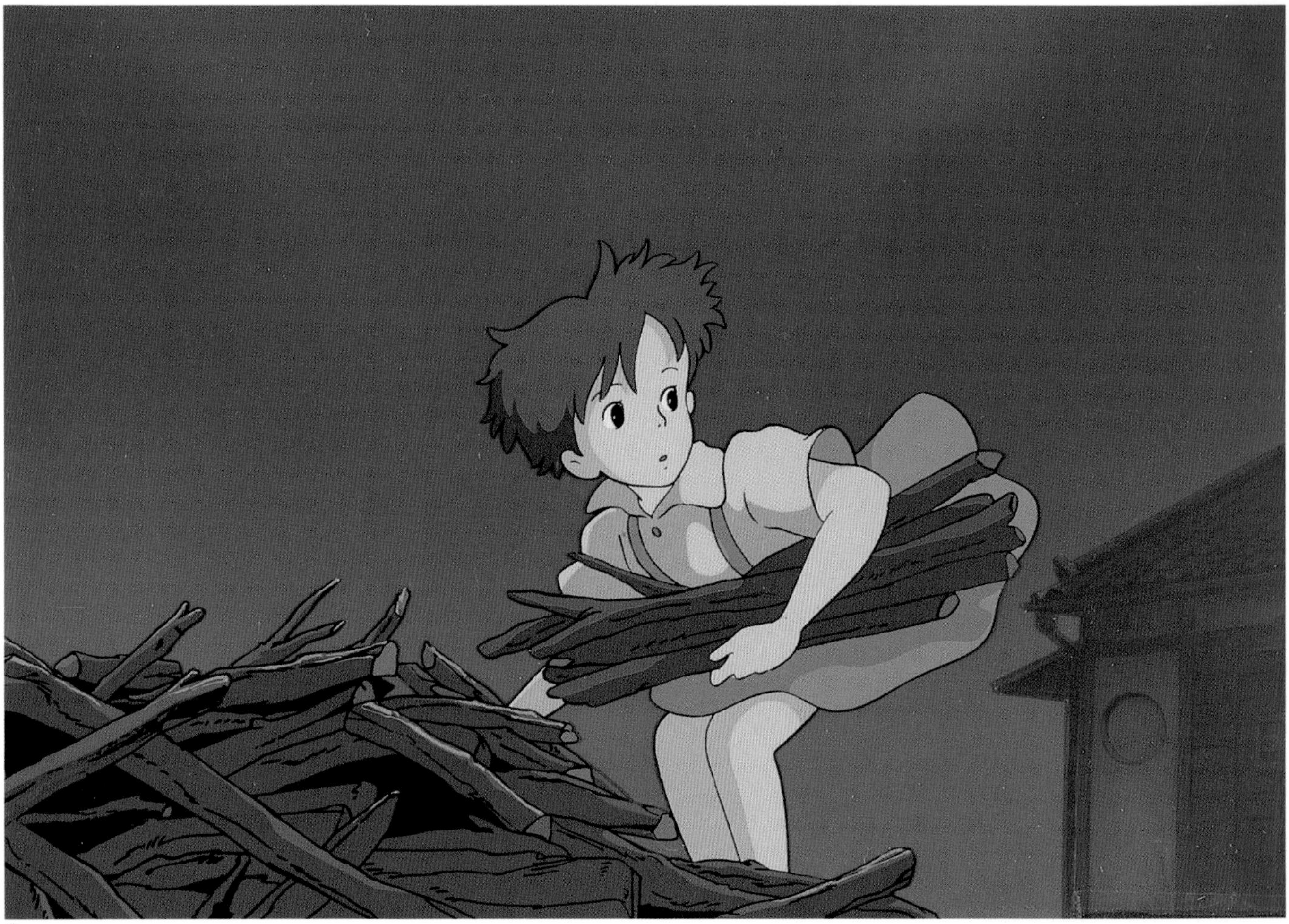

1

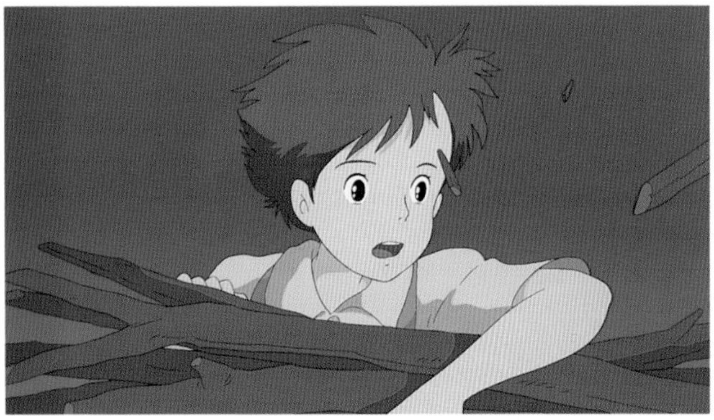

3

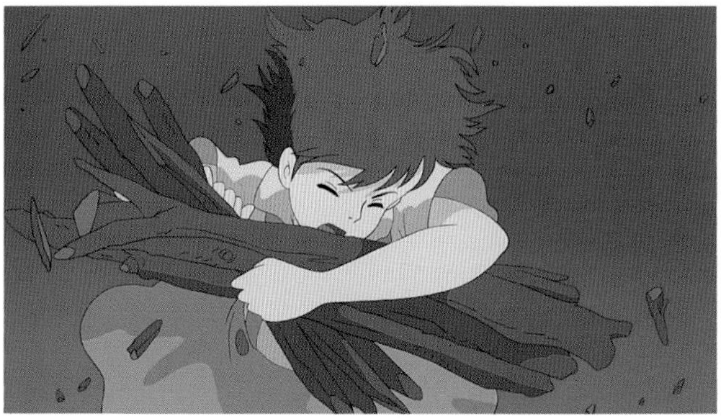

4

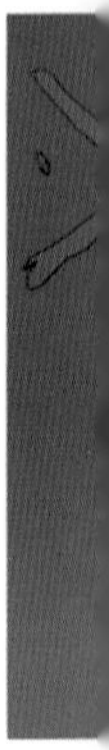

5

1-6 The gust of wind blowing against Satsuki as she gathers firewood. The sudden flurry blows away the dry branches, leaves, and her wood. Later she discovers the wind came from the Cat Bus. *(cel art)*

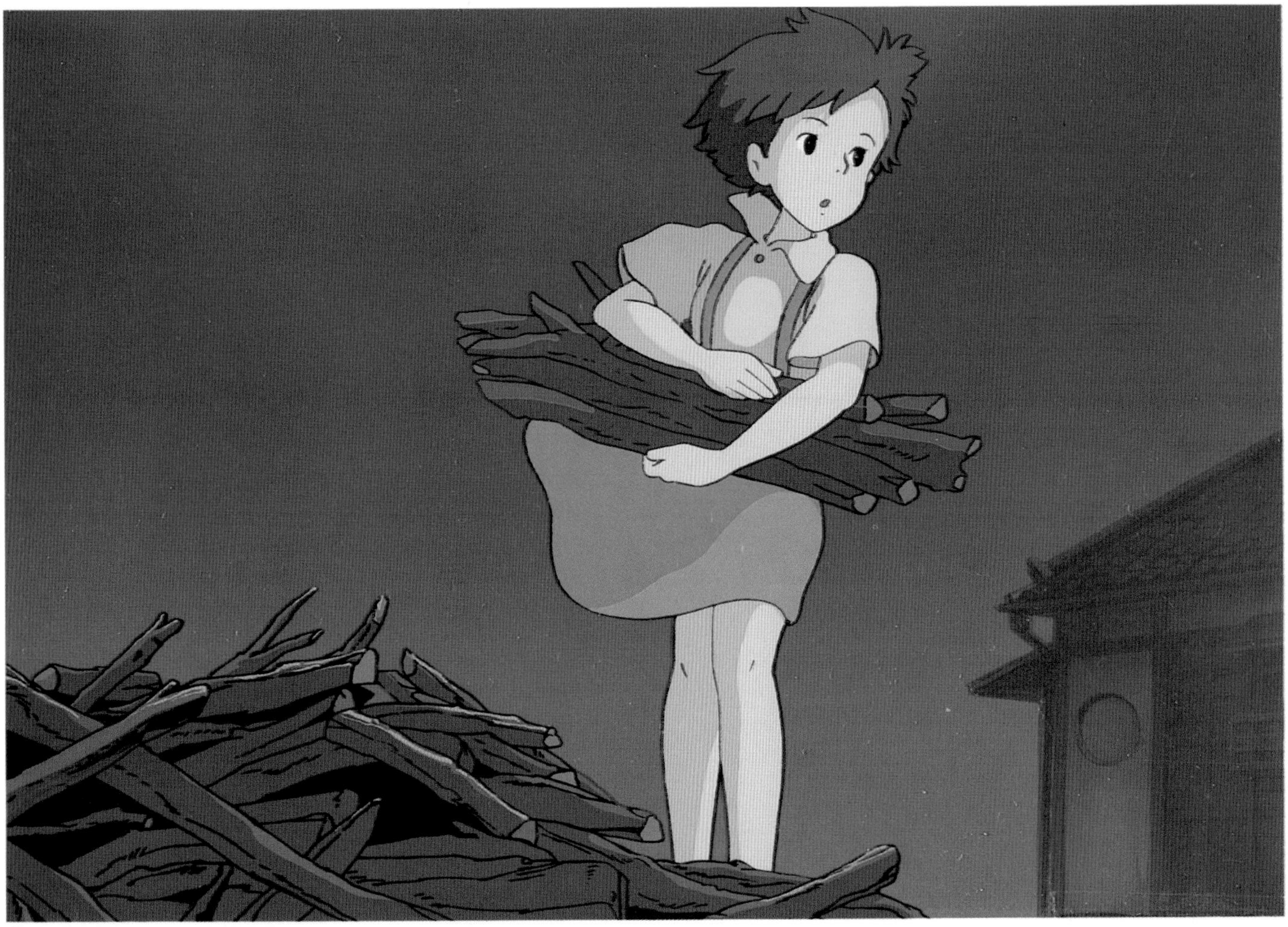

2

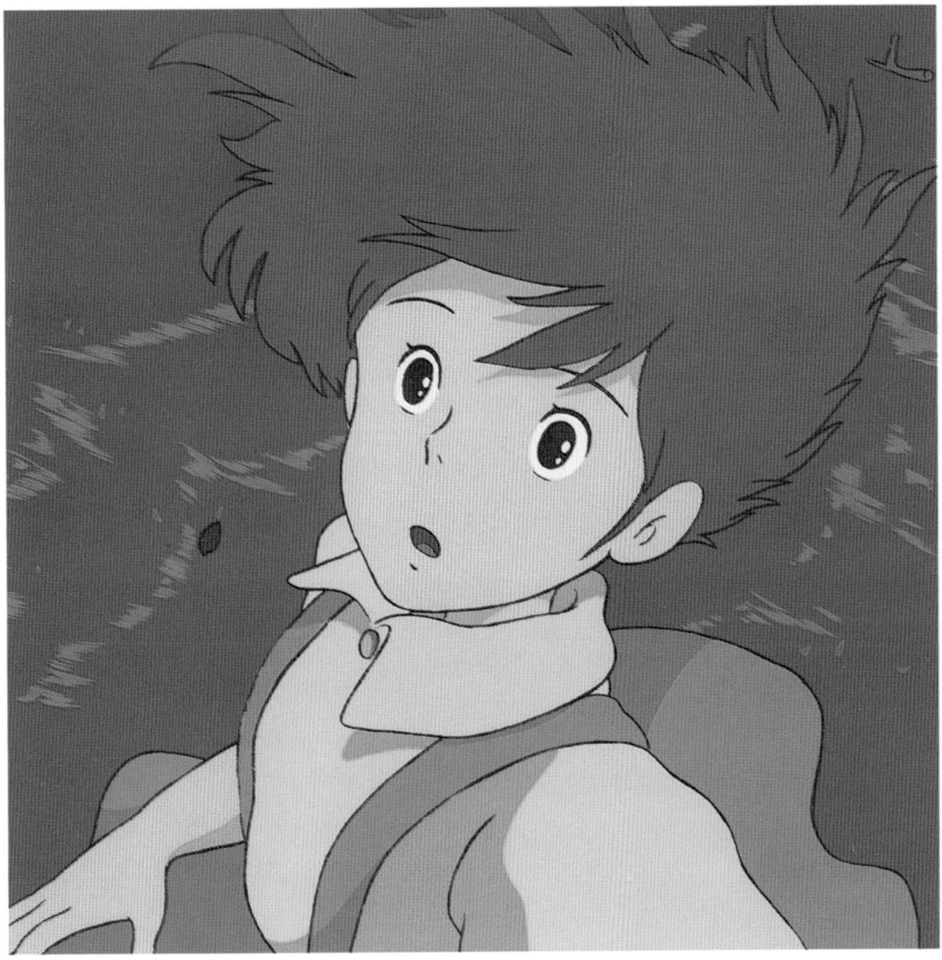

6

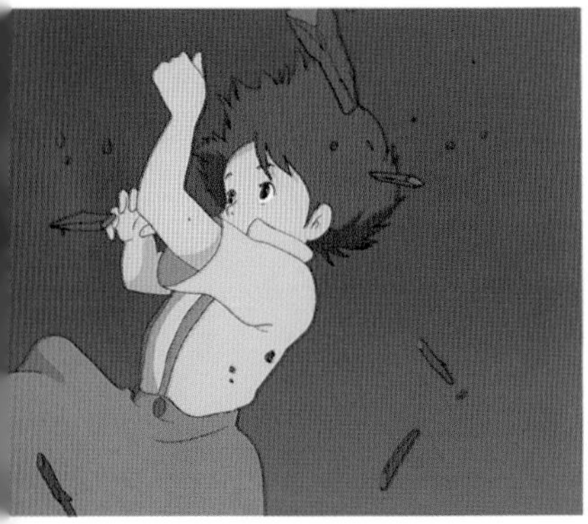

1, 2 The family takes a bath. Mei looks up, worried, while Satsuki turns to follow the sound of the wind. *(cel art)*

3 The wind suddenly dies down, and an owl's low cry startles Satsuki. She immediately rinses herself and steps into the bathtub without her soap. *(film)*

5 The three take a bath. *(concept sketch)*

"I actually wanted to have a storm scene. I thought of depicting a suspenseful day that starts with a storm forecast on the radio and ends with the aftermath the following morning. For kids, a storm is a kind of carnival event. A single day depicting that would be far more thrilling to a child than some diabolical character who's out to rule the world." *(Miyazaki)*

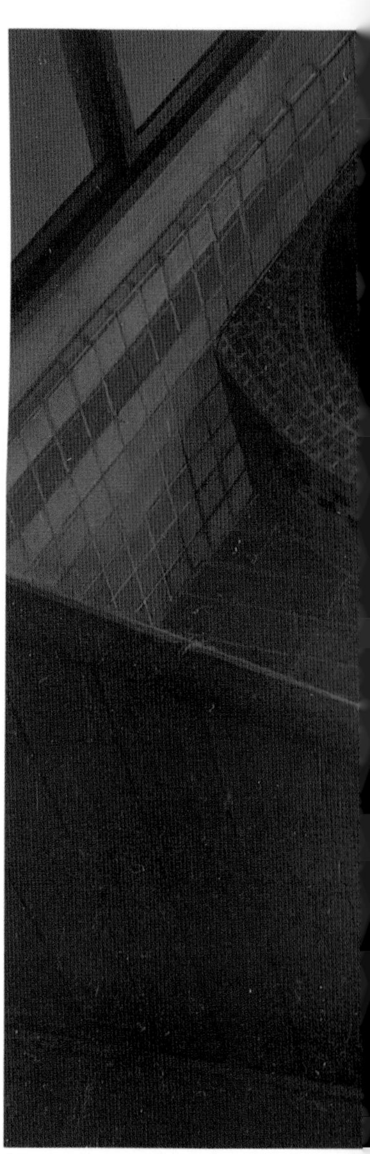

1

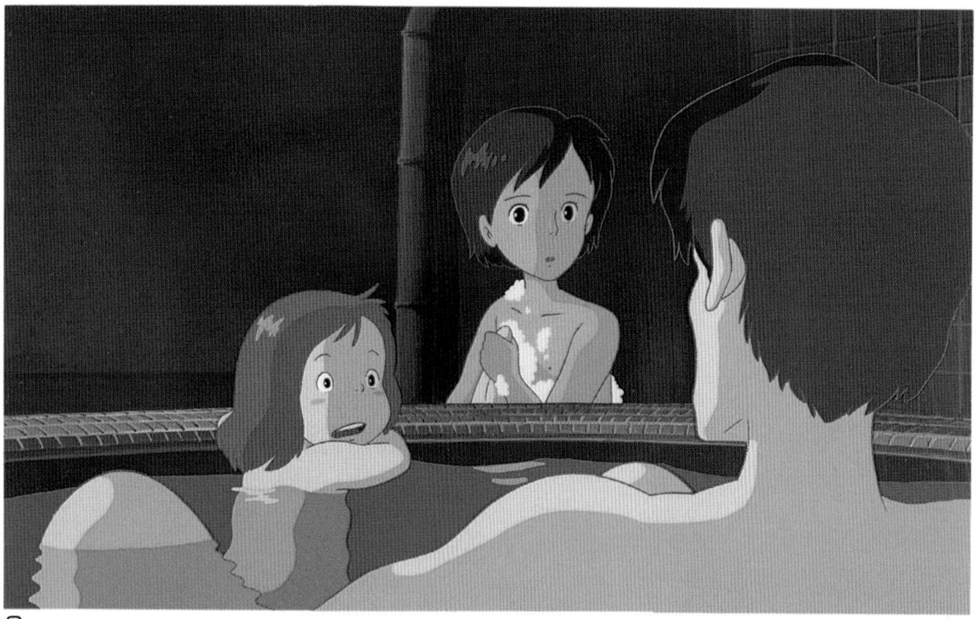

2

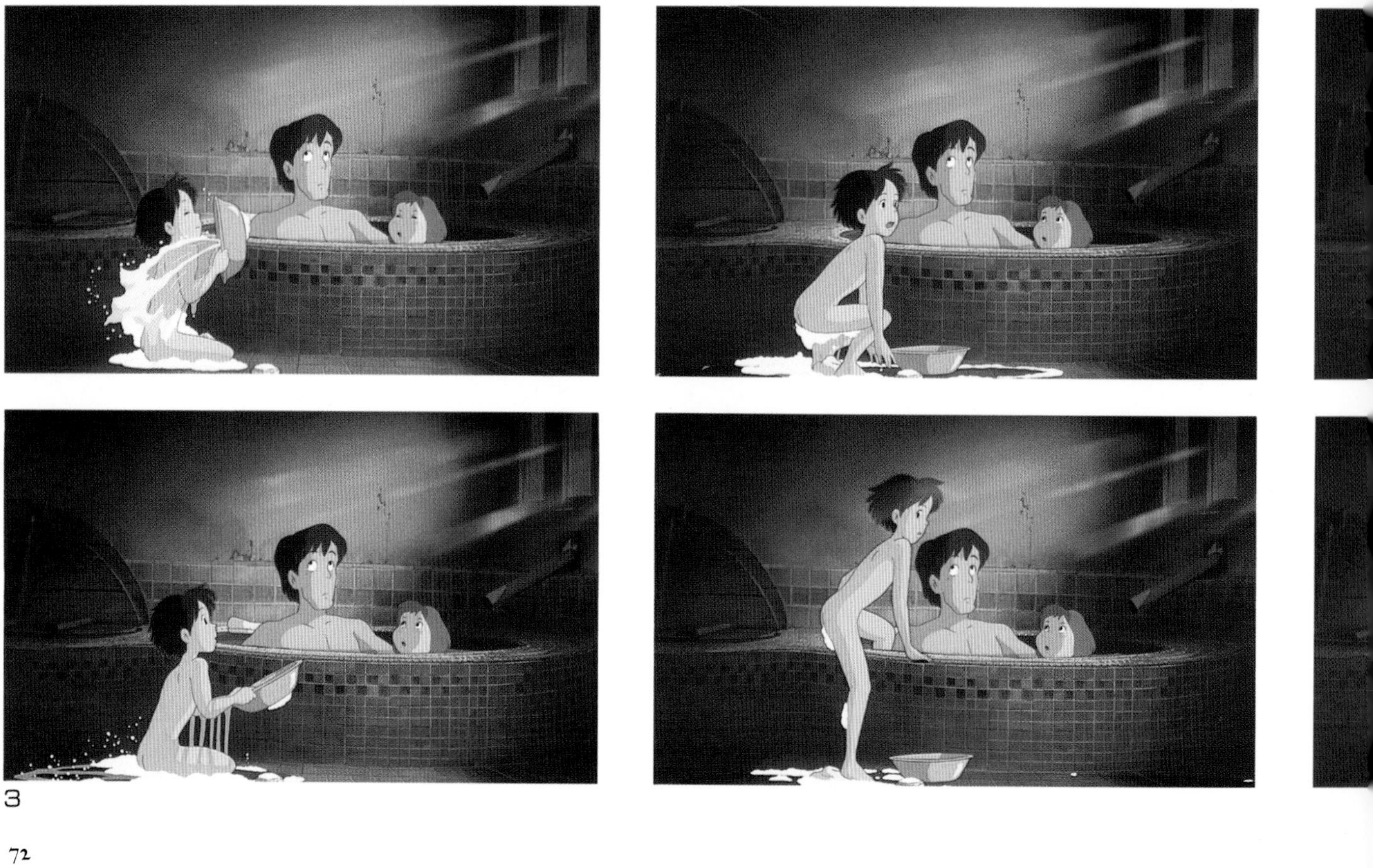

3

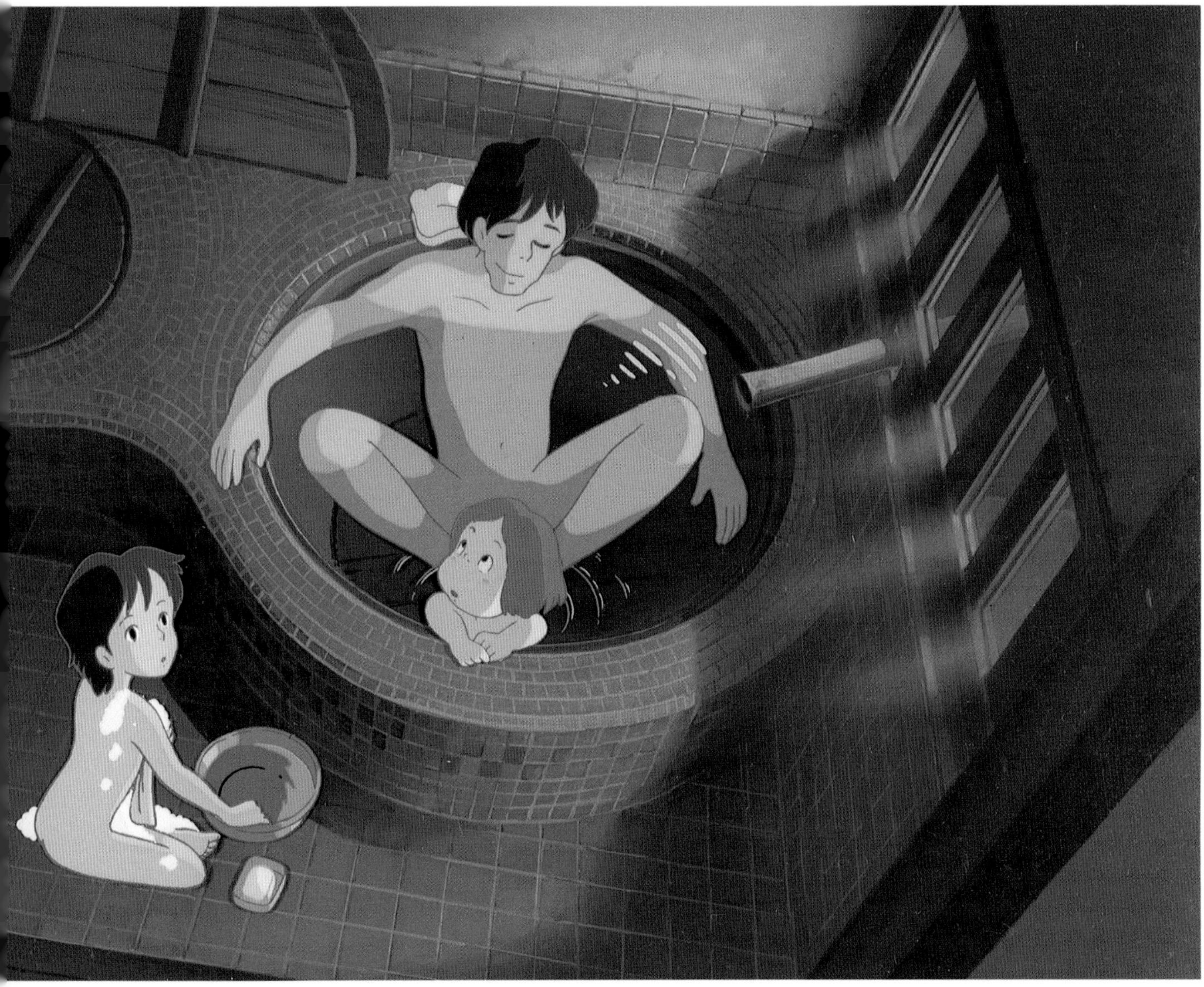

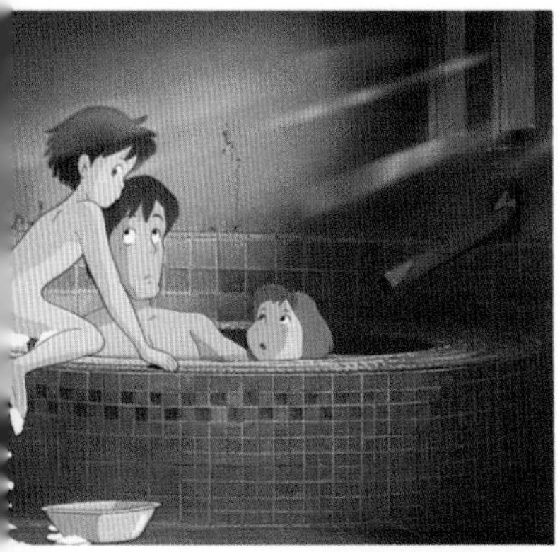

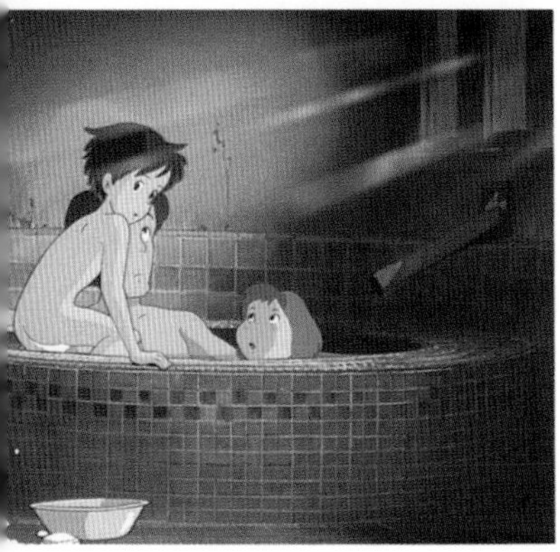

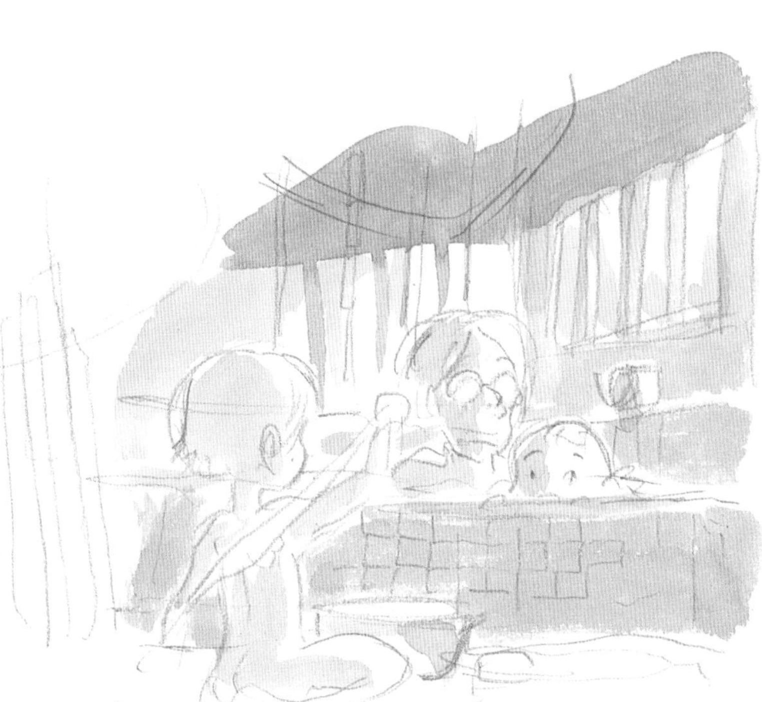

4

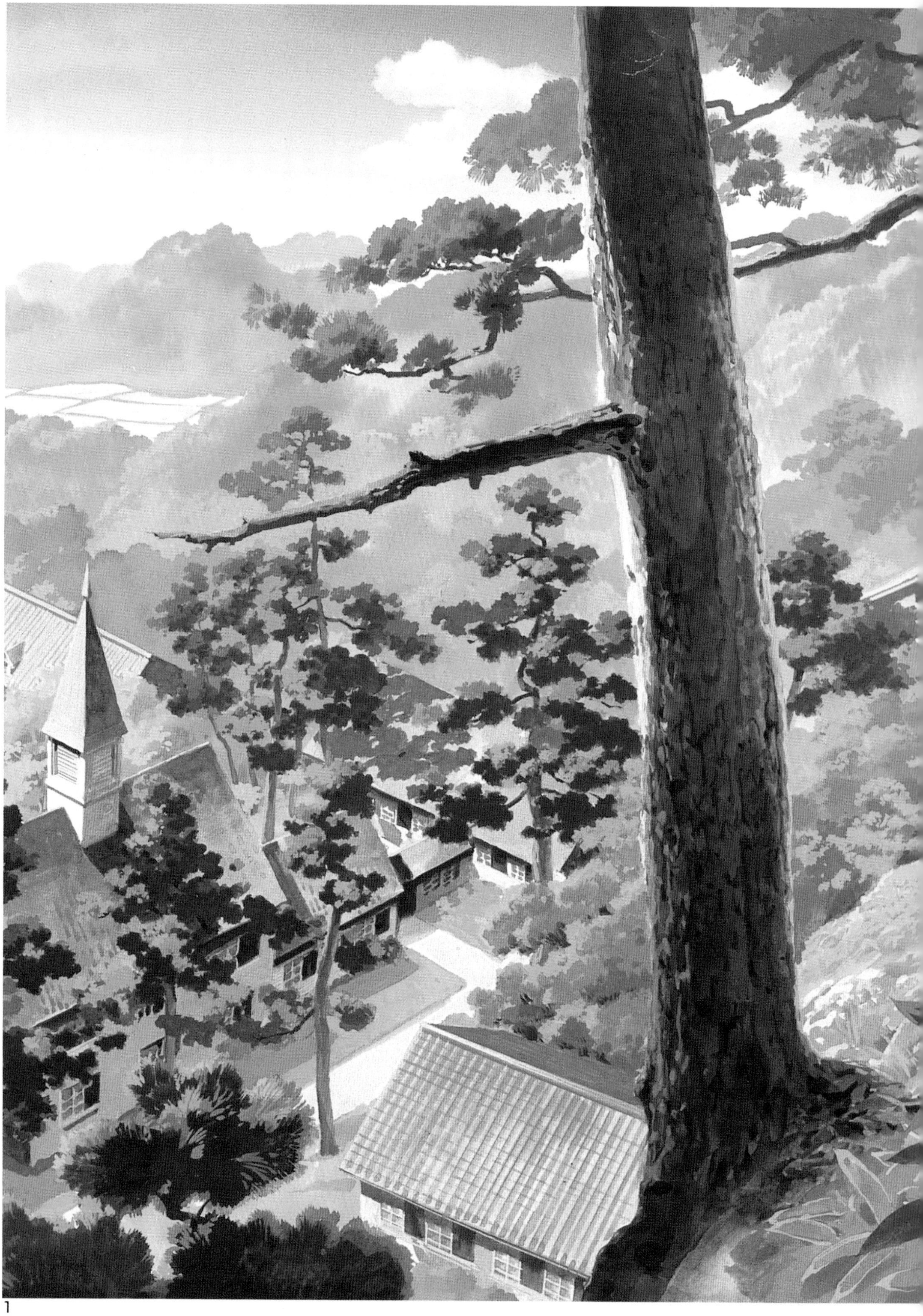

1

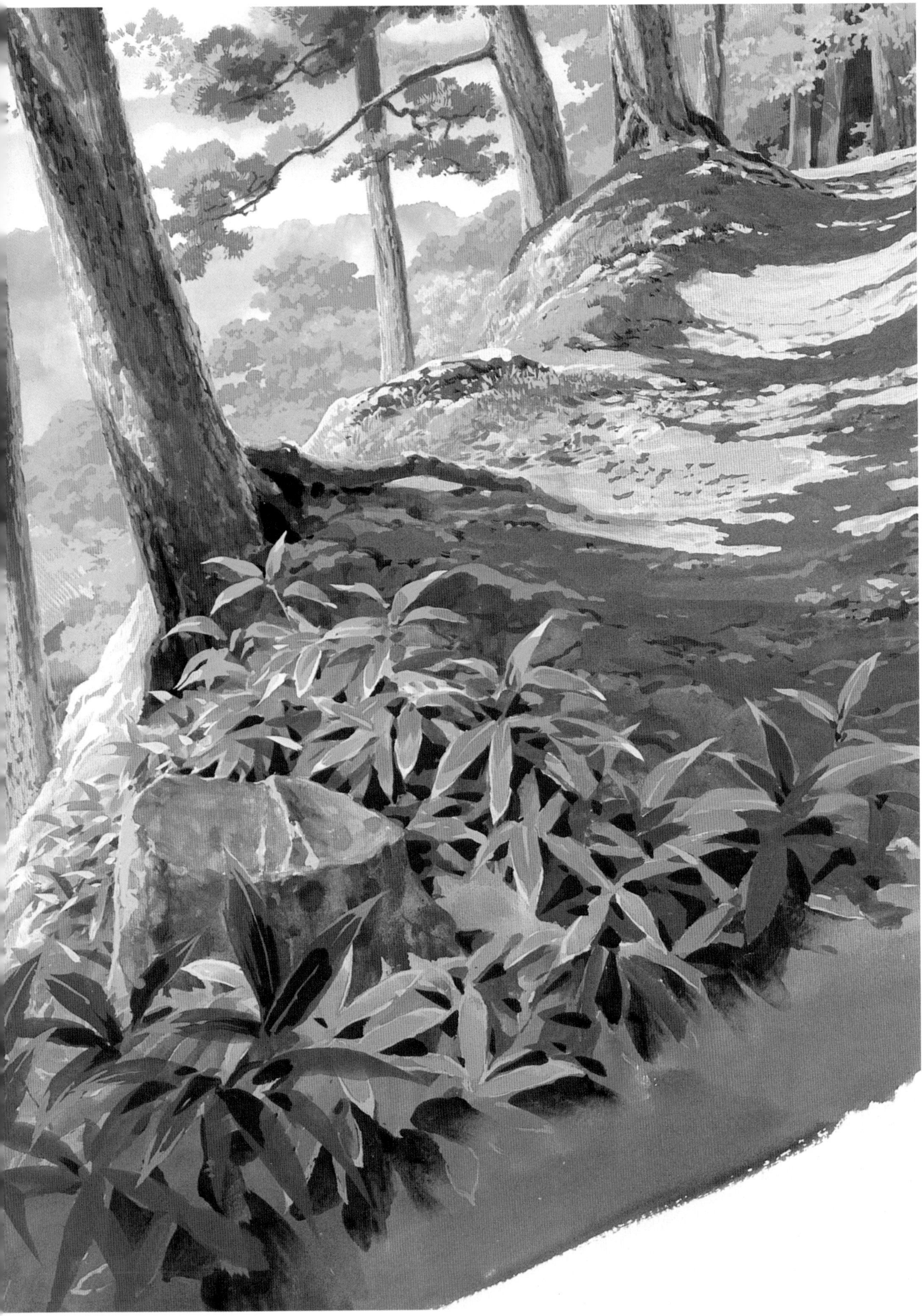

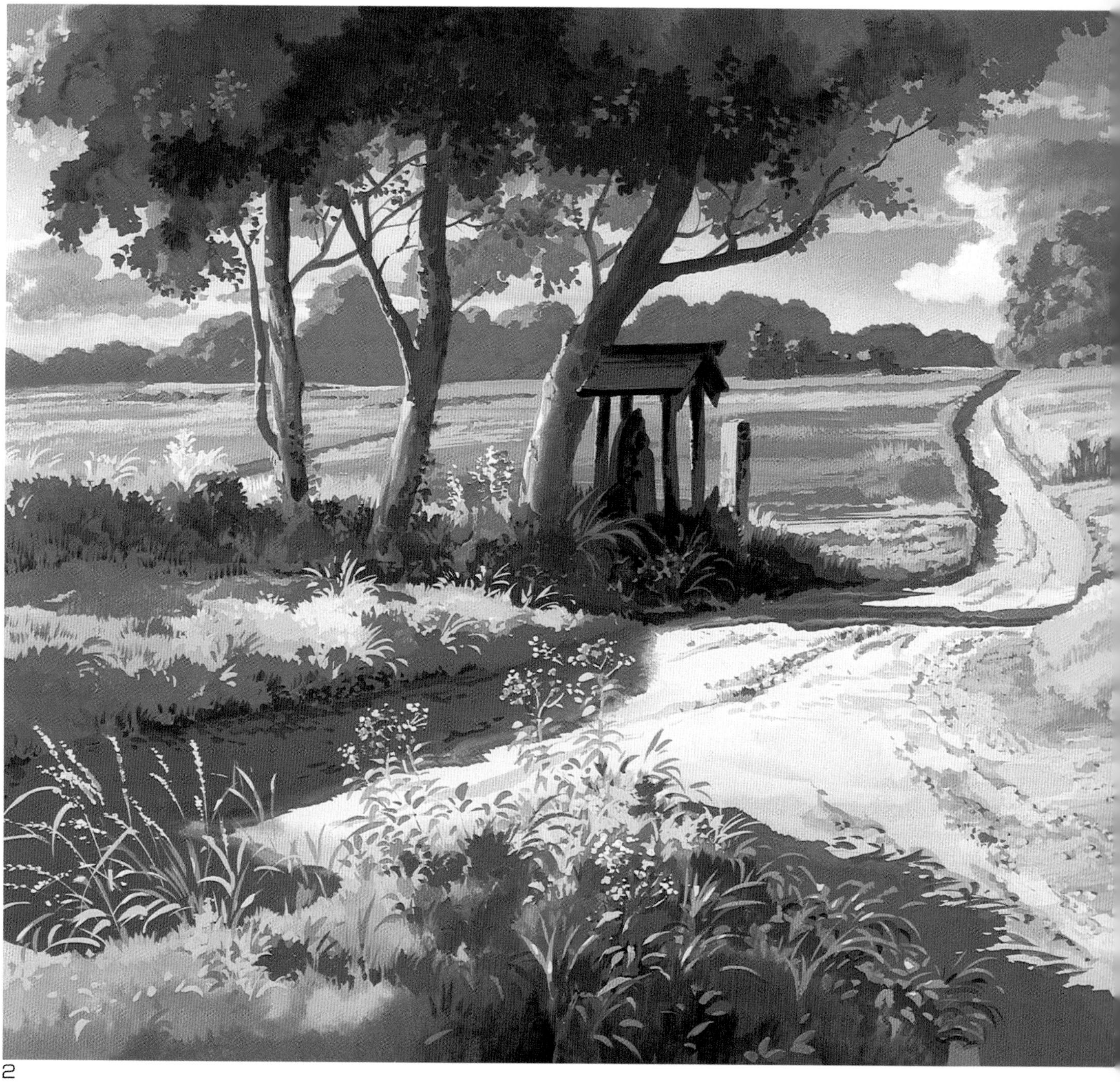

2

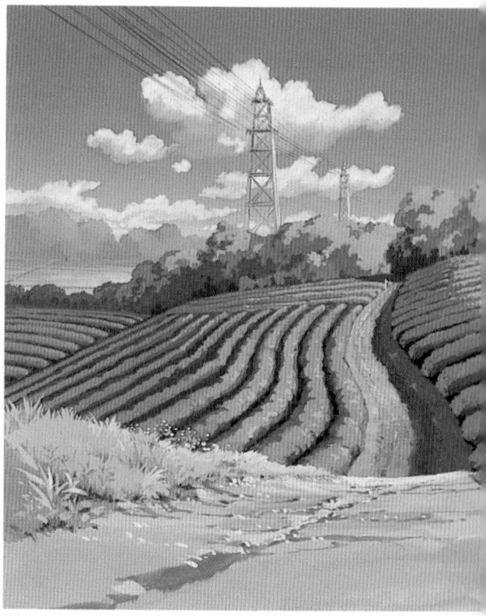

4

1 The pine forest ridge offers a view of the hospital.

2 The fork in the road with the Jizo statue leads to Shichikokuyama.

3 The father and daughters take a bicycle ride to Shichikokuyama. *(cel art)*

4 Hill of the tea fields. *(background)*

5 The bridge over Matsui River on the outskirts of town.

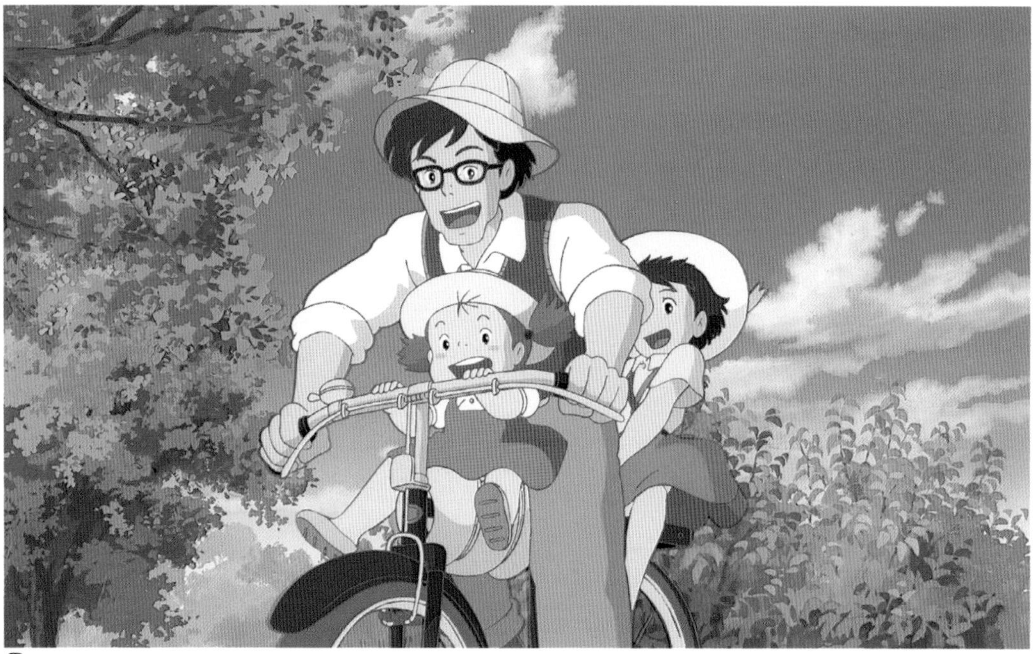
3
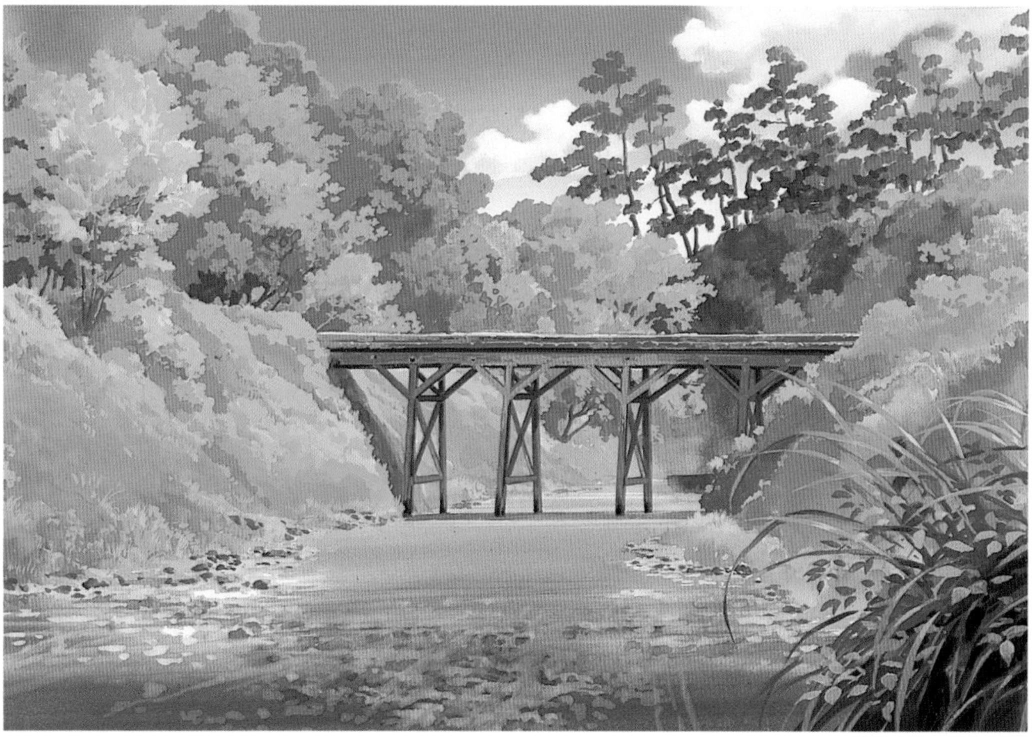
5
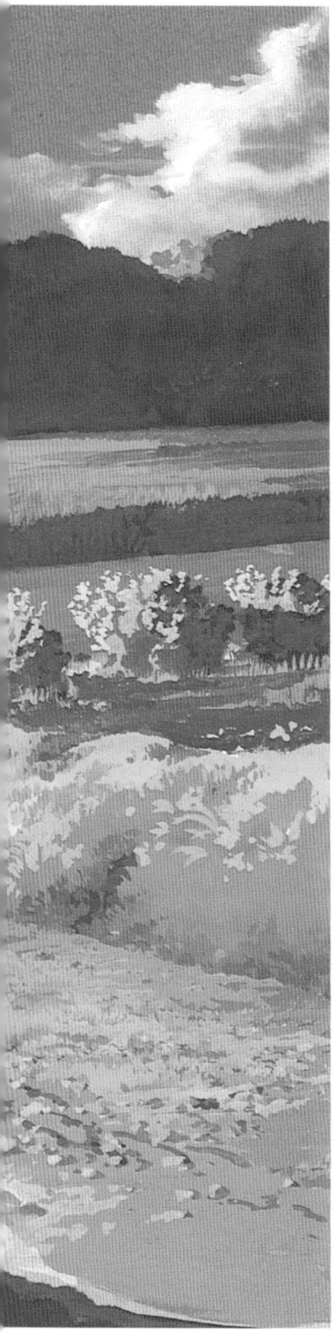
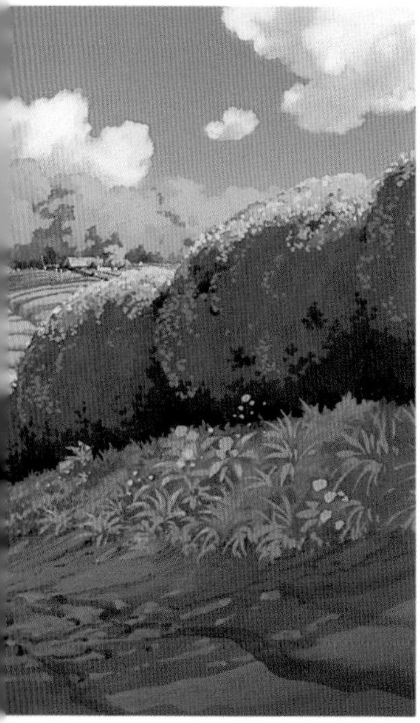

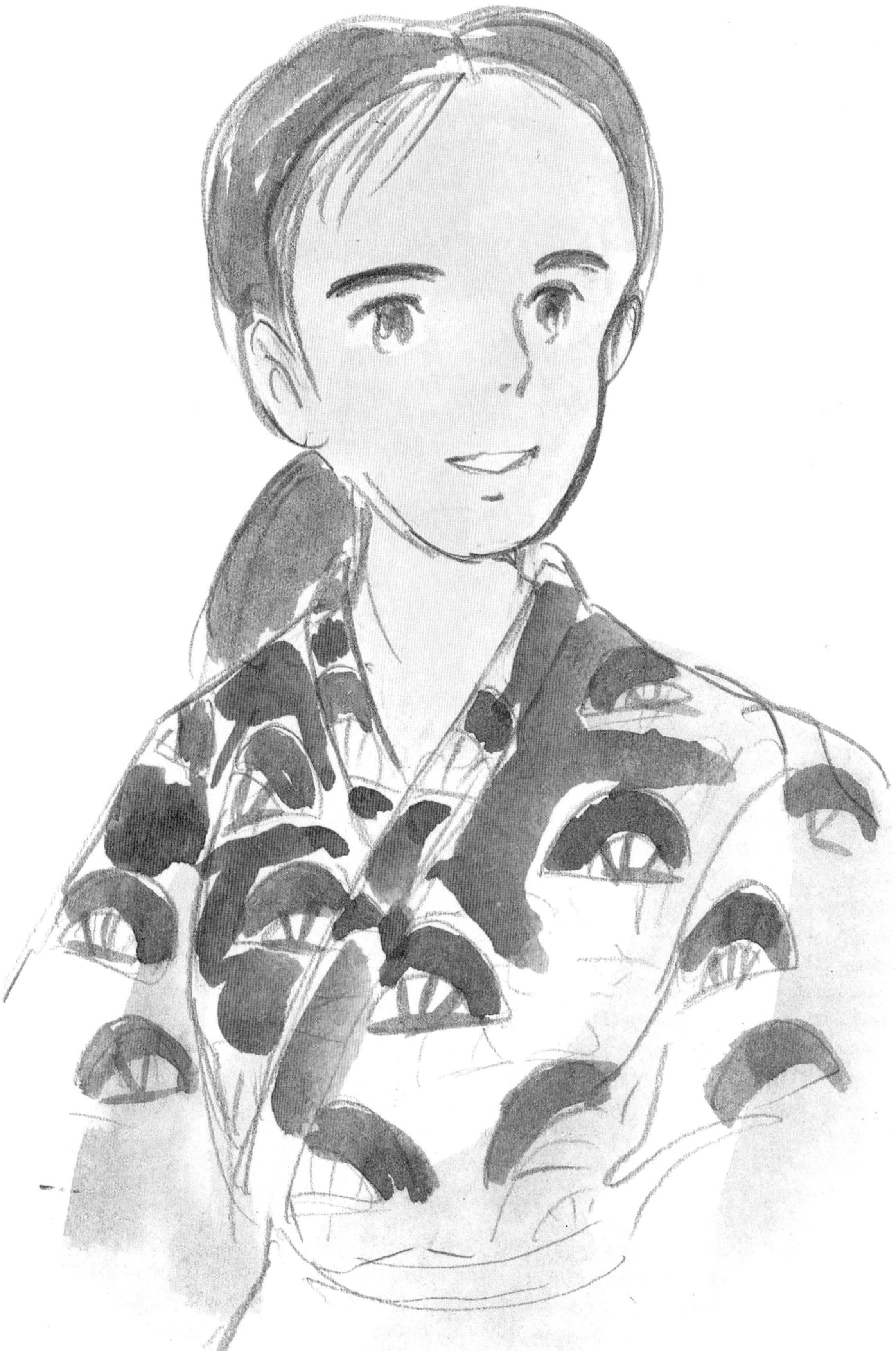

1

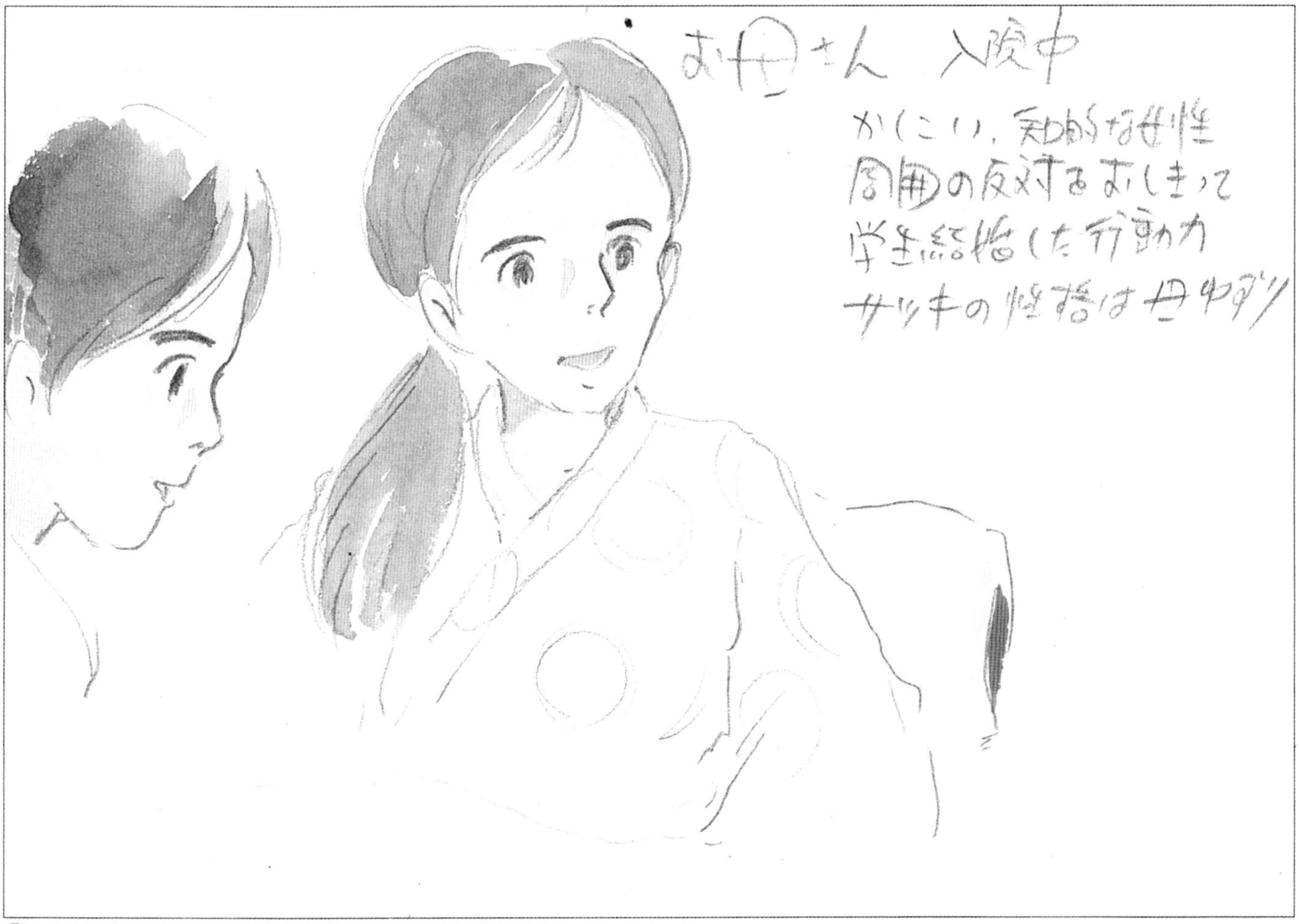
お母さん 入院中
かしこい、知的な女性
周囲の反対をおしきって
学生結婚した行動力
サツキの性格は母ゆずり

2

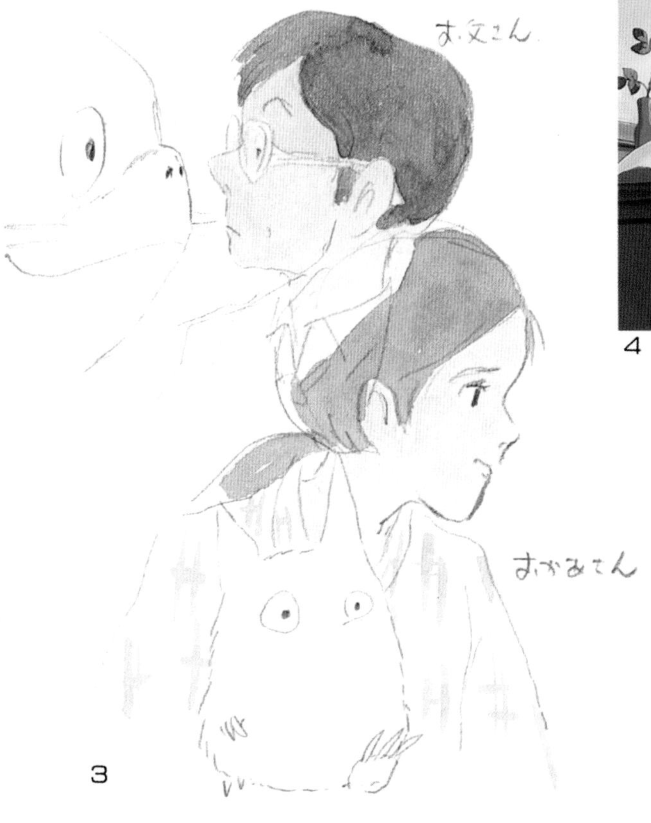
お父さん
おかあさん

3

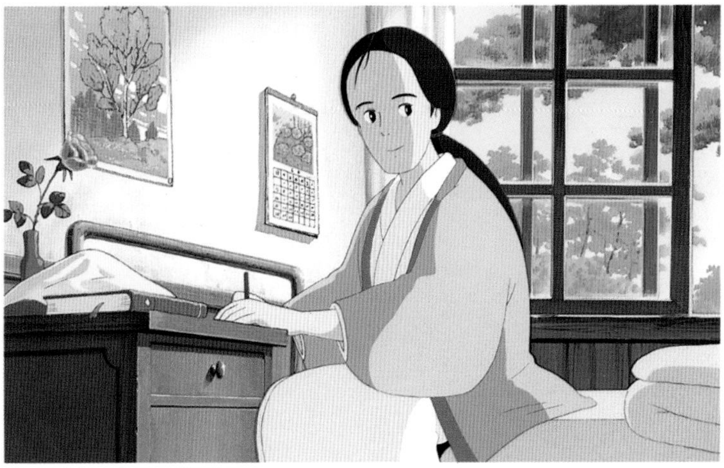

4

1 Mother. (Yasuko Kusakabe) *(concept sketch)*

2 Mother. *(character design)*

3 Father and mother. *(initial character design)*

4 Mother sitting on her bed as she writes a letter. *(cel art)*

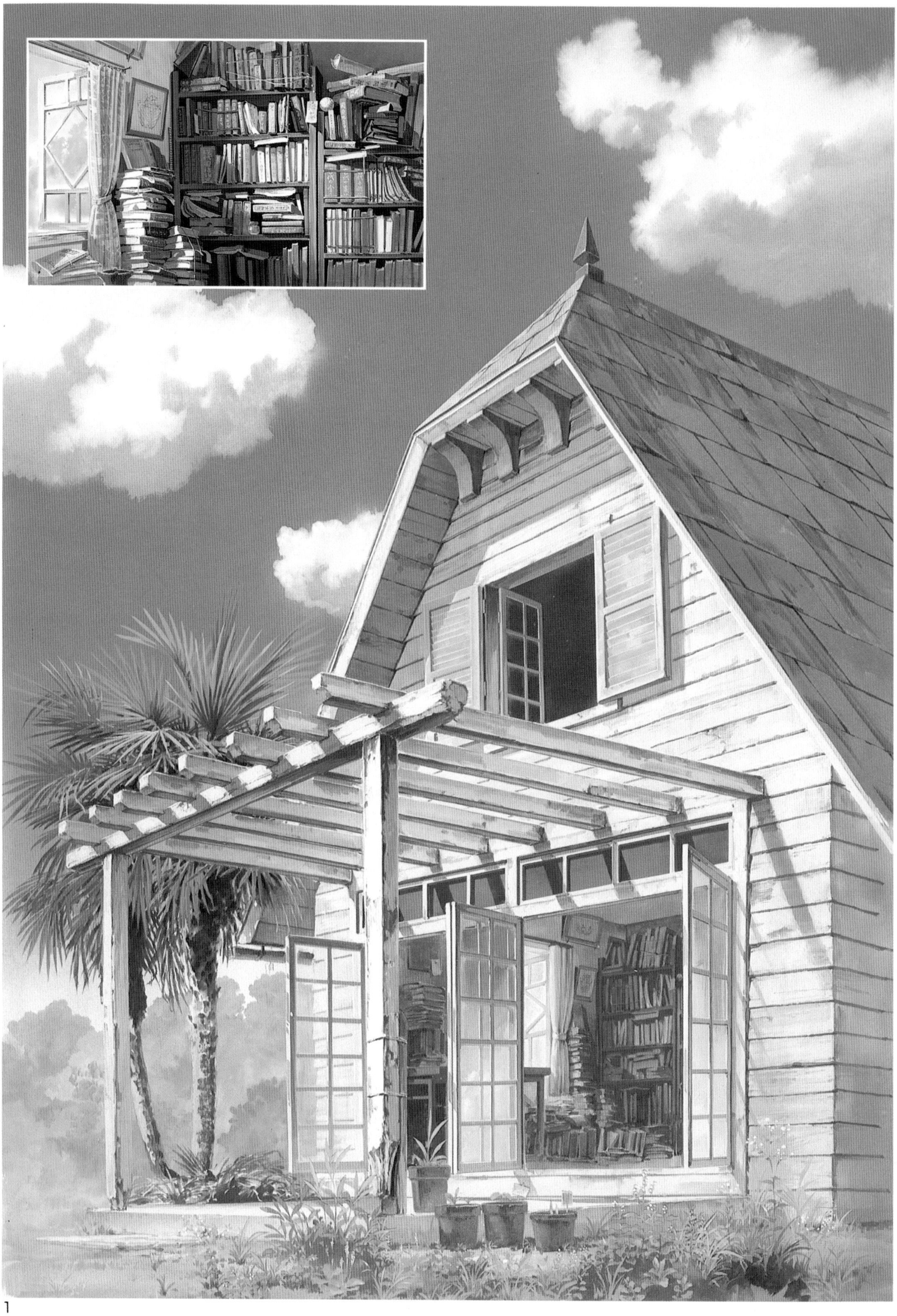

1

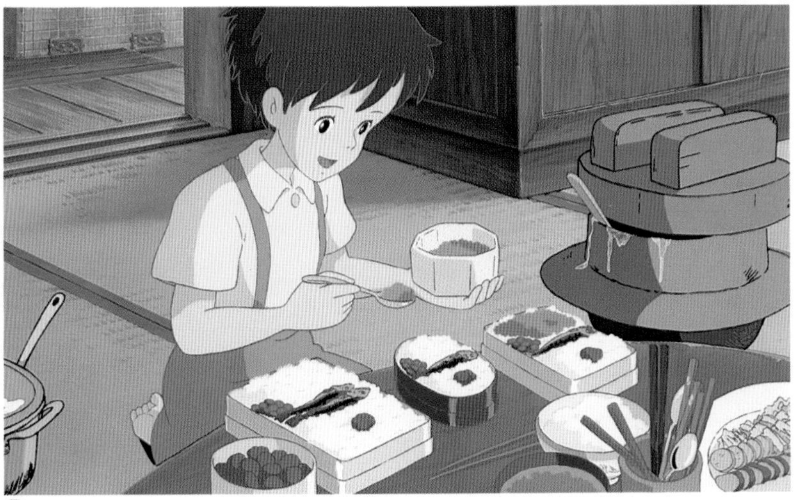

2

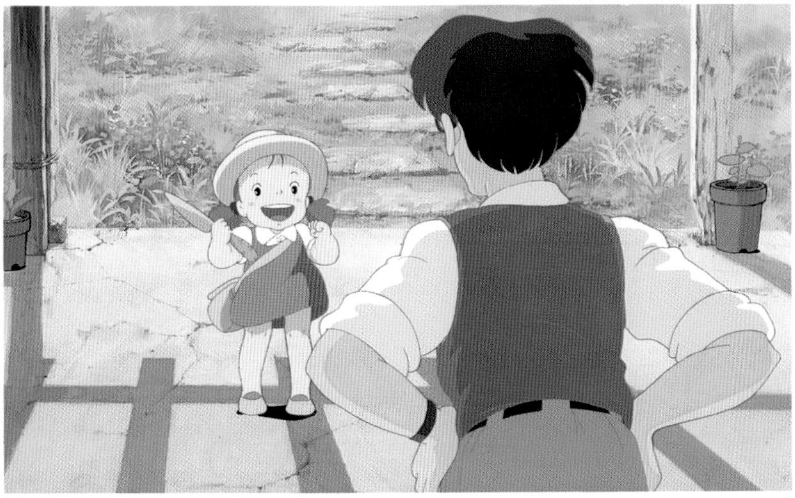

3

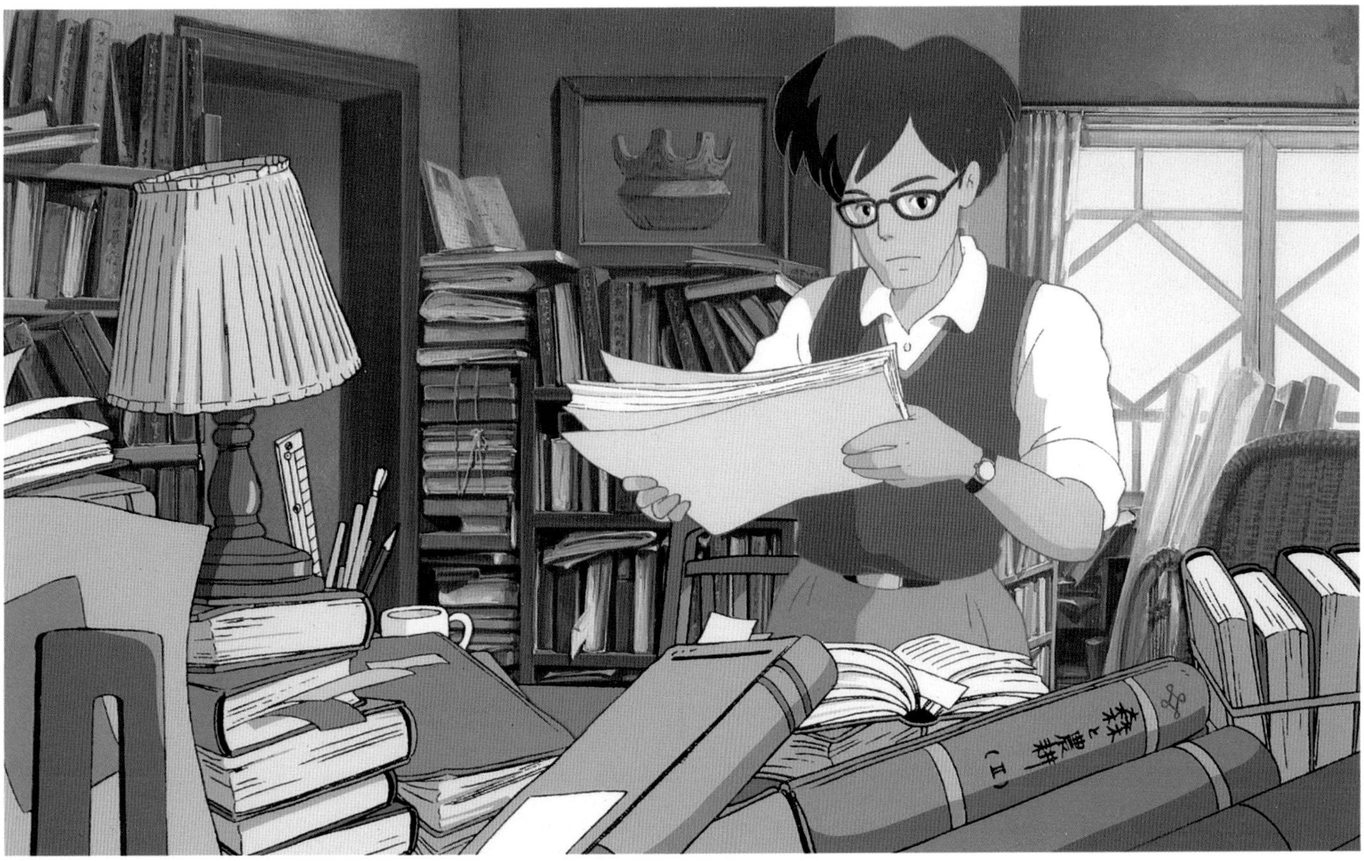

4

1 A clear June morning. *(background)*

2 Satsuki packing her family's lunch. *(cel art)*

3 Mei dressed up like Satsuki. *(cel art)*

4 Father going over his manuscript. He looks quite serious. *(cel art)*

"Many Japanese homes used to have Western-style additions. Actually, this house is only half built. The yard was supposed to be well kept, but the house was abandoned. The previous occupant was ill and died there. It was a villa built as a retreat for a tuberculosis patient. The house languished after the patient died. That's the story behind the house." *(Miyazaki)*

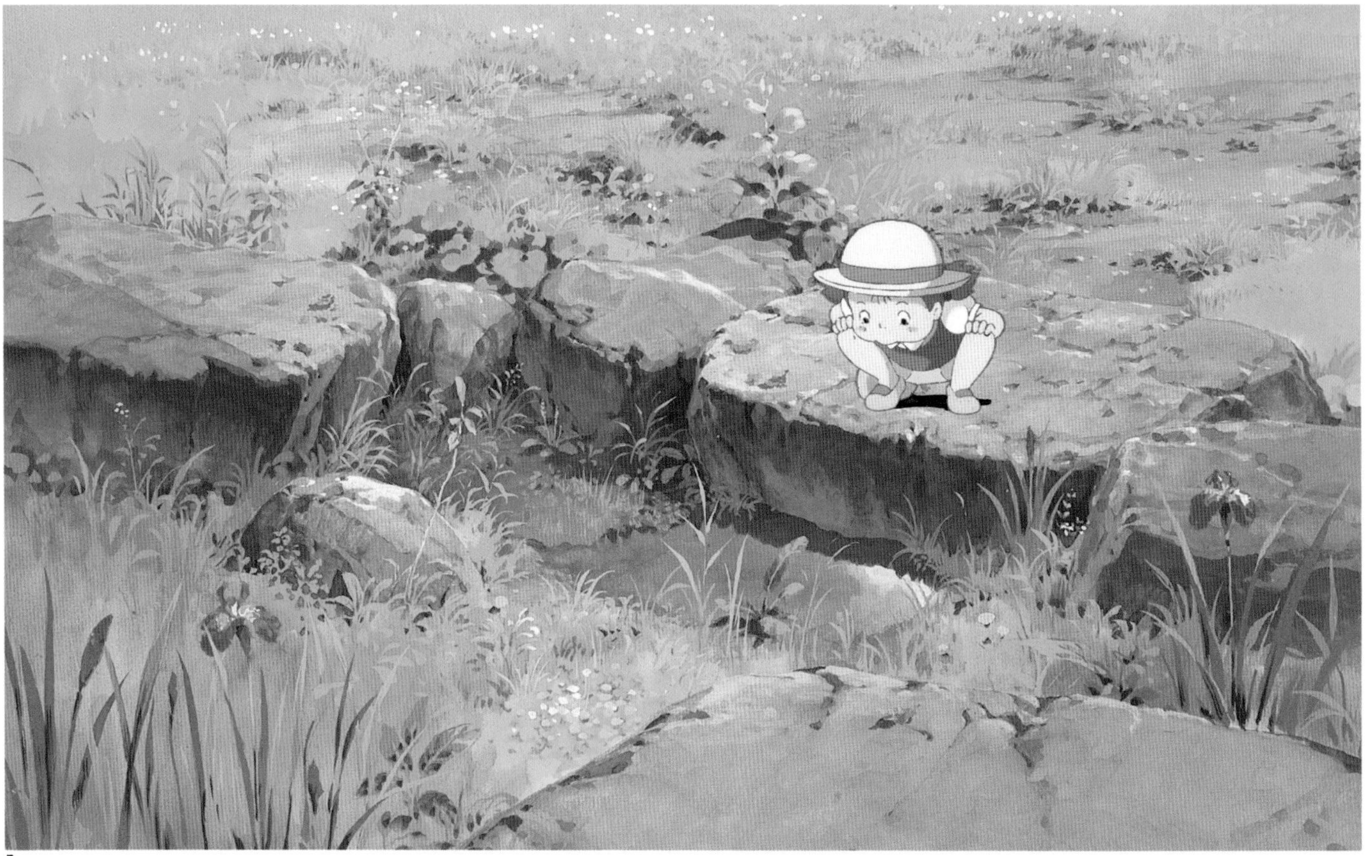

1

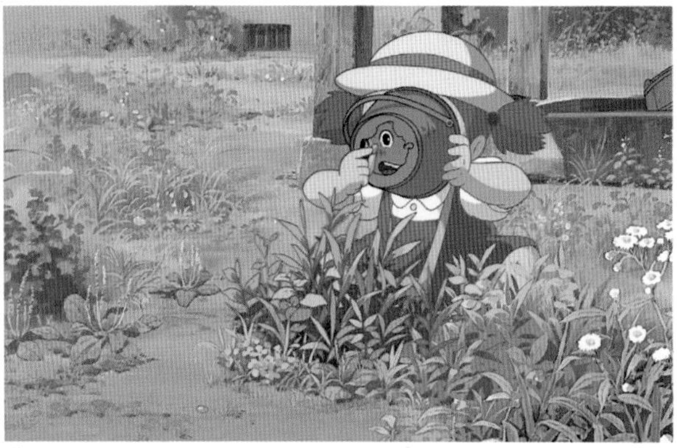

2

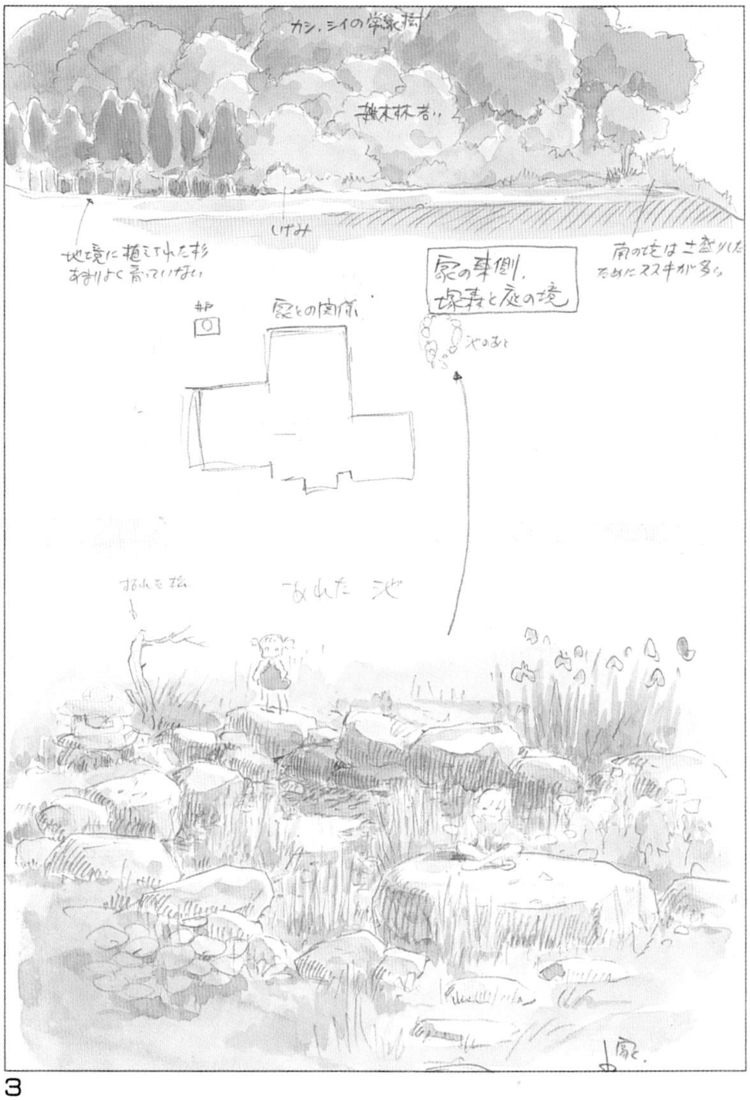
カシ，シイの常緑樹
雑木林
地境に植えられた杉
あまりよく育っていない
南の境は土盛りしたために ススキが多い
家の東側，
塚森と庭の境
家との関係
池のあと
あれた池

3

1 Mei staring into the shallow pond. *(cel art)*

2 Mei looking through a bucket with a hole. *(cel art)*

3 The bottom of the shallow pond. *(design board)*

4 Big Totoro (Big Toto), Medium Totoro (Mid Toto), Little Totoro (Mini Toto). *(character design)*

"Miyazaki said he wanted the yard soil red because of the red loamy layers of the Kanto district. I always thought of soil as basically dull, either black or gray, so that was really hard for me. I kept on adding red and asked him whether this was what he wanted, and he would just say, `No, I want more red!´ [*laughs*]. That's how we ended up with that extreme color." *(Oga)*

4

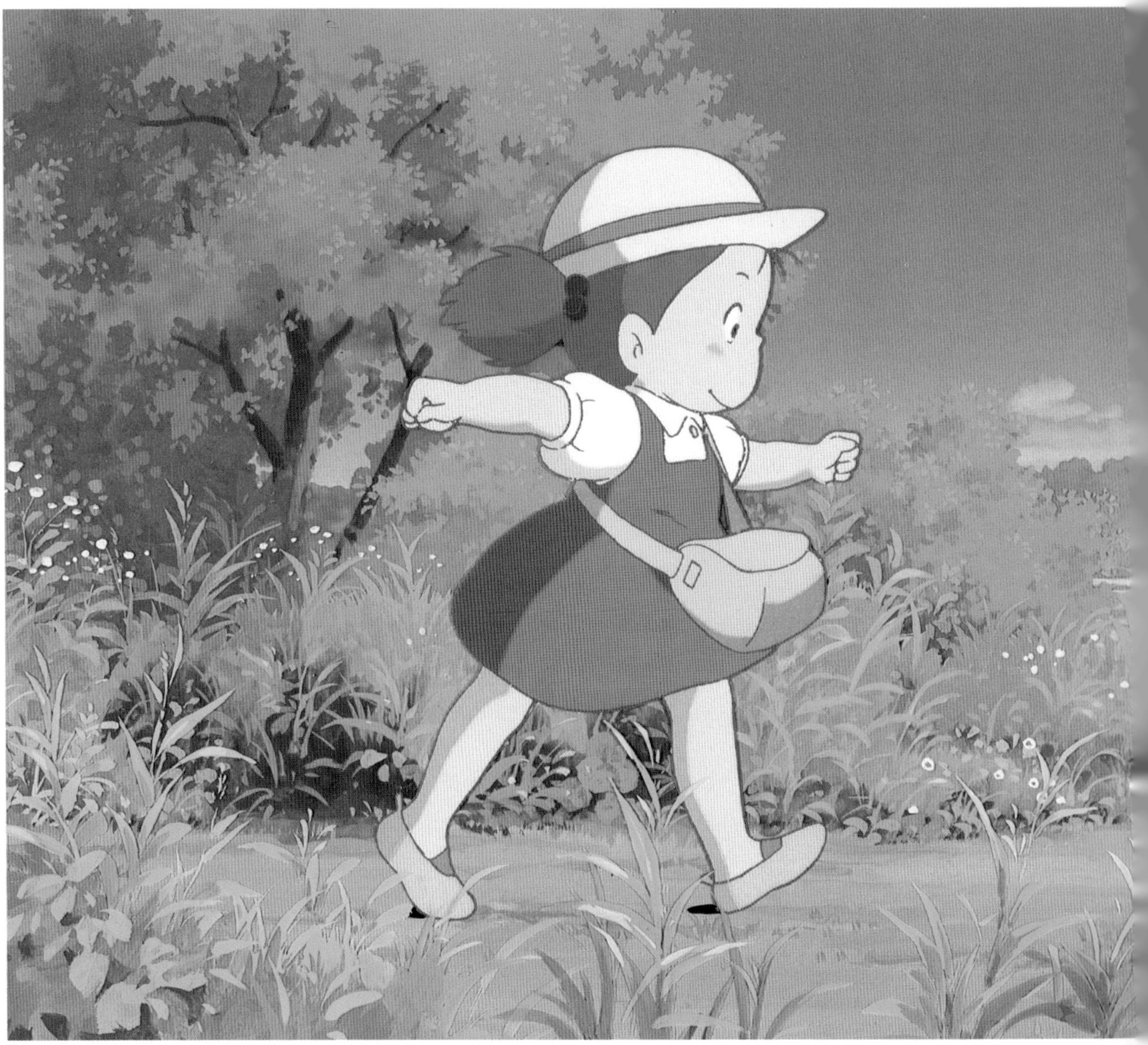

1

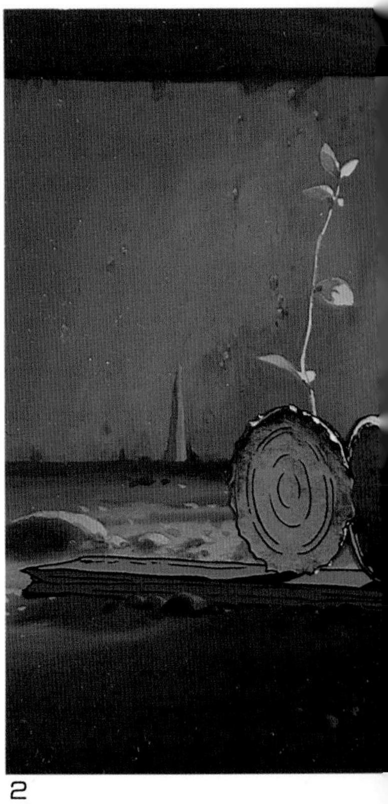

2

1 Mei following Little Totoro. *(cel art)*

2 Mei peeks under the floor with rusty cans and soda bottles strewn about. *(cel art)*

3 Medium Totoro and Little Totoro dash off once Mei spots them. *(cel art)*

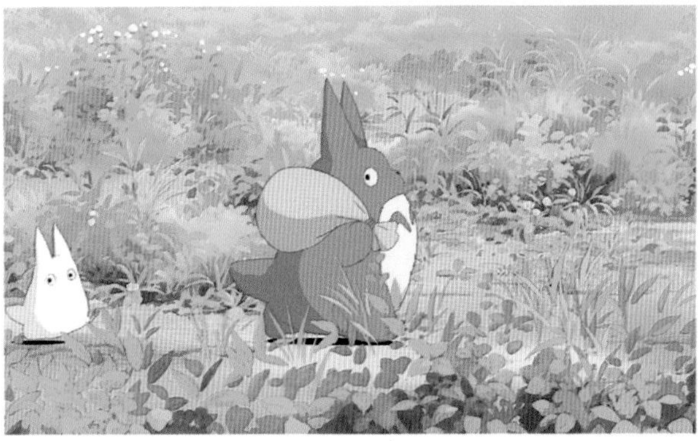
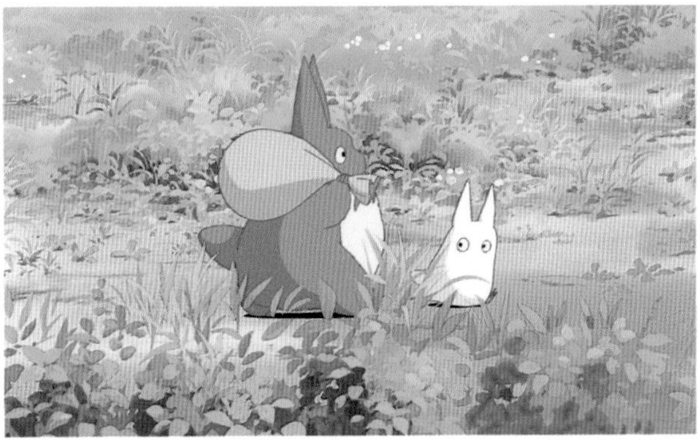
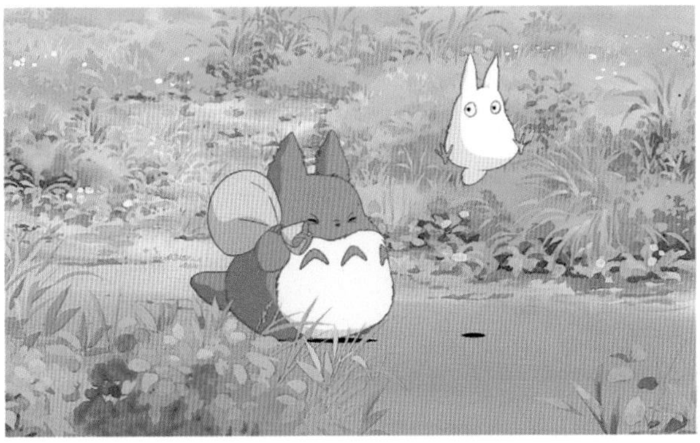
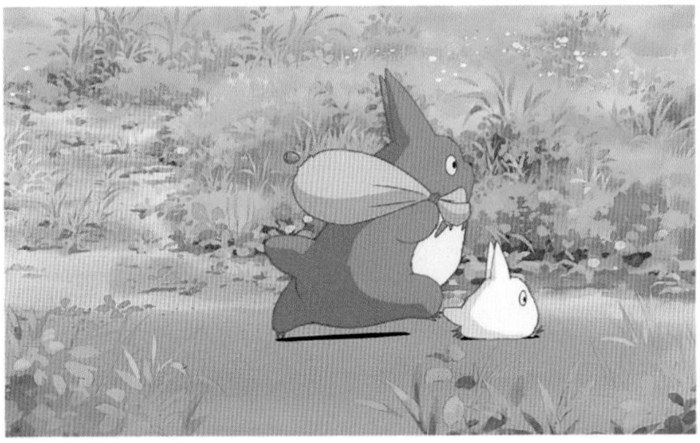
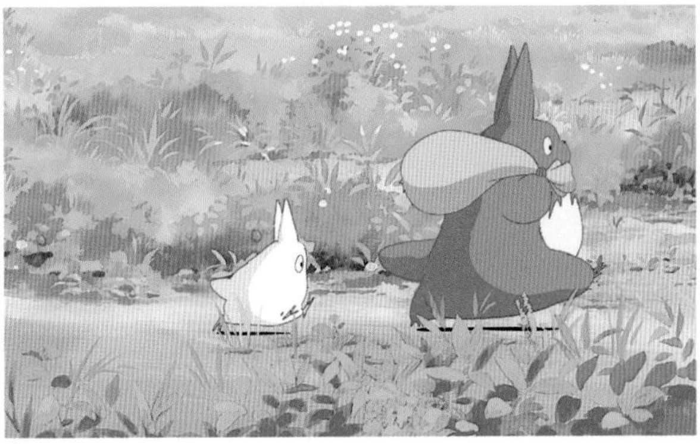
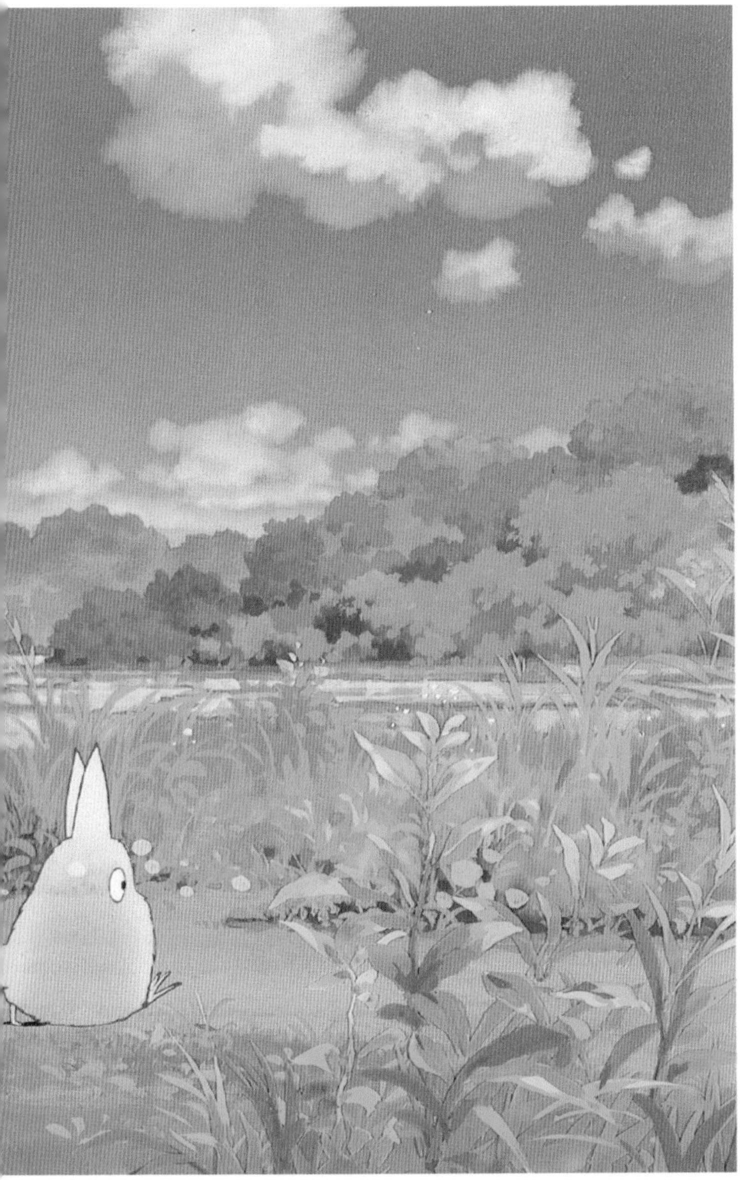
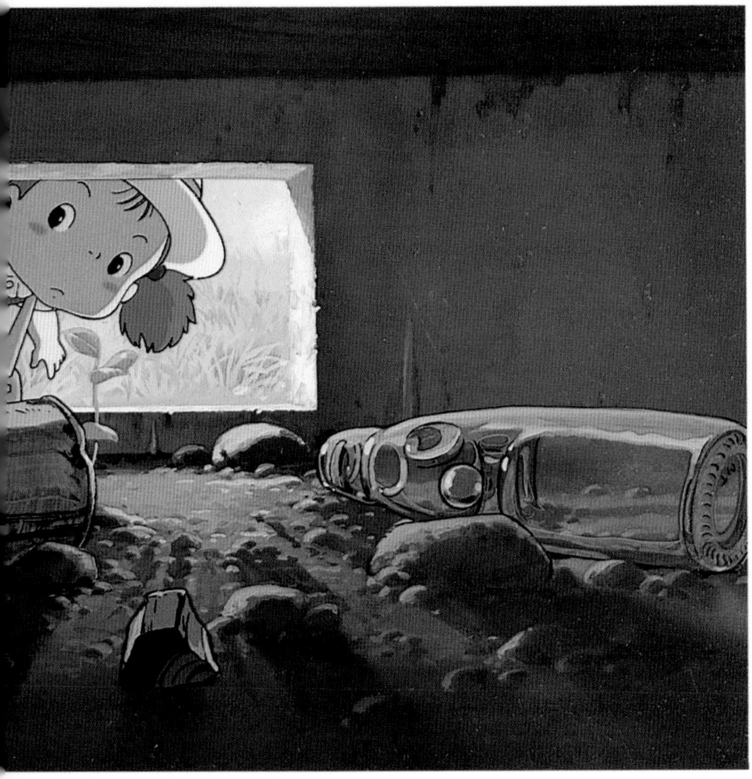

3

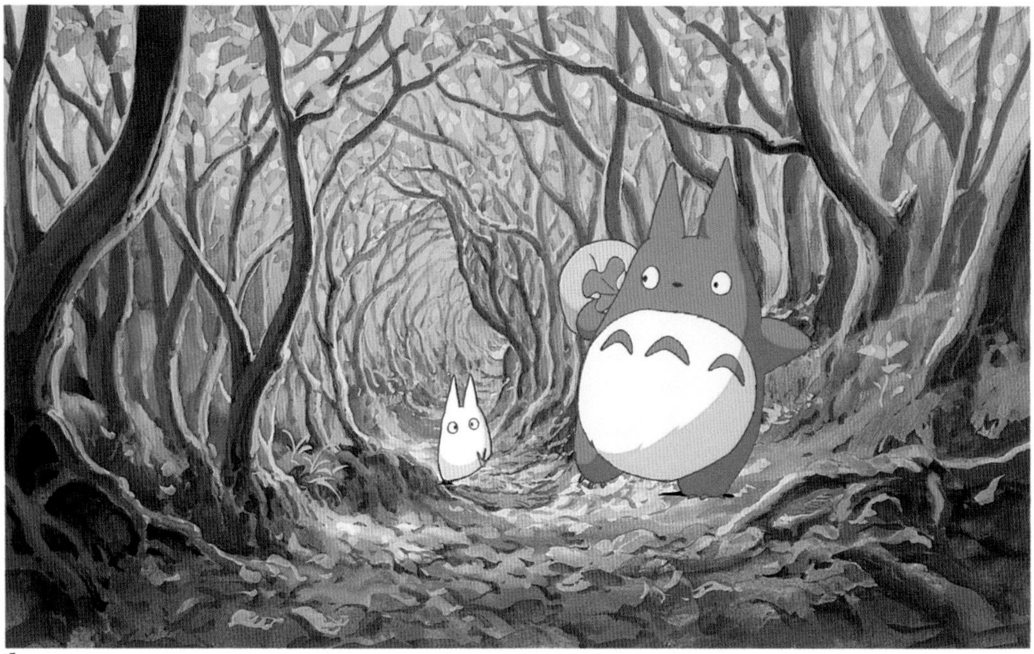
1

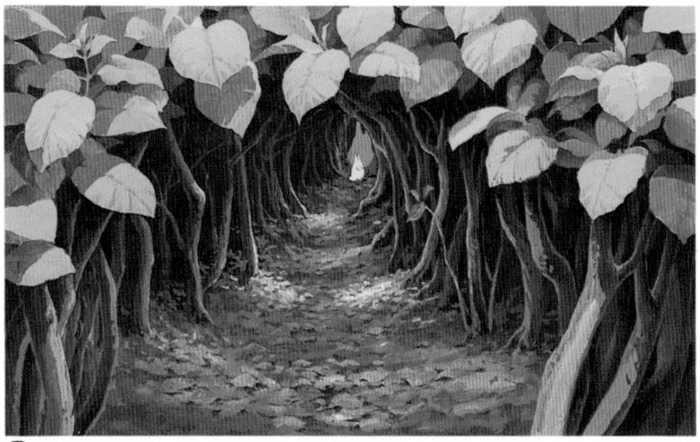
2

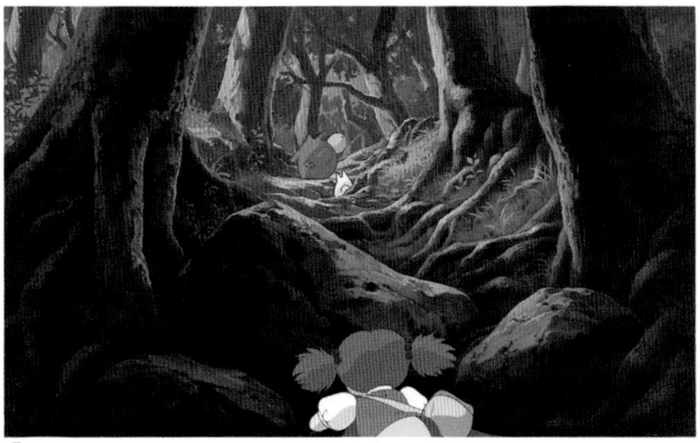
3

1-3 Medium Totoro and Little Totoro enter the dark forest through the tree tunnel. *(cel art)*

4 The entrance leading to the Totoros' cave. *(background)*

"We drew the tree tunnel without having a clear idea what kind of tree it was. It's a pretty low thicket...not like sawtooth oak or quercus serrata oak. It's more like azaleas. I had a larger version of these trees in mind when I drew them." *(Oga)*

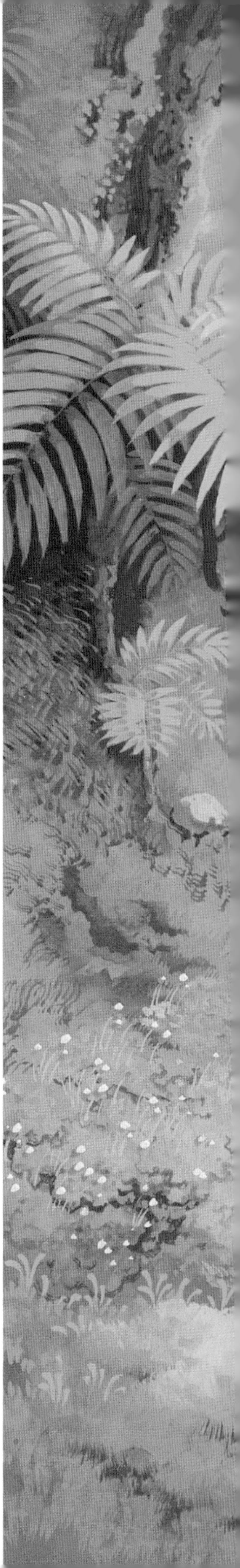
4

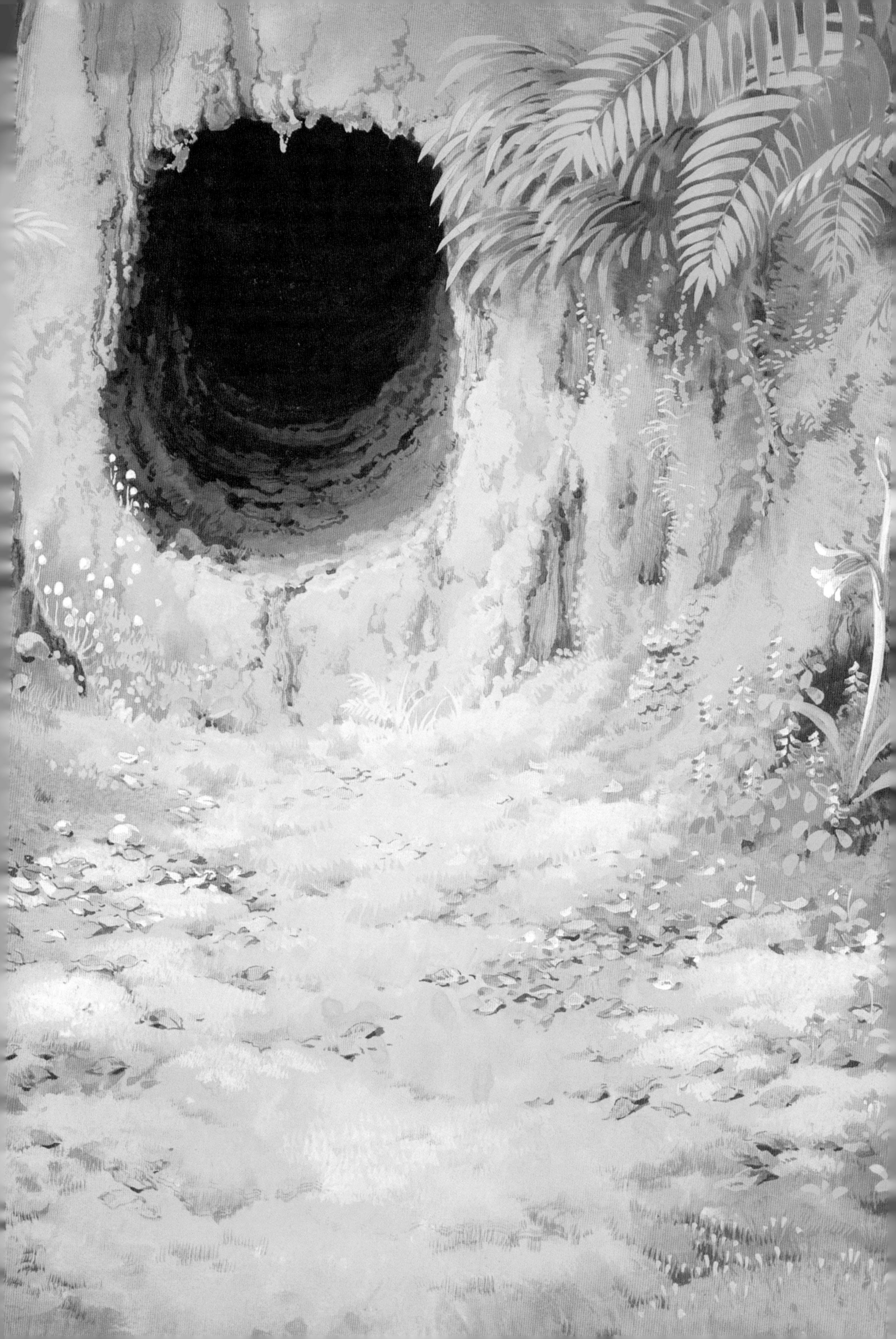

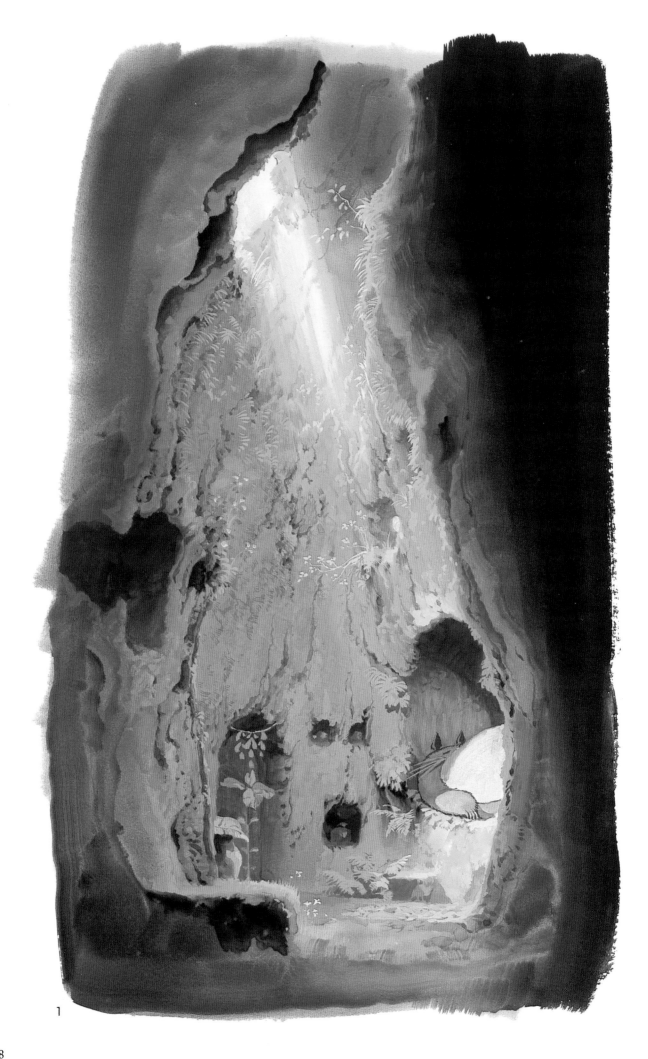

1

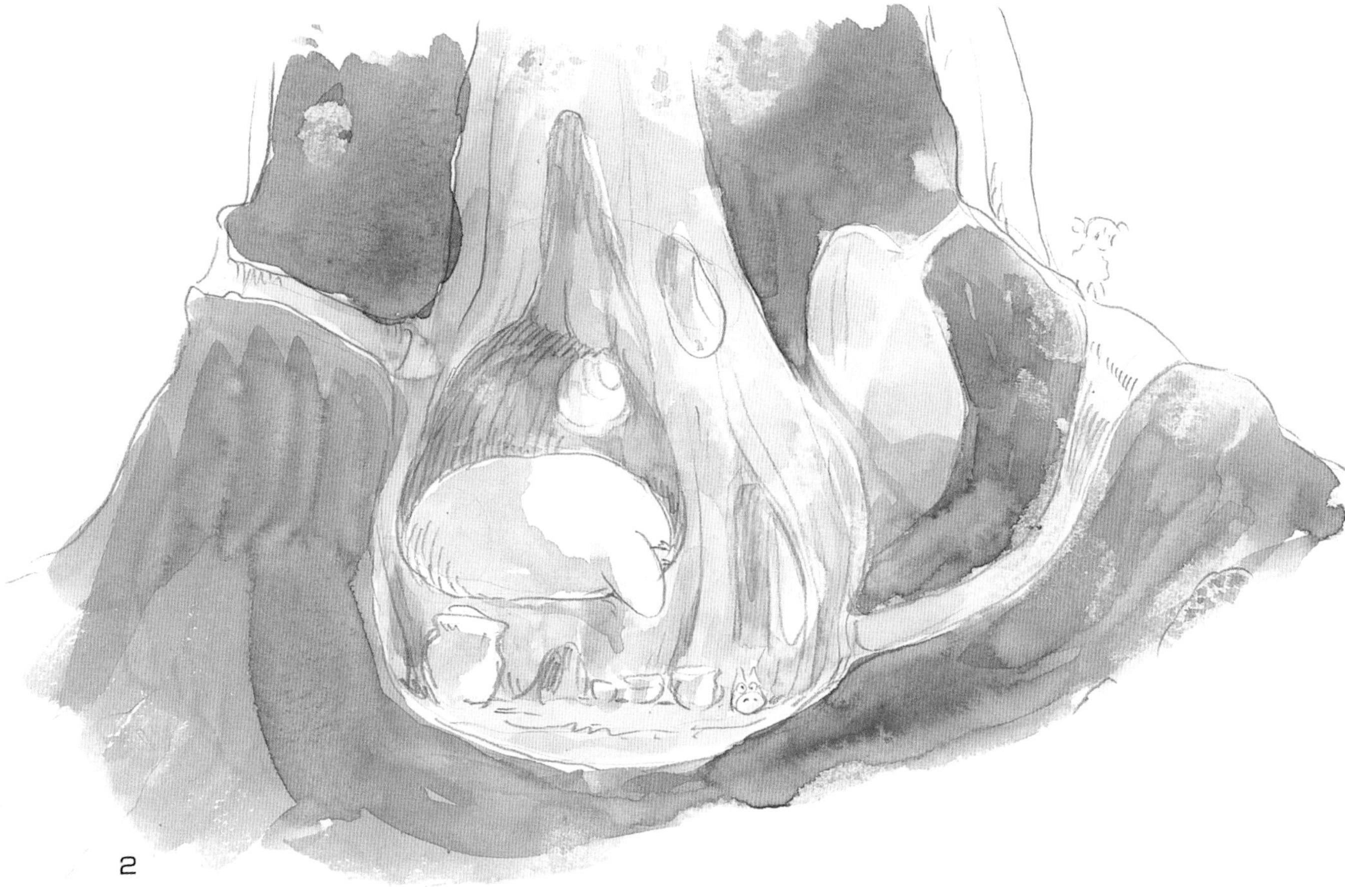

2

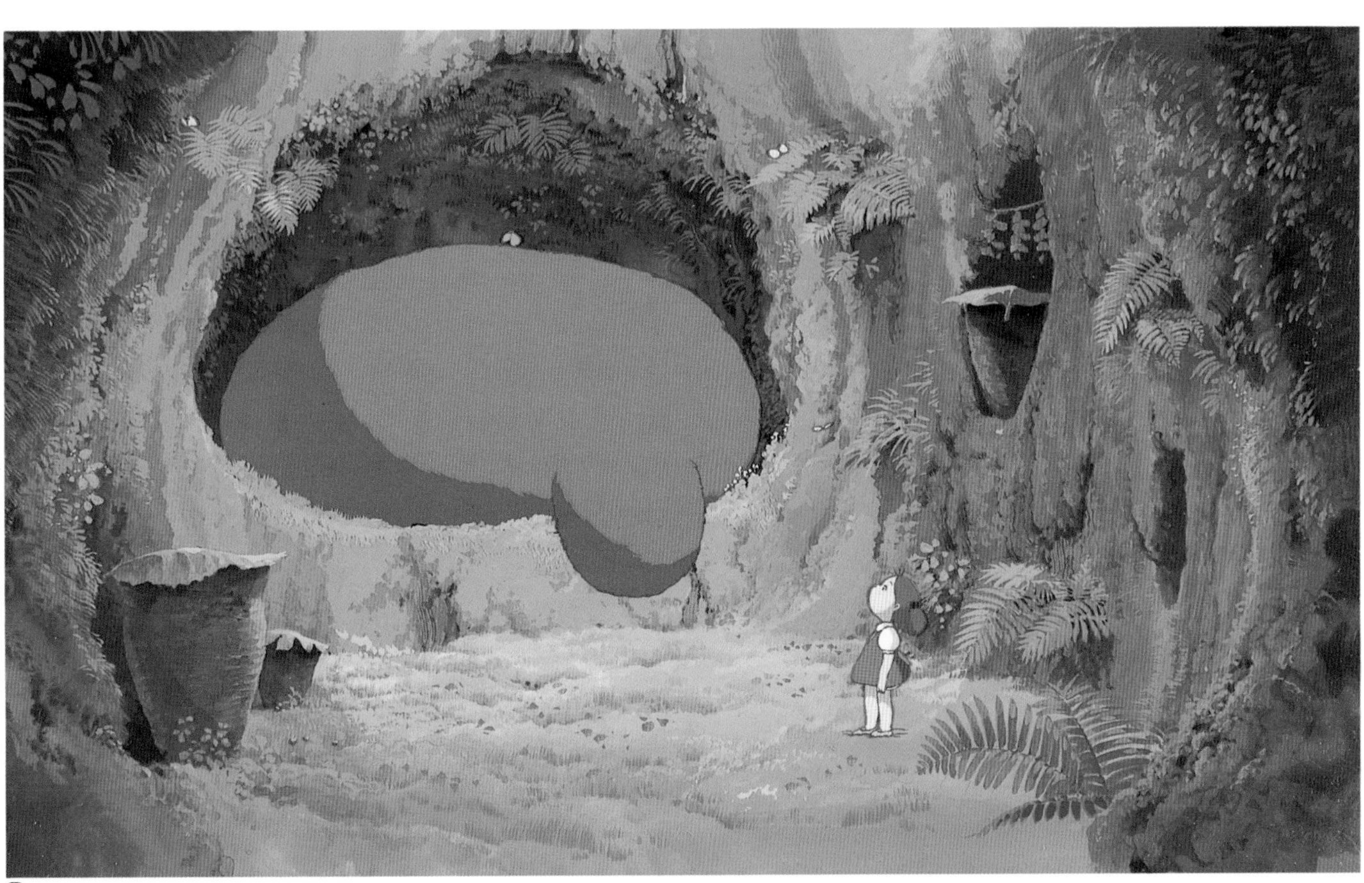

3

1 Totoro's cave. *(concept art)*

2 Cross section of Totoro's cave. *(concept sketch)*

3, 7-9 Mei encounters Totoro. *(cel art)*

4-6 Totoro and Mei. *(storyboard)*

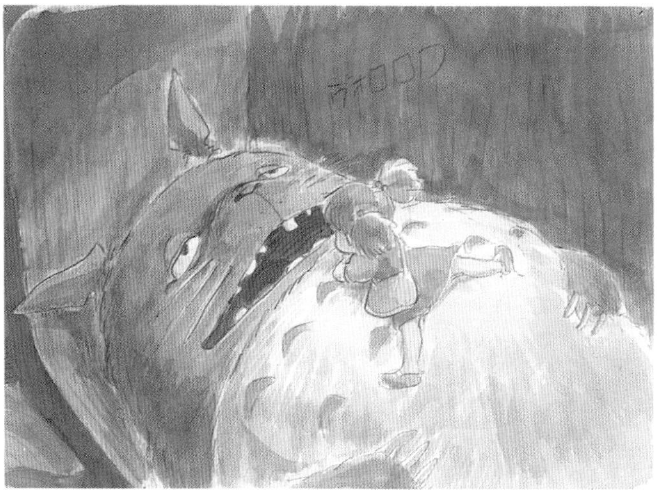
ウオロロロ

4

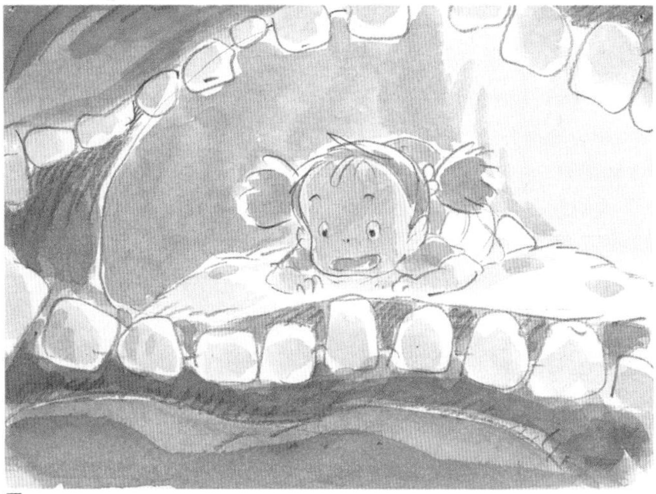

5

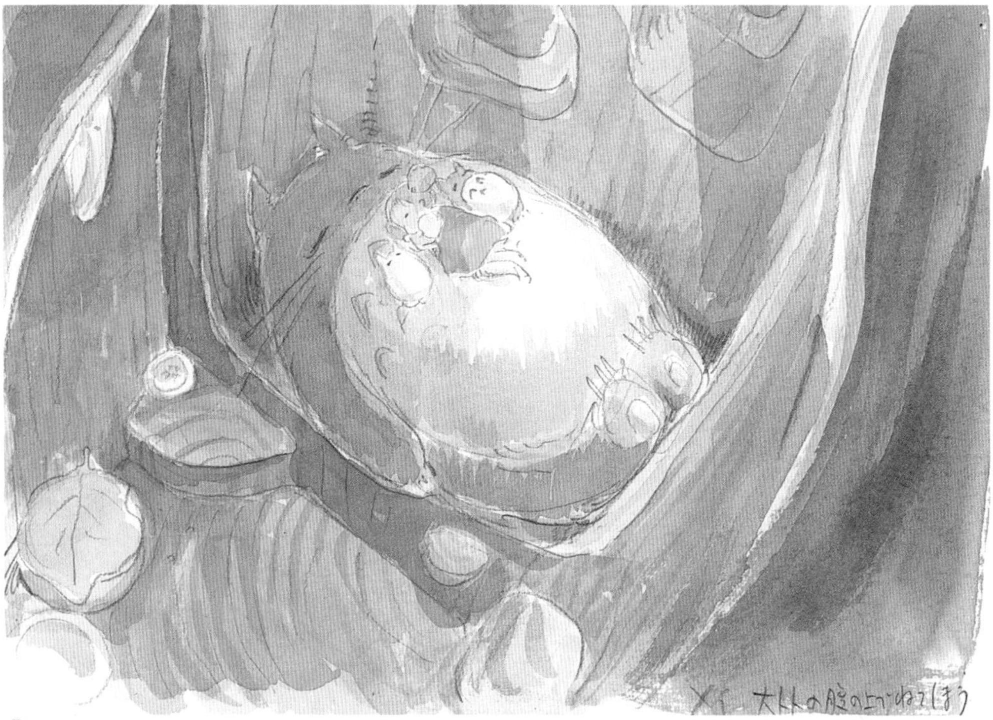
メイ 大トトの腹の上でねてしまう

6

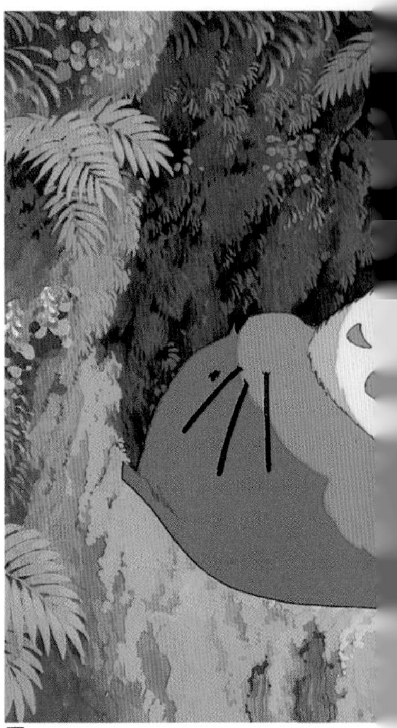

7

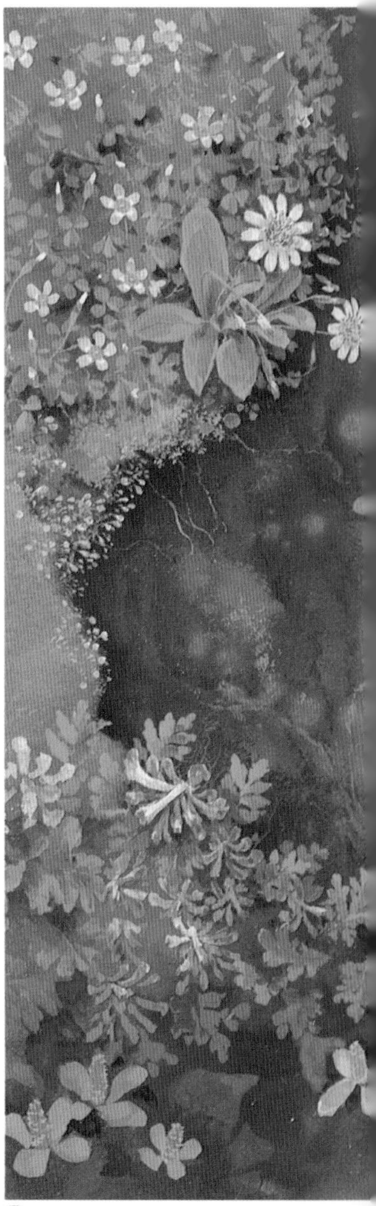

9

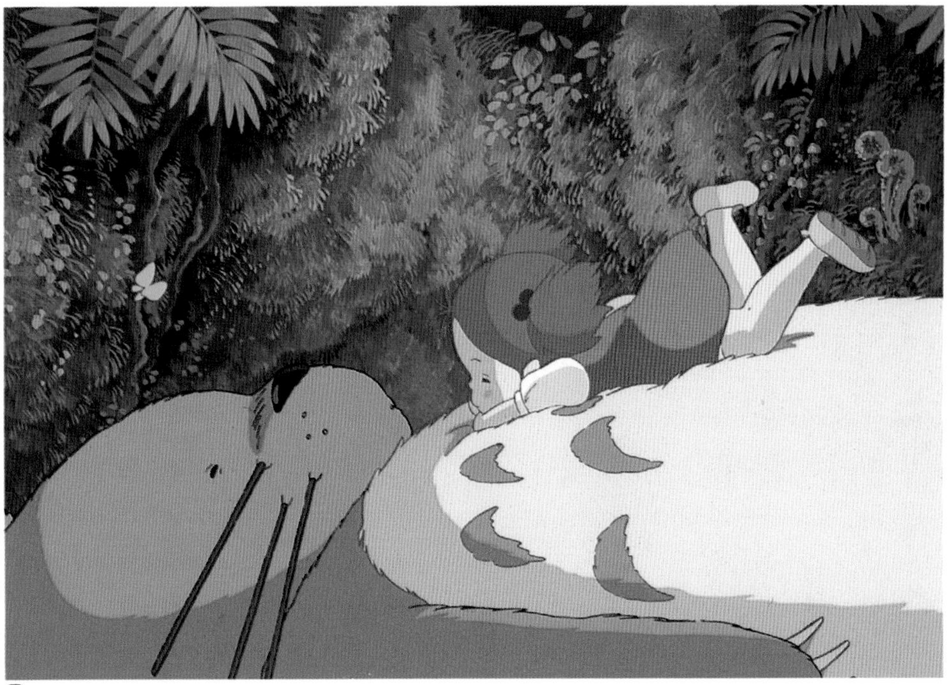

8

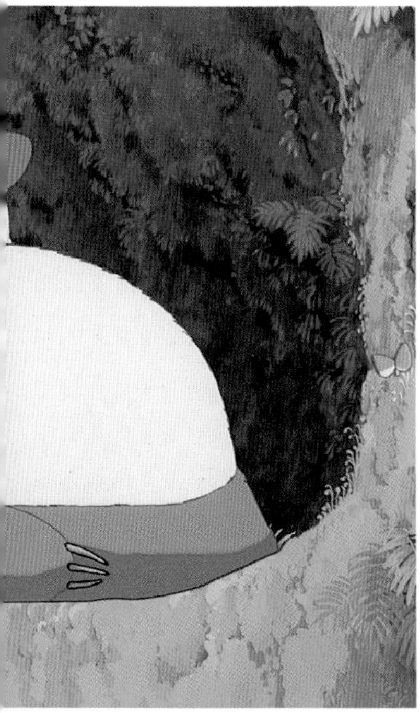

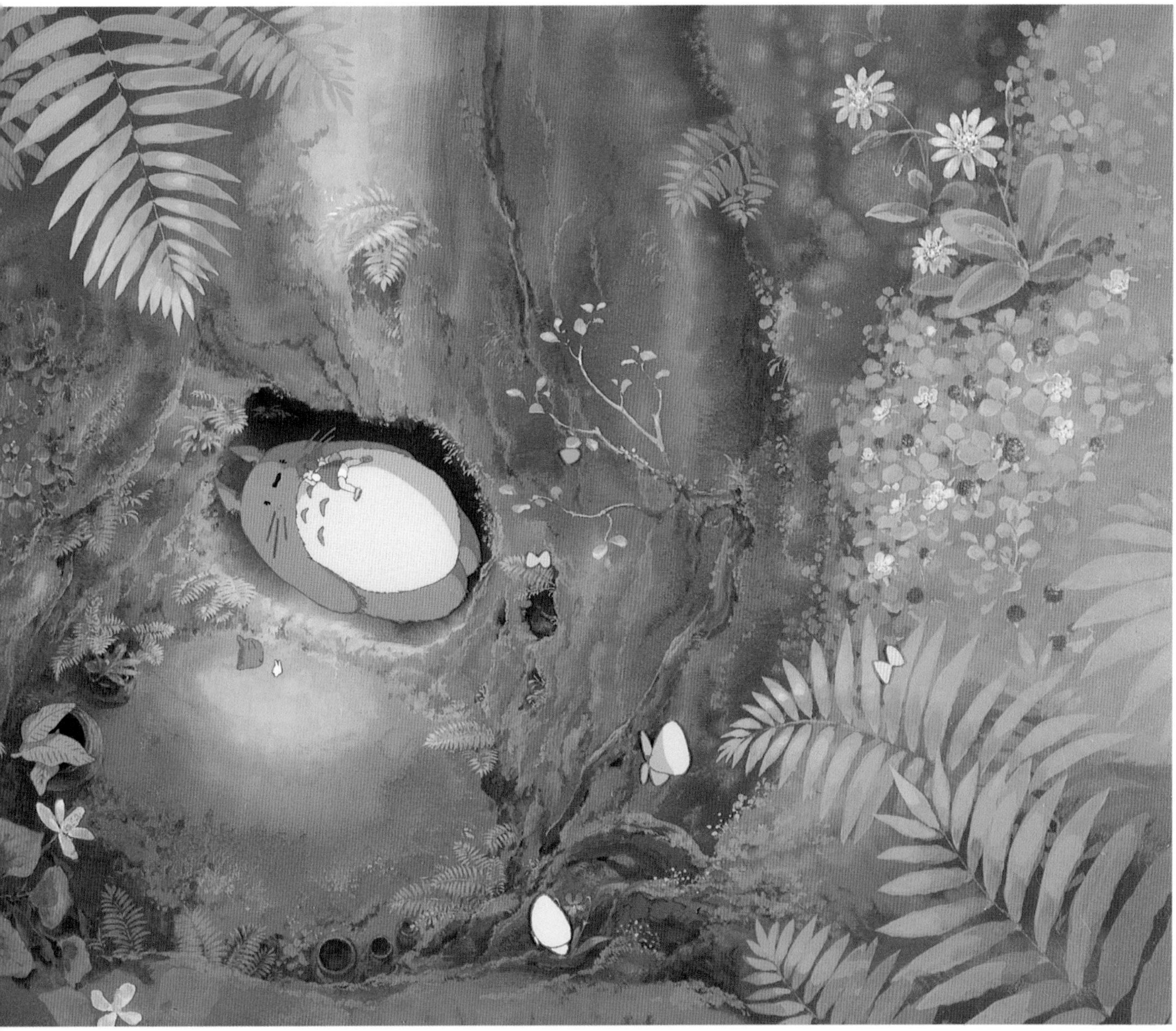

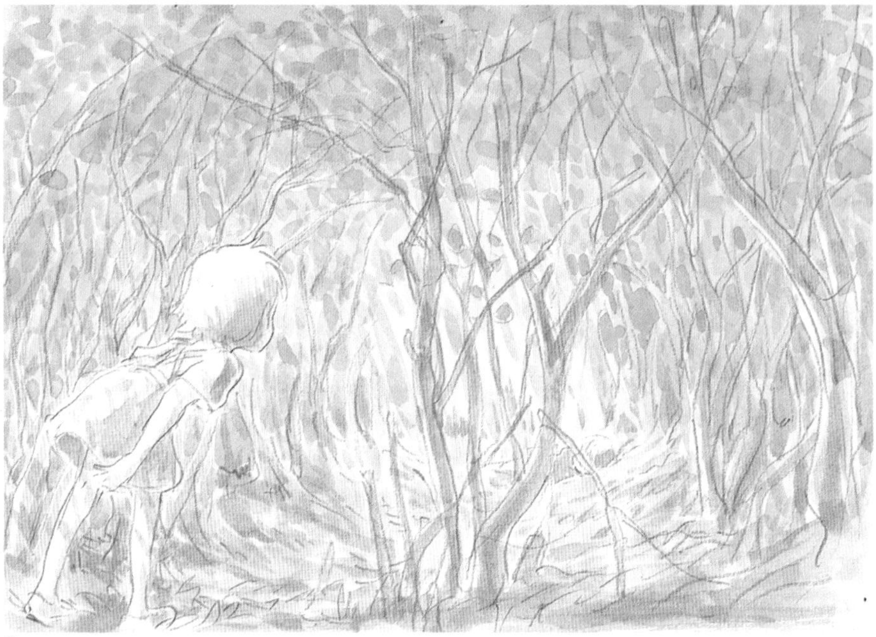

1

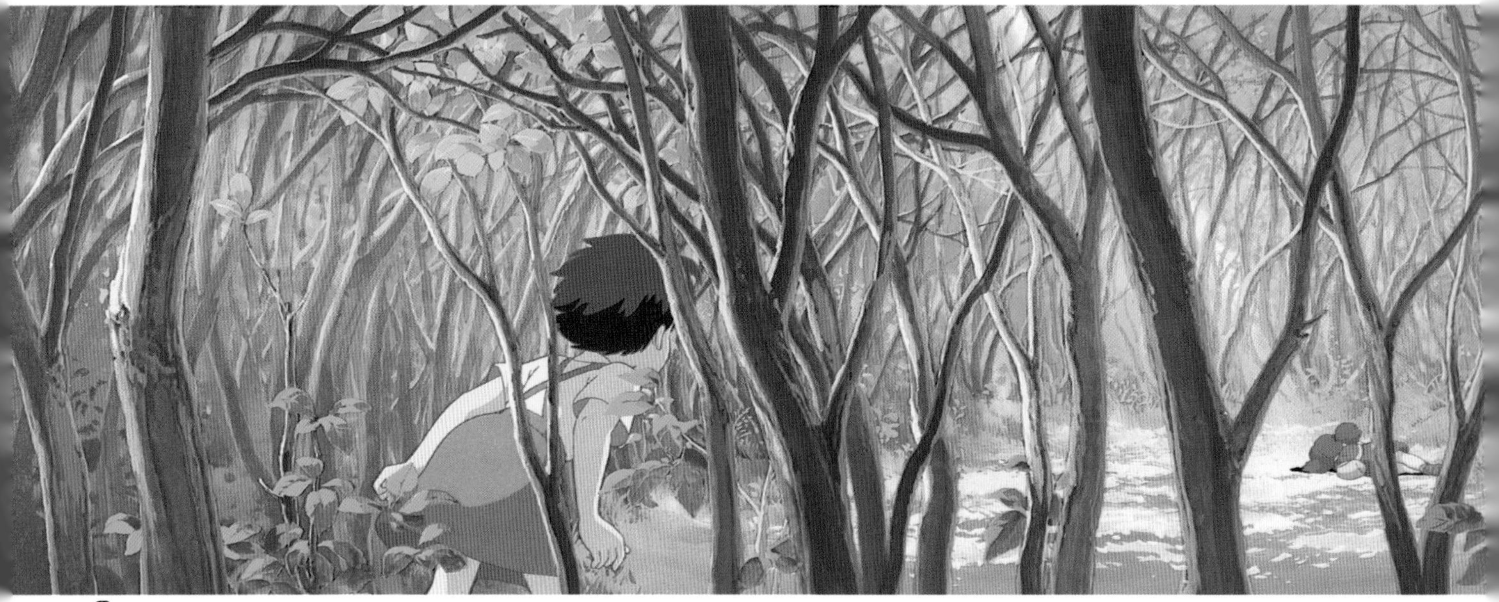

2

1 Satsuki finds Mei in the tree tunnel. *(storyboard)*

2 Same scene. *(cel art)*

3 Satsuki composing a letter to her mother. *(concept sketch)*

4 Big camphor tree next to a Suitengu shrine. *(background)*

"This was my first serious attempt to draw a towering tree, and I found it quite enjoyable. I fancied working on its sheer size. When you draw something large like that, whether it's a tree or a field, you can't convey its size by simply filling up the entire space. You have to leave out a portion. I made it look as if there's more beyond what's drawn by having the light cross through, or by adding fine moss at the edges. I labored over these details to make the tree look massive." *(Oga)*

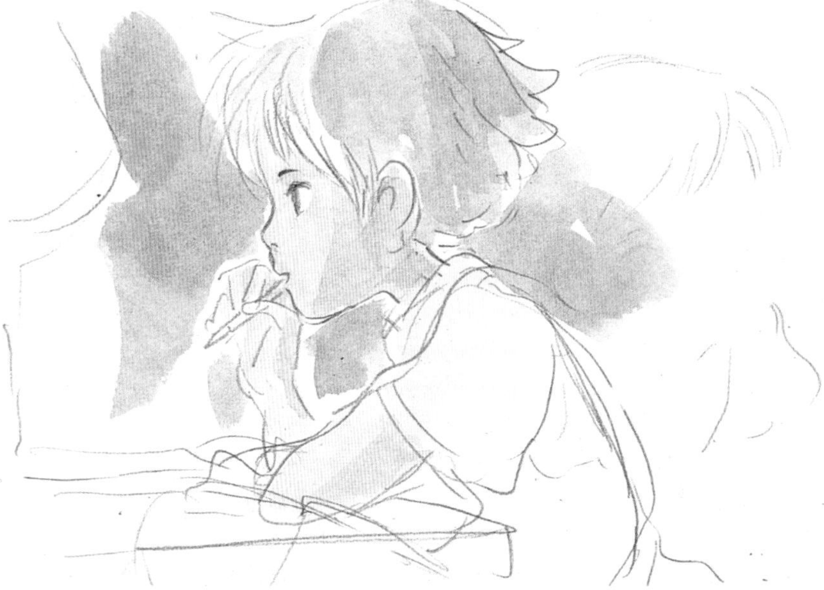

3

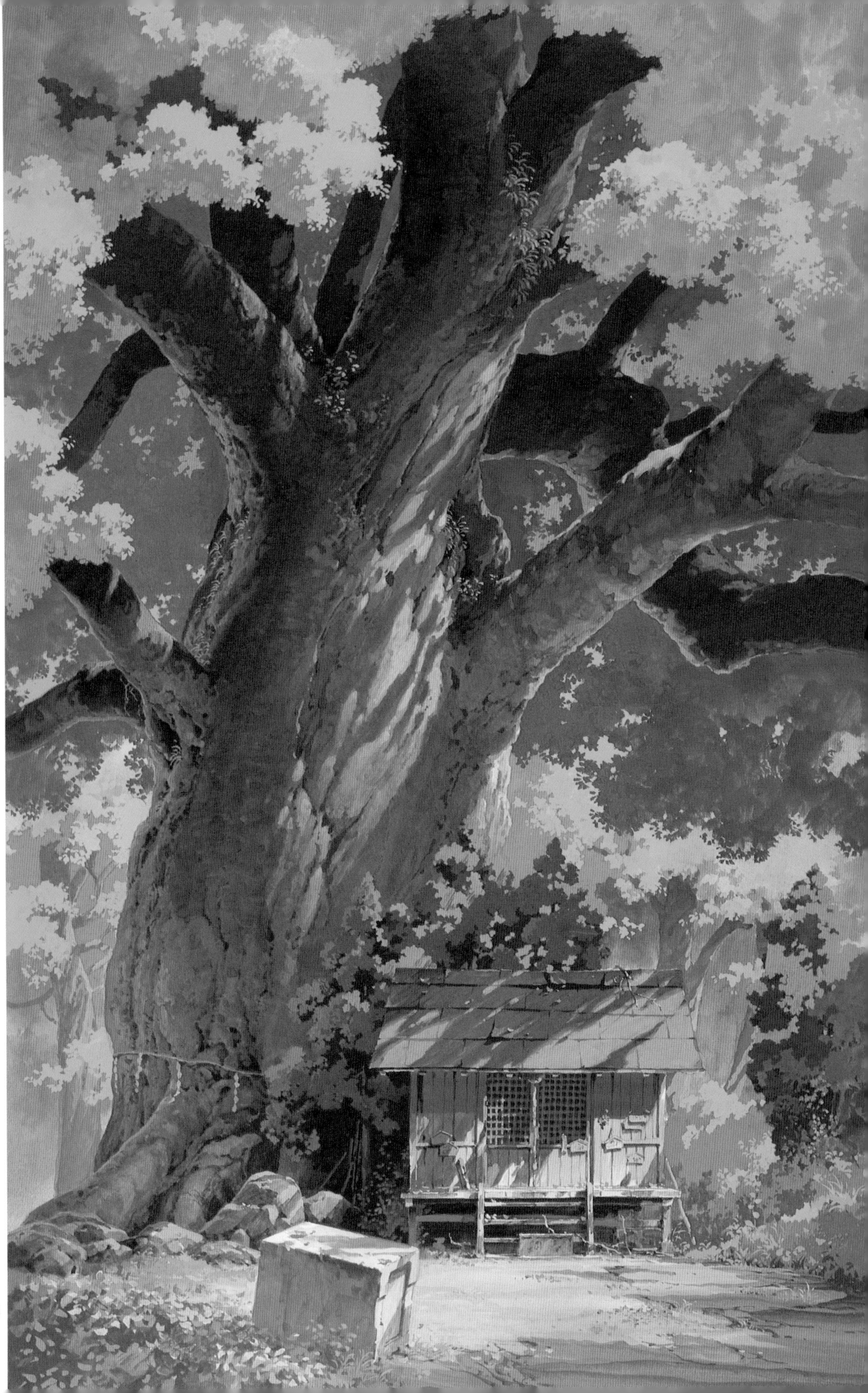

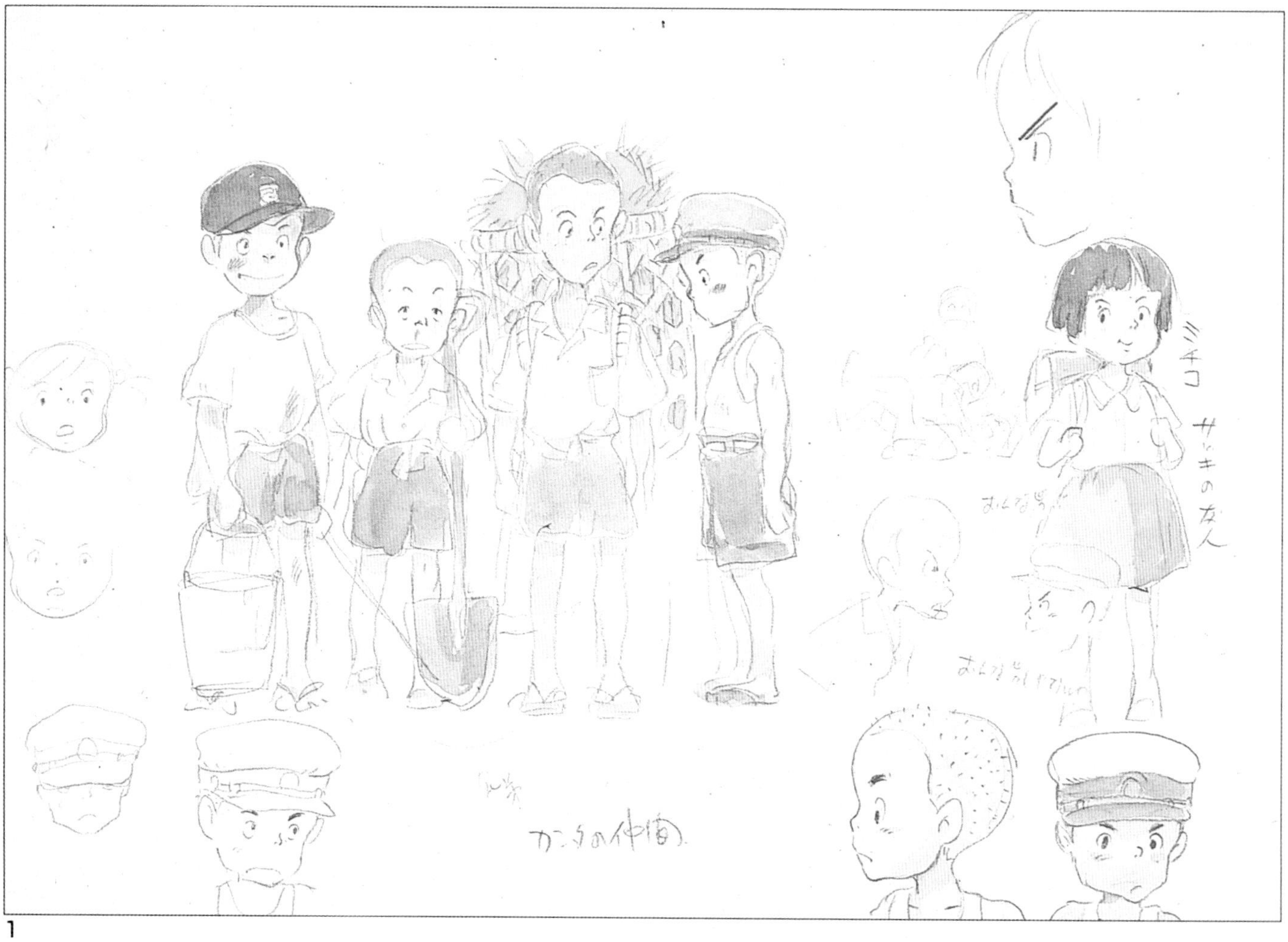
ミチコ
サツキの友人
カンタの仲間.

1

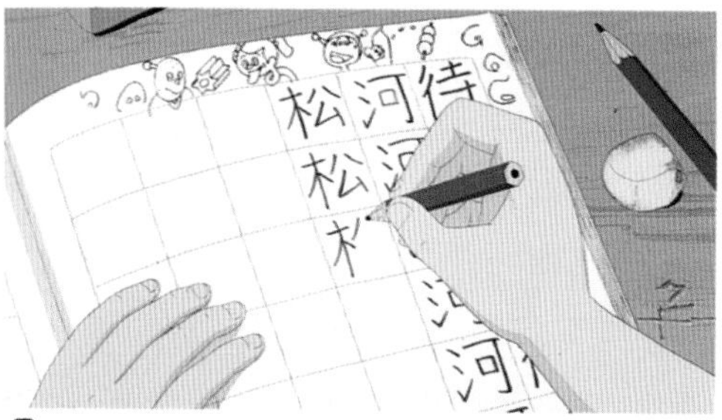
松河待

2

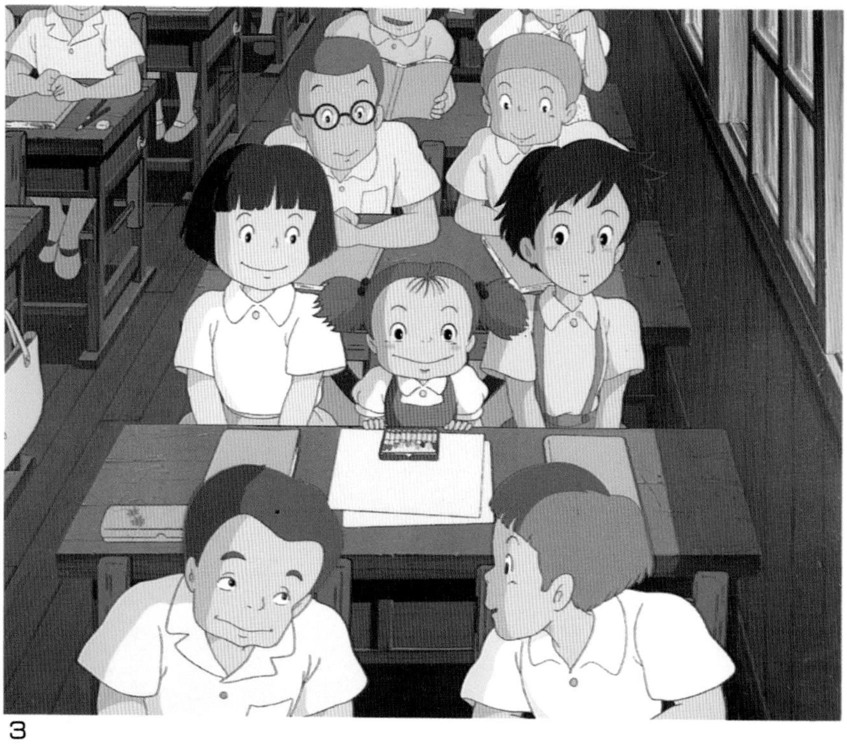

3

1 Kanta's friends. *(character design)*

2 Kanta practicing his kanji. Shigeru Sugiura's comic art is scribbled in the margins. *(film)*

3 Mei sits between Satsuki and Michiko. Satsuki looks ill at ease. *(cel art)*

4, 5 The elementary school in the morning when the kids arrive. The same school now darkened by the ominous rain clouds above as the kids leave. *(backgrounds)*

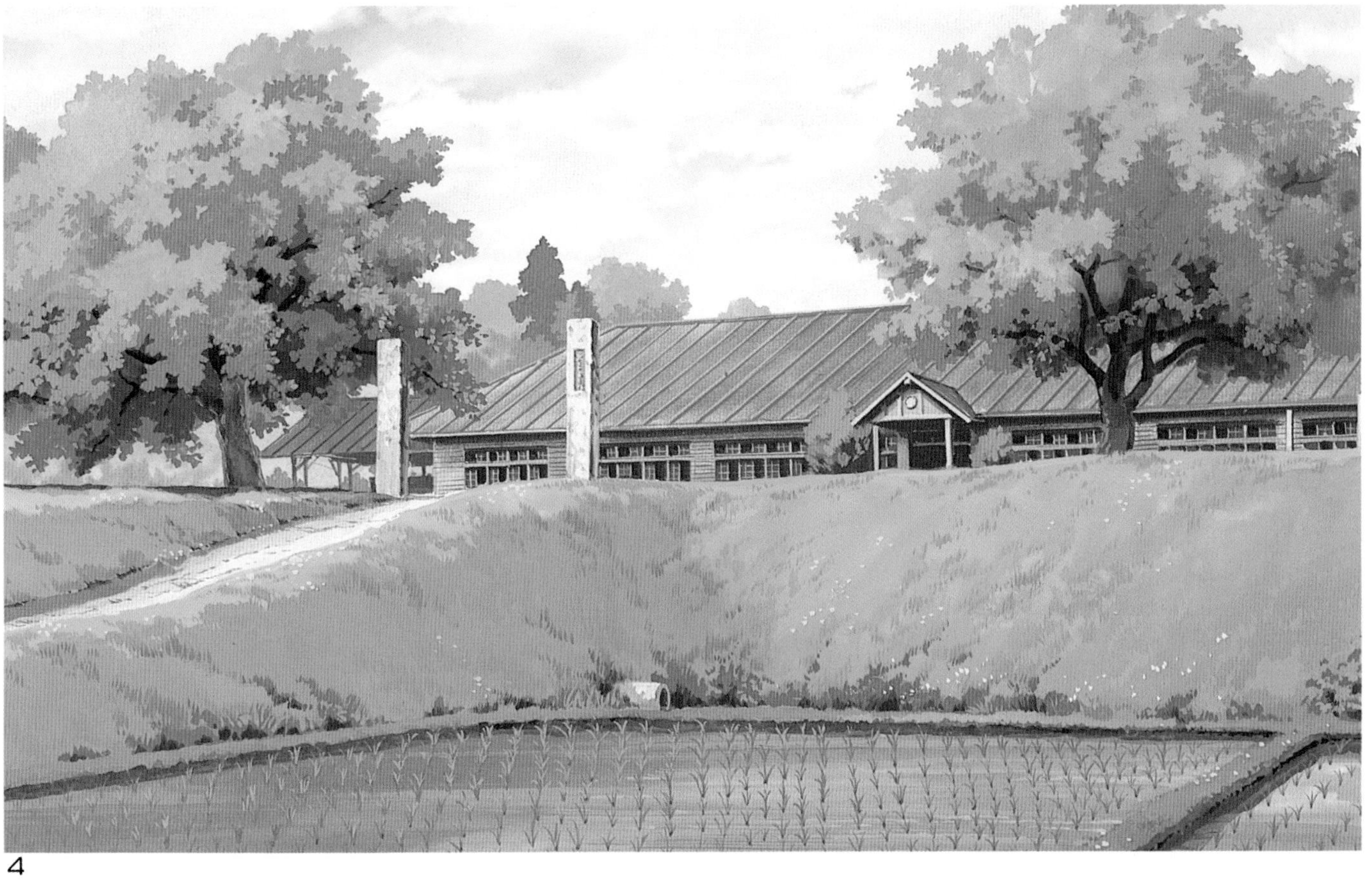
4

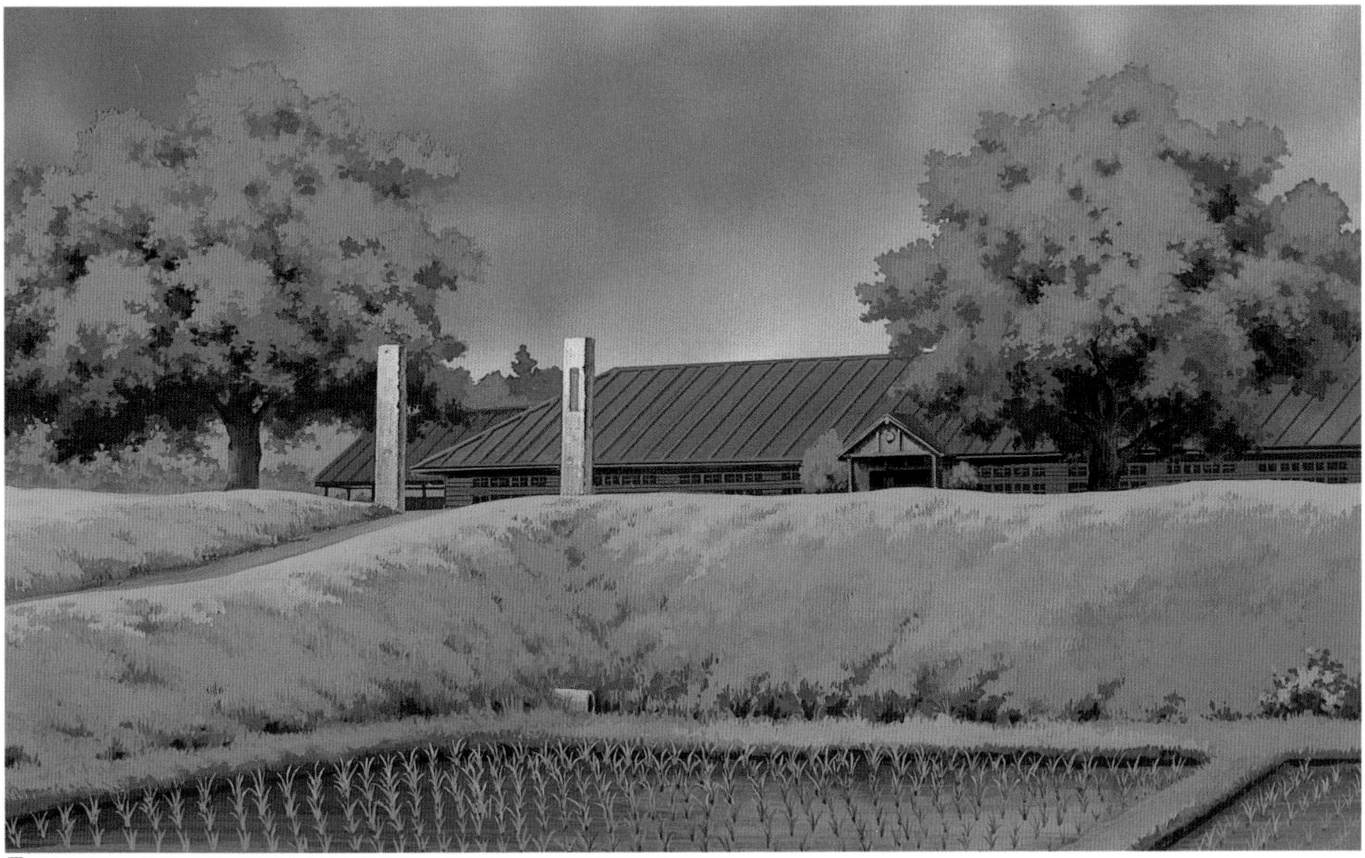
5

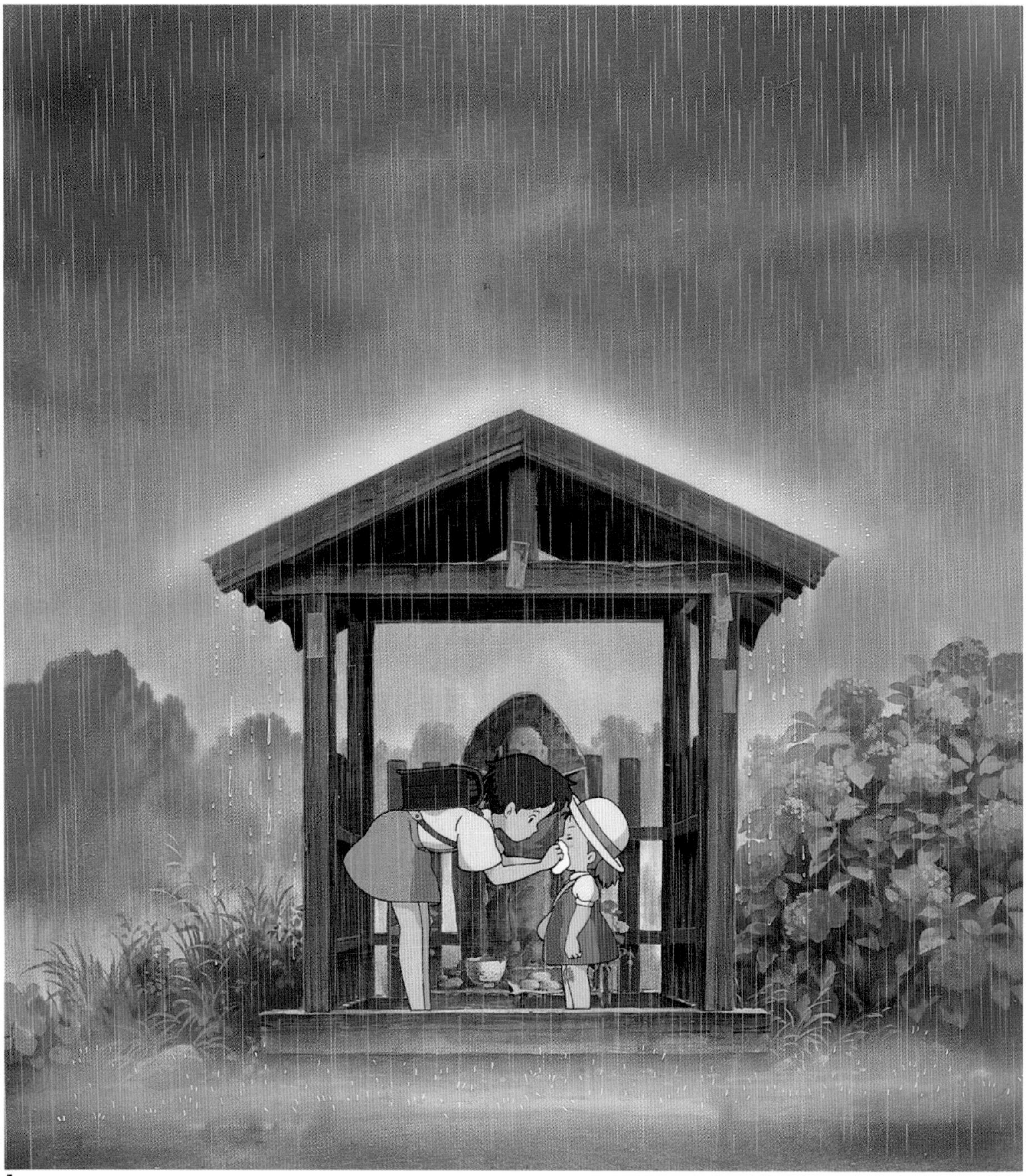

1

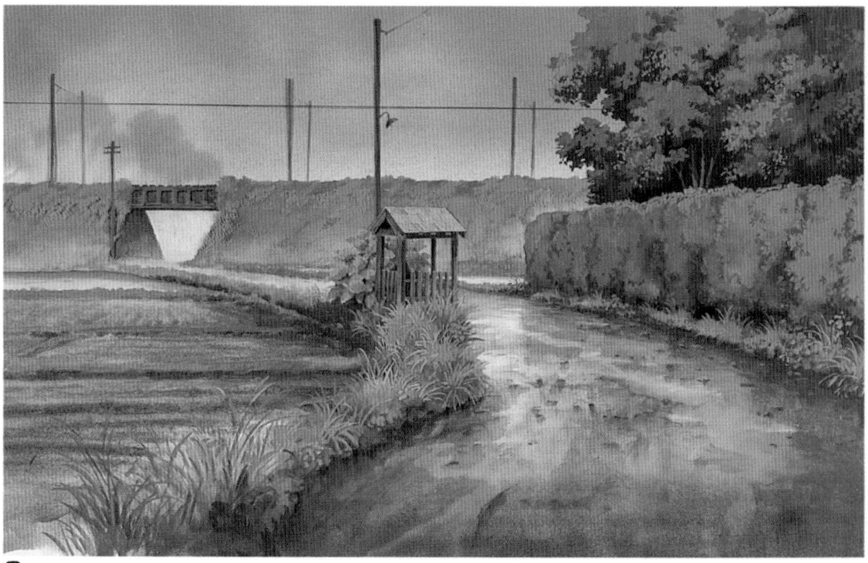

2

1 Satsuki wipes Mei's face with a handkerchief underneath the Jizo statue's shed. *(cel art)*

2 Jizo statue by the Toden railway. *(background)*

3 Road with Jizo statue. *(concept art)*

4 Rainy landscape. *(background)*

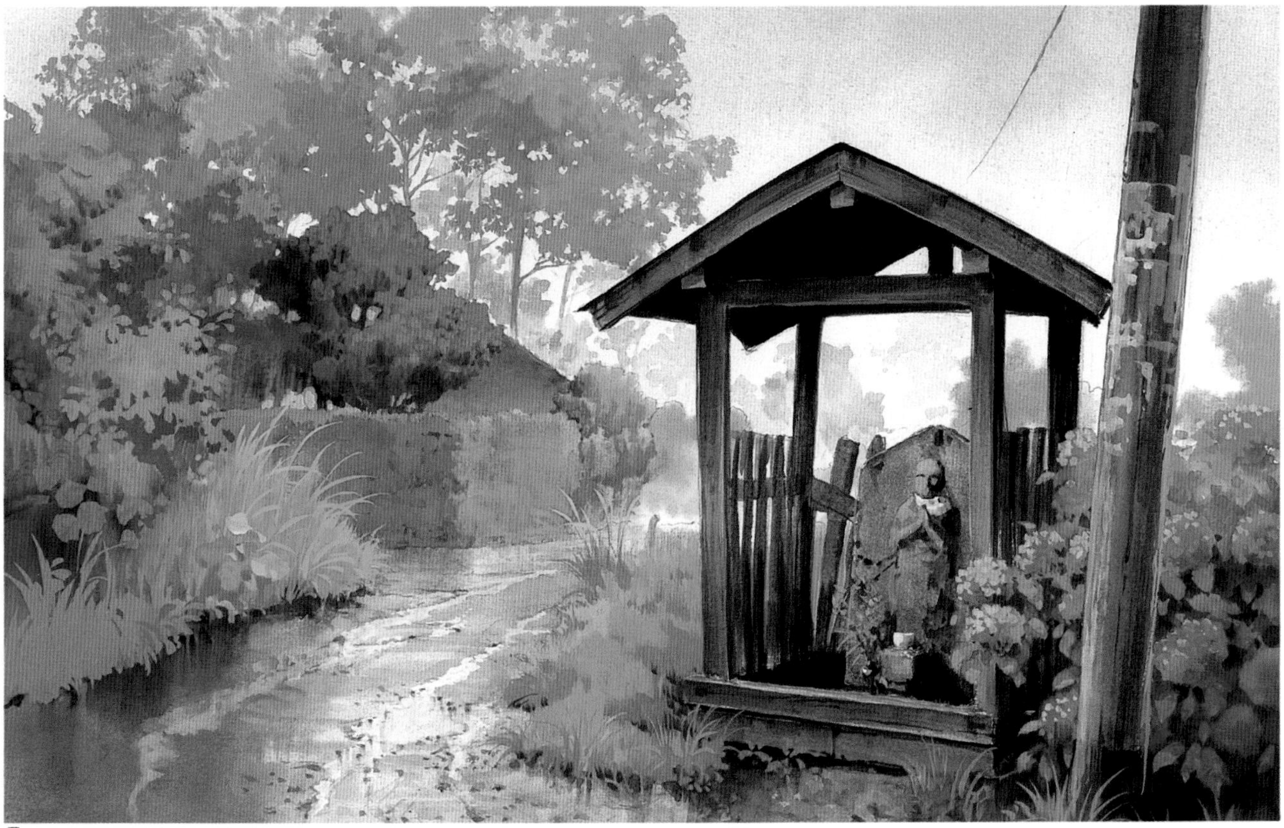

3

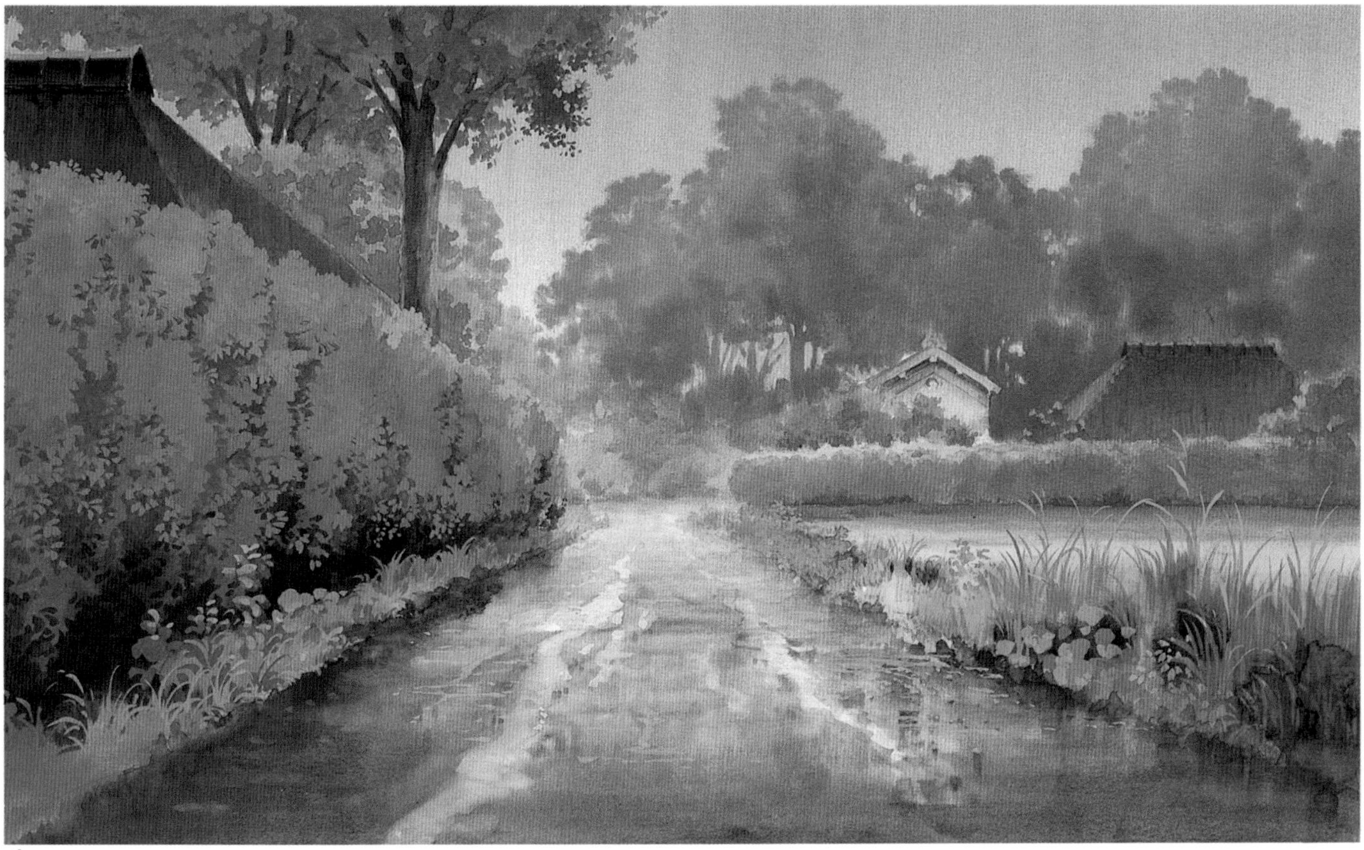

4

1

2

1   Kanta's main house in the late afternoon mist.
    *(background)*

2   Vicinity of Granny and Kanta's house. *(concept
    sketch)*

3, 4   Entrance to Kanta's house. Contrast between lit and
       unlit interior. *(background)*

5   Living room of Kanta's house. The room and sliding
    doors are overlays. *(background)*

6   Kanta's house with minor clouds above. *(background)*

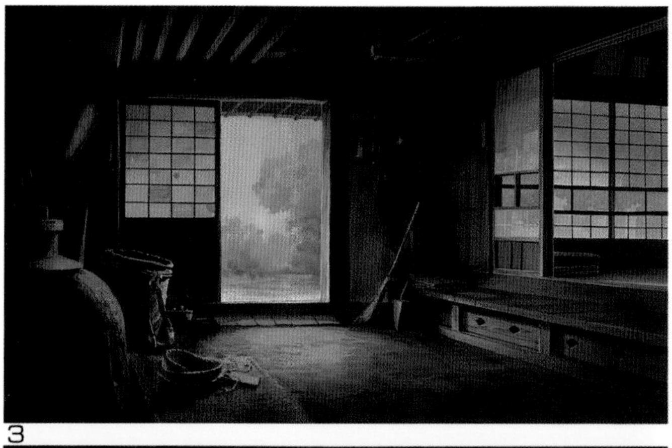

3

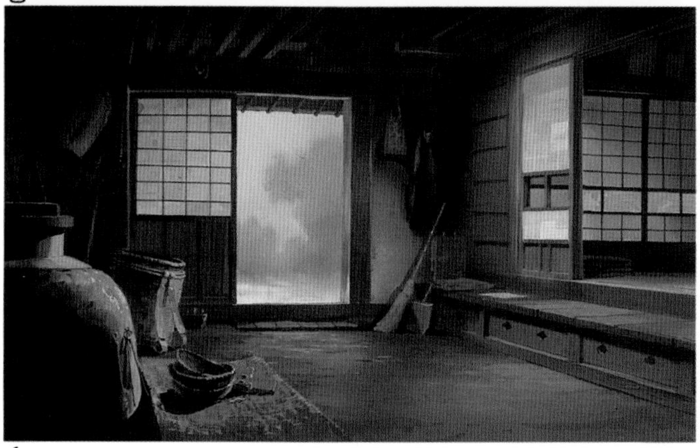

4

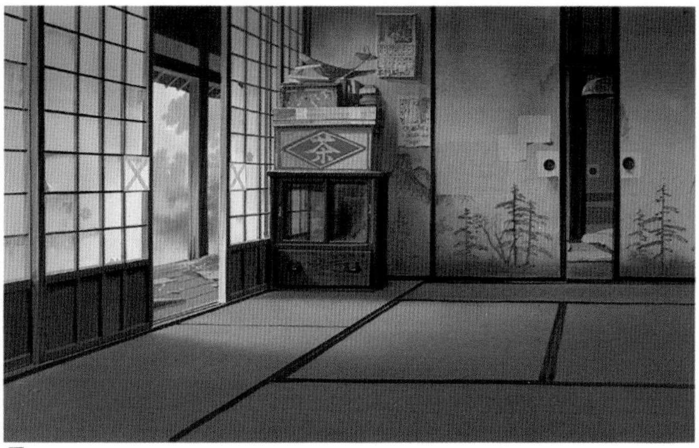
茶

5

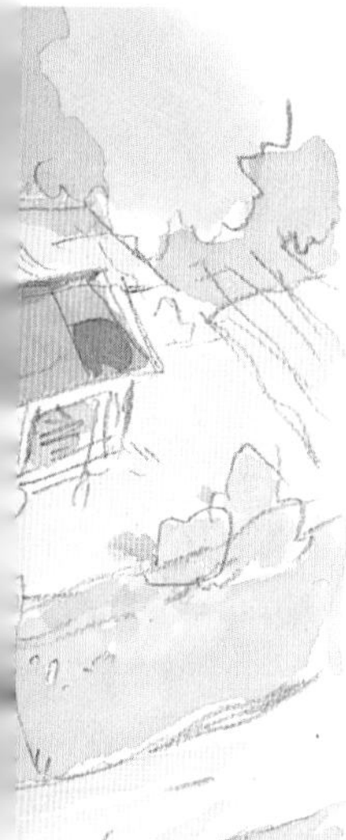

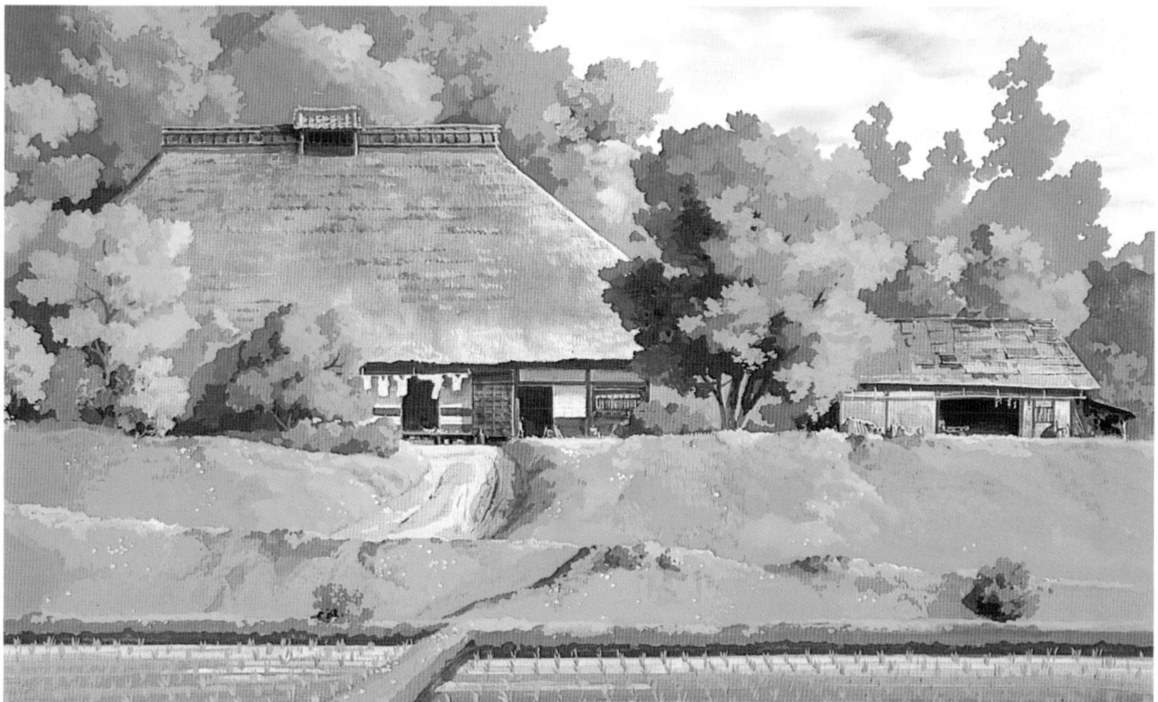

6

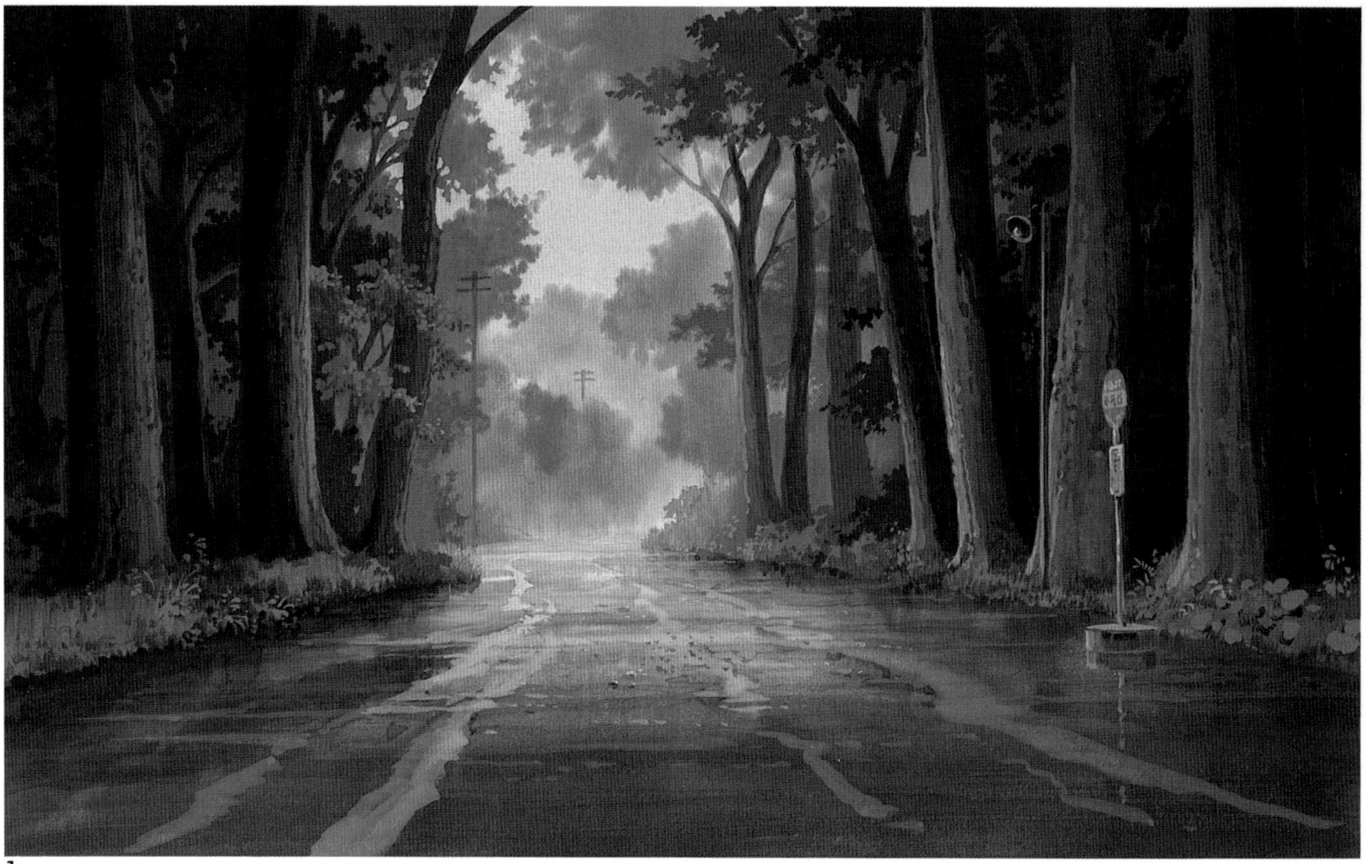

1

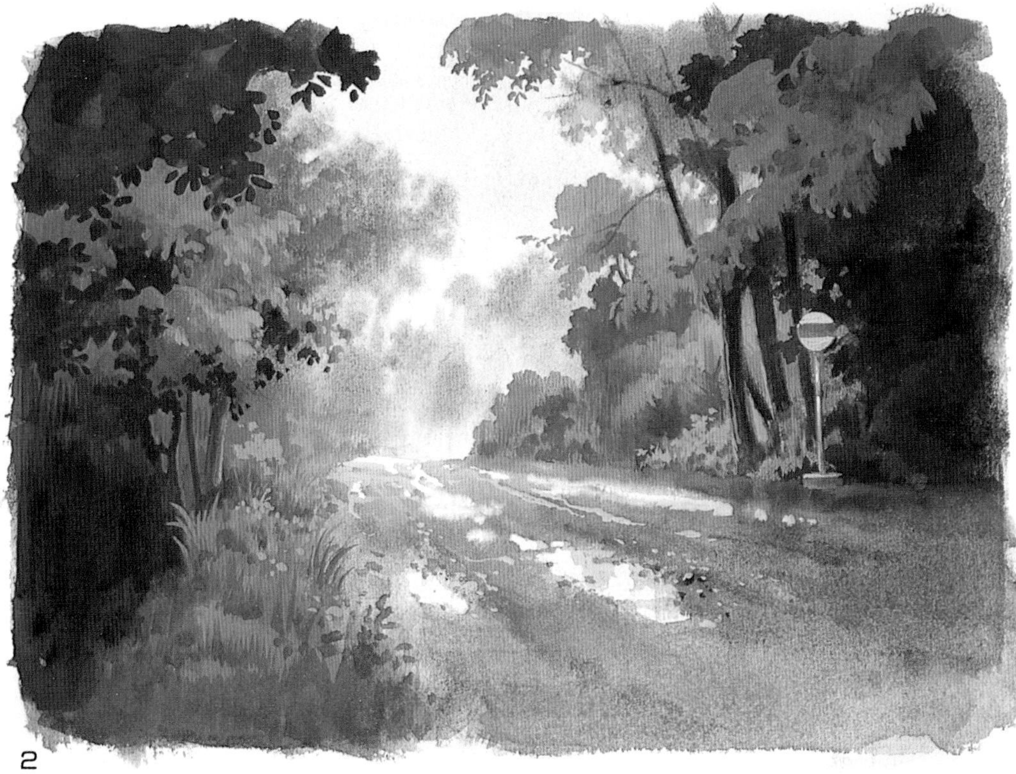

2

1 Inari statue bus stop at dusk. *(background)*

2, 3 Rain drenched Inari statue bus stop. *(concept art)*

4 Bus stop at night illuminated by street lamp. *(background)*

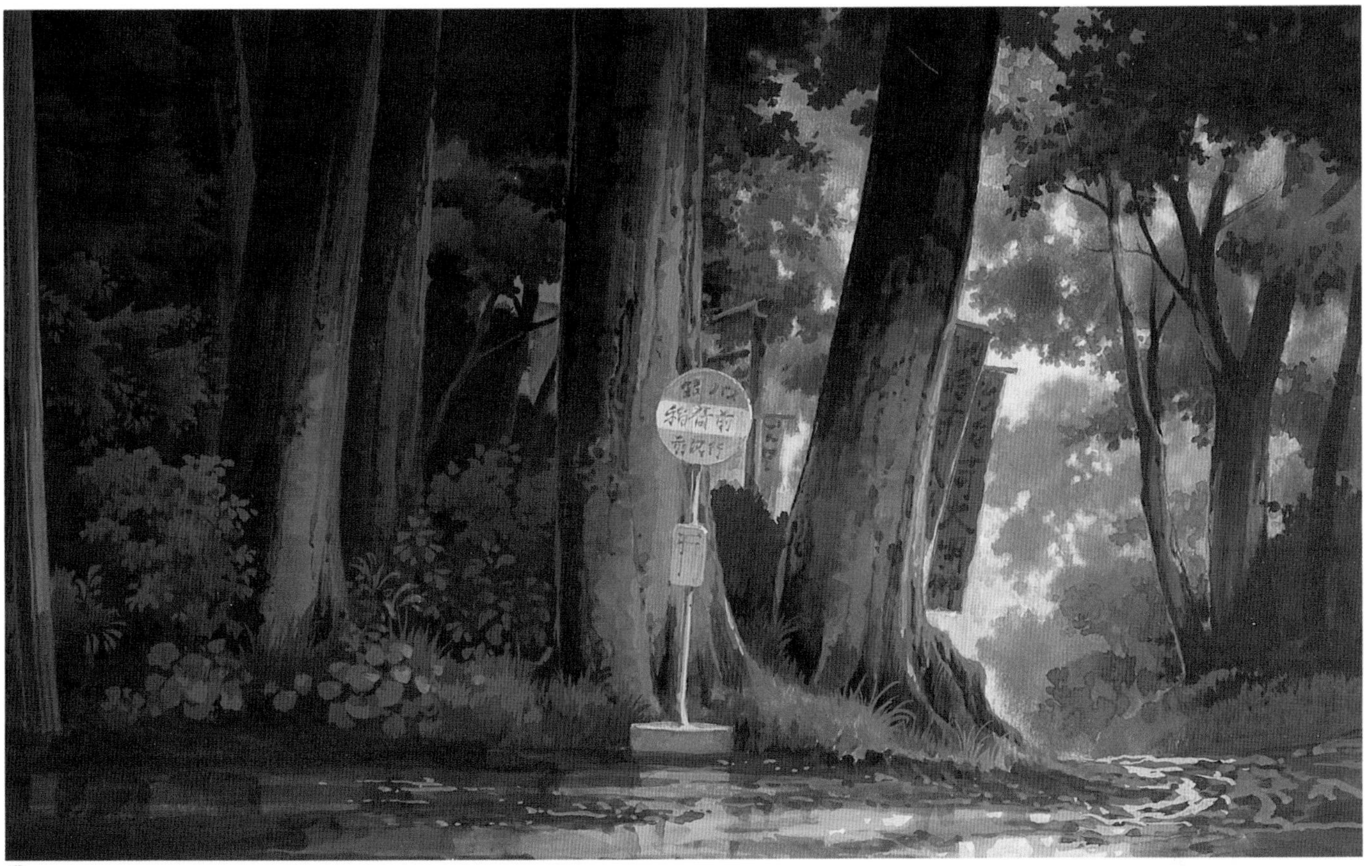
稲荷前

3

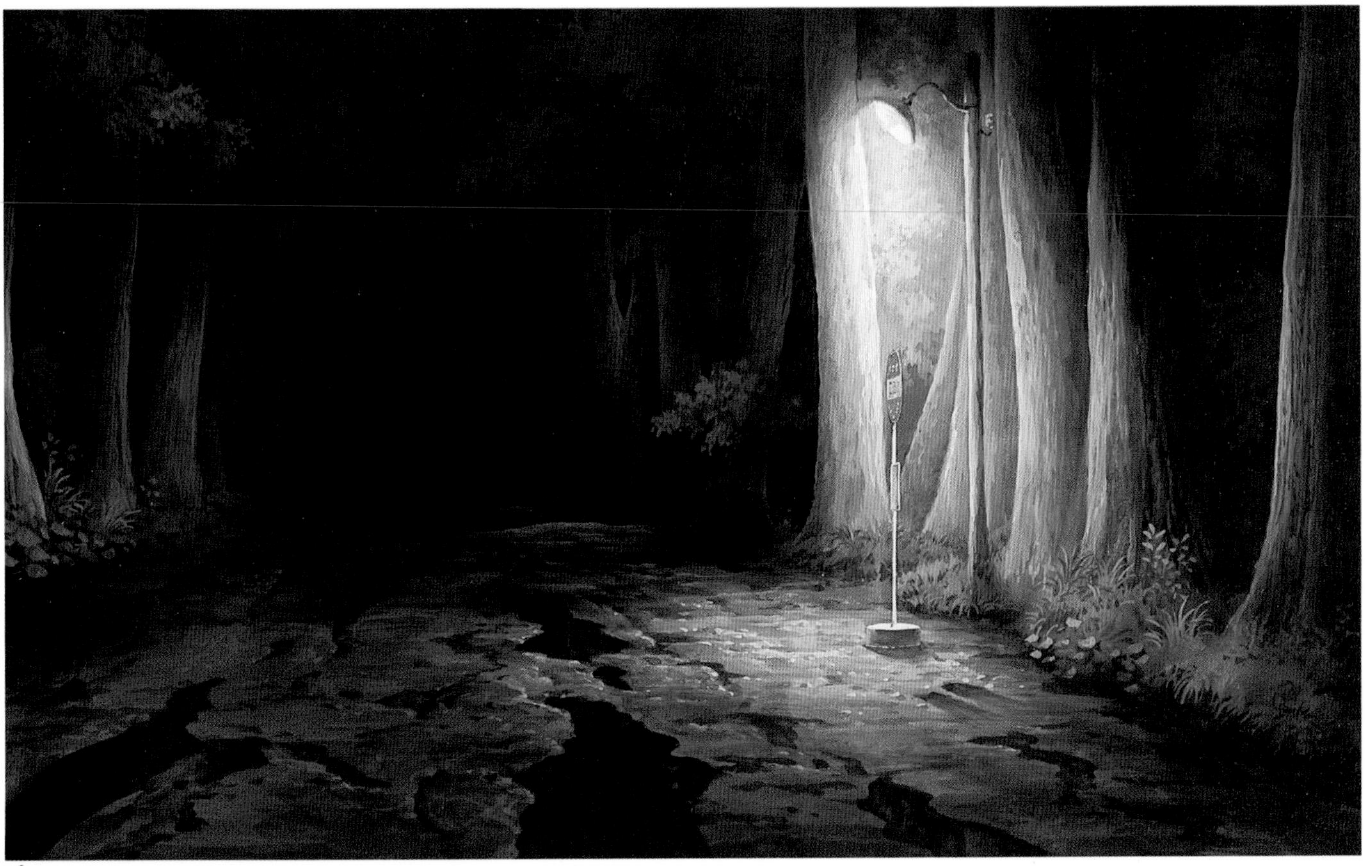

4

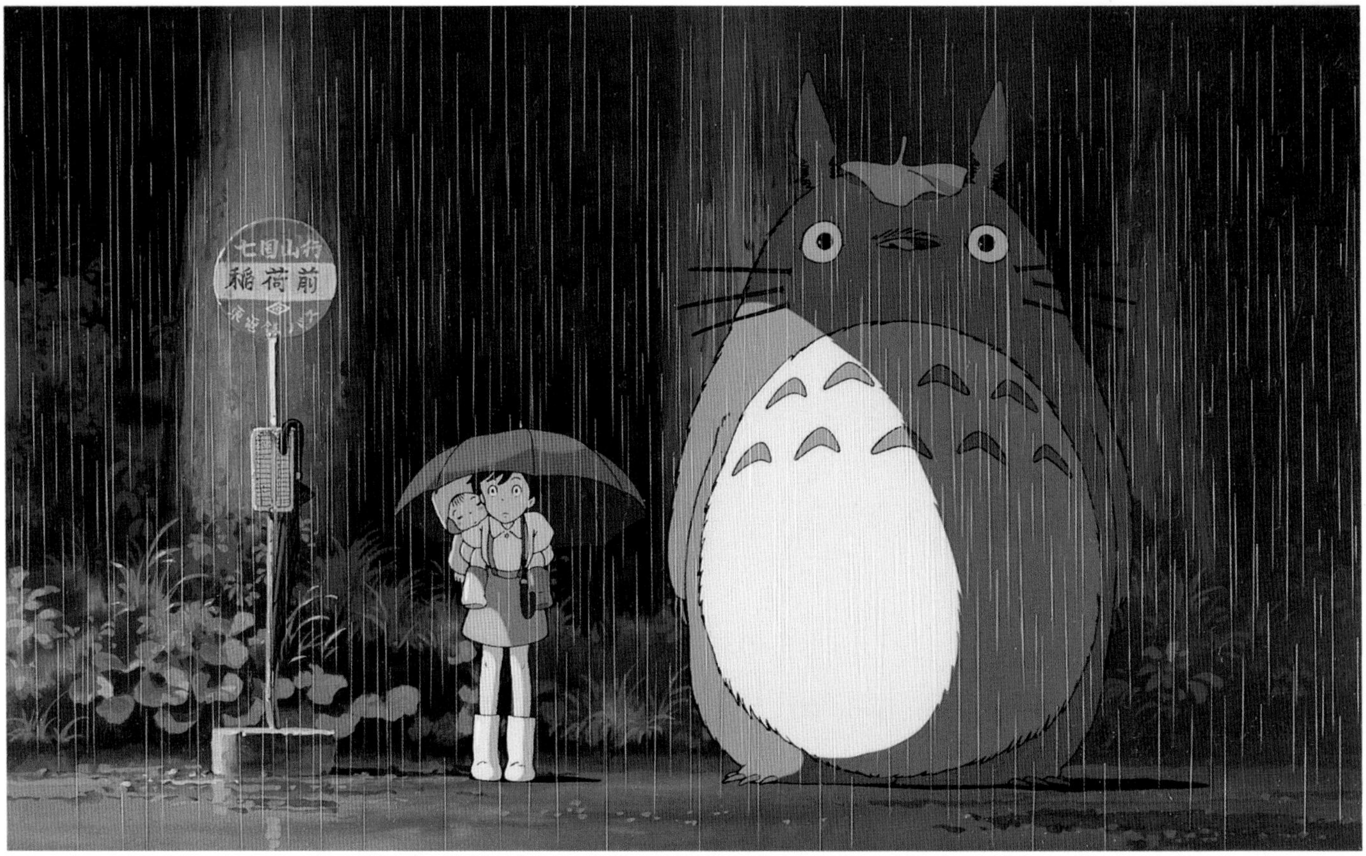
七国山行
稲荷前

1

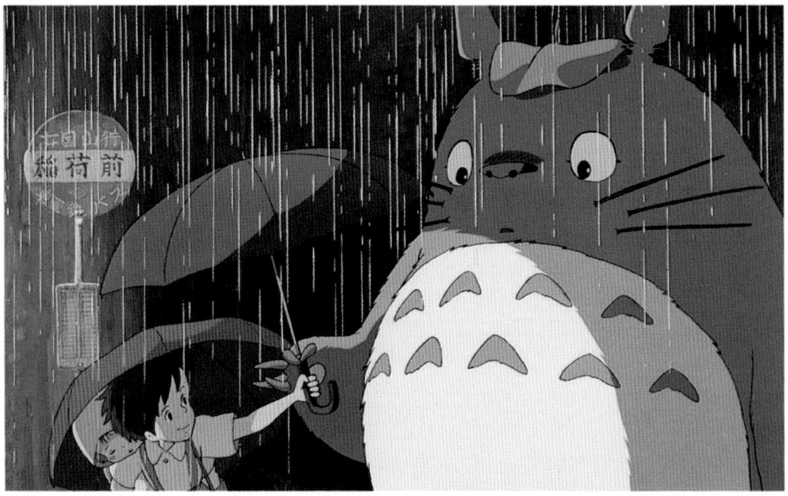
七国山行
稲荷前

2

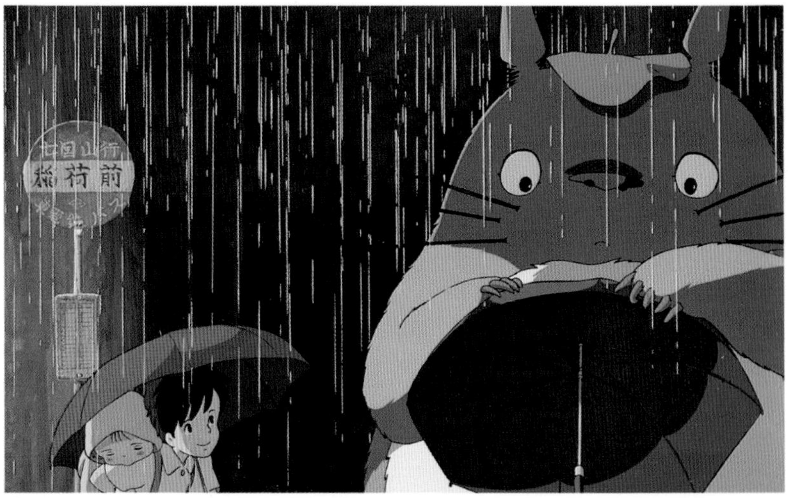
七国山行
稲荷前

3

1-5 Satsuki's encounter with Totoro. Totoro grasps the umbrella Satsuki hands him, not knowing what it's for. *(cel art)*

6 Totoro character design.

"I wanted Totoro to be massive. It wouldn't work if he had a long neck, so we made him pudgy. He's not a spirit; he's only an animal. I believe he lives on acorns. He's supposedly the forest keeper, but that's only a half-baked idea, a rough approximation. It would be more accurate to consider him a creature that modern Japanese had to make up out of desperation." *(Miyazaki)*

6

出るとき　　　すかっとの時

足つこッッとさげて

4

5

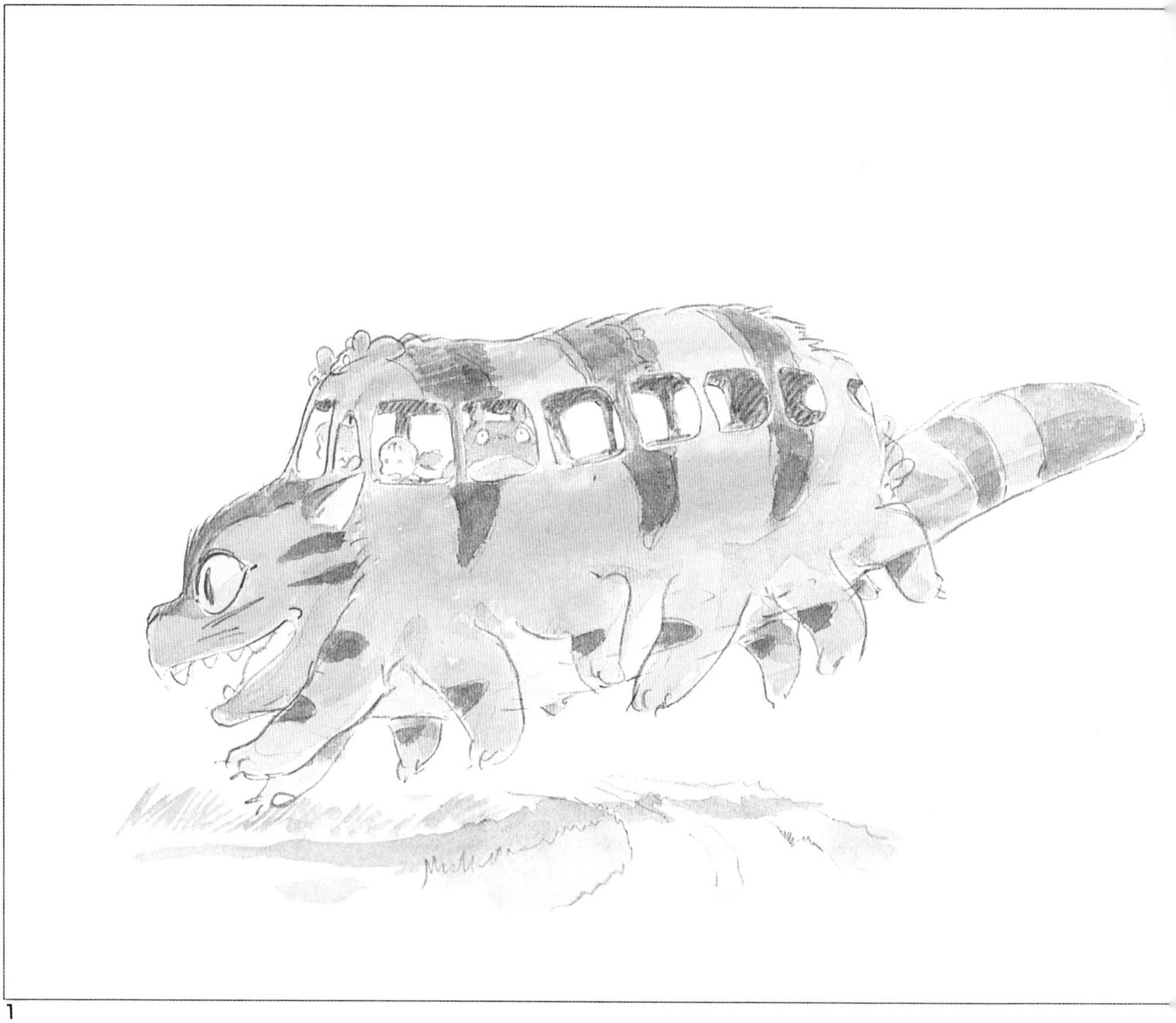

1

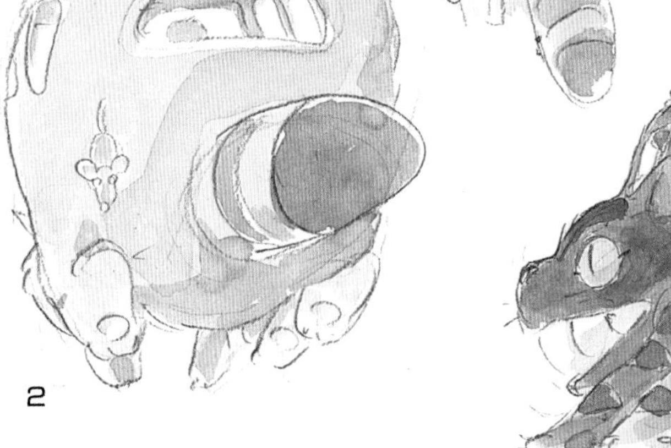

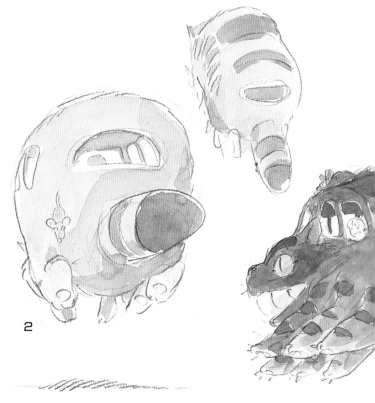

2

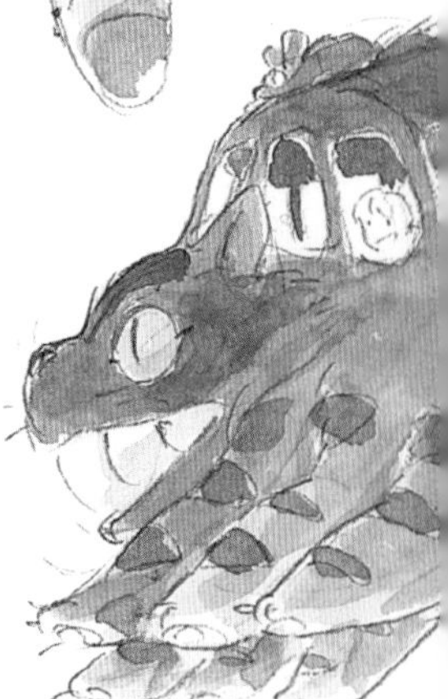

1-2 The Cat Bus. *(character design)*

3 The Cat Bus grinning upon seeing Satsuki and the others. *(film)*

"The Cat Bus is always grinning. As long as it's running, it's happy [*laughs*]. The Cat Bus once assumed the shape of a rickshaw carrier, but the sight of a bus rumbling by excited it so much it turned itself into one." *(Miyazaki)*

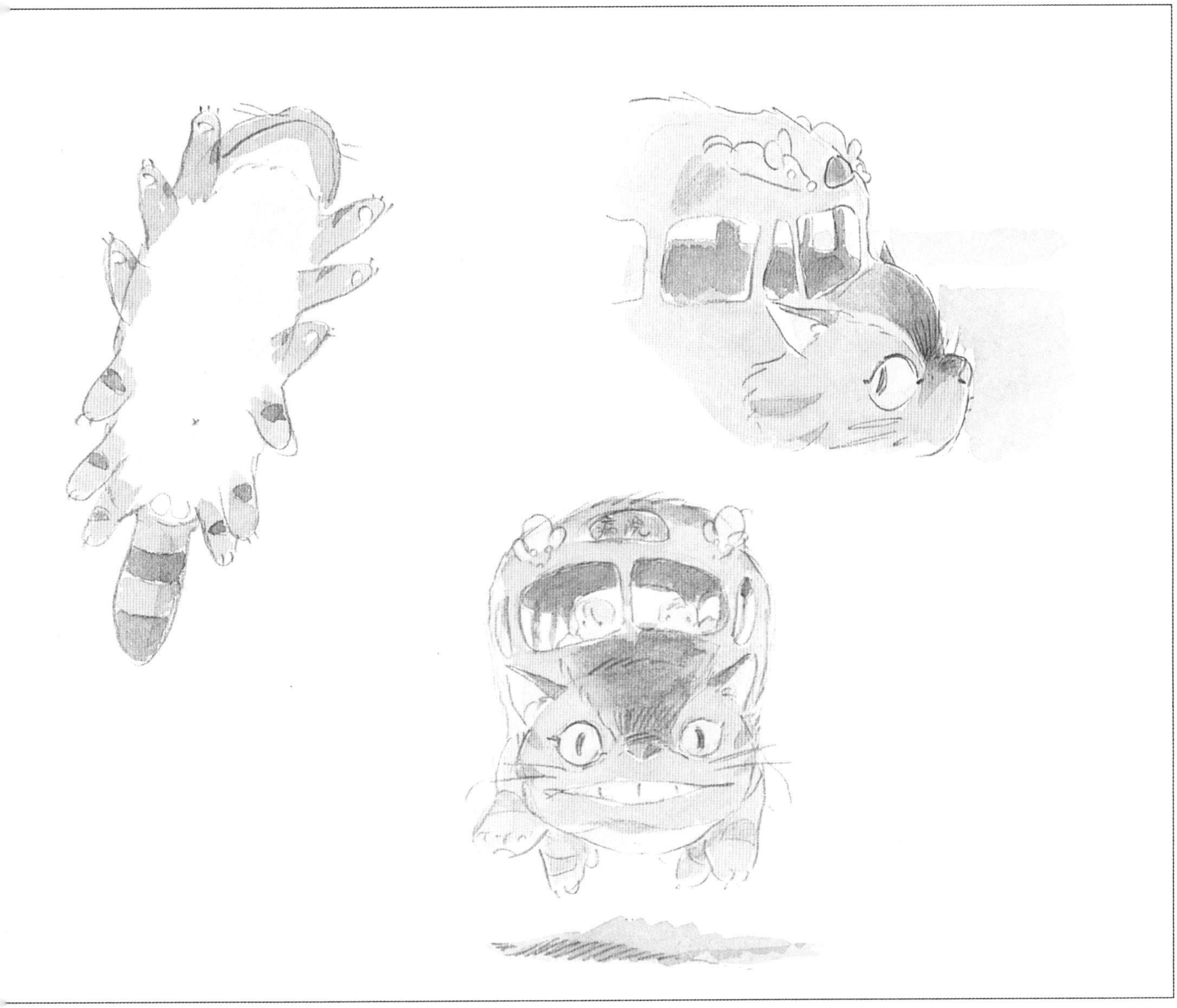

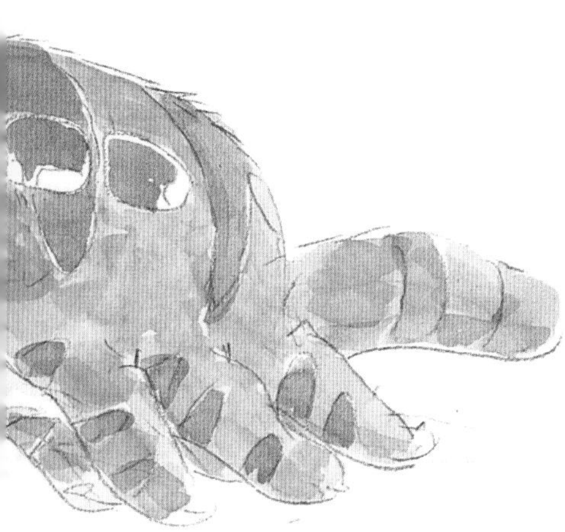

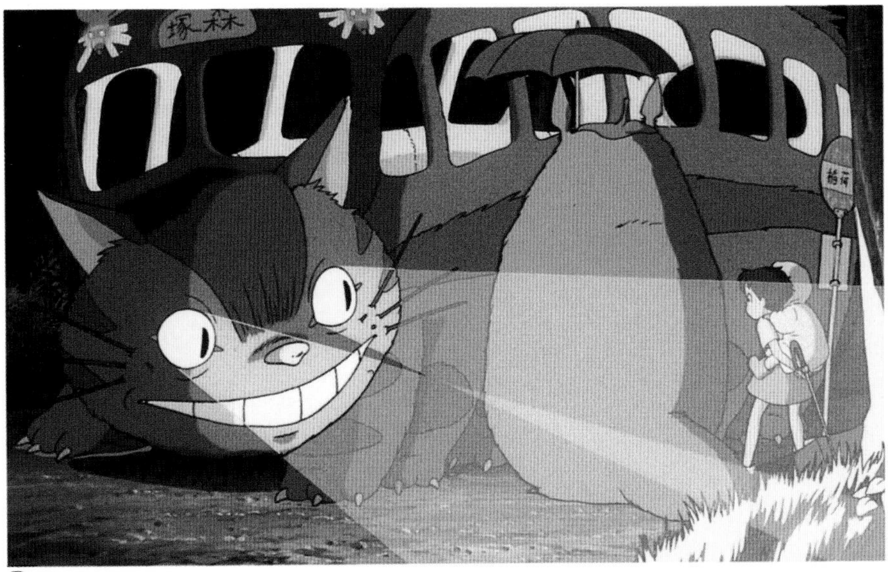

3

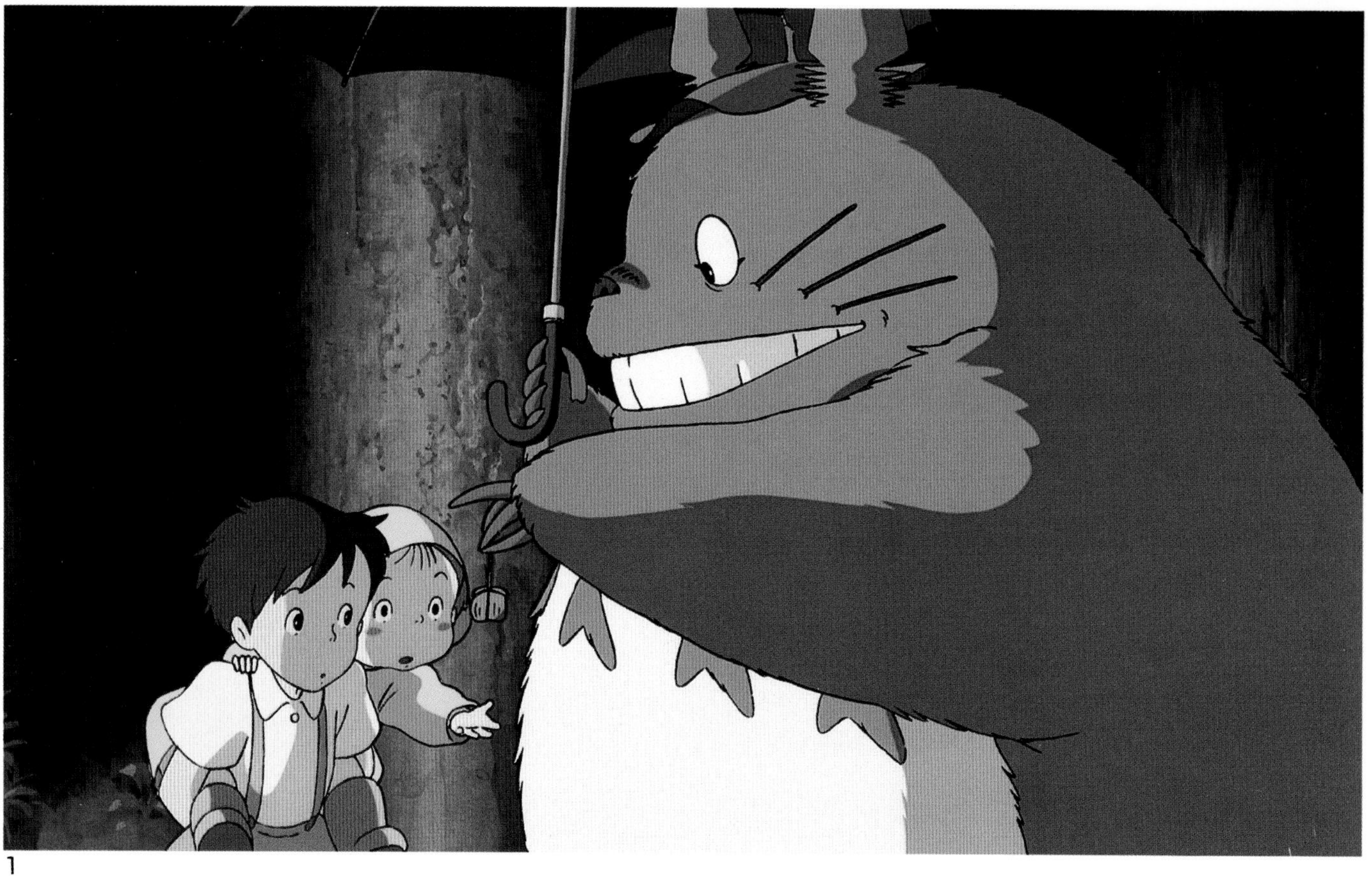

1

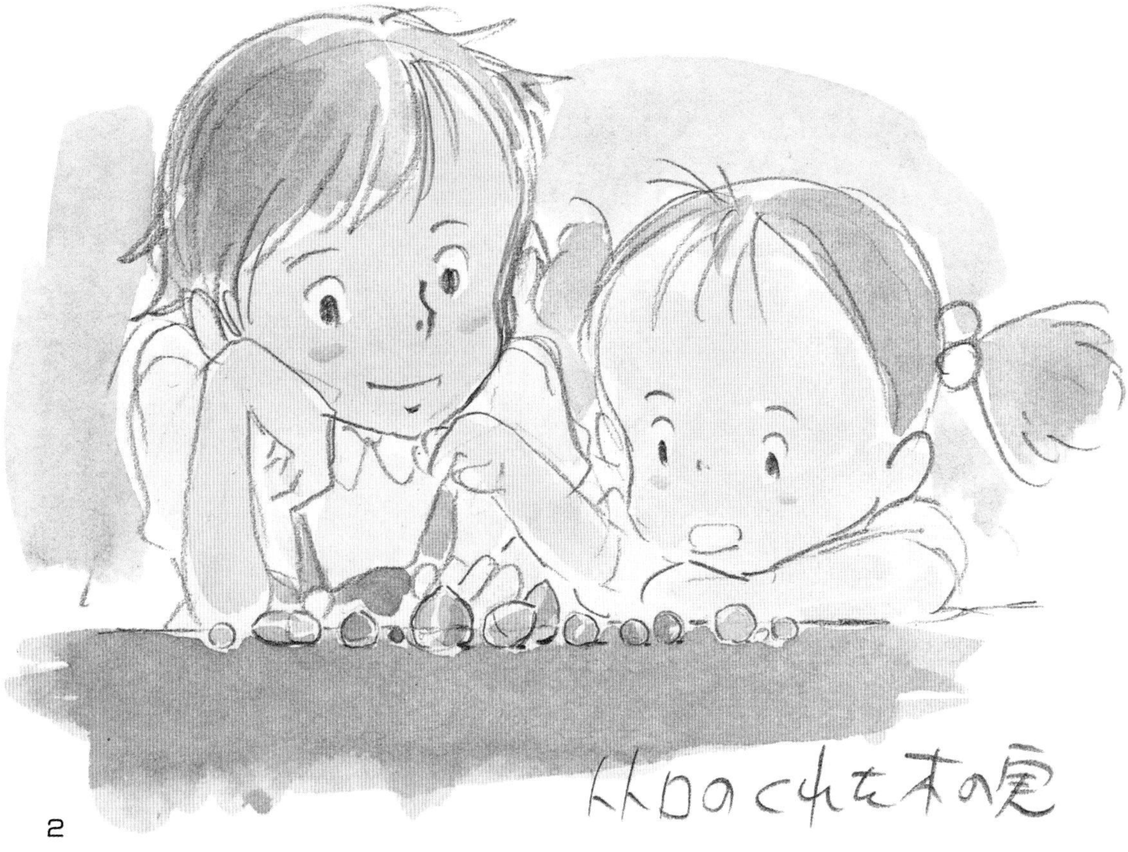
トトロのくれた木の実

2

1 Big Totoro offers a small gift to the bewildered Satsuki and Mei. *(cel art)*

2 Satsuki and Mei gaze at Totoro's gift—acorns. *(concept sketch)*

3, 4 Satsuki and Mei hugging their father as he gets off the bus. They prance around in joy. *(cel art)*

5, 6 Satsuki's letter makes her mother smile. *(cel art)*

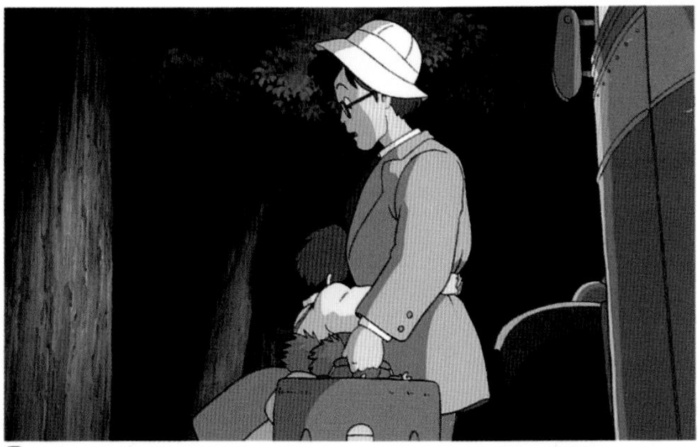
3

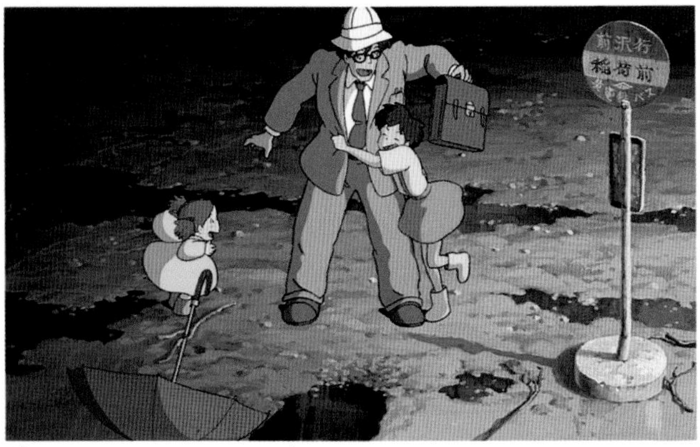
4

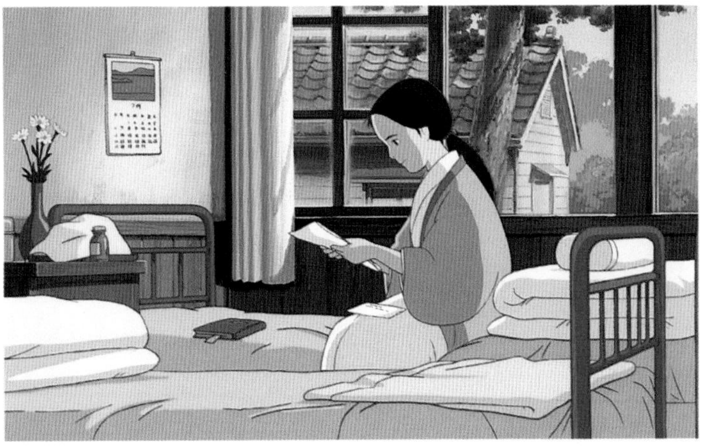
5

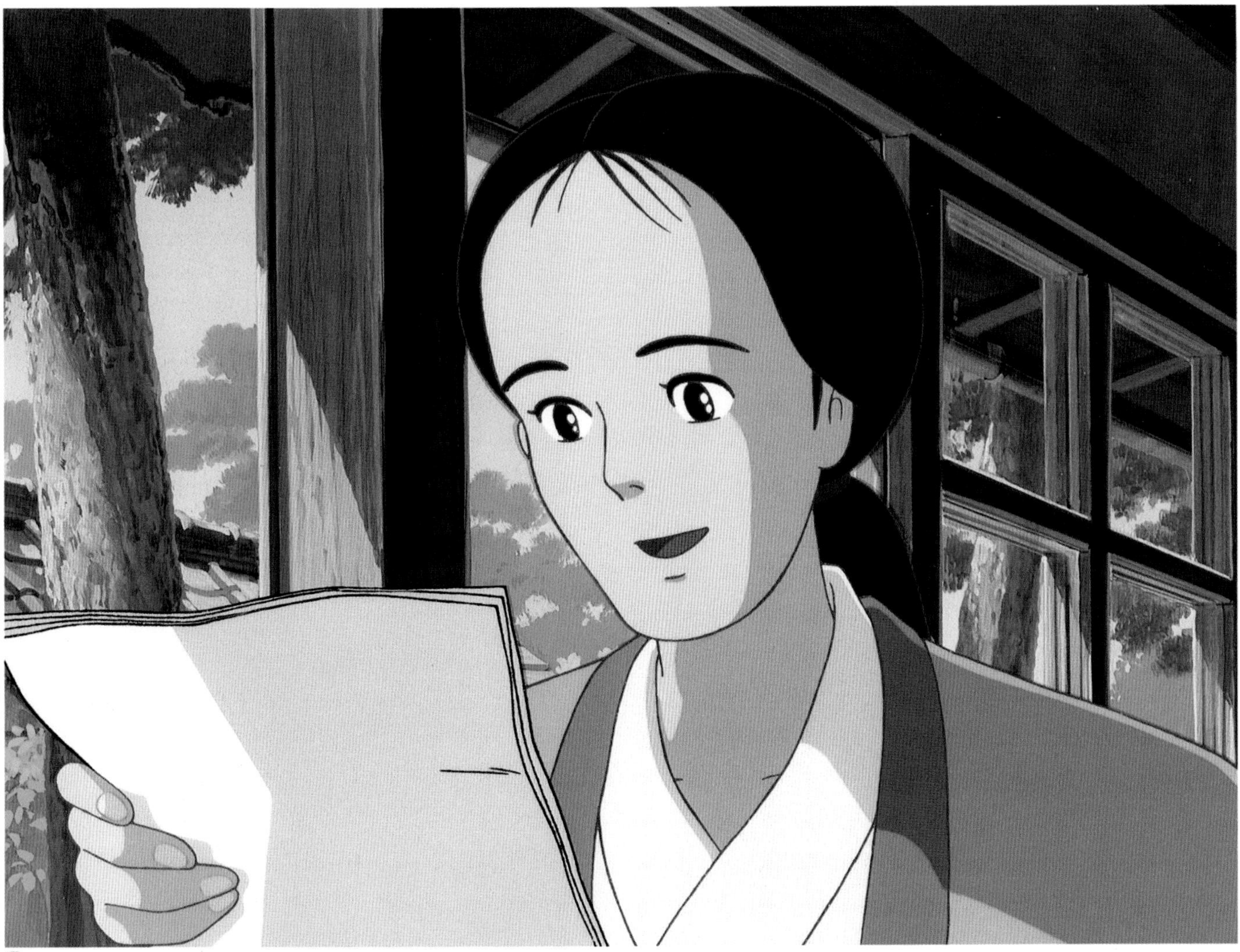
6

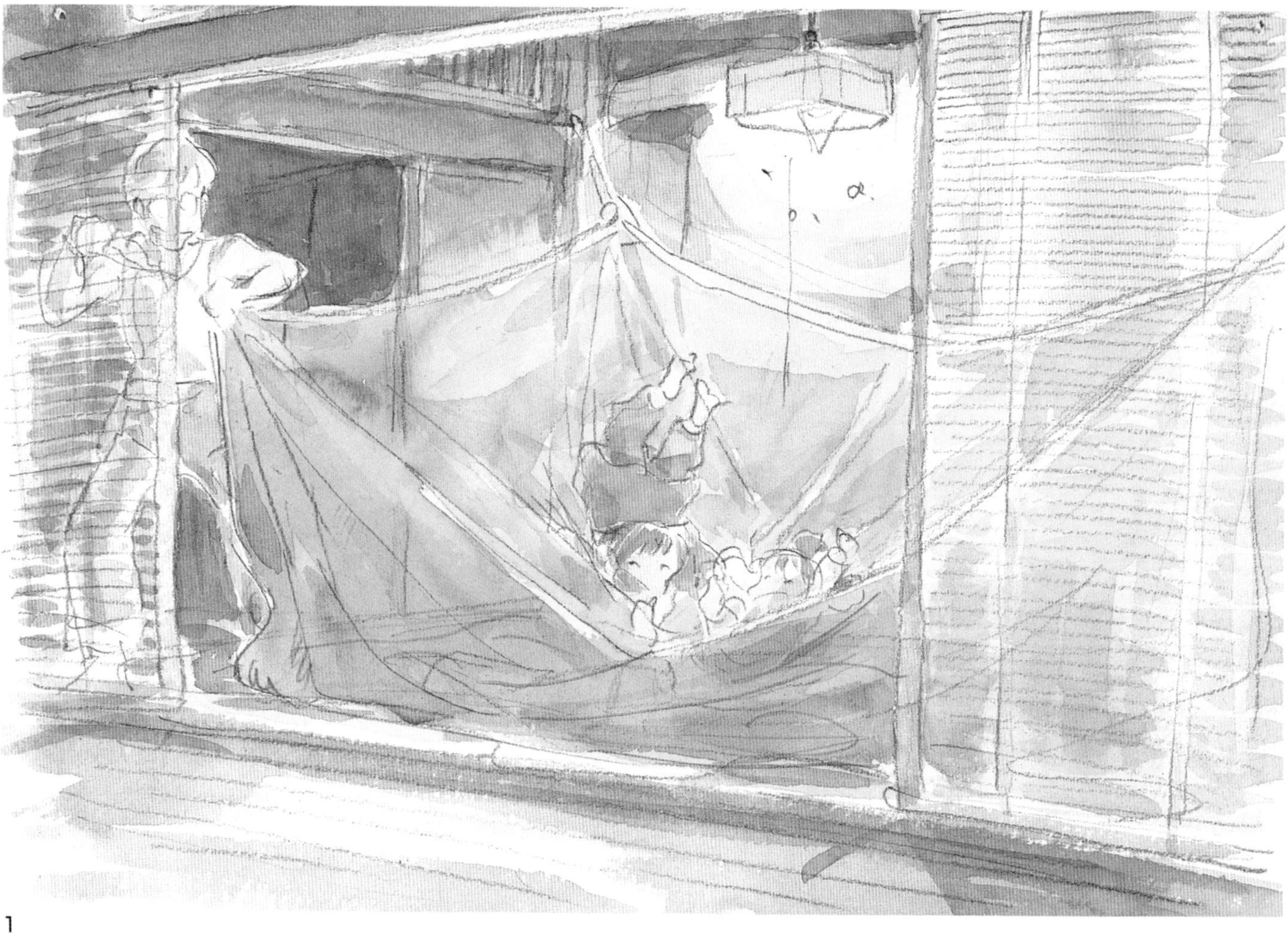

1

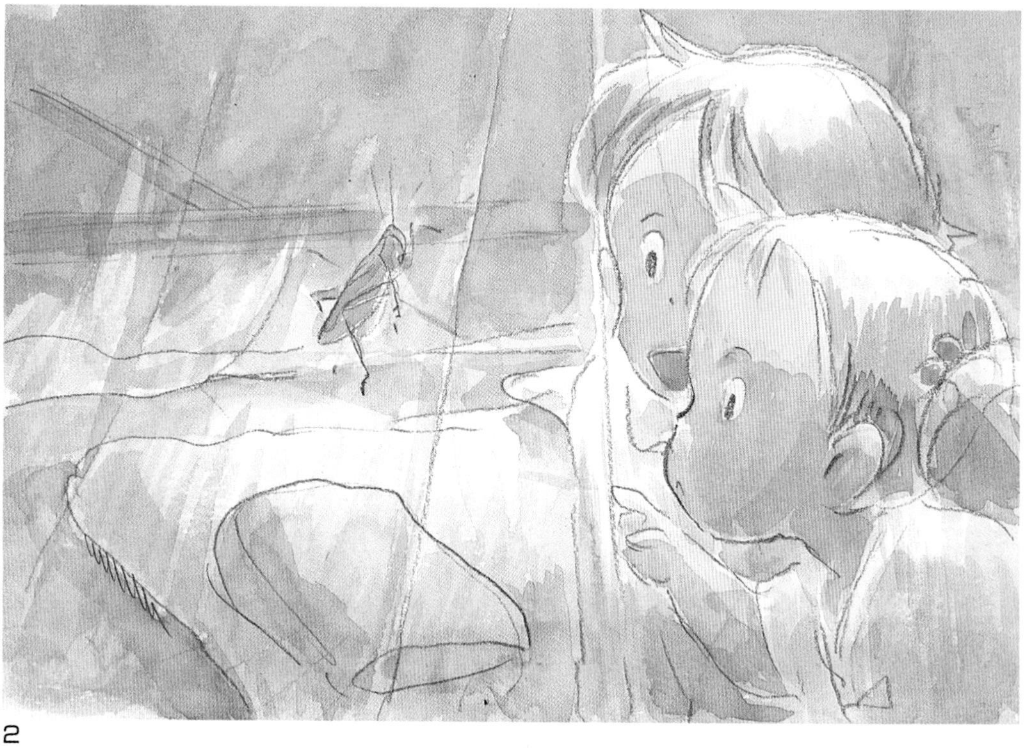

2

1, 2 Satsuki and Mei romp on top of the hanging mosquito net. Mei stares at the grasshopper that lands on the net. *(concept art)*

3 Satsuki sleeping peacefully. *(cel art)*

4 Satsuki and Mei stare at the procession of Totoros in Mei's yard under the moonlight. *(cel art)*

5 Satsuki and Mei in their pajamas. The storm door with a peephole (never used). *(character design)*

3

4

雨戸の
のぞき窓.

5

ハロー4つ
になる!!

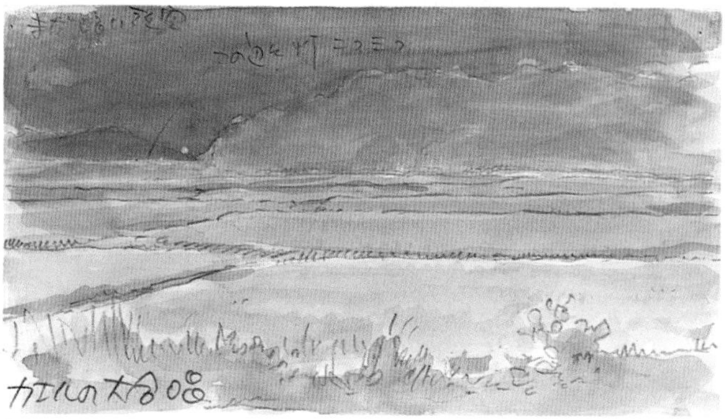
カエルの大合唱

1

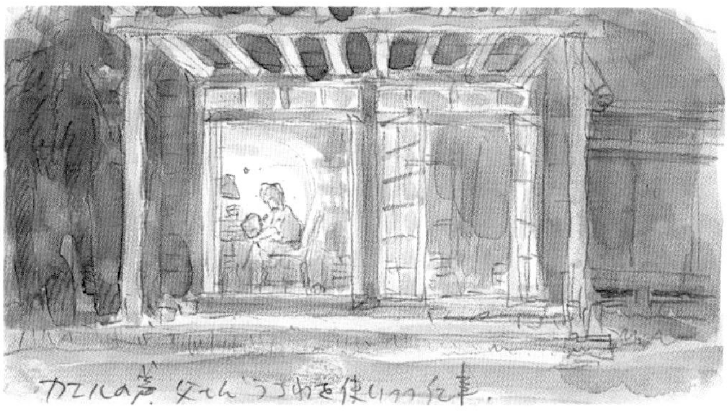
カエルの声. 父さん うちわを使いつつ仕事.

2

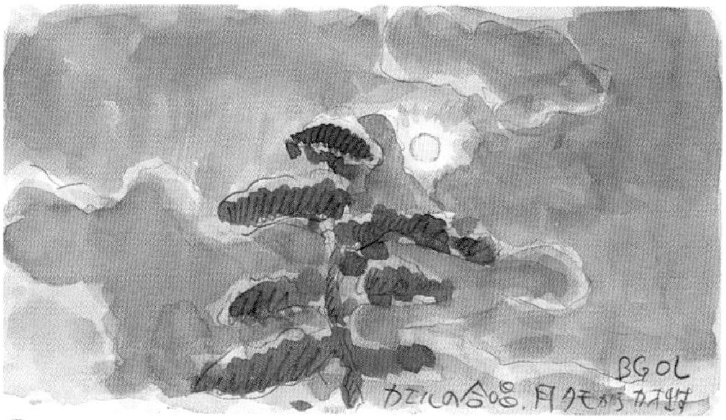
BG OL
カエルの合唱. 月クモが

3

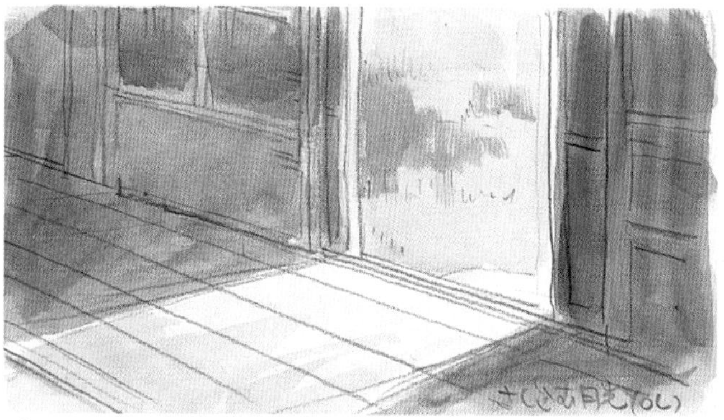
さしこむ月光 (OL)

4

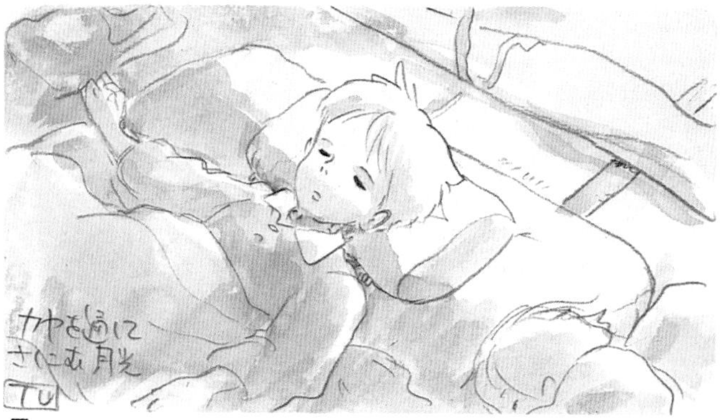
カヤを通して
さしこむ月光
TU

5

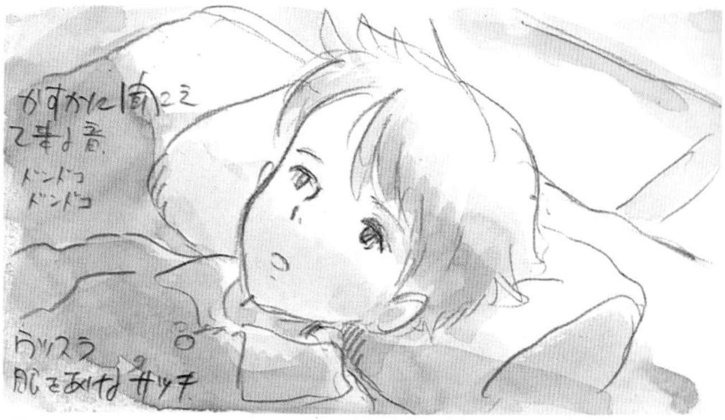
かすかに聞こえて来る音.
ドンドコ
ドンドコ
ウッスラ
眼をあけるサツキ

6

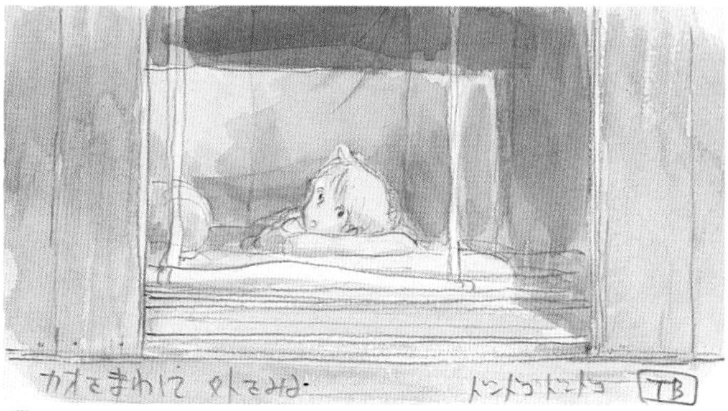
カオをまわして 外をみる.
ドンドコドンドコ
TB

7

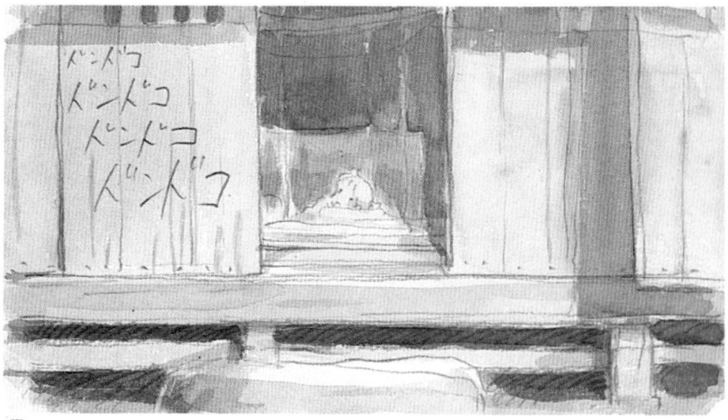
ドンドコ
ドンドコ
ドンドコ
ドンドコ

8

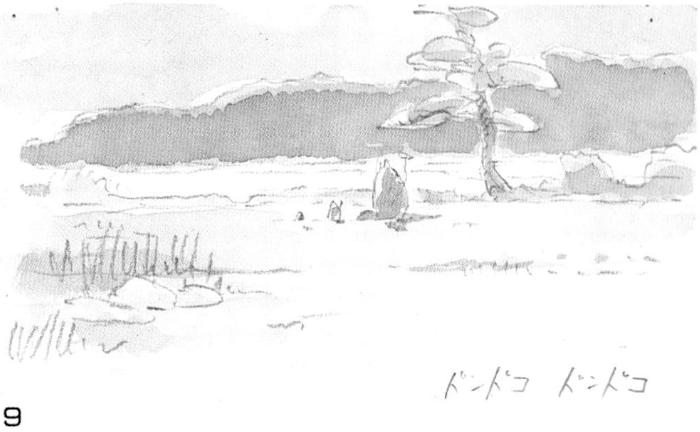
ドンドコ ドンドコ

9

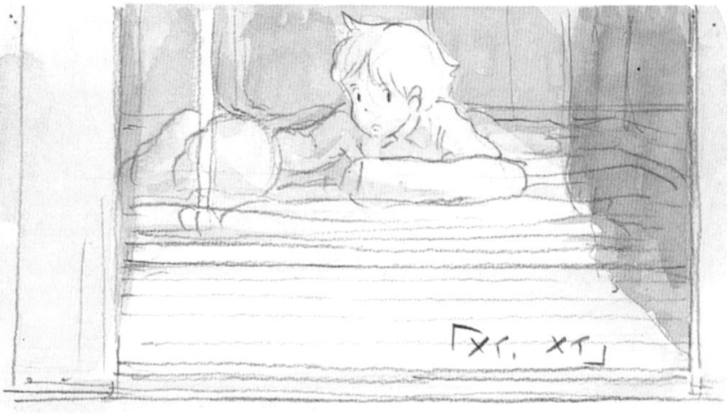
「メイ、メイ」

10

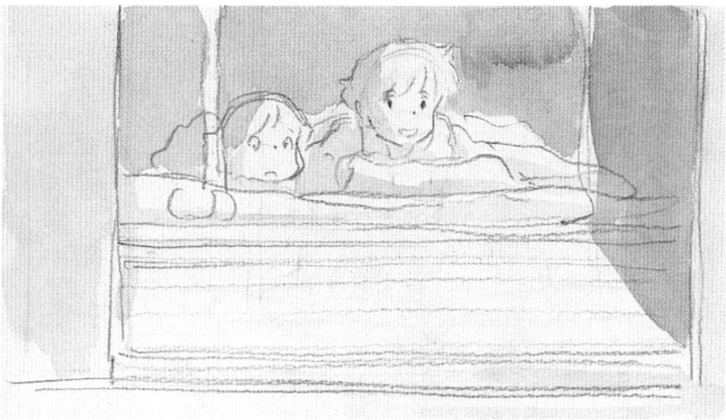

11

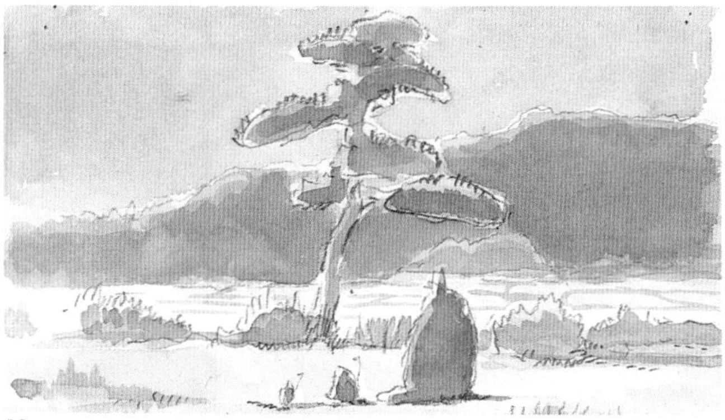

12

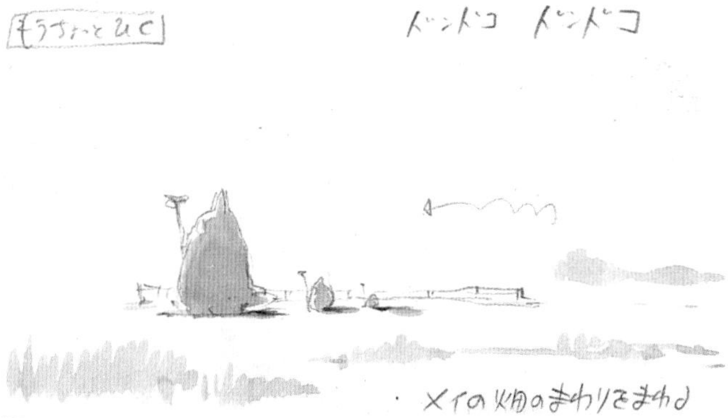
もうちょっとひく
ドンドコ ドンドコ
・メイの畑のまわりをまわる

13

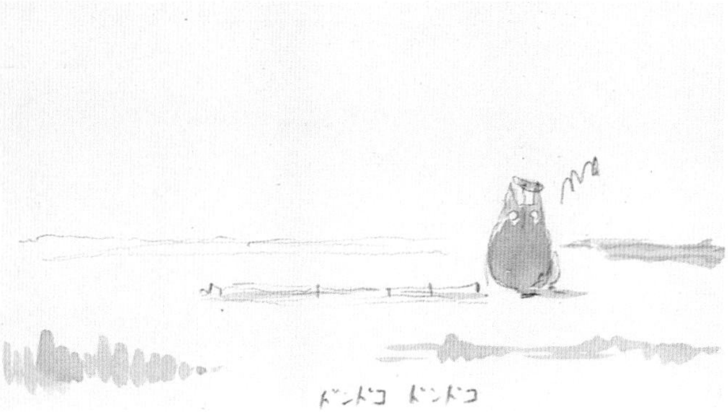
ドンドコ ドンドコ

14

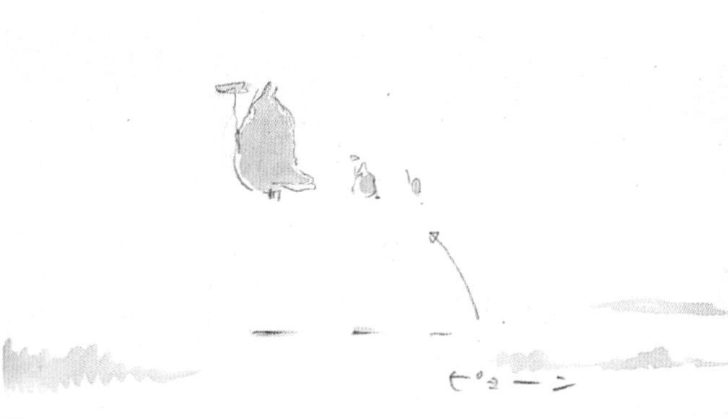
ピョーン

15

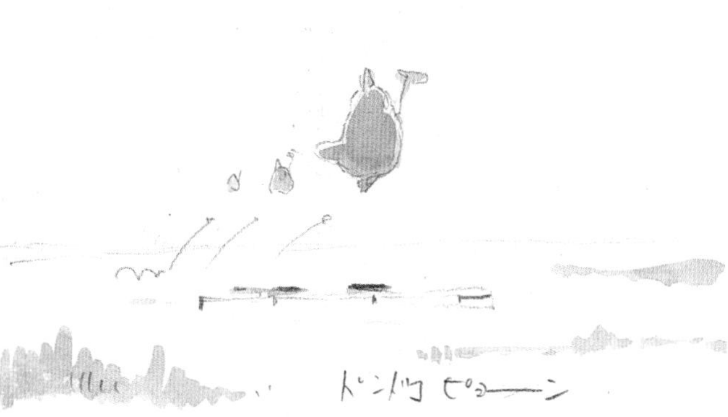
ドンドコ ピョーン

16

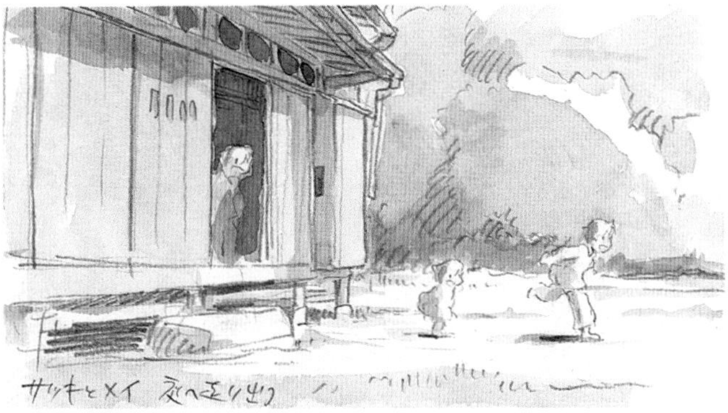
サツキとメイ 庭へ走り出る

17

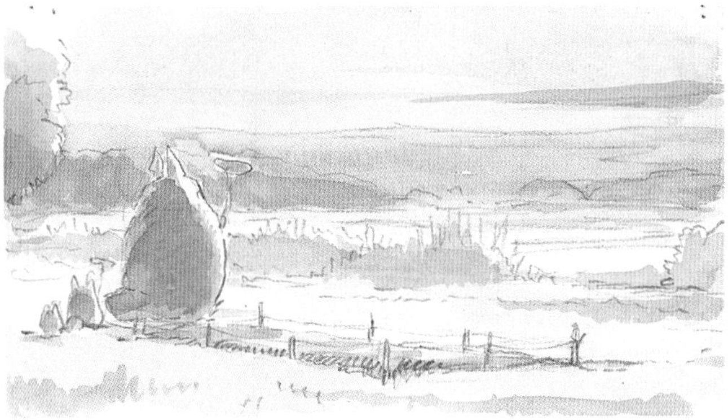

18

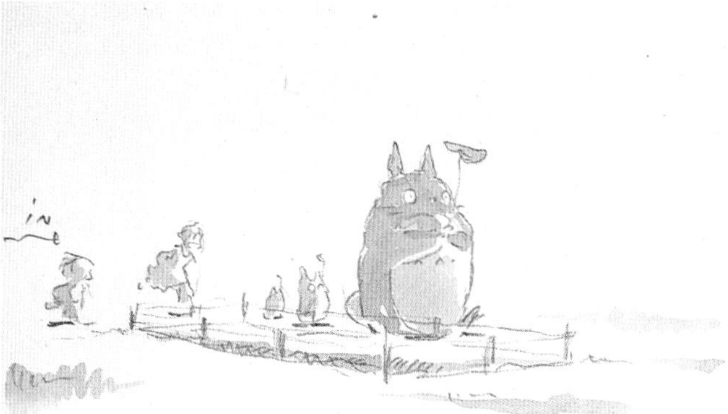
IN

19

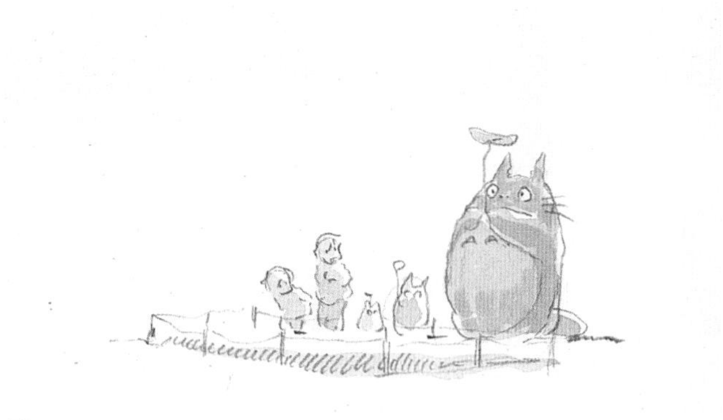

20

21

22

サツキとメイ
見たり見まねが
手ねる

ちぢんで

北重たのびより

23

24

25

A.C

アナグミ

26

27

28

29

30

ヌママ

ノビロオ…

ボコ!!

一瞬 光をともすか

アアッ!!

112

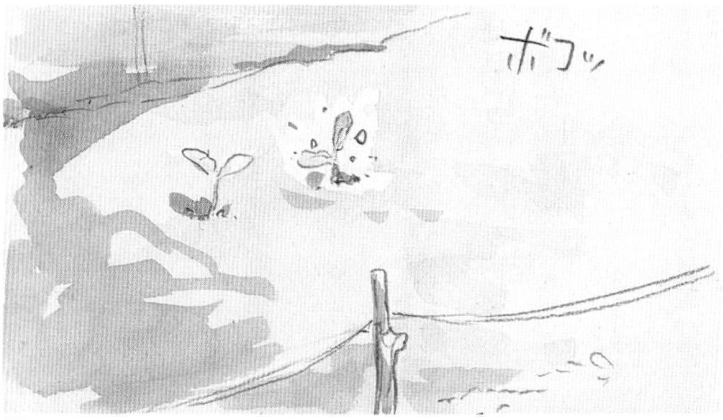
ボコッ

31

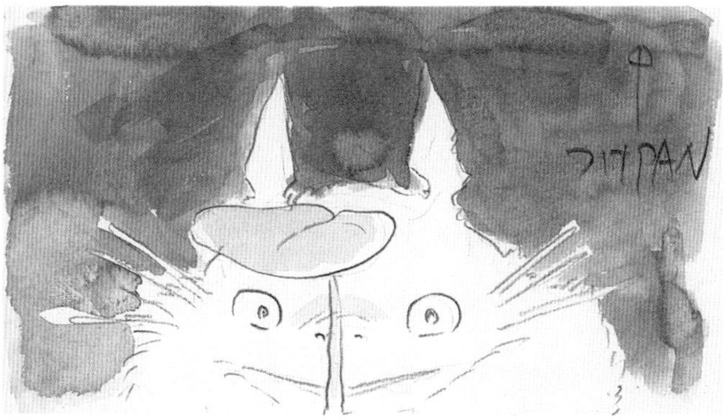
フォロPAN

32

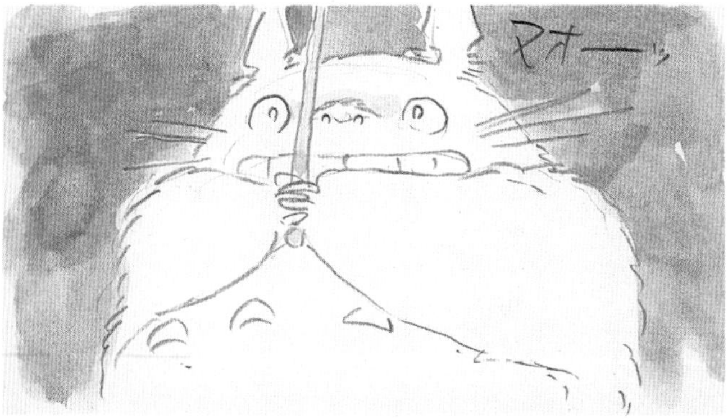
ヤオーッ

33

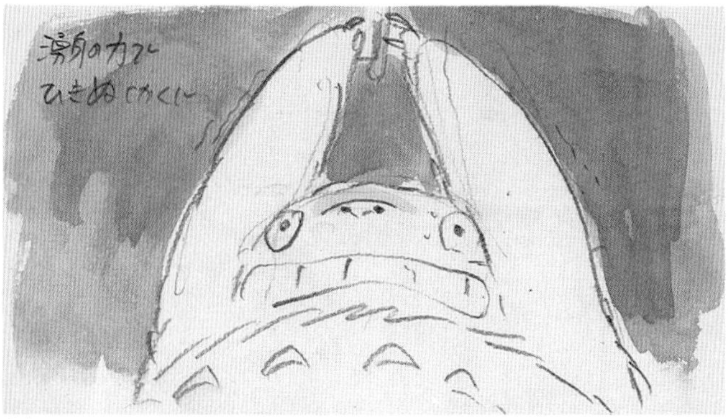
渾身の力で
ひきぬくかんじ

34

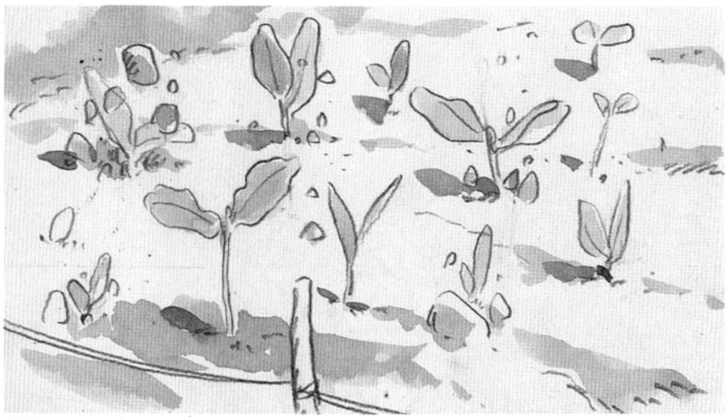

35

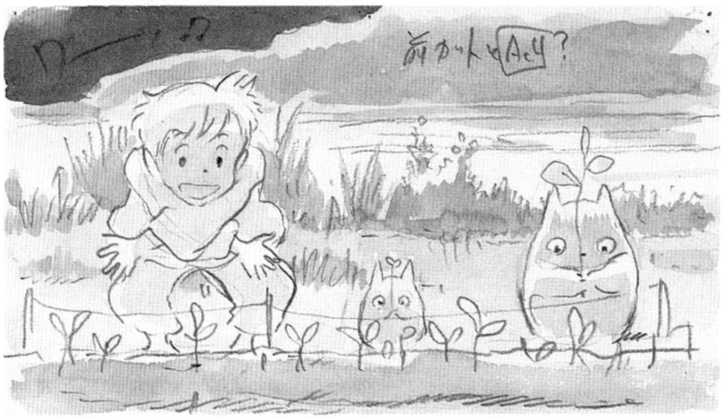

36

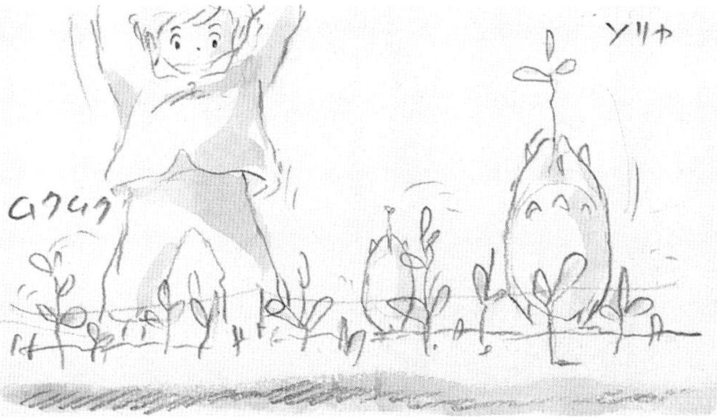
ソリャ
ムクムク

37

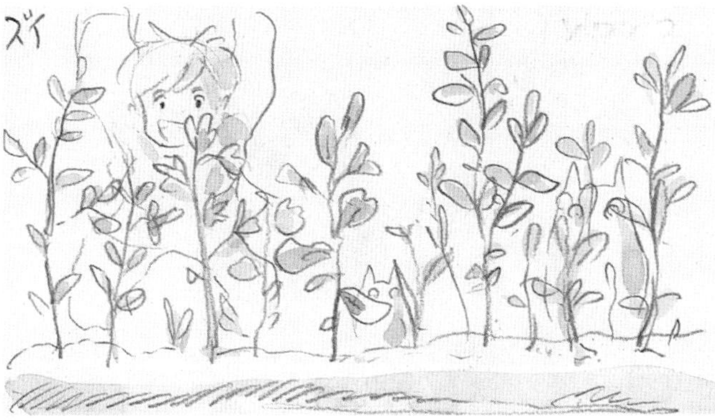
ズイ

38

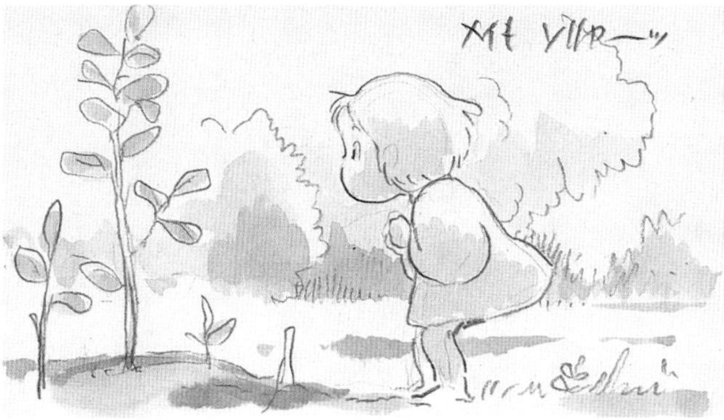
メイも ソリャーッ

39

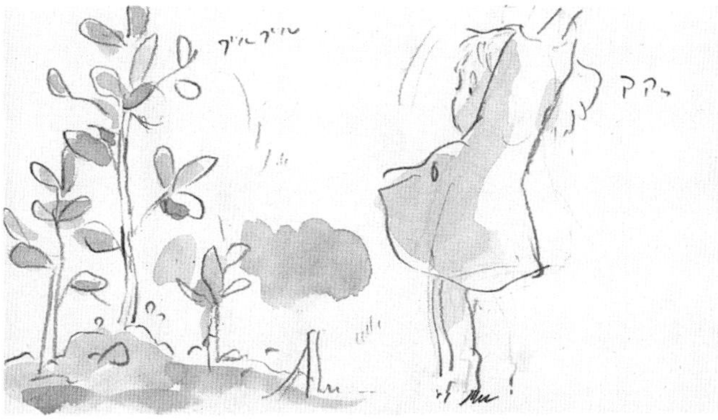
ブルブル
アア

40

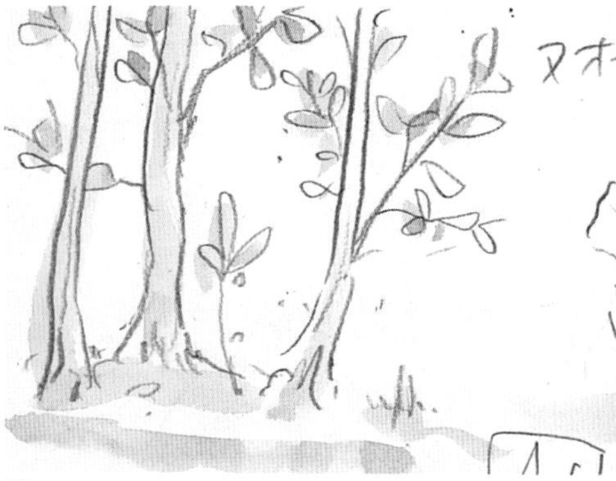
アオー
ドテッ

41

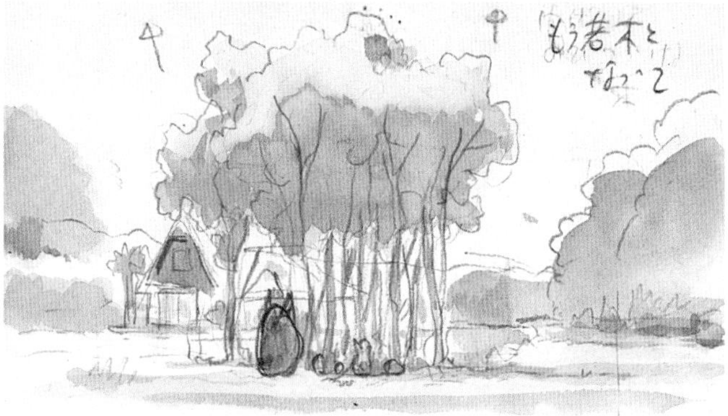

42

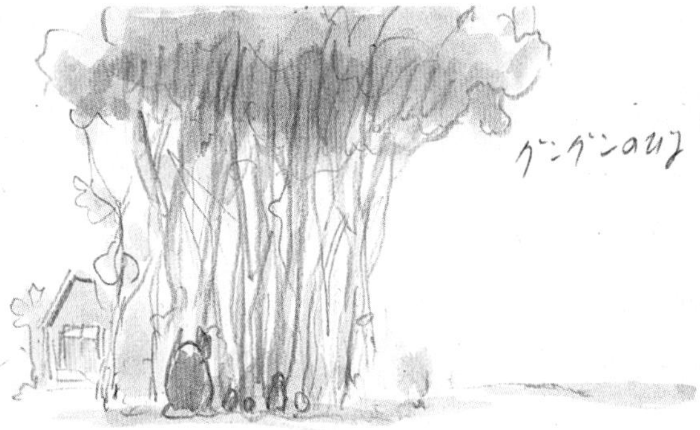
グングンのびる

43

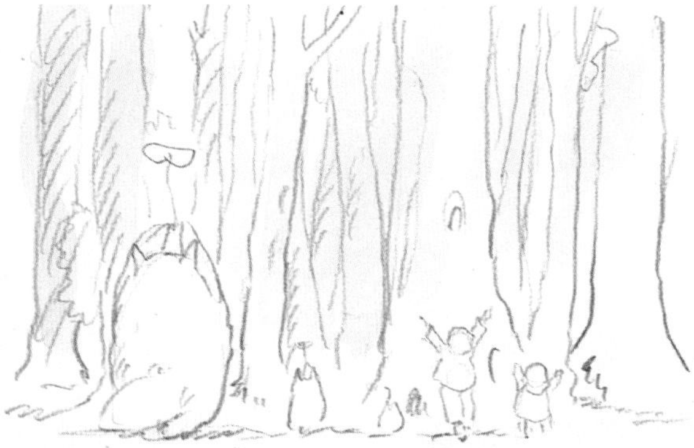

44

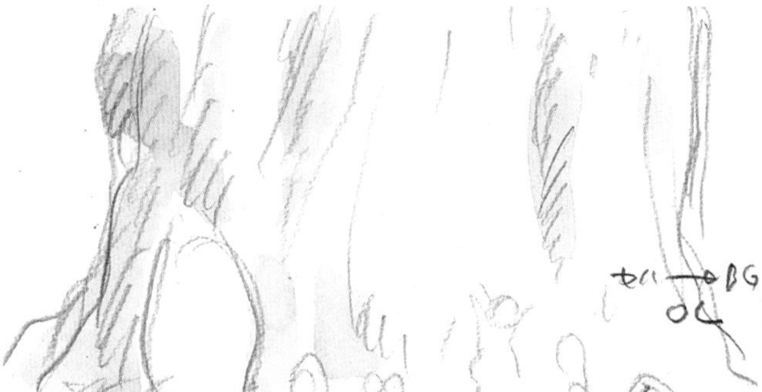
セル→BG
OL

45

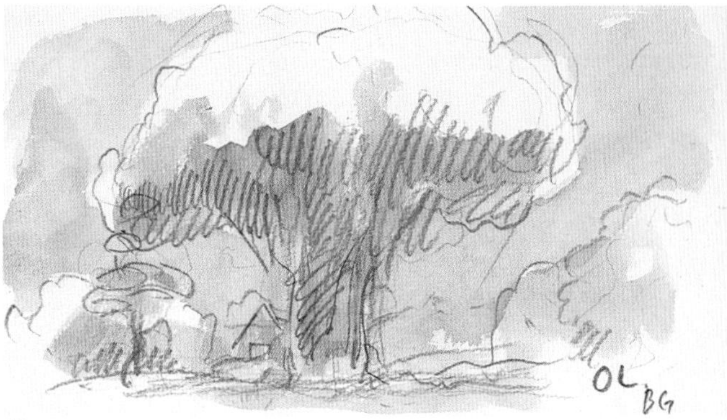
OL BG

46

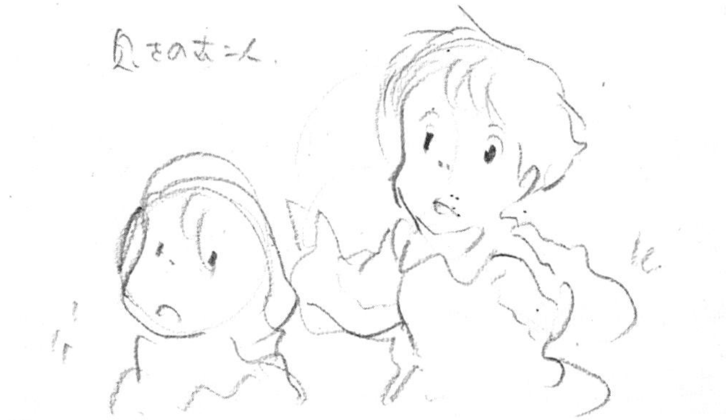

47

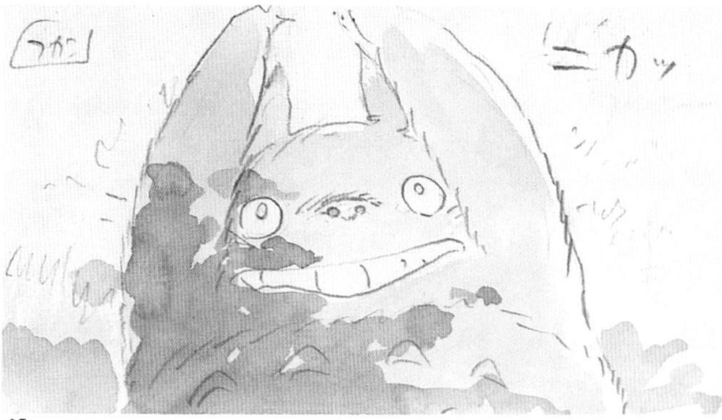
フカン
ニカッ

48

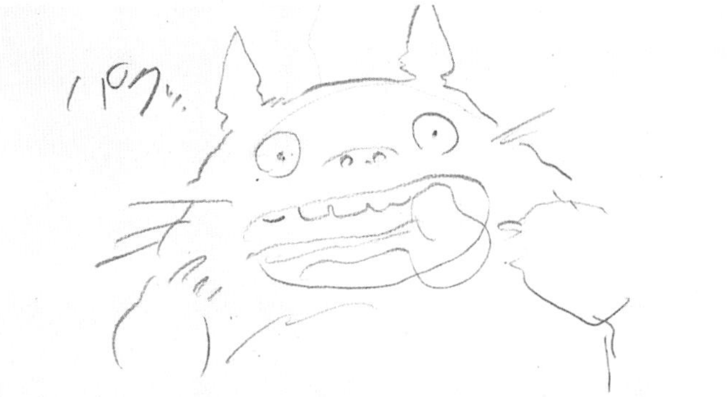
パクッ

49

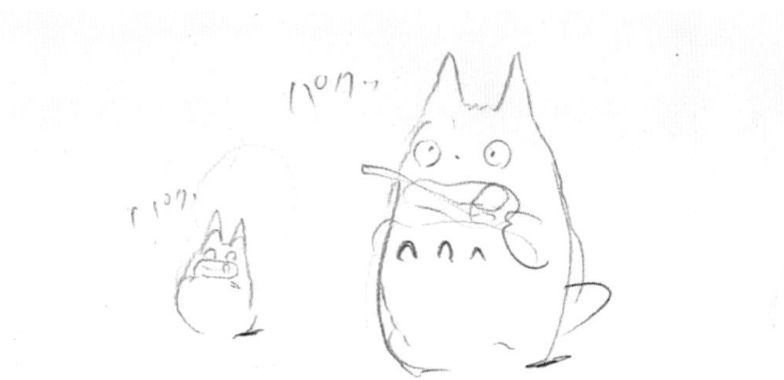
パクッ
パクッ

50

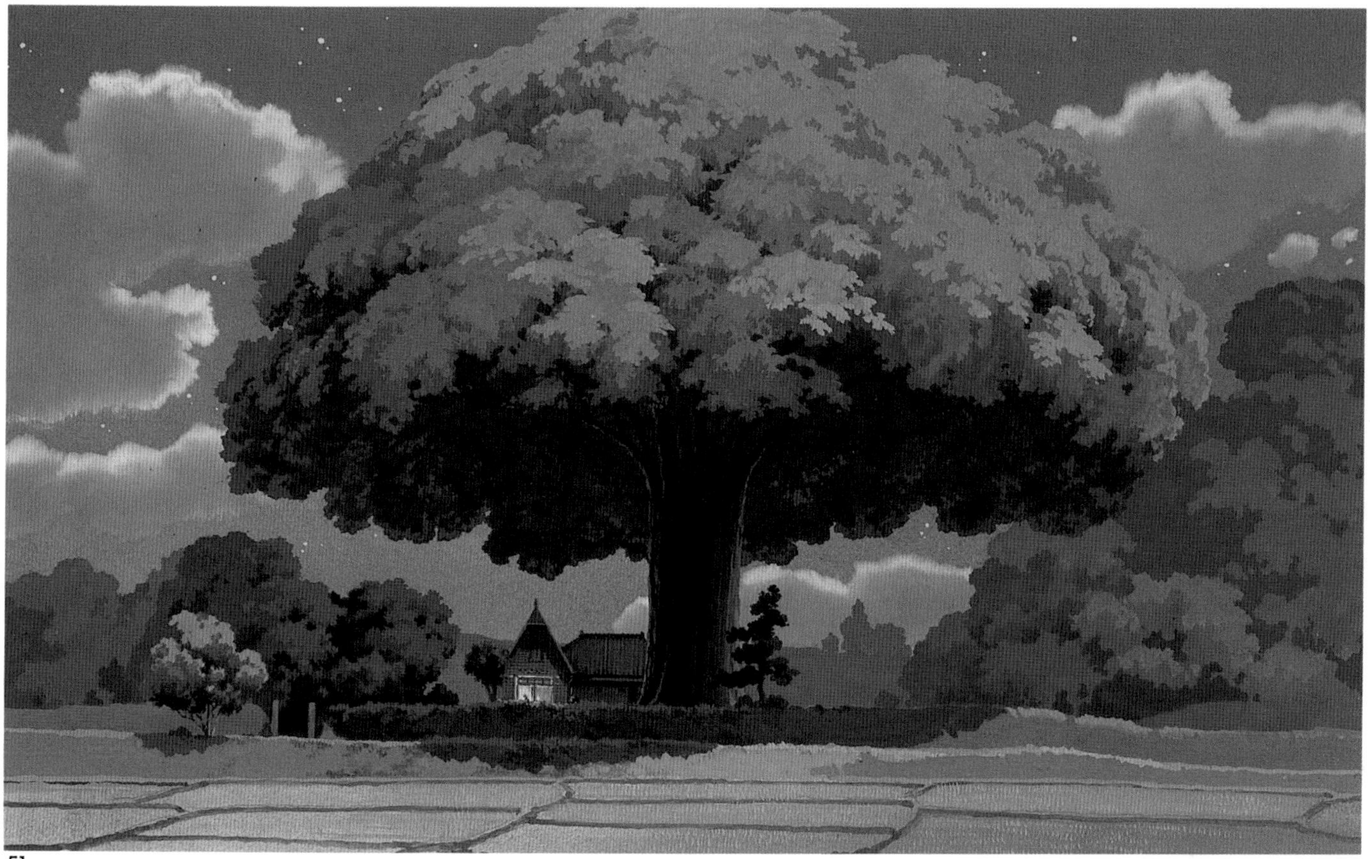

51

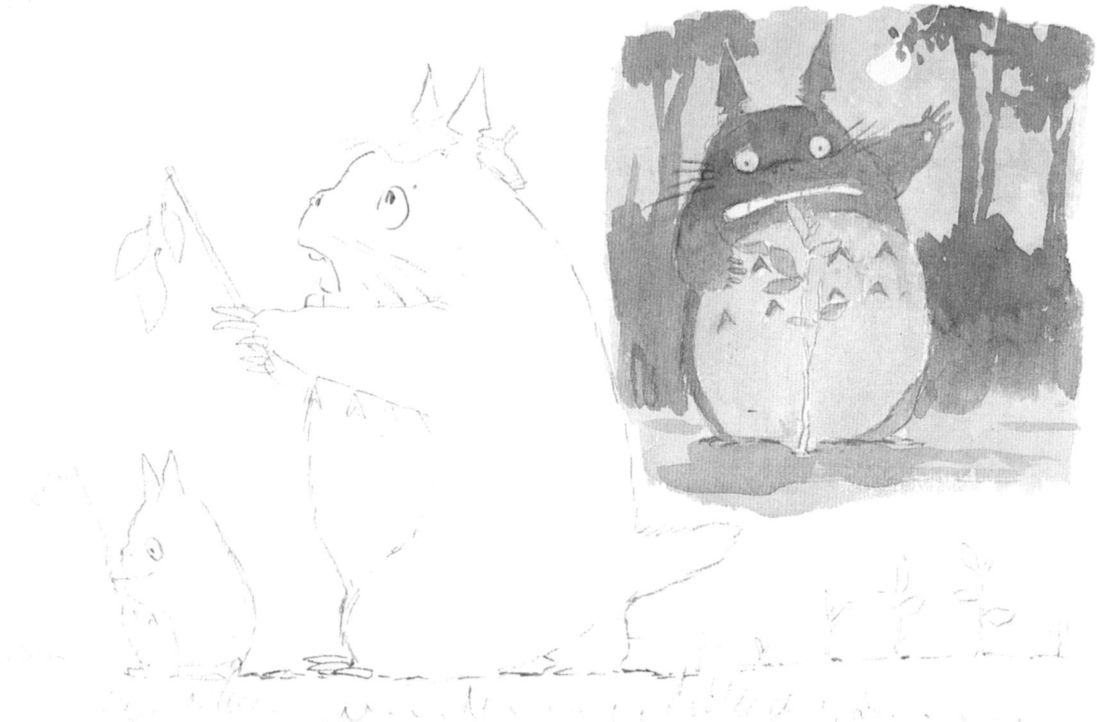

52

1-50 The acorn Mei planted sprouts to the Totoros' drum dance until it grows into a huge tree. *(storyboards)*

51 The towering tree bathed in moonlight. *(background)*

52 Totoros do their drum dance. *(concept sketch)*

1

2

1 Totoro flies into the sky as Satsuki and Mei hang onto it. *(concept sketch)*

2 Totoro rides into the sky with a spinning top. *(concept art)*

3-6 Once it hurls the top and puffs up its chest, Totoro has Satsuki and Mei grab onto it as it hops on the top so they can fly away. *(cel art)*

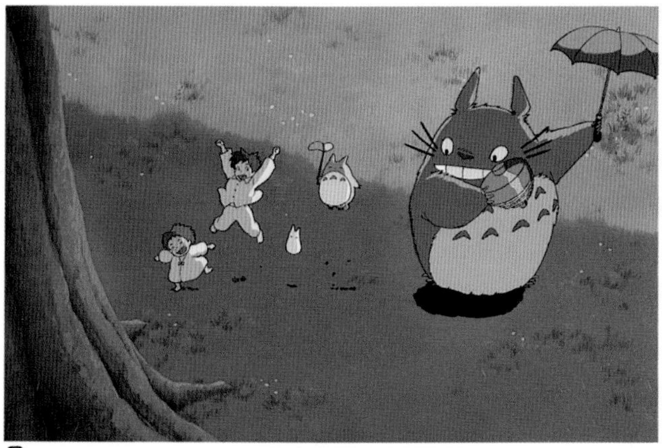

3

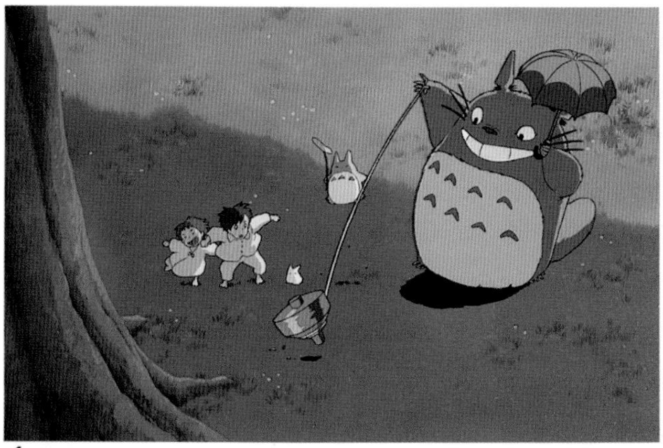

4

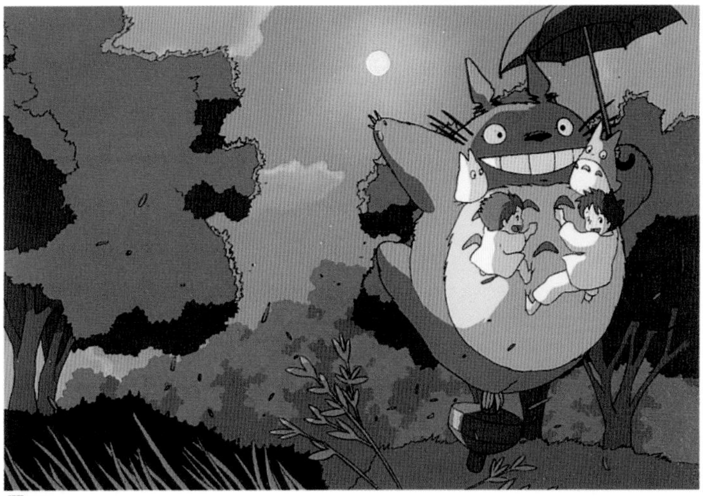

5

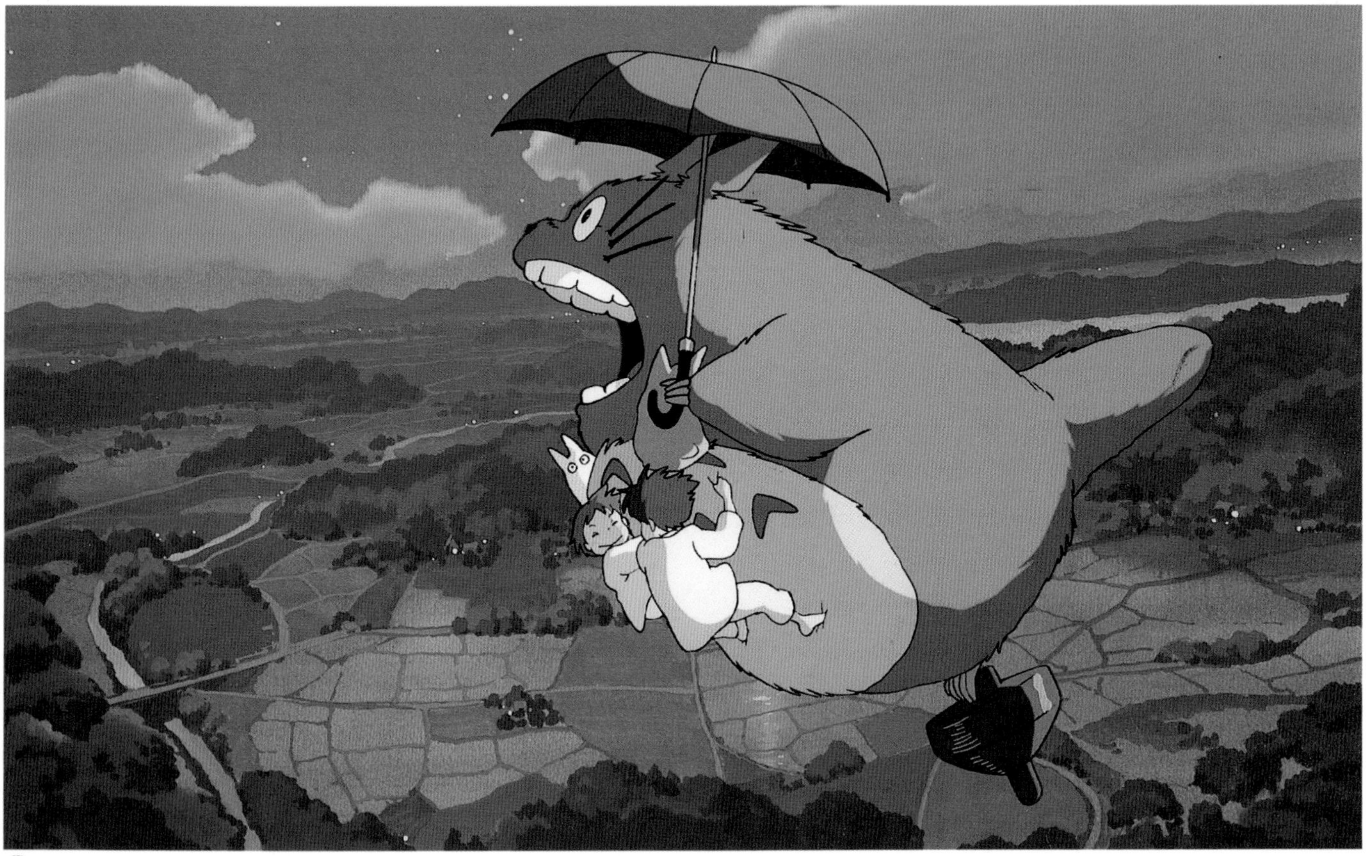

6

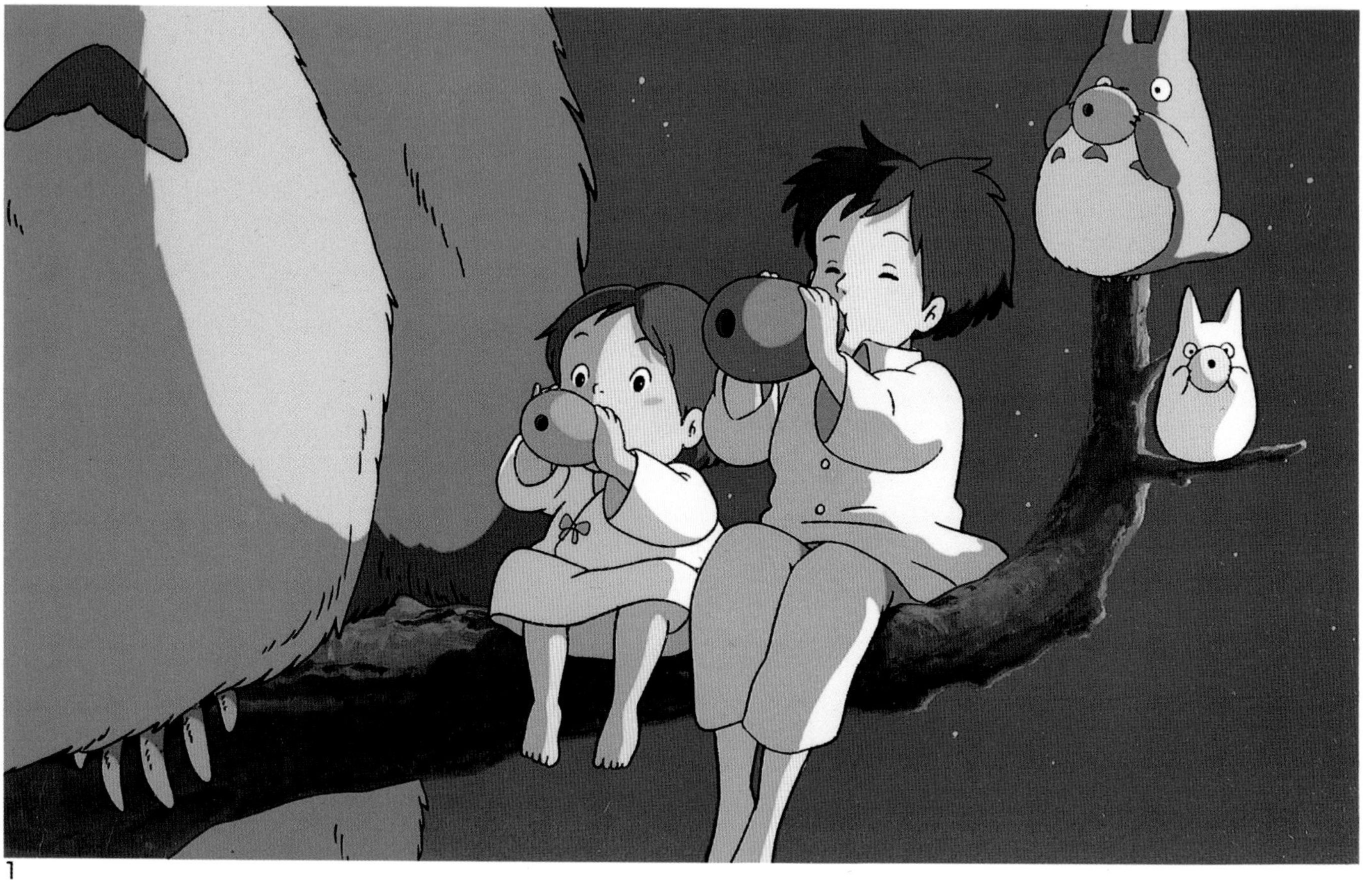

1

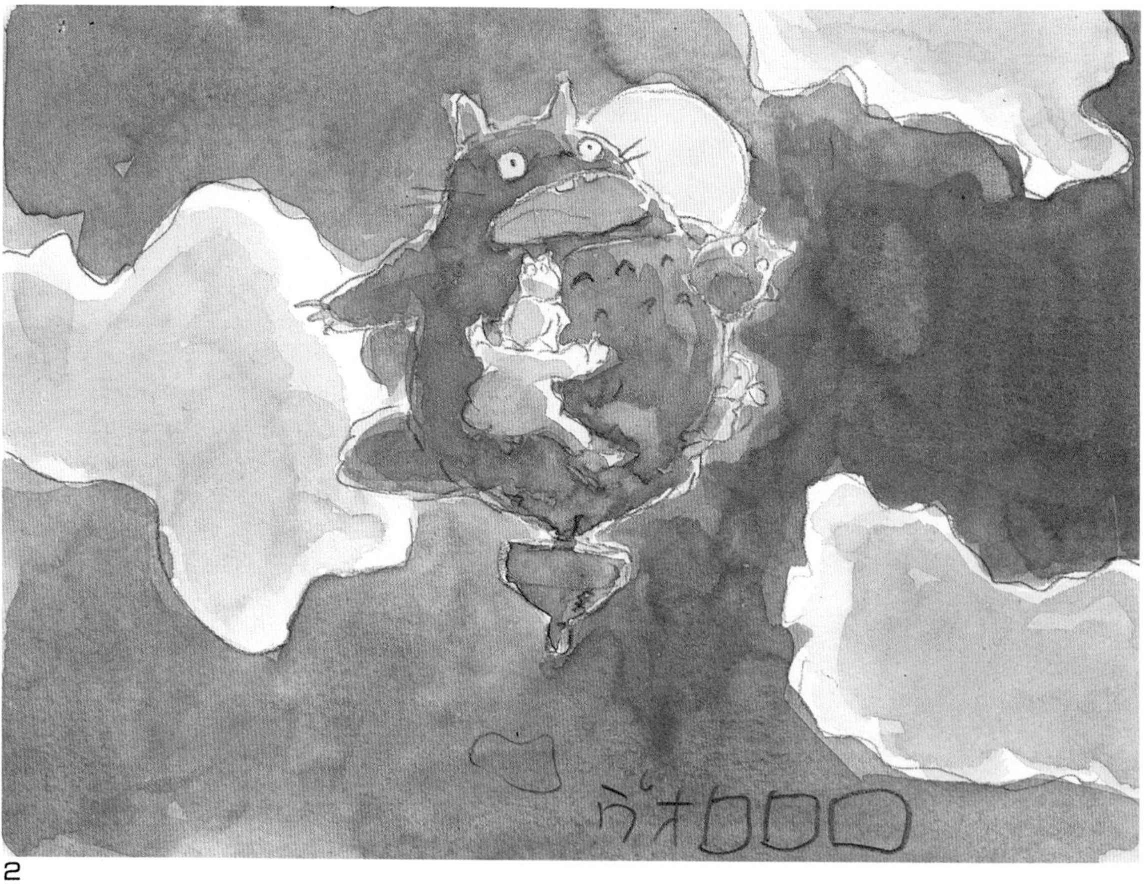
ヴオロロロ

2

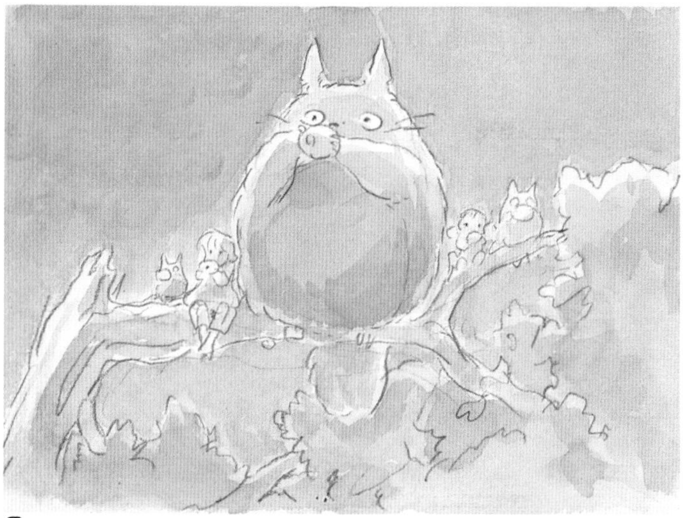

3

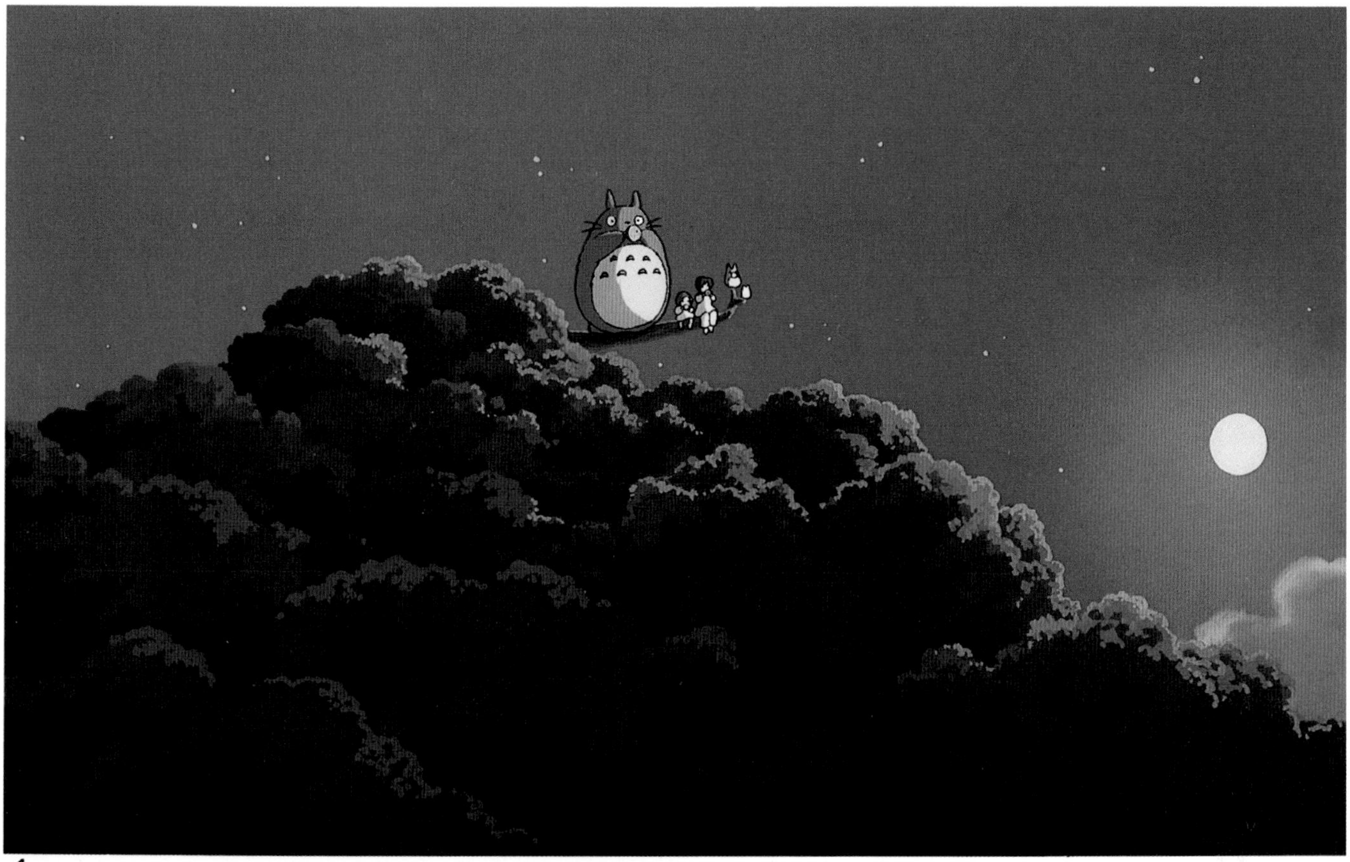

4

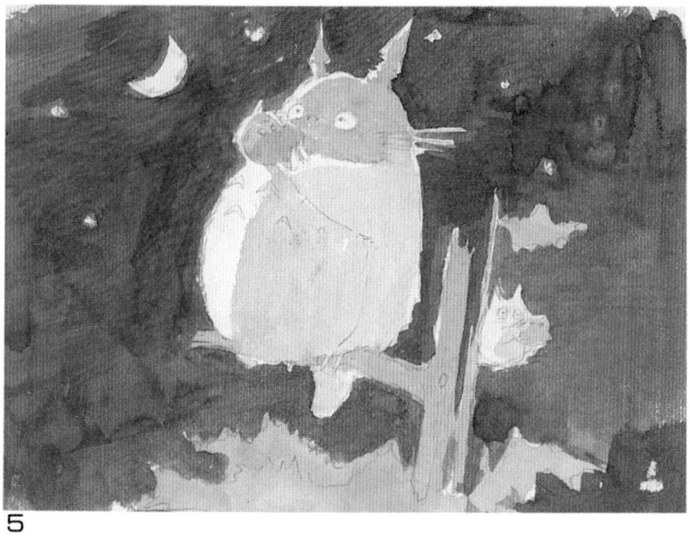

5

1 Satsuki and Mei join the Totoros in blowing into their ocarinas on top of the big camphor tree. *(cel art)*

2 Totoro flying in the sky with Satsuki and Mei clutching onto it. *(storyboard)*

3 Totoros blowing into their ocarinas on top of the big camphor tree. *(storyboard)*

4 Same as above. *(cel art)*

5 Totoros blowing into their ocarinas. *(concept sketch)*

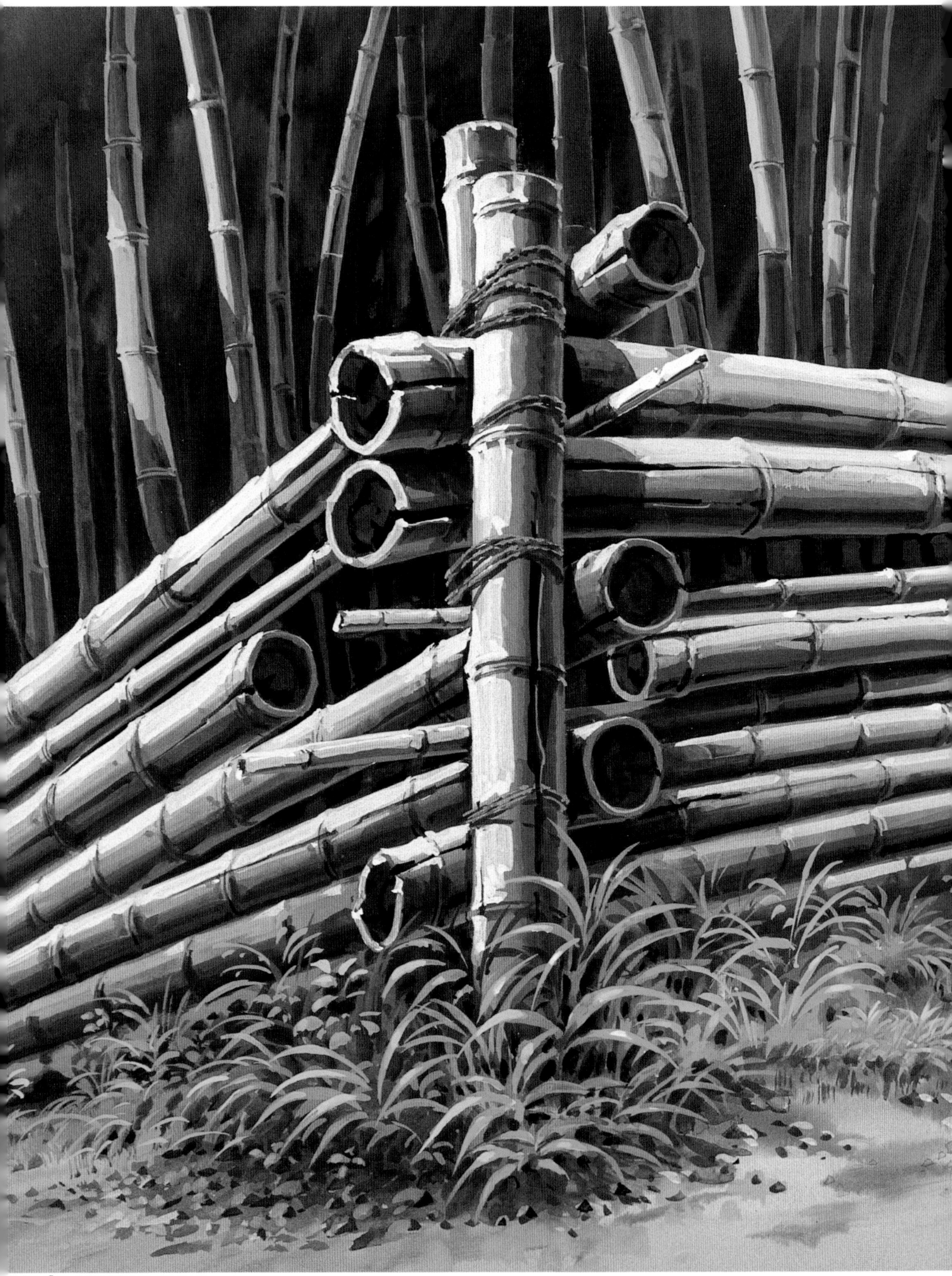

1

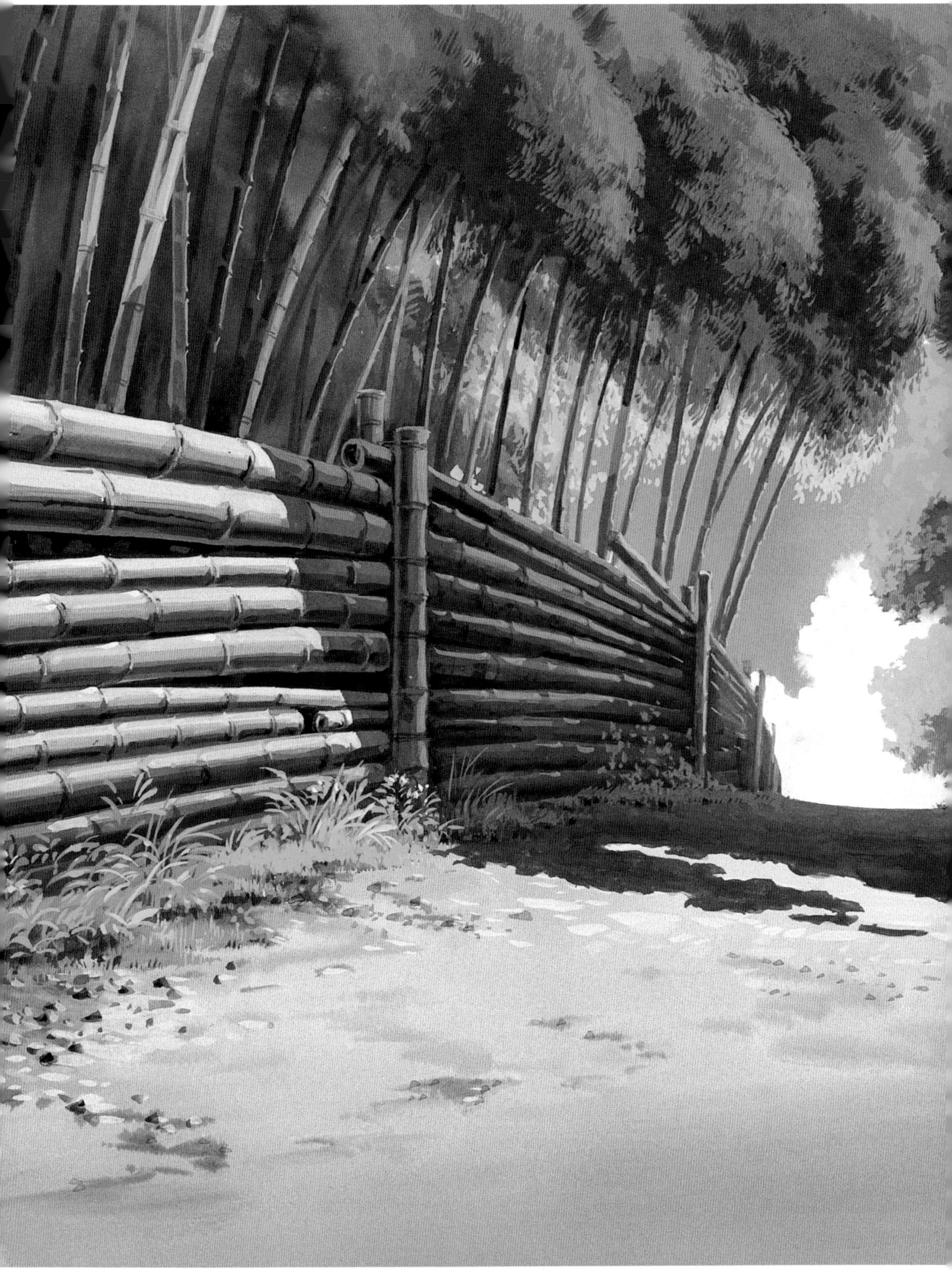

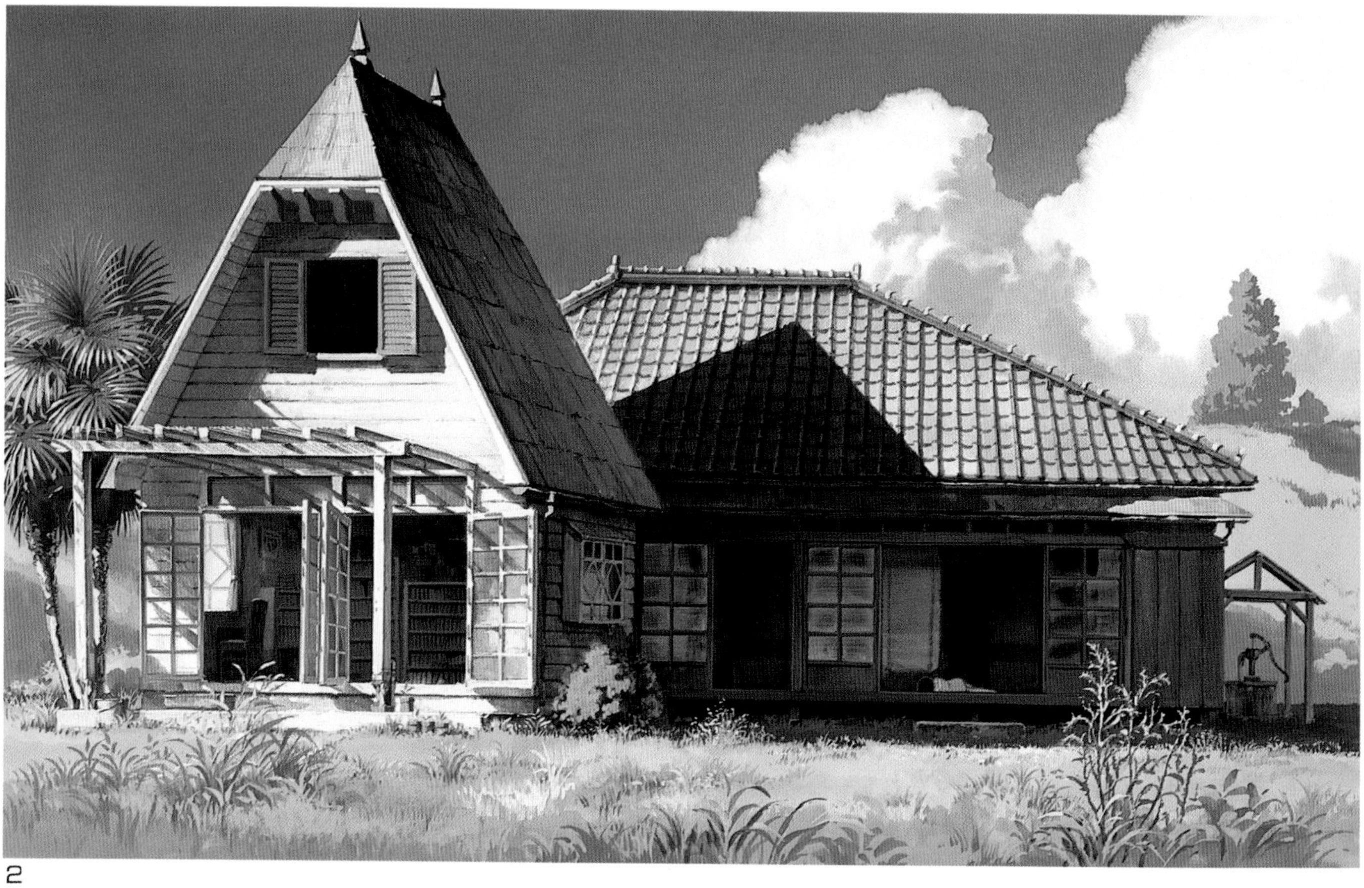

2

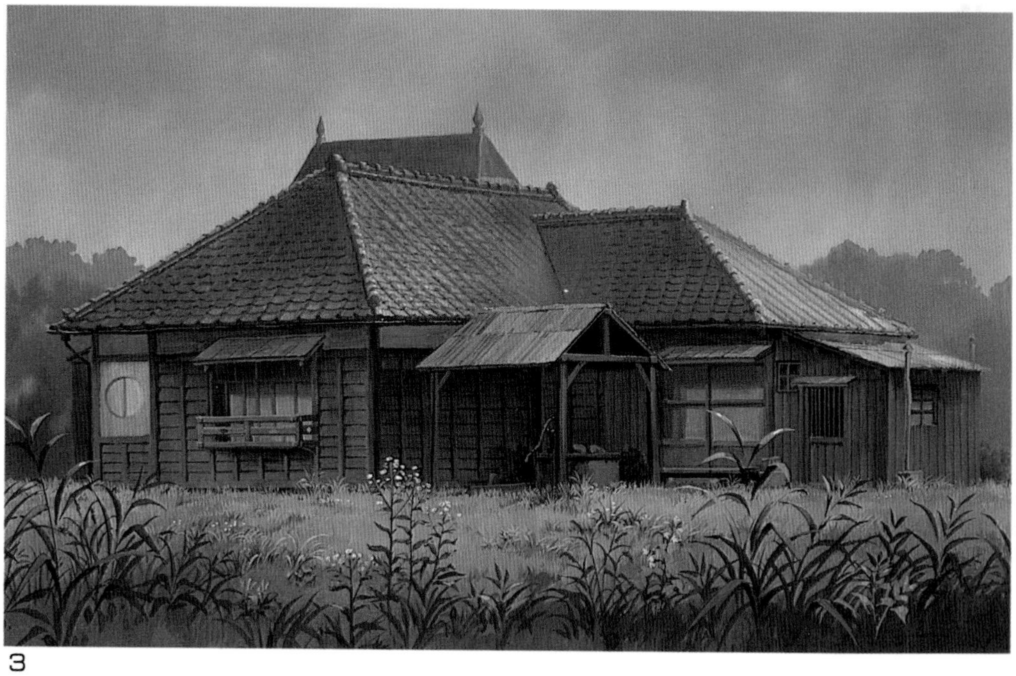

3

1 Bamboo wall in the bright summer sunlight. *(background)*

2 Late August afternoon at the Kusakabe residence. *(background)*

3 Late June sundown. Kusakabe residence after rain. *(background)*

4 Kusakabe residence in May. The sunlight is darker than the same light in August. *(background)*

5 July, the moonlight scattering across the night sky above the Kusakabe residence. *(background)*

4

5

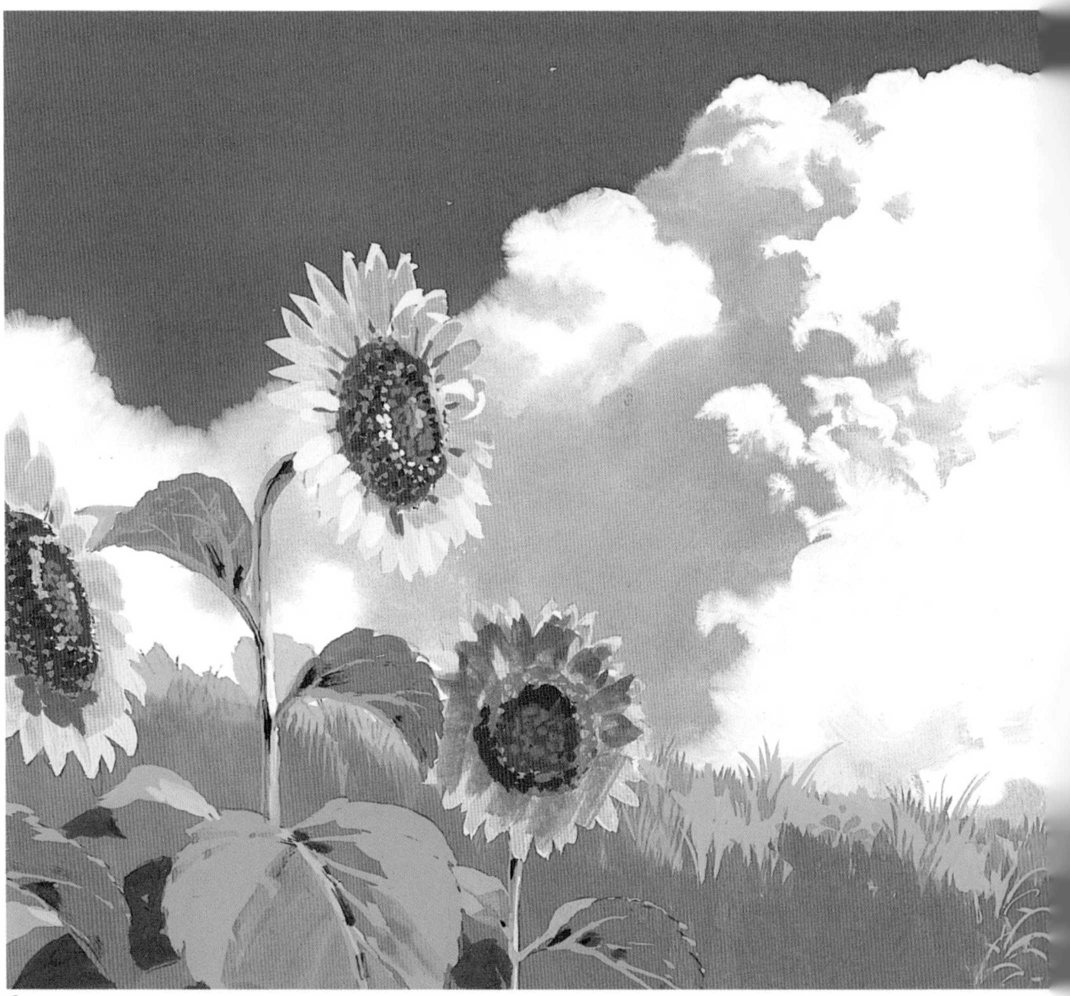

1

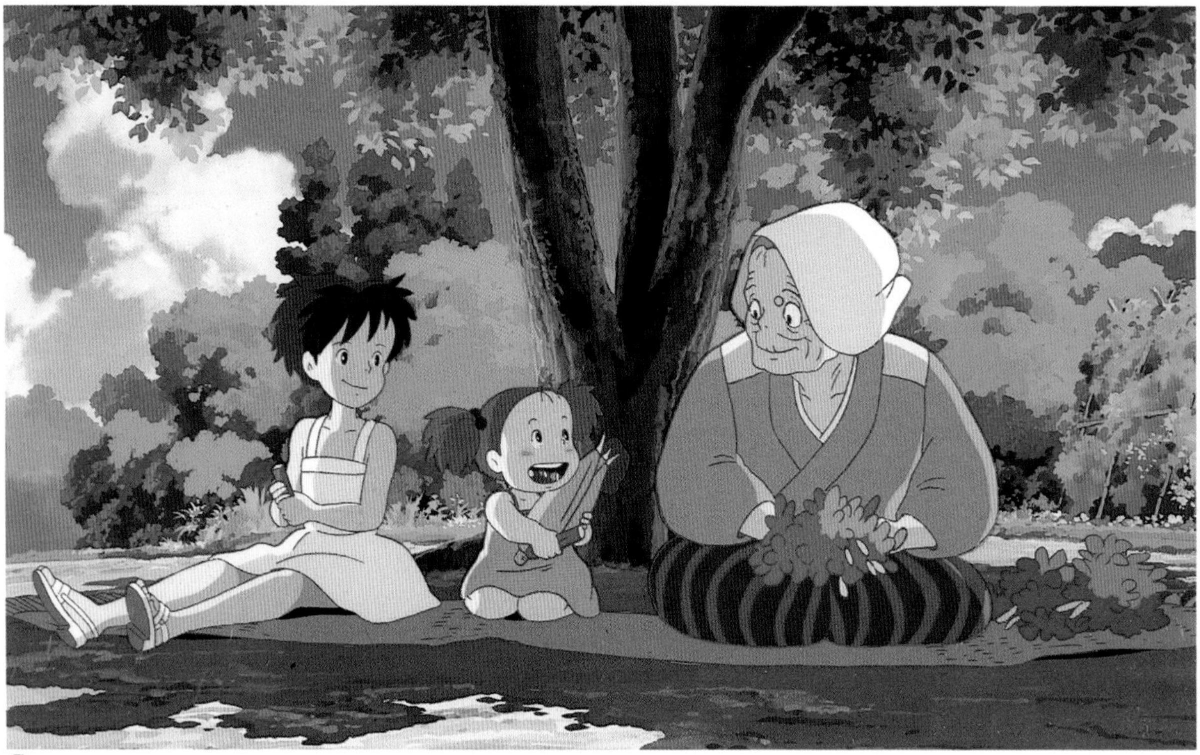

2

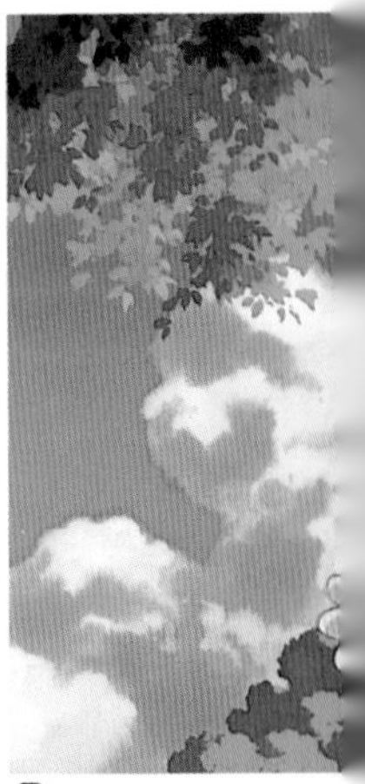

3

1 Sunflowers blossom under the water bank. *(background)*

2 Satsuki and Mei chewing on cucumbers in the tree shade. *(cel art)*

3 Chewing on a fresh cucumber. *(background)*

4-6 Road lined with Holly Hedges. Bamboo alley, hedge around Kanta's head family house.

4

5

6

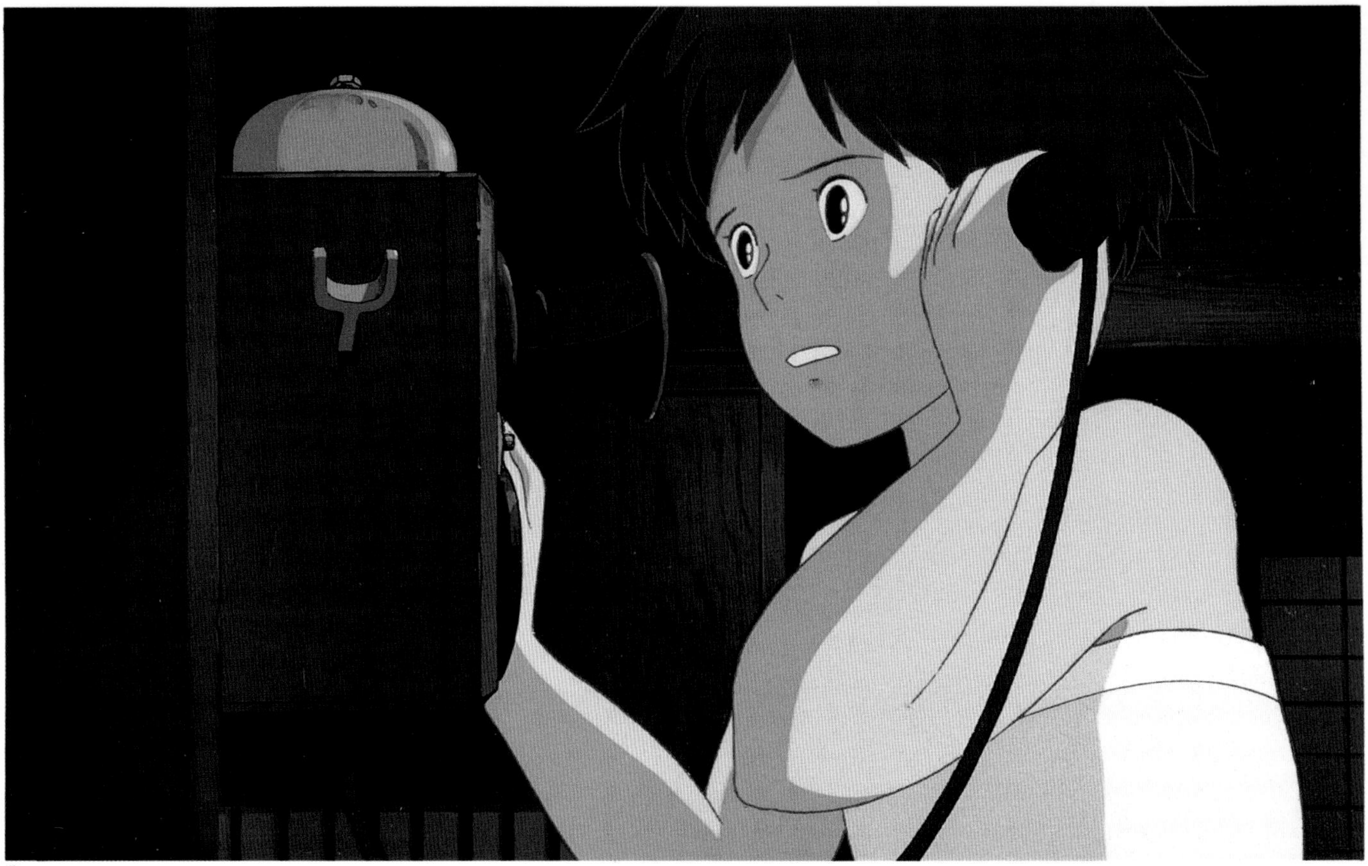

1

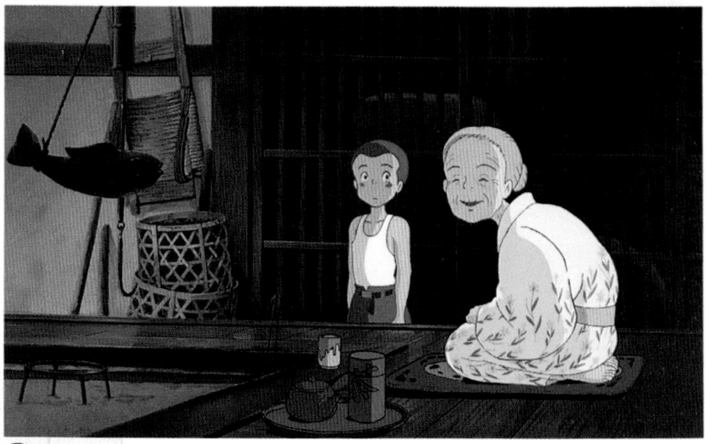

2

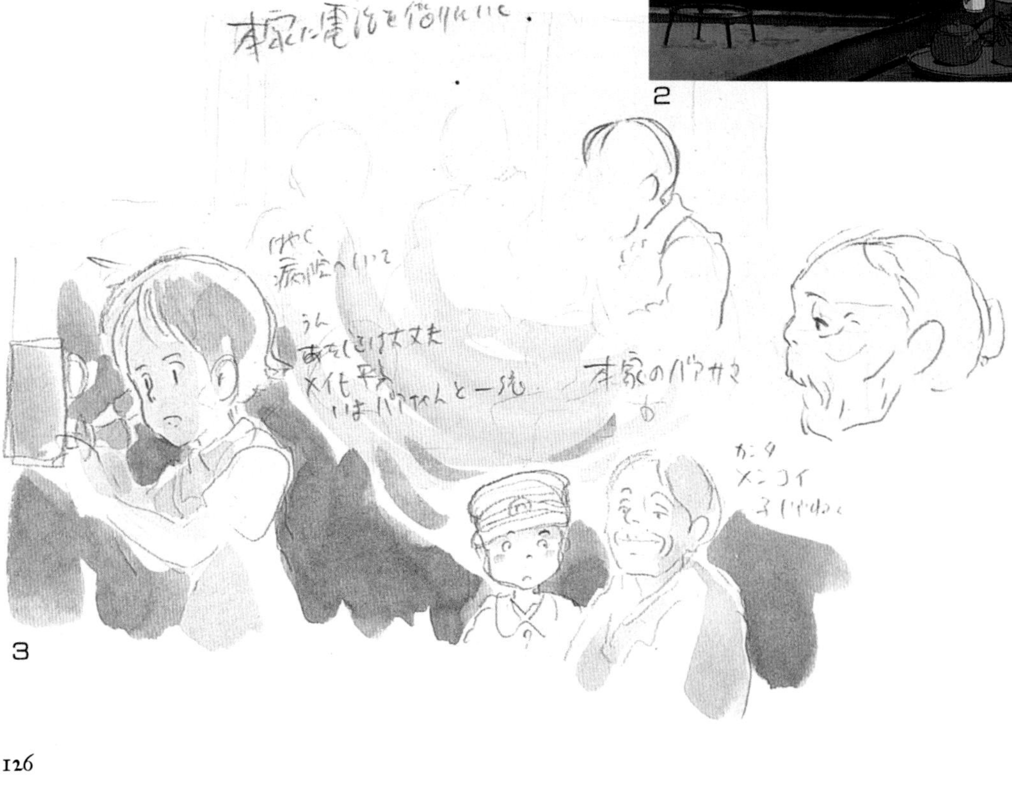
本家に電話を借りにいく.
はやく
病院へいって
うん
あたしは大丈夫
メイも平気
いまバアちゃんと一緒
本家のバアサマ
カンタ
メンコイ
子じゃねぇ

3

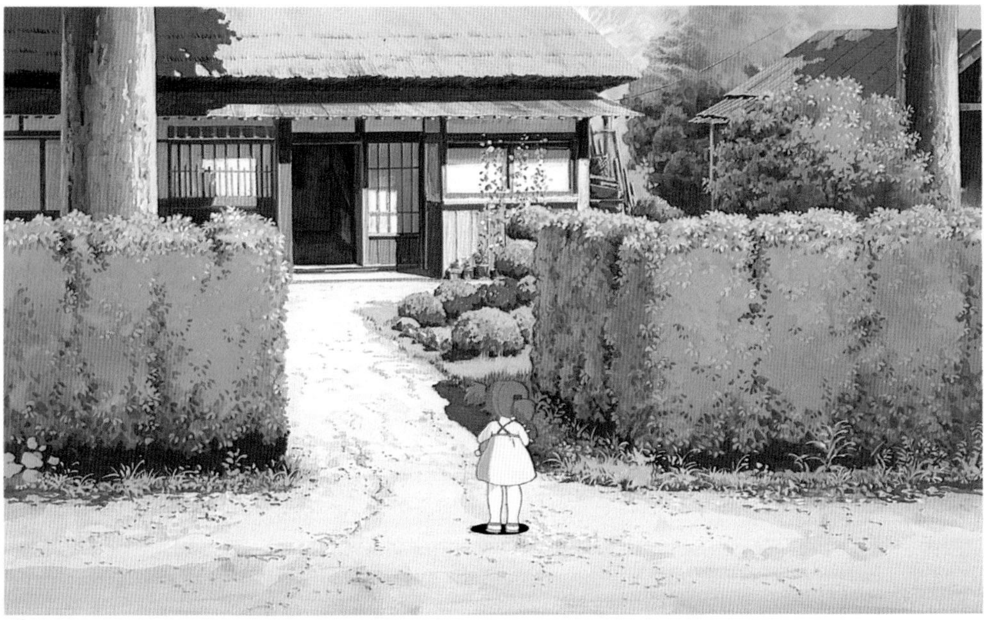

4

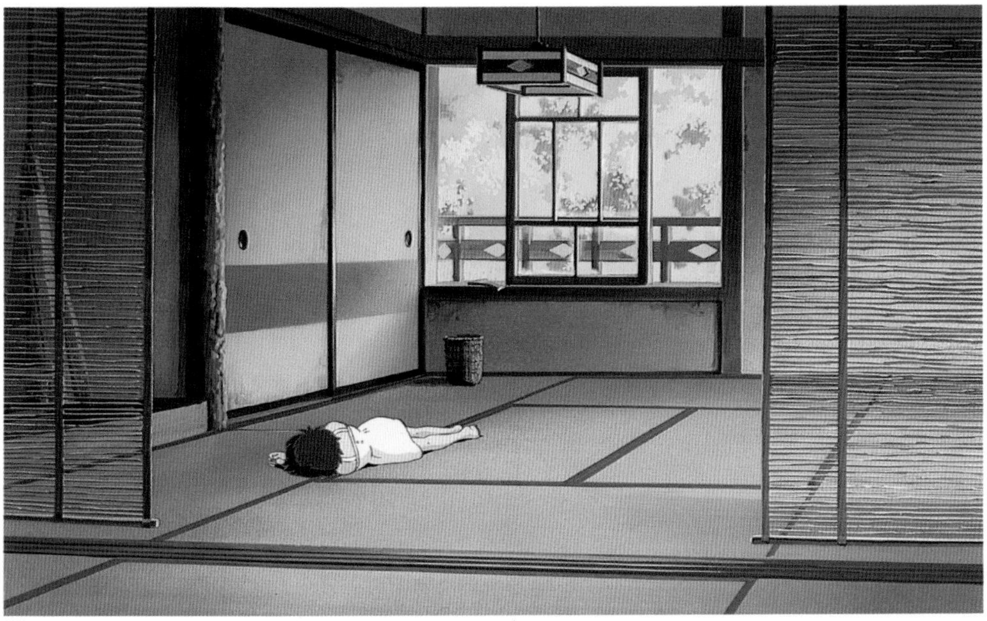

5

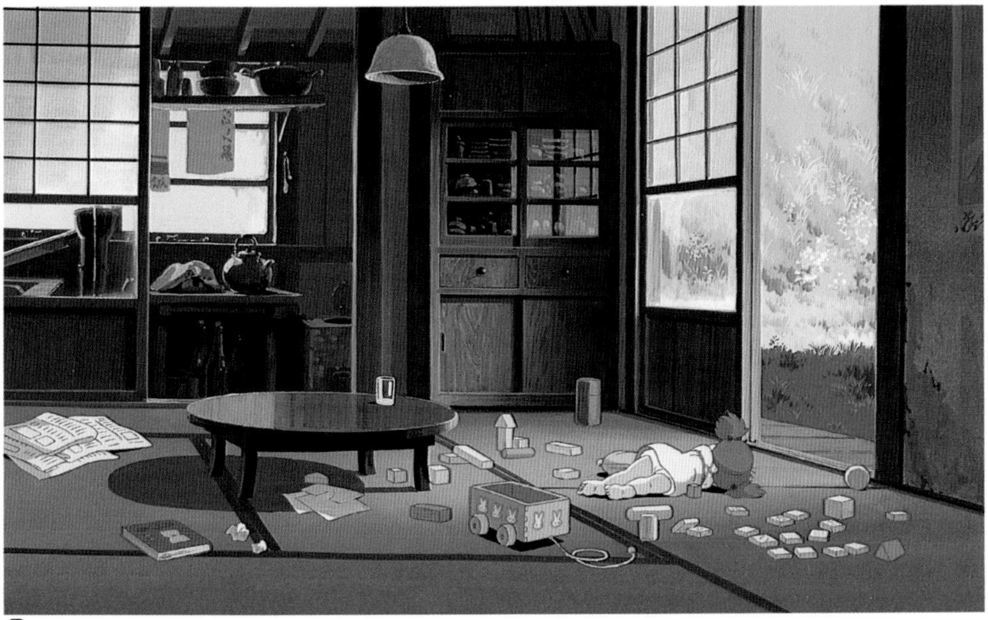

6

1 Satsuki borrows the phone at Kanta's uncle's house. *(cel art)*

2 The matriarch of Kanta's family adores Satsuki while a nervous Kanta looks on. *(cel art)*

3 Concept sketches of 1, 2.

4 Mei waits in front of the head family's house.

5, 6 Satsuki napping in the living room and Mei who falls asleep hugging a corn husk in the dining room.

"Parents misunderstand kids. For instance, they might react to this situation by saying, `How could they be so heartless and sleep through this? They are so clueless.´ But the kids aren't heartless at all. They can hardly stand. Sleeping is their form of self-defense. So the fact that they're sleeping only indicates how dire their situation is." *(Miyazaki)*

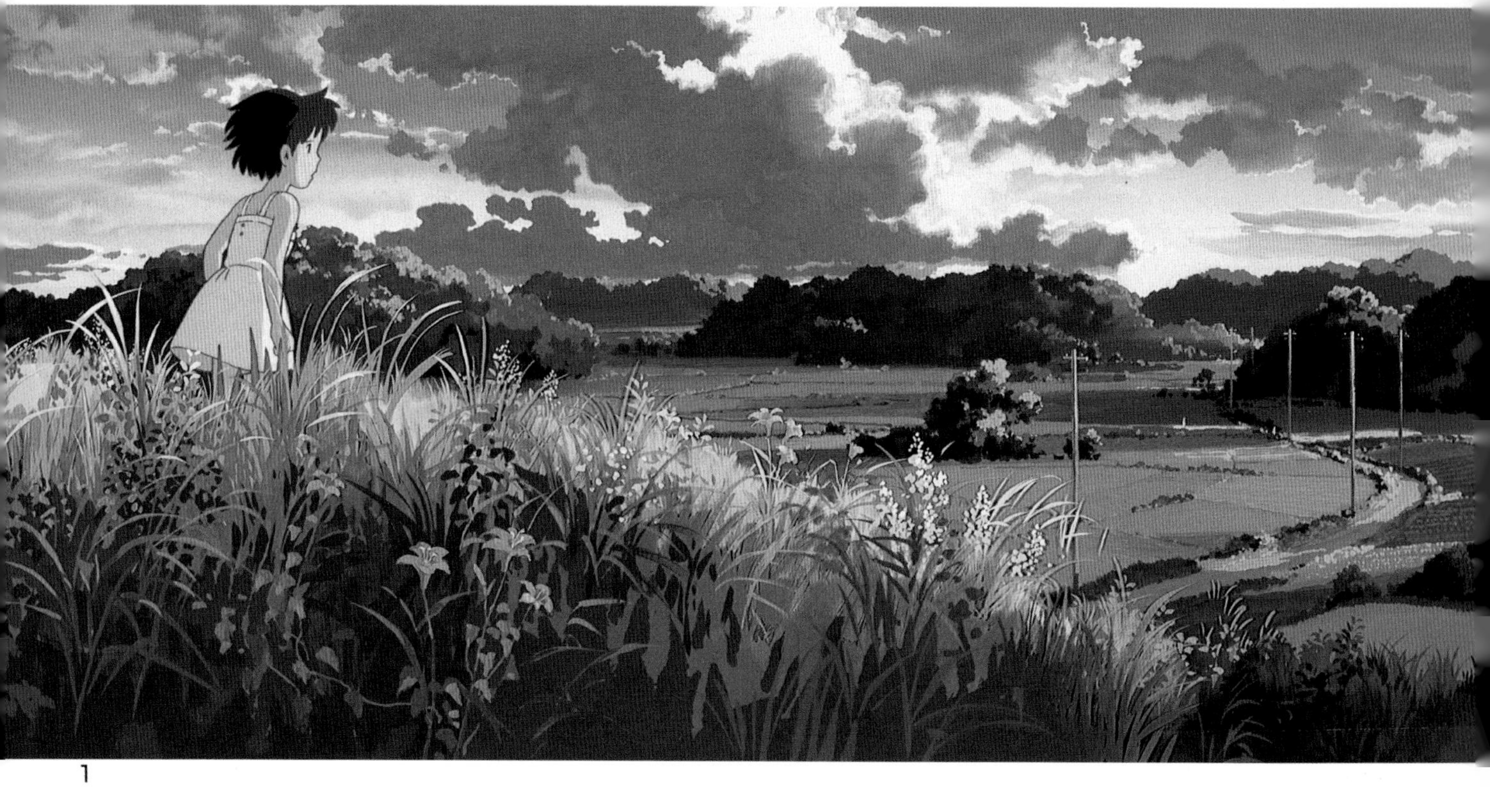

1

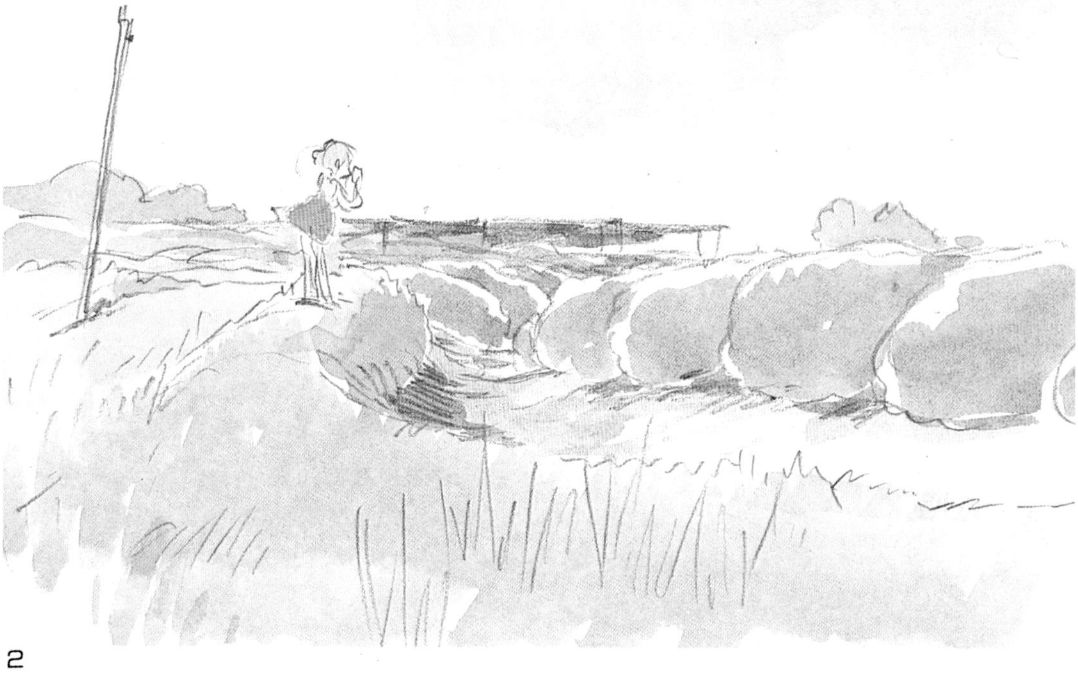

2

1 From the small hillside bathed in the remaining light, Satsuki looks for Mei. *(cel art)*

2, 3 Satsuki looks for Mei, who's lost. *(concept sketch)*

4 Satsuki runs as fast as she can, holding her sandals. *(cel art)*

5 Kanta looks for Mei, straddling an adults' bicycle. *(cel art)*

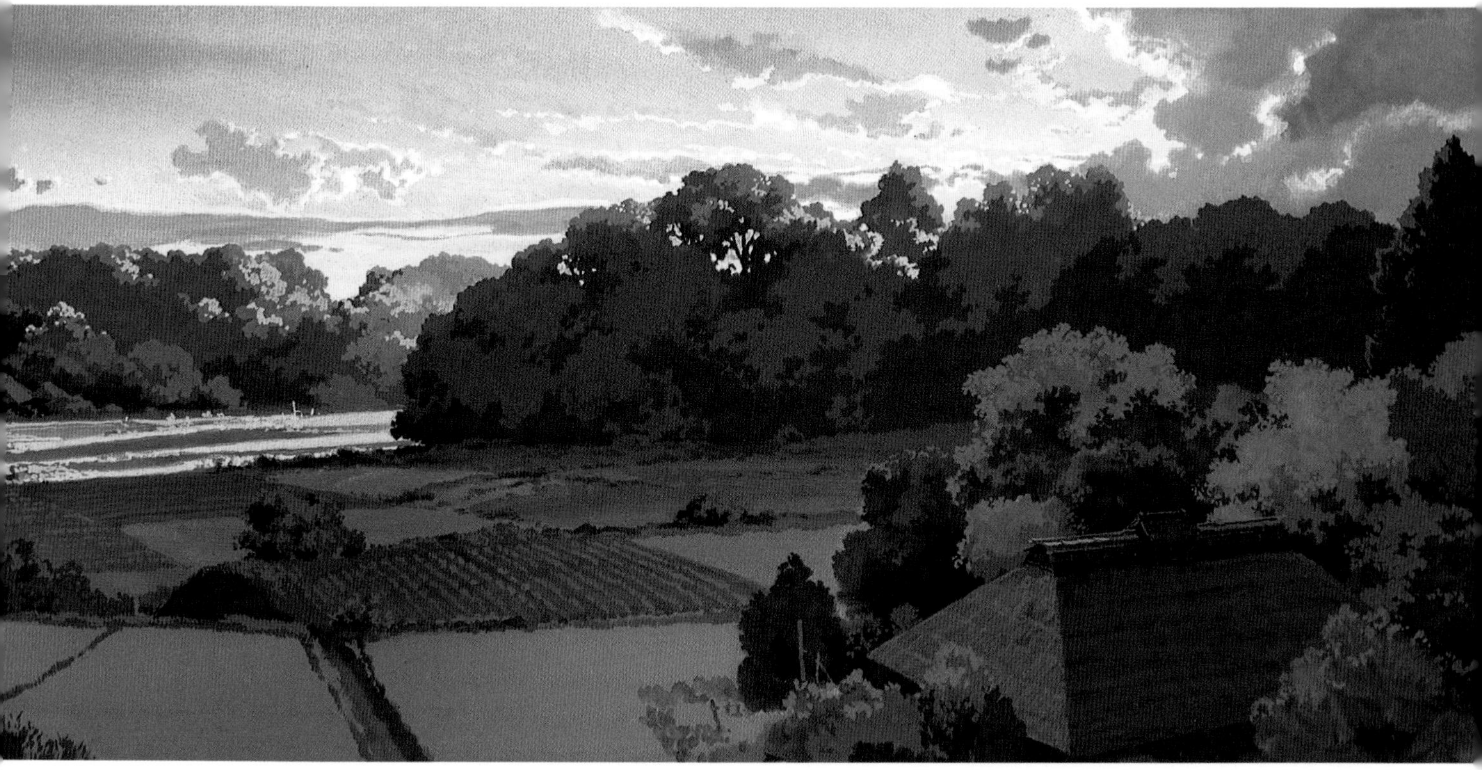

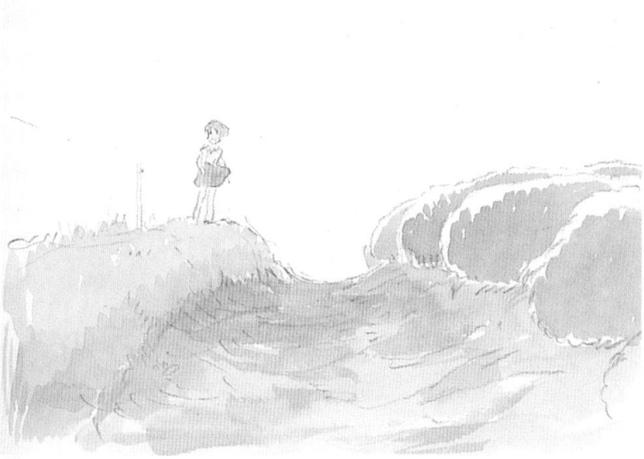

3

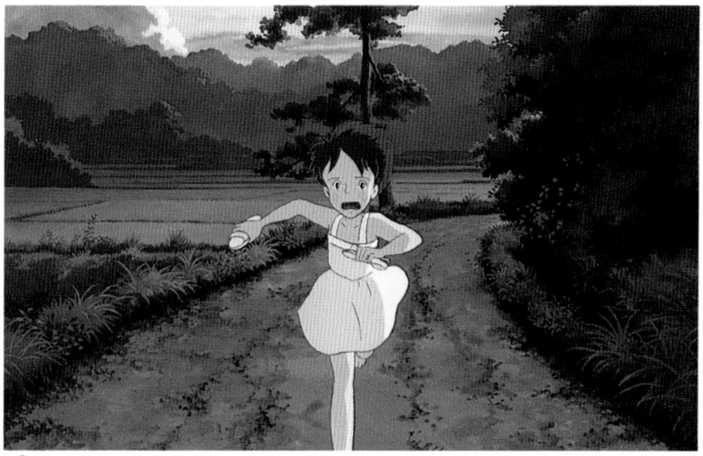

4

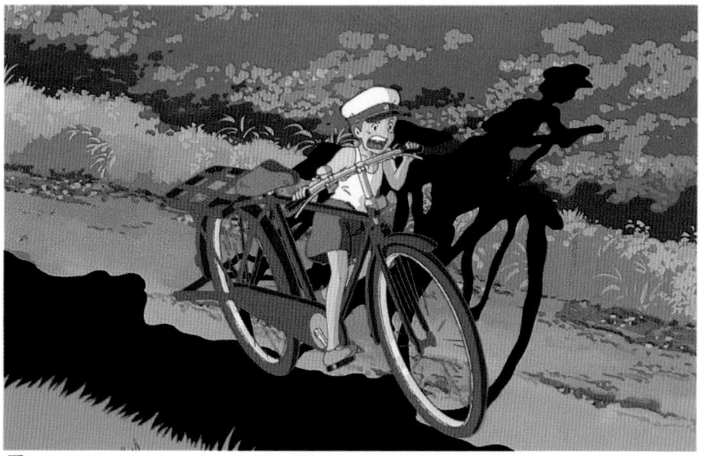

5

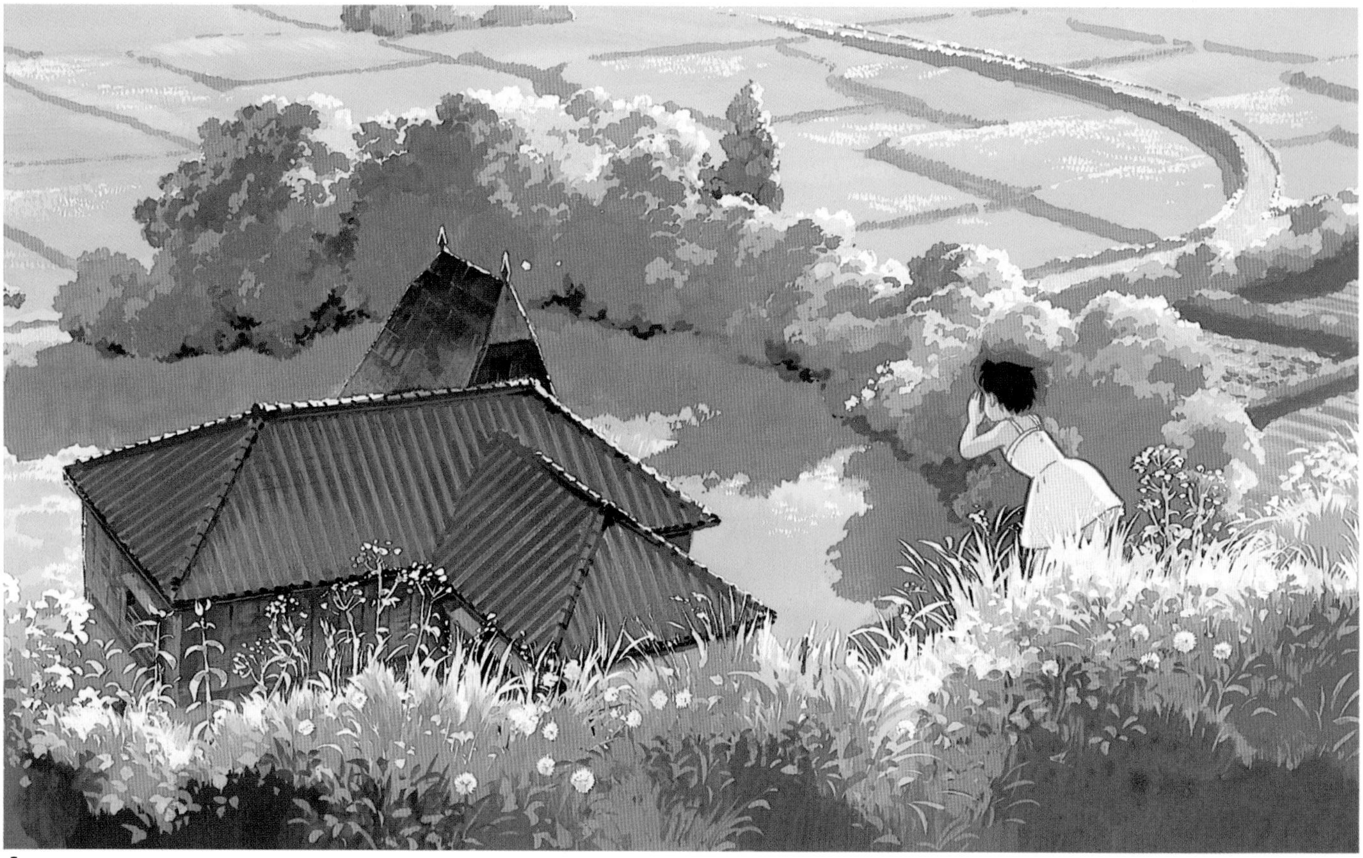

1

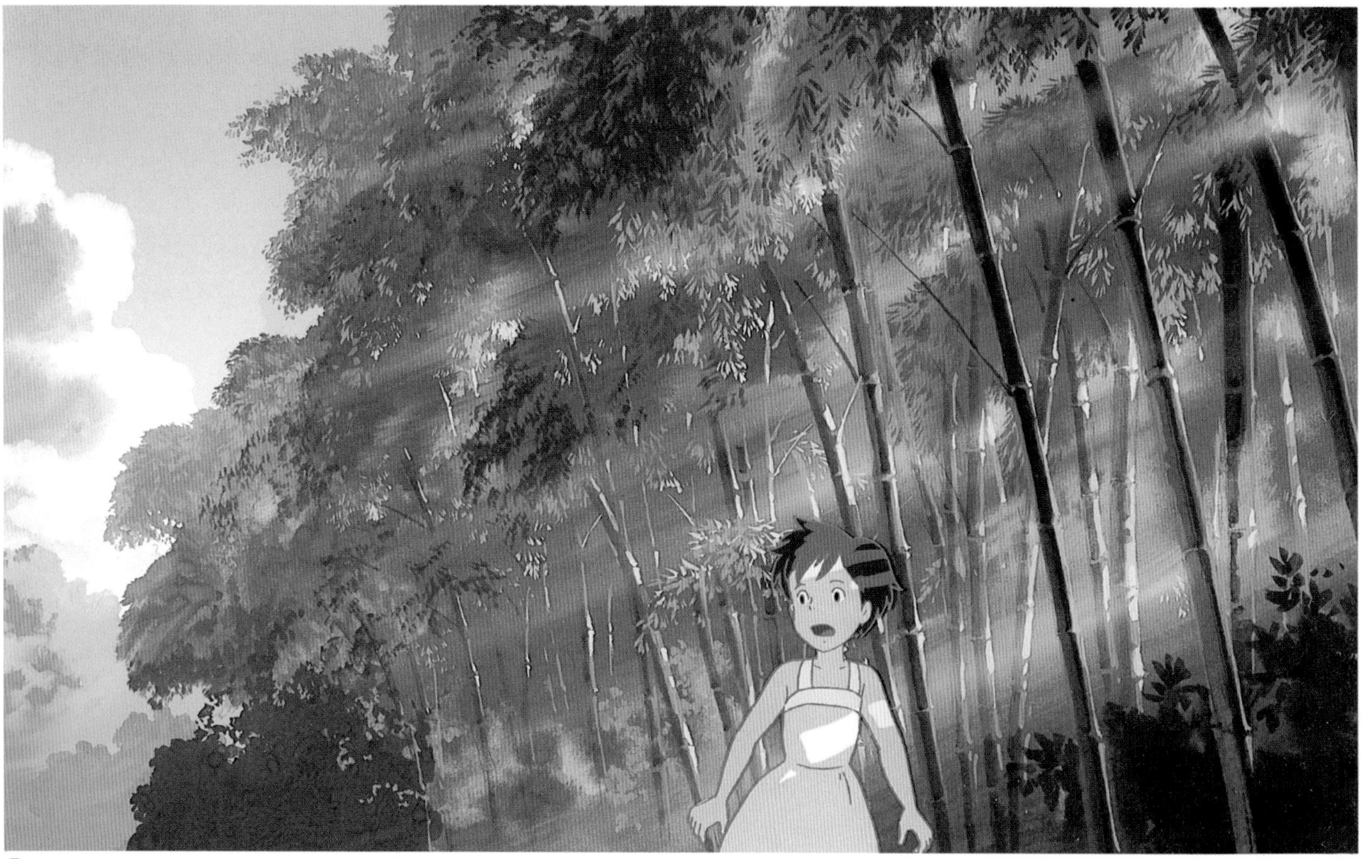

2

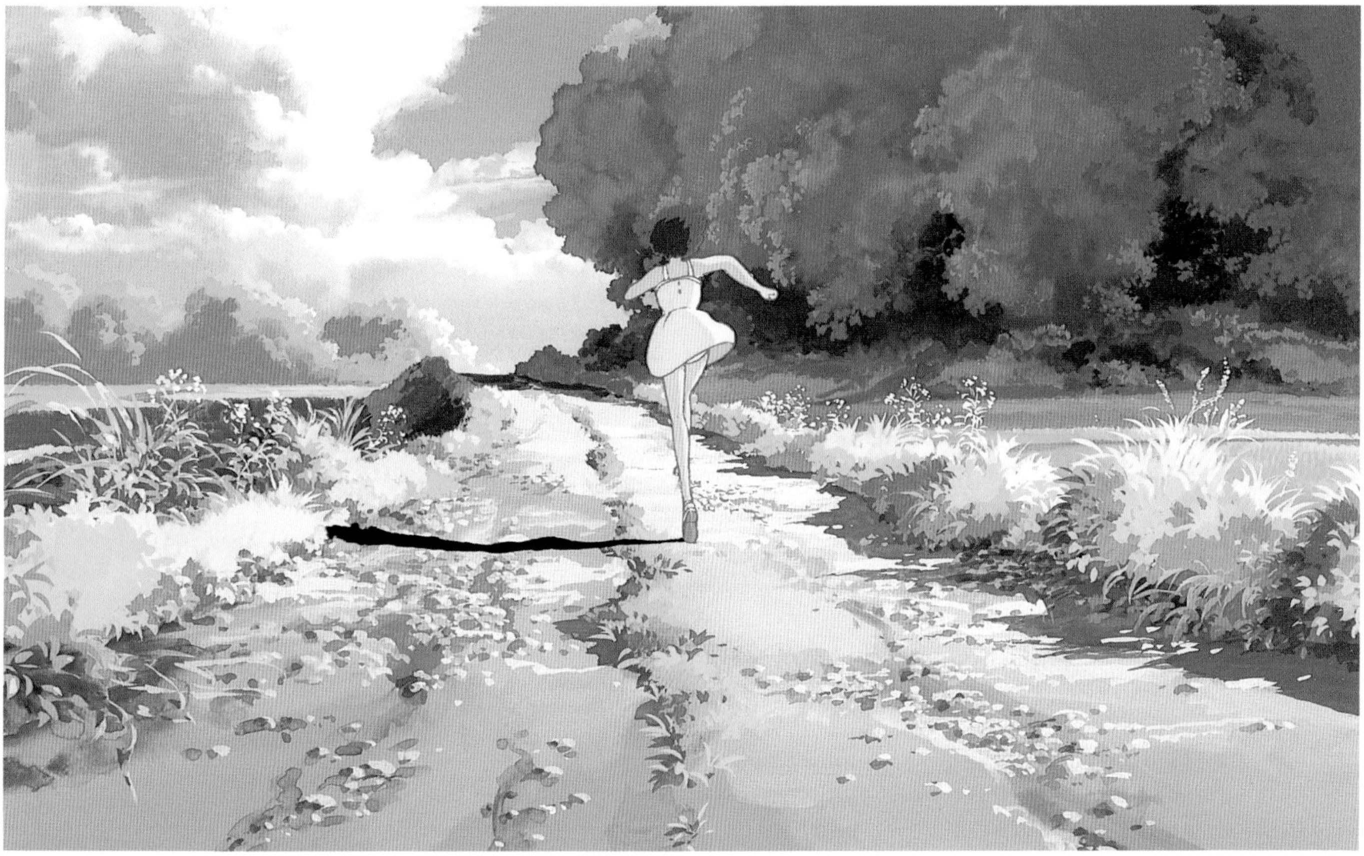

3

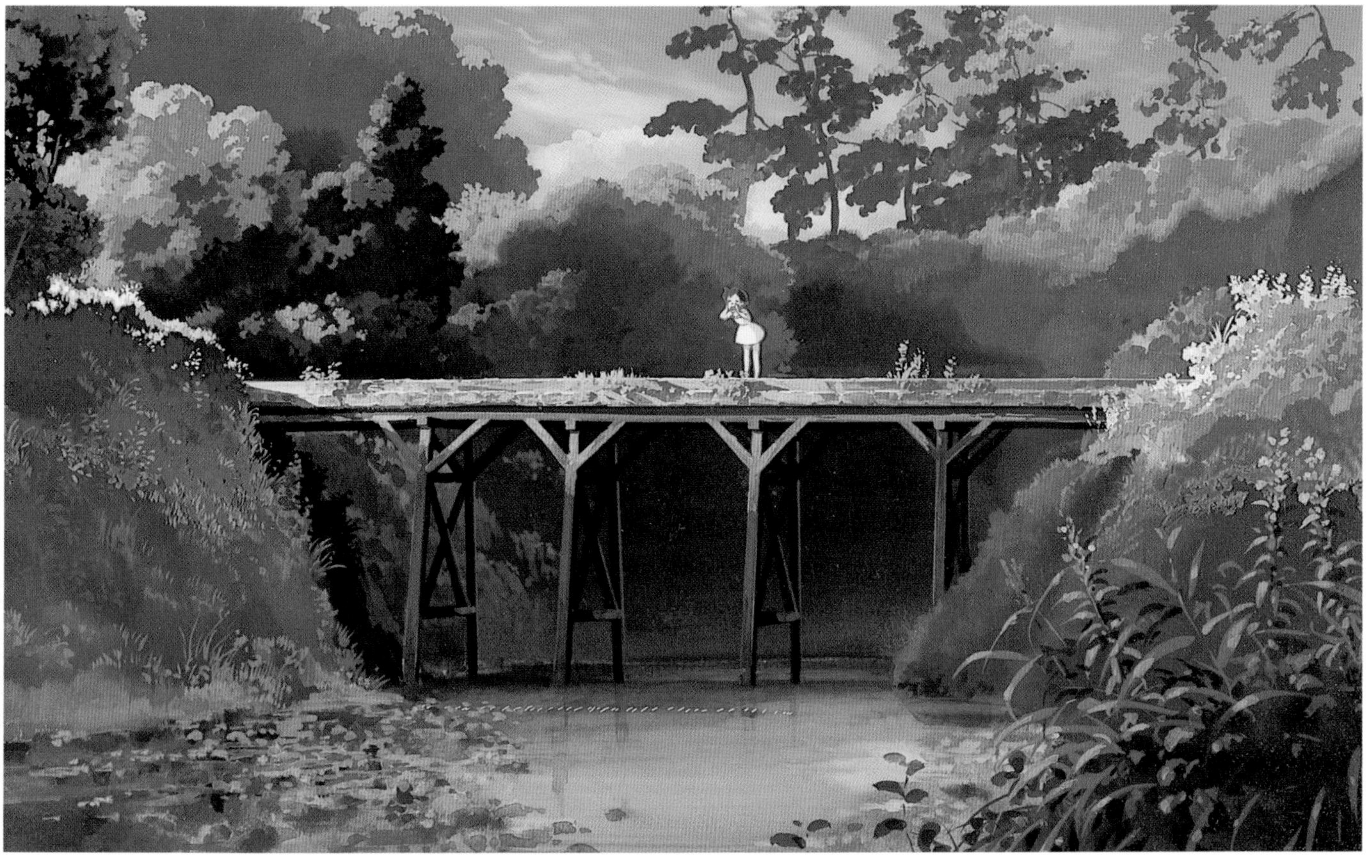

4

1-4 Scenes of Satsuki searching for Mei *(cel art)*

1 The secret passageway's gate cloaked in the dusk light. *(concept art)*

2 Sunset after the brightest hour of the day. *(background)*

"Dusk light isn't really red even when the sun sets quite a bit. The red around the sun can only be seen through a telescope, and the red only appears after sunset. That's why we avoided tinting the light with red." *(Oga)*

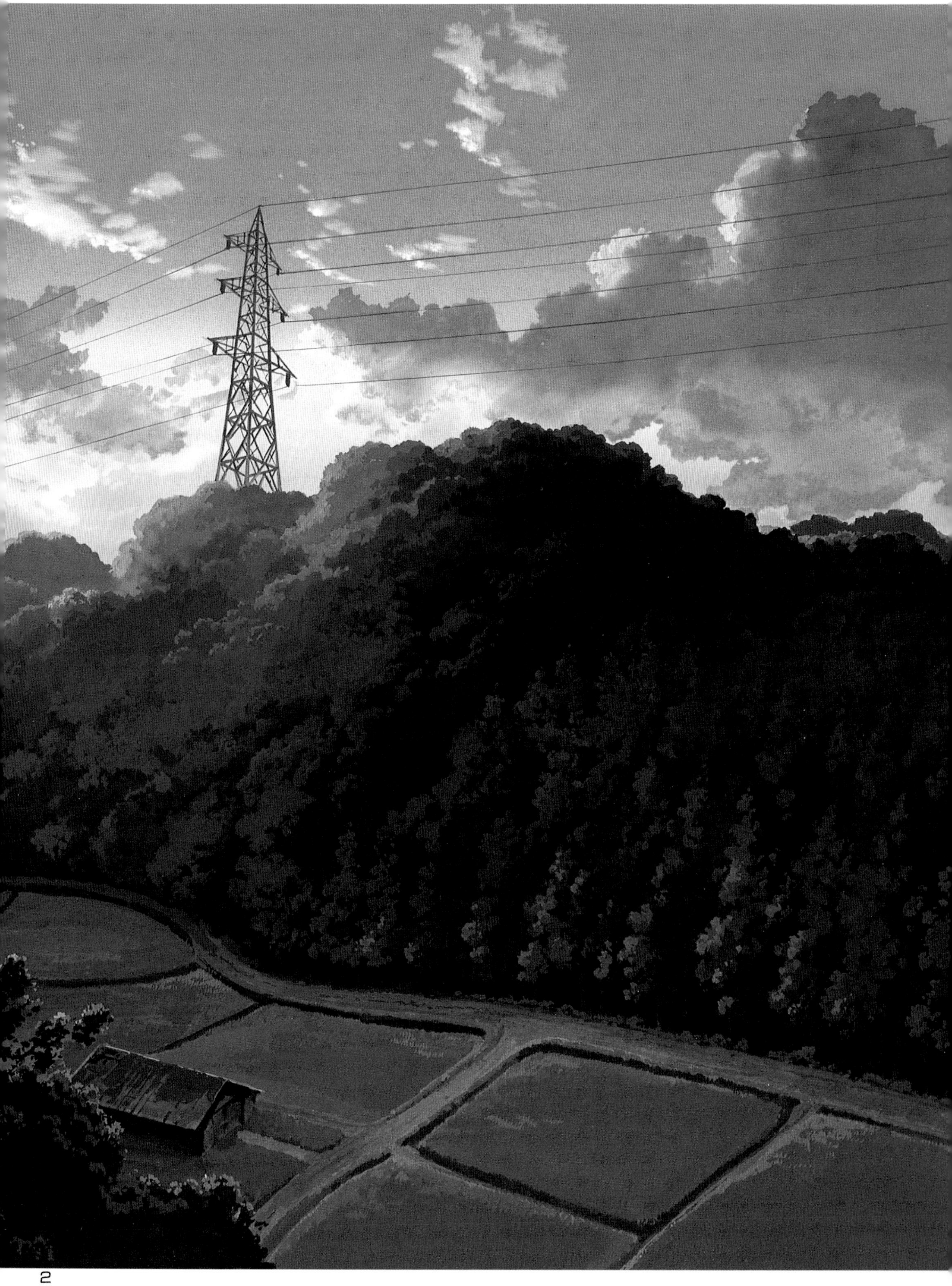

2

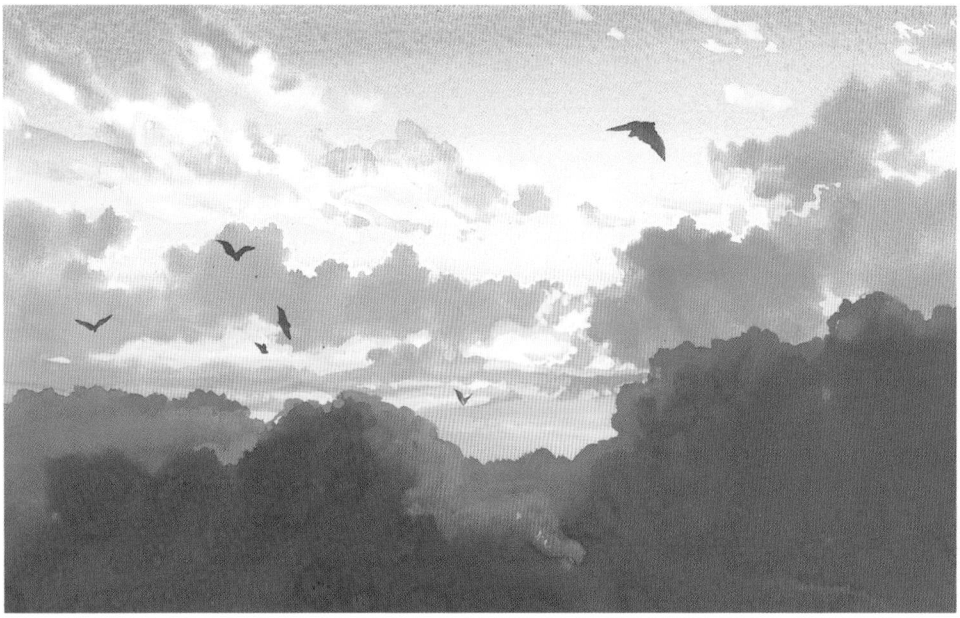
1

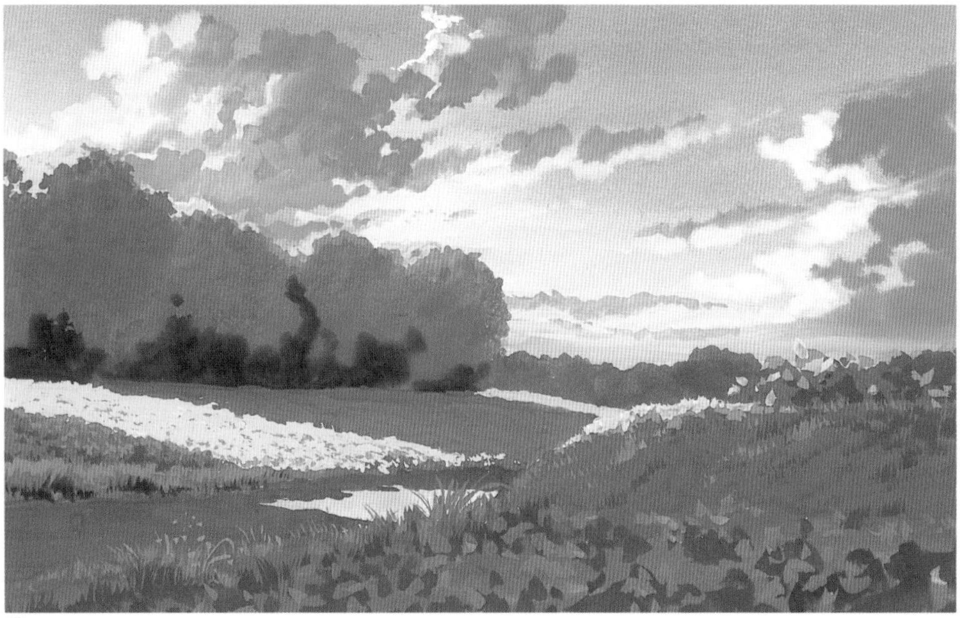
2

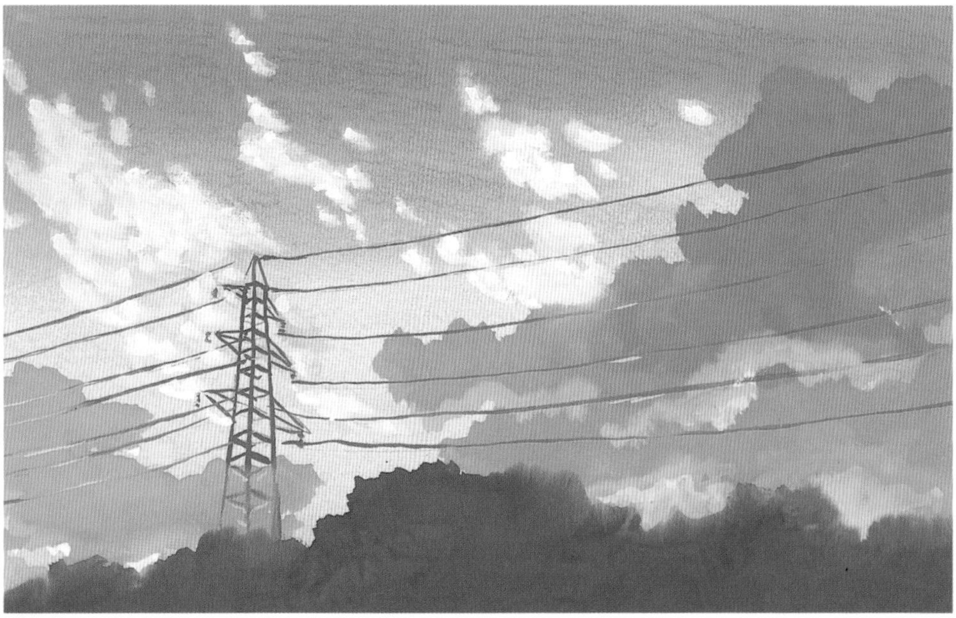
3

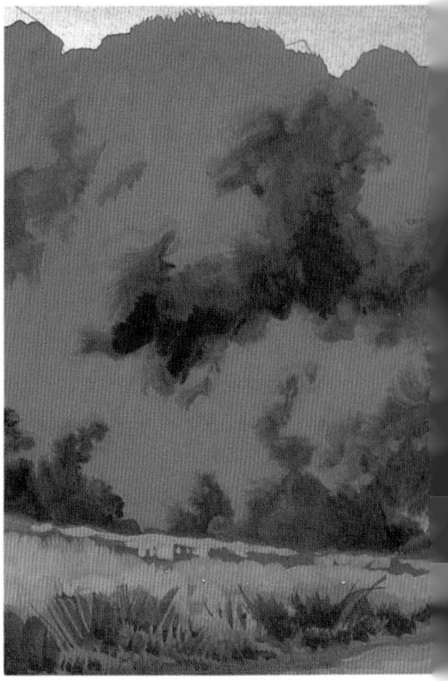
4

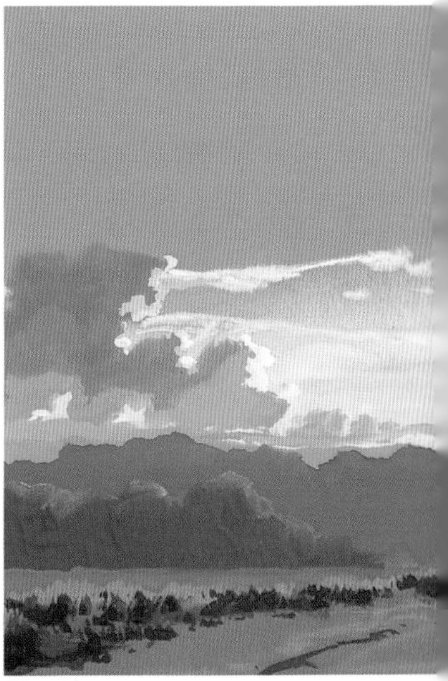
5

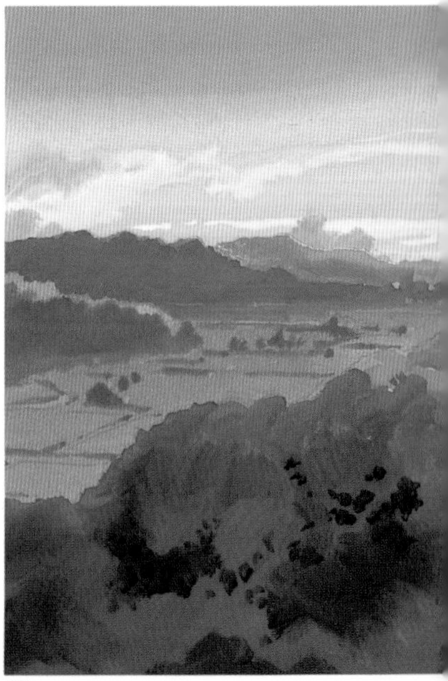
6

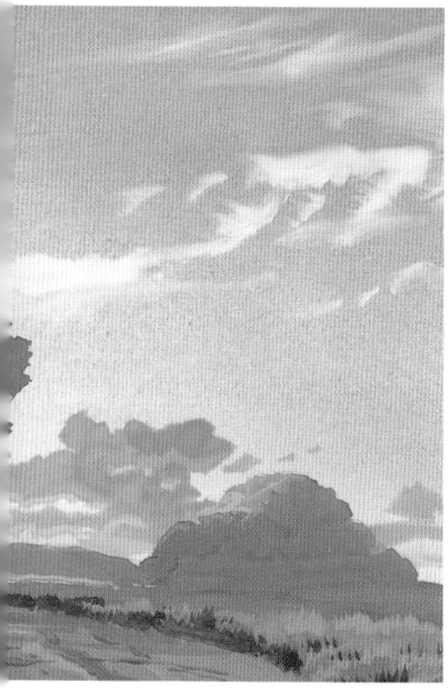

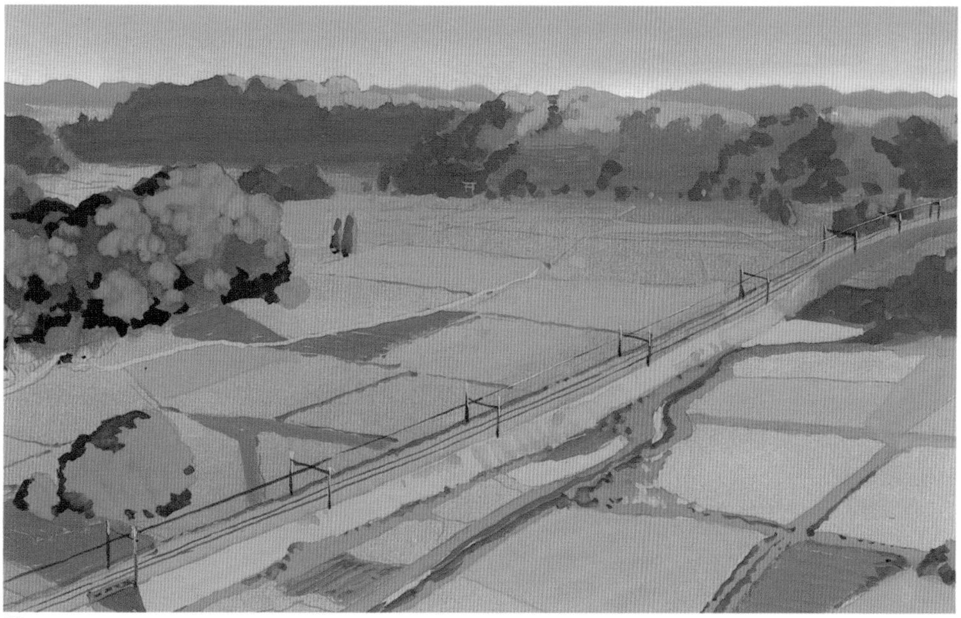

7

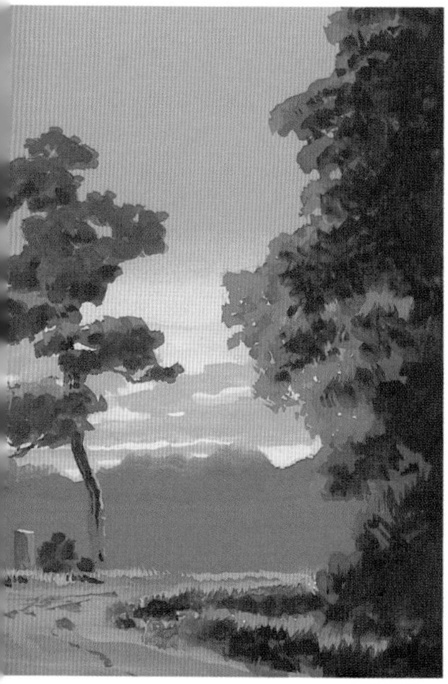

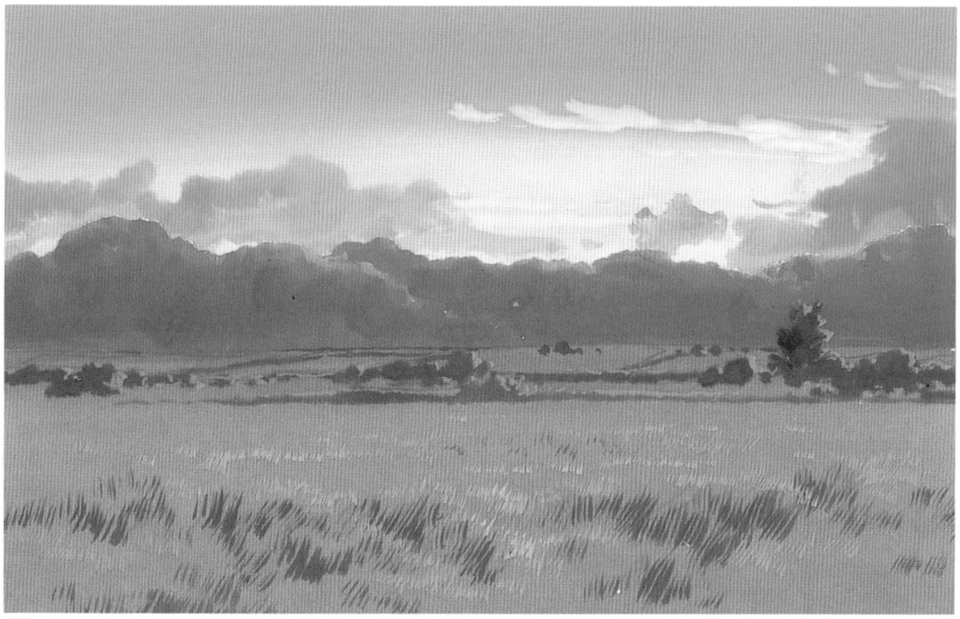

8

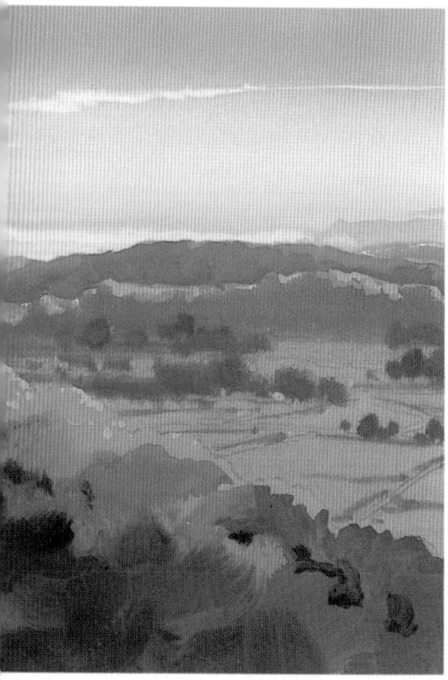

1-8 In order to depict sunset, art boards were drawn for every shot during the scene where Satsuki looks for Mei who has lost her way.

"I'm always conscious of lighting. The image can't be interesting without [proper] lighting. The entire last quarter of the last sequence begins with the noon sun gradually tipping west as it sets, and then ends with the afterglow as it fades into the night. I'm sure Oga had a difficult time completing this sequence. We thought of having it get dark somewhere in the middle, but that would have been too much. It would have been like, `It's sunset. Look how bright red it is,´ which would have been the easy way out. We tempered the afterglow instead. Darkness is creeping in when they come home from the hospital, so the tones for the backgrounds should also be getting darker. I don't think the execution was perfect, but by restraining flashy colors, we were able to faithfully depict the shift in light and colors over the last quarter of the final sequence." *(Miyazaki)*

1 Satsuki climbing the tunnel leading to Totoro's tunnel. The tunnel is filled with soot sprites and mock mushrooms (creatures disguised as mushrooms). *(cel art)*

2 Satsuki leaps out of the wall tunnel into Totoro's cave. *(cel art)*

3 Totoro's cave *(background)*

"At first, we were thinking of a dug-out hollow with a wooden grain, but it just didn't look right. What Miyazaki had in mind was a clean cave, like an arts and crafts room. When wood looks smooth in a drawing, the grain has to be clear, so it ends up looking like new building material. So we ended up abandoning that idea. Instead, we decided to add moss. But you know how moist moss is. The Totoros probably wouldn't find that very enticing, so we illuminated the interior to get rid of the musky feel, adding pretty flowers in bloom, and created a different world. That's how that scene evolved." *(Oga)*

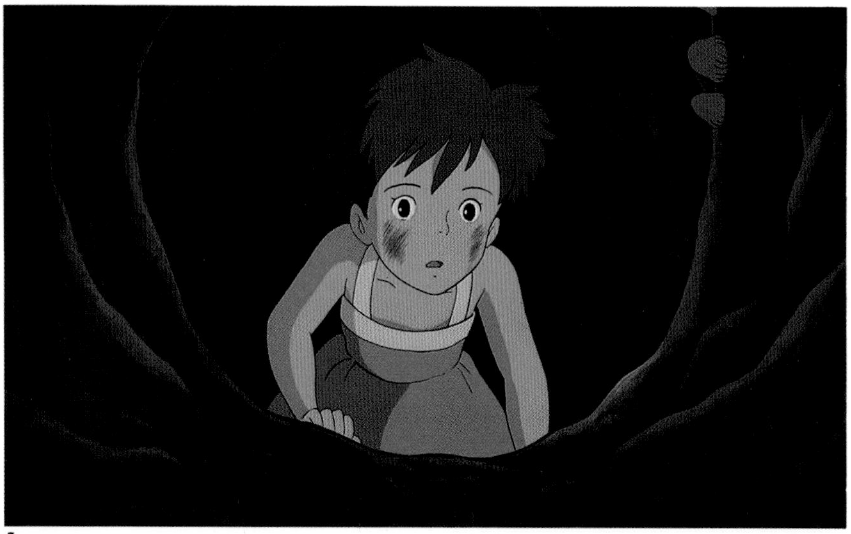

1

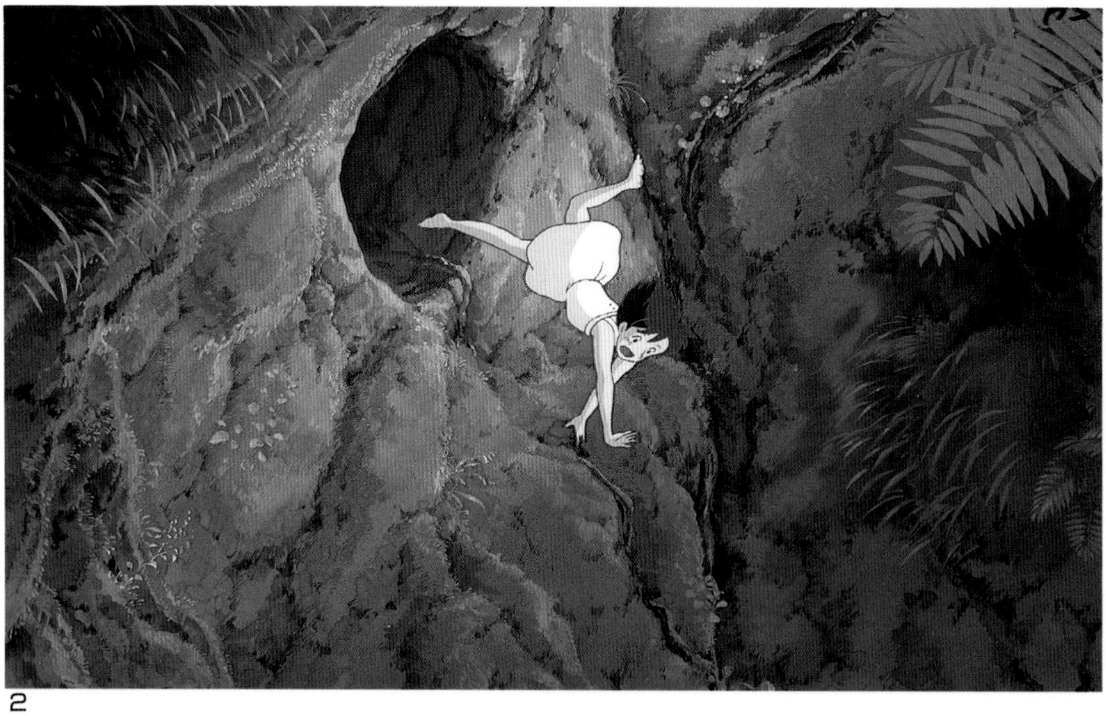

2

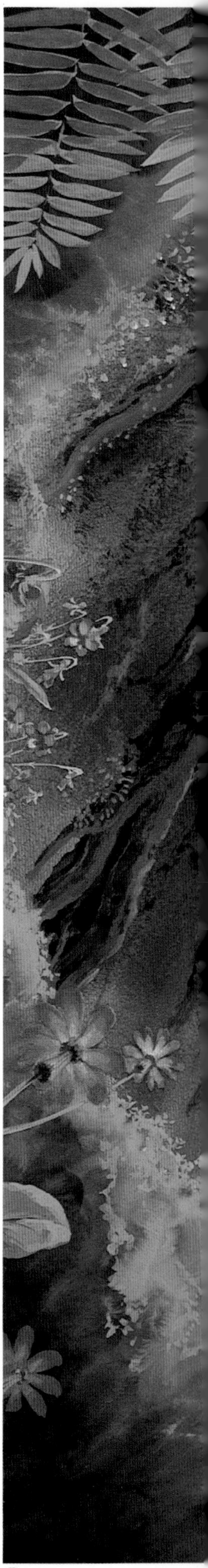

3

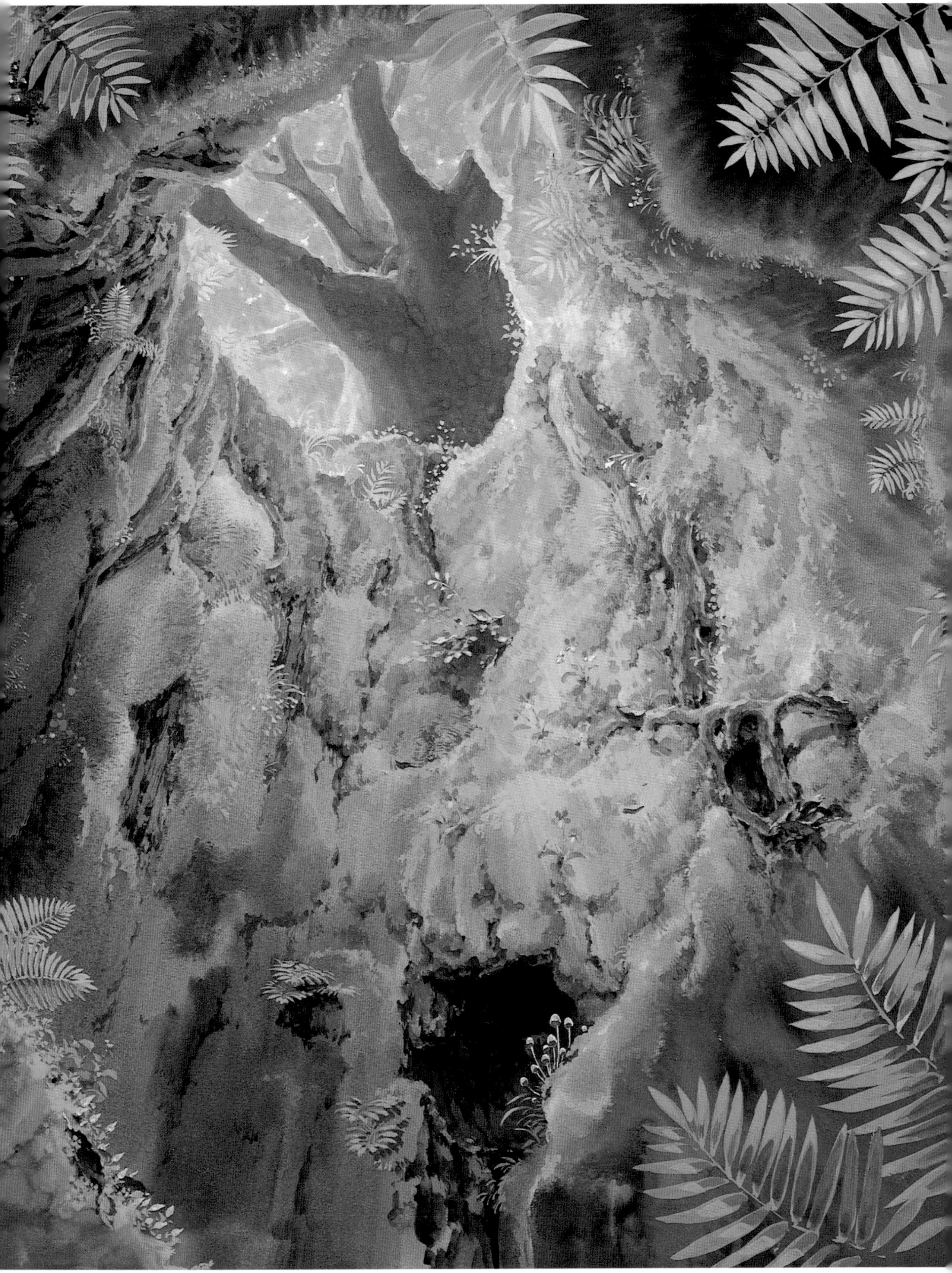

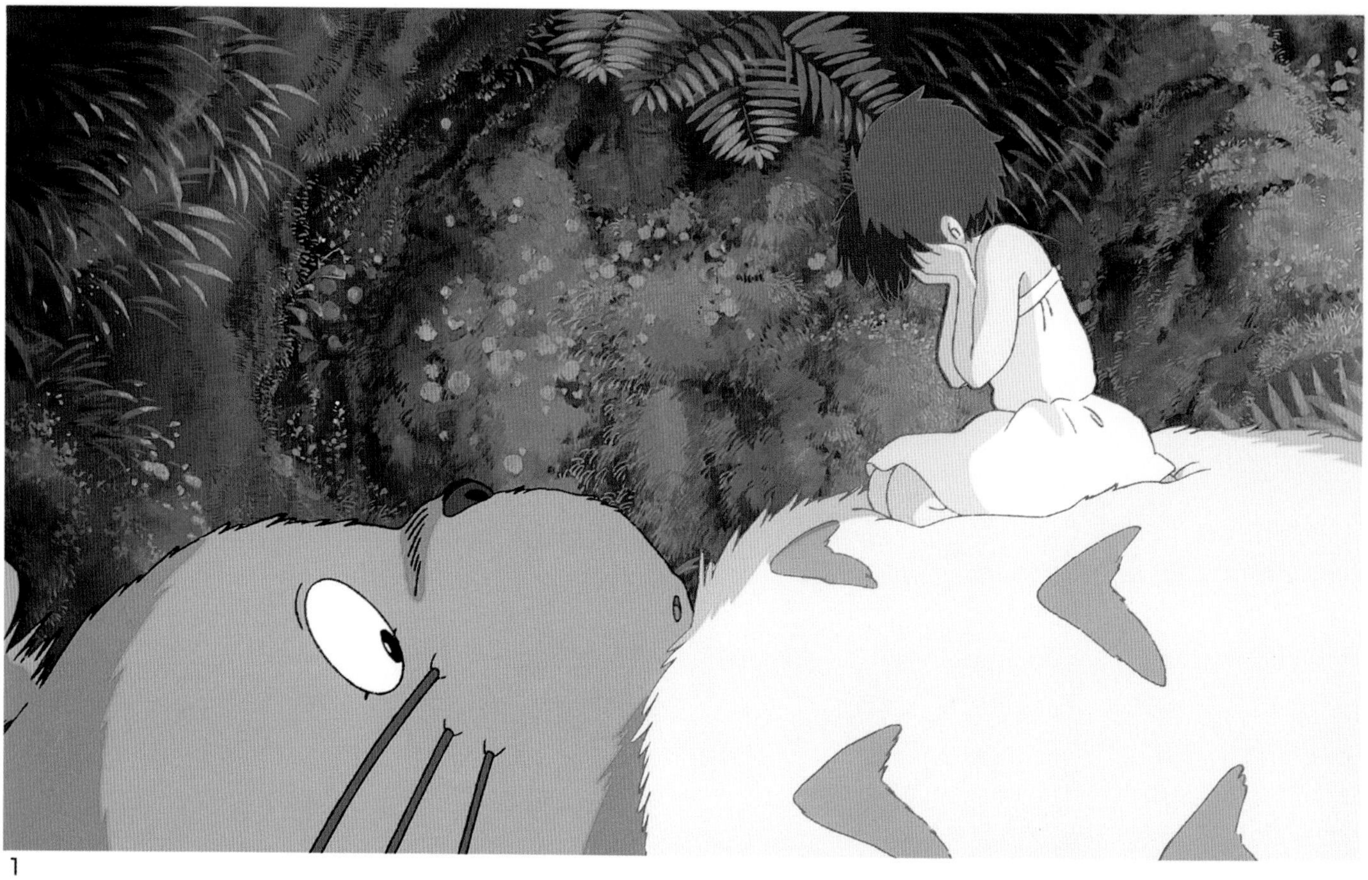

1

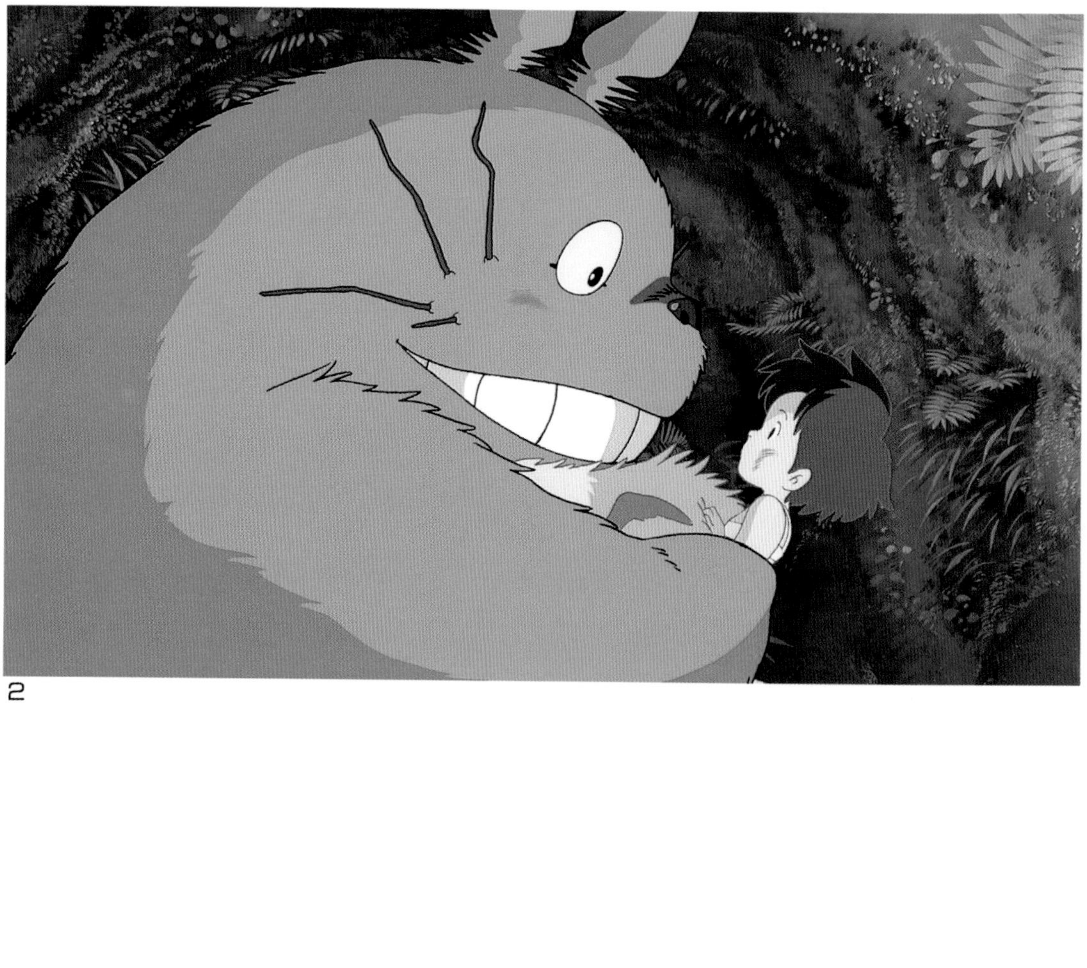

2

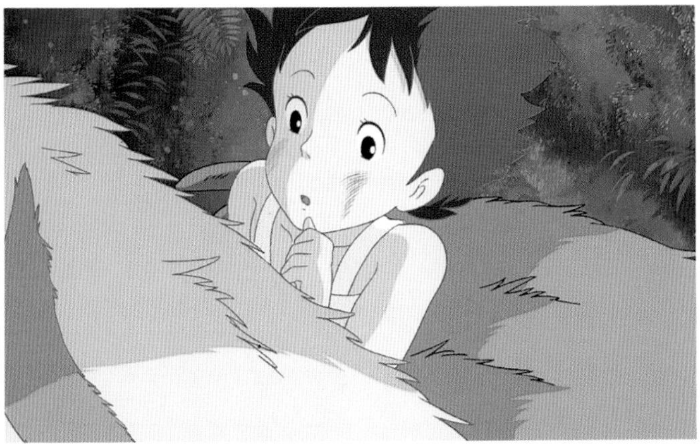
3

1 Satsuki bursts into tears, covering her face, as she kneels on Totoro's chest. *(cel art)*

2 Totoro gets up and holds Satsuki up to its chest, staring at her. *(cel art)*

3-9 Suddenly it cries and leaps, still holding her. They emerge on top of the camphor tree. It takes a deep breath and then lets out a roar. *(cel art)*

"What was hard to tell was whether Satsuki's request prompted Totoro to look for Mei and call the Cat Bus. I assumed that was the case, but some of our staff only thought Satsuki looked cute [*laughs*], and that was all [ *laughs*]." *(Miyazaki)*

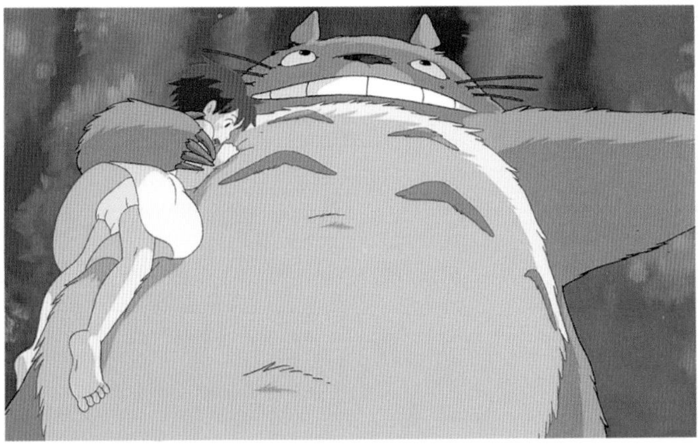
4

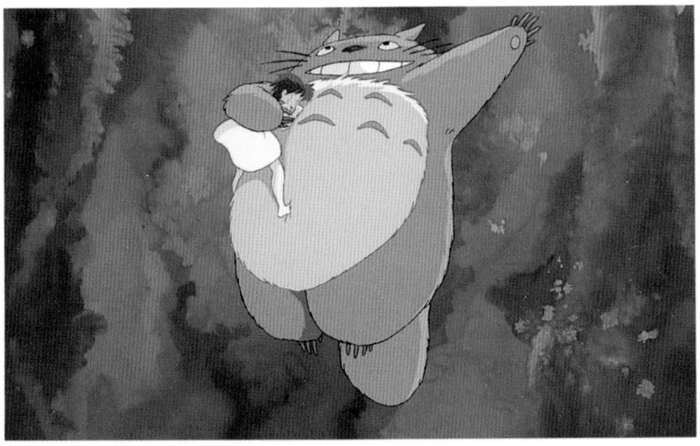
5

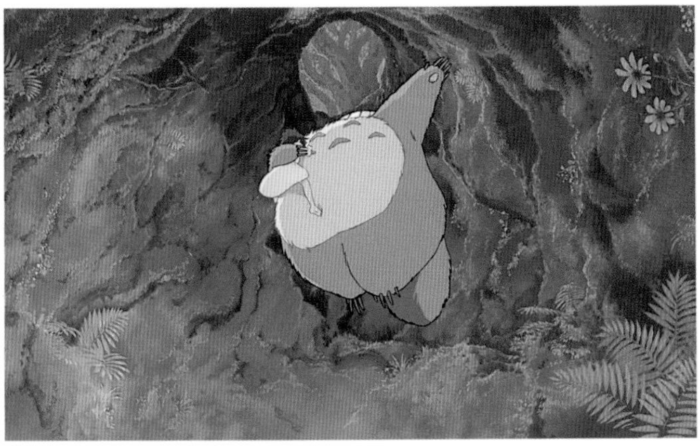
6

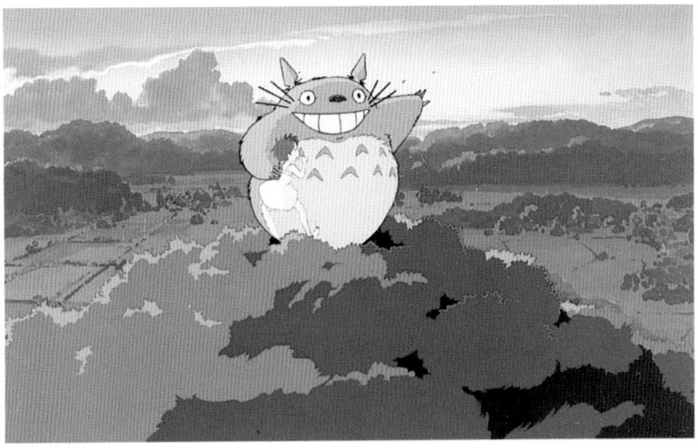
7

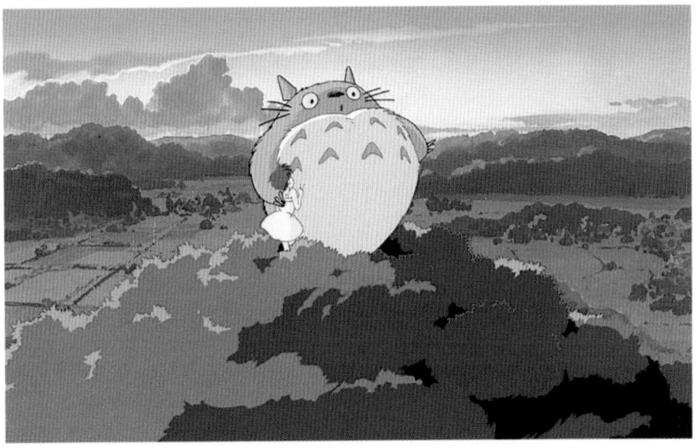
8

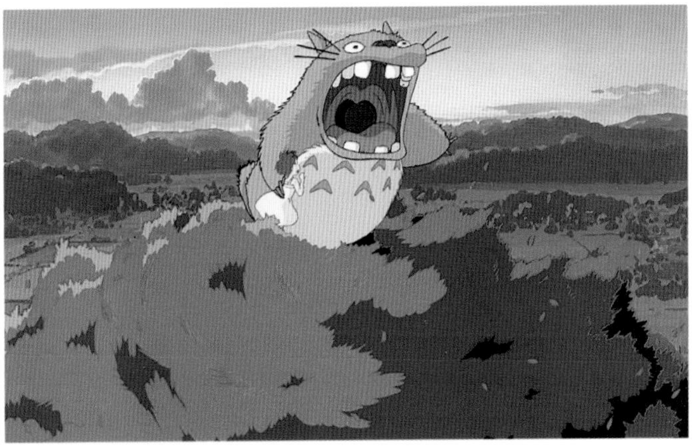
9

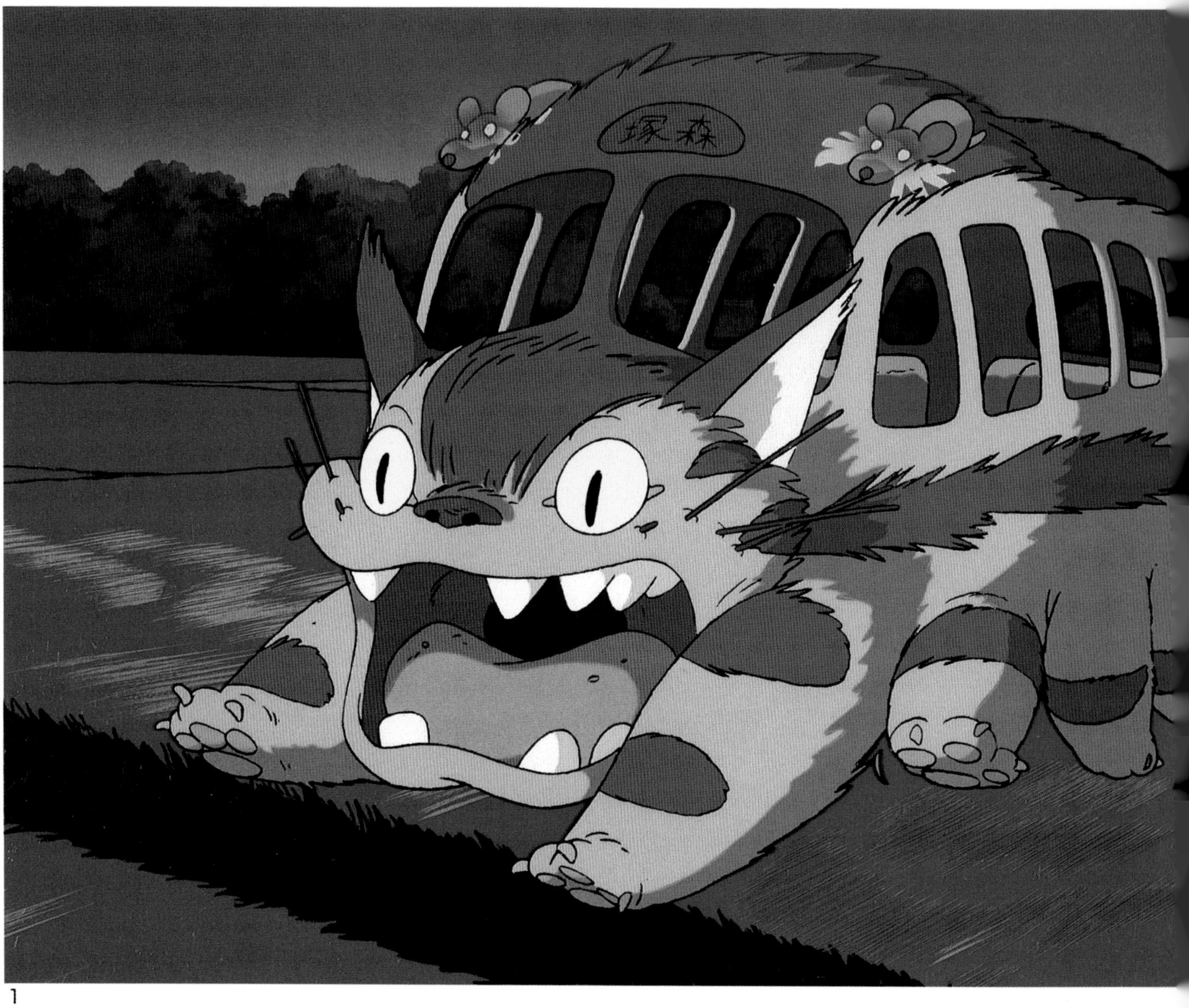
塚森

1

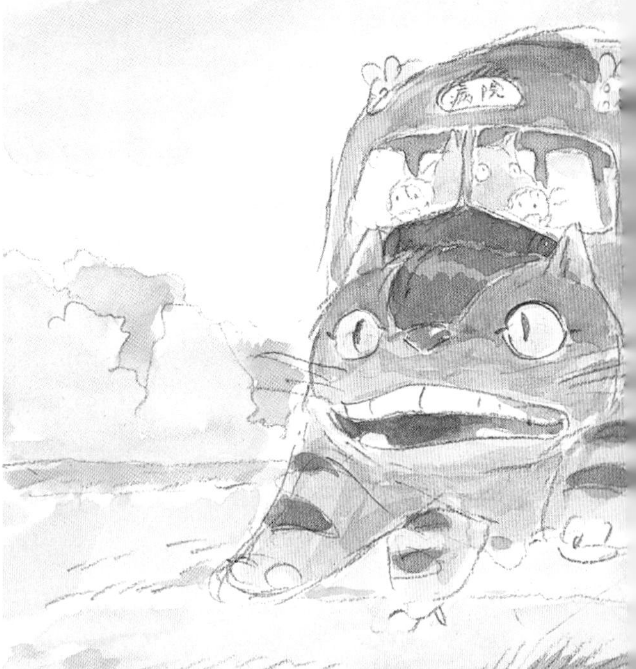
病院

2

1 The Cat Bus rushes in, responding to Totoro's call. *(cel art)*

2 Concept sketch for 1.

3 Wearing a grin, the Cat Bus stops by Satsuki and Totoro. *(cel art)*

4 Satsuki sits on the cozy fur seat. *(cel art)*

5 Totoro waves to the Cat Bus as it departs. *(cel art)*

"When Totoro stays behind as Satsuki rides the Cat Bus toward the end, some people said, `That's harsh.´ But it wouldn't have worked if it rode with them, consoled her, and joined them in looking through the hospital window. Totoro can't be too touchy-feely with them. It can't be too giving. The rest is up to the Cat Bus." *(Miyazaki)*

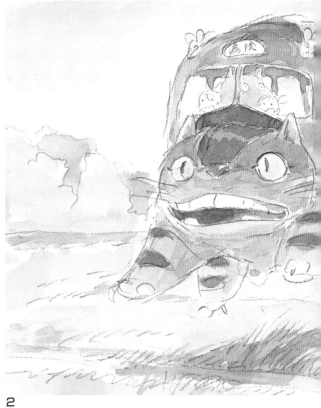

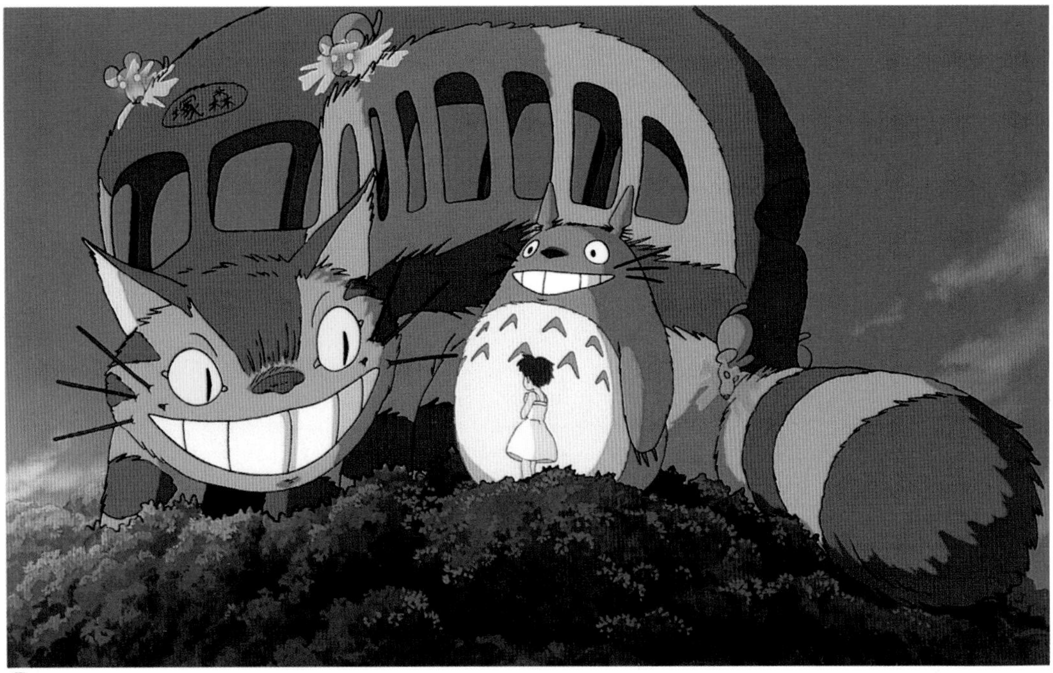
塚森
3

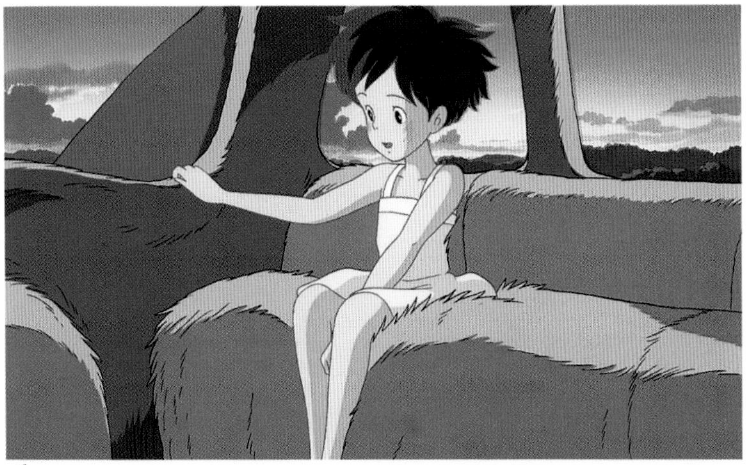
4

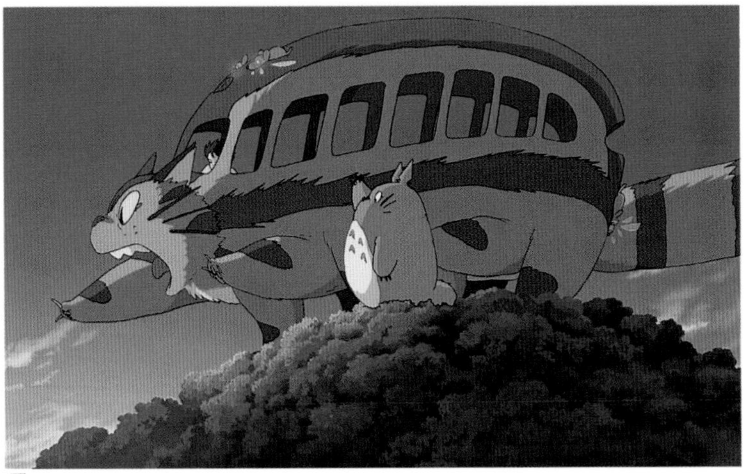
5

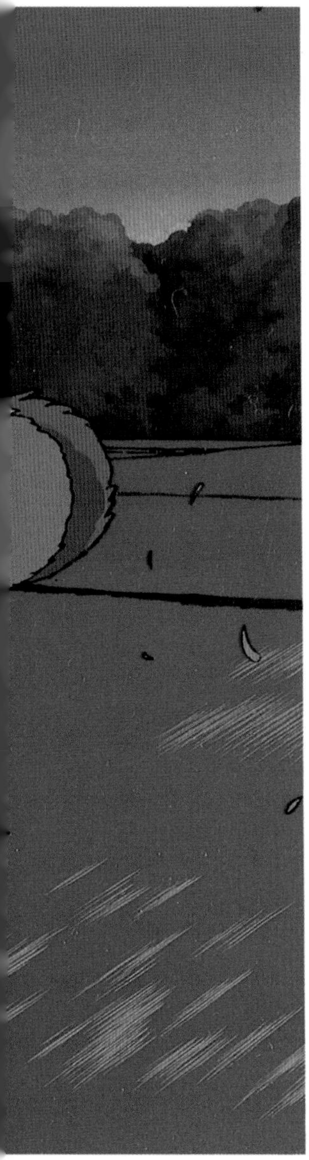

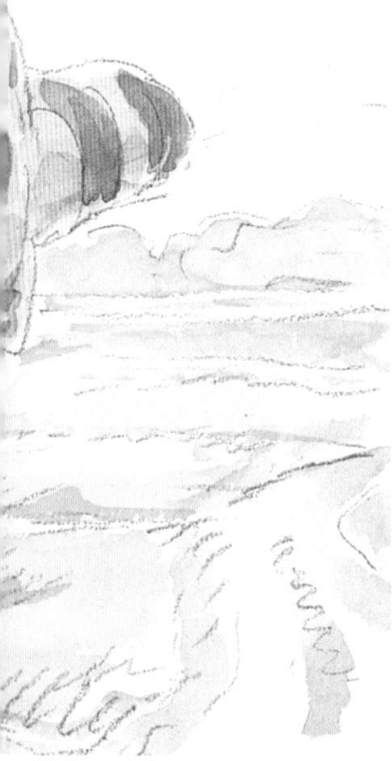

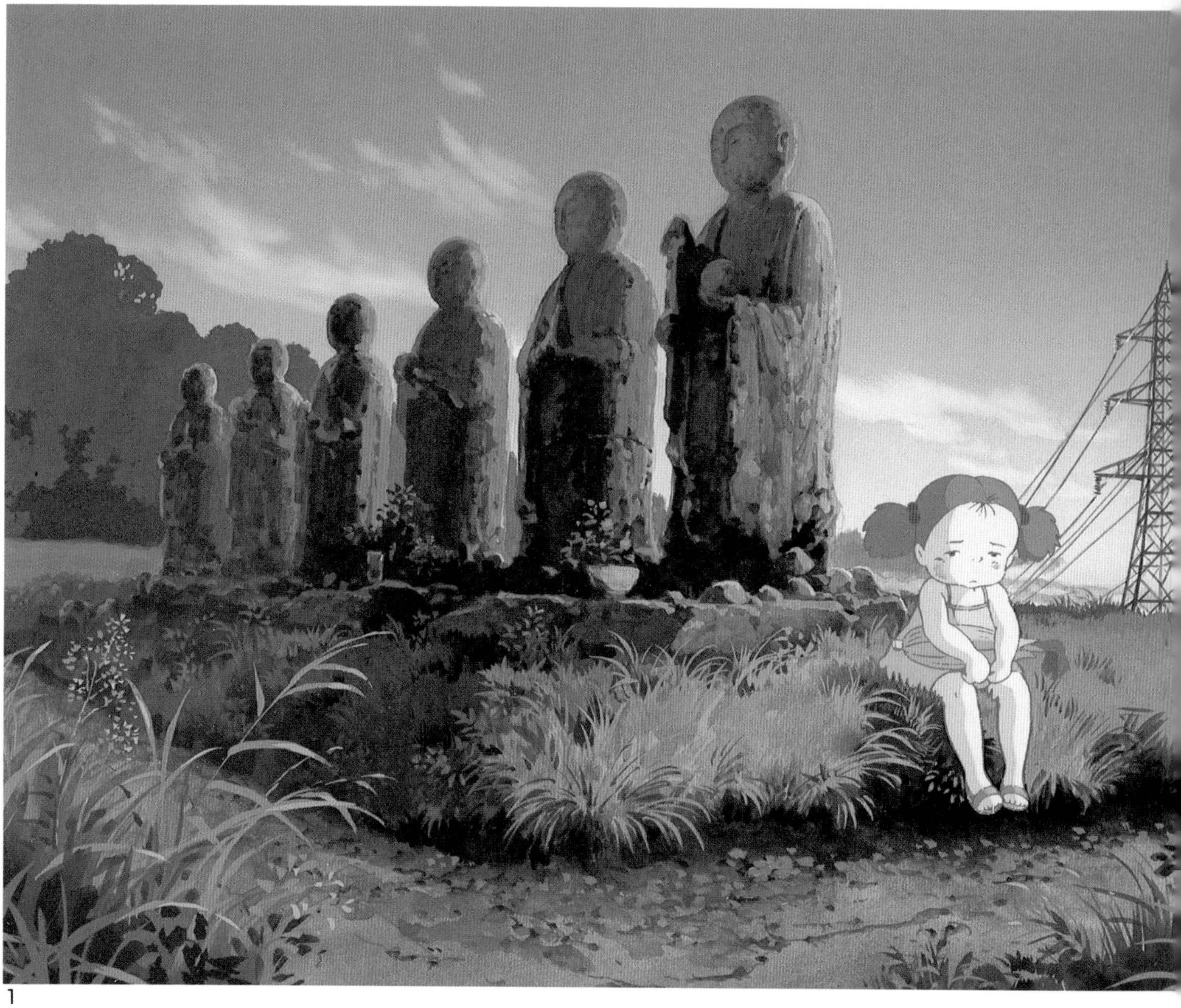

1

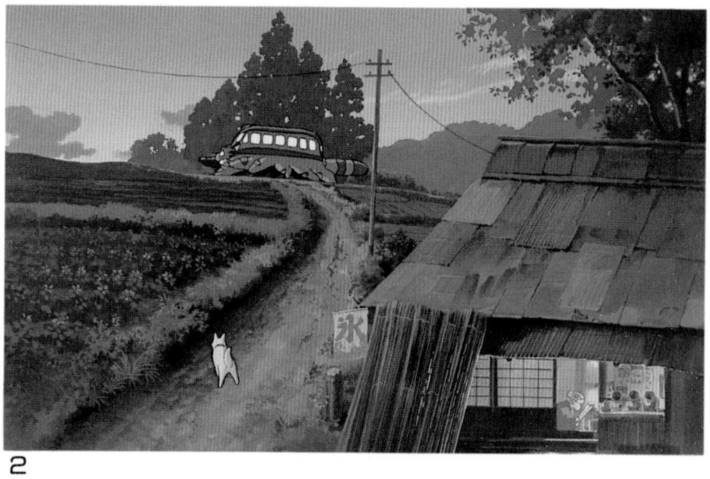
氷

2

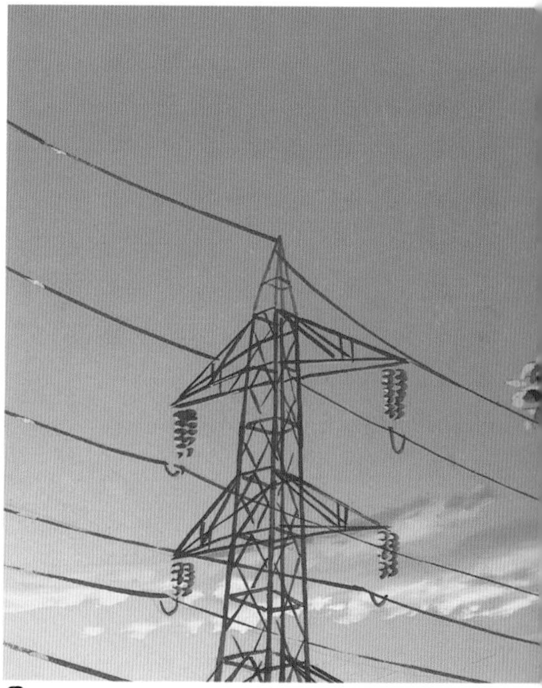

3

1 Mei crouched over by the Rokujizo statues. *(cel art)*

2 The Cat Bus runs up the hillside by the teahouse on the outskirts of the town. A dog jumps and barks. *(cel art)*

3 The Cat Bus runs on the high power line. *(concept art)*

4 Satsuki hugs the nose of the Cat Bus when she learns it's taking them to Shichikokuyama Hospital. *(cel art)*

5 Satsuki and Mei sit on top of the pine tree with the Cat Bus. *(cel art)*

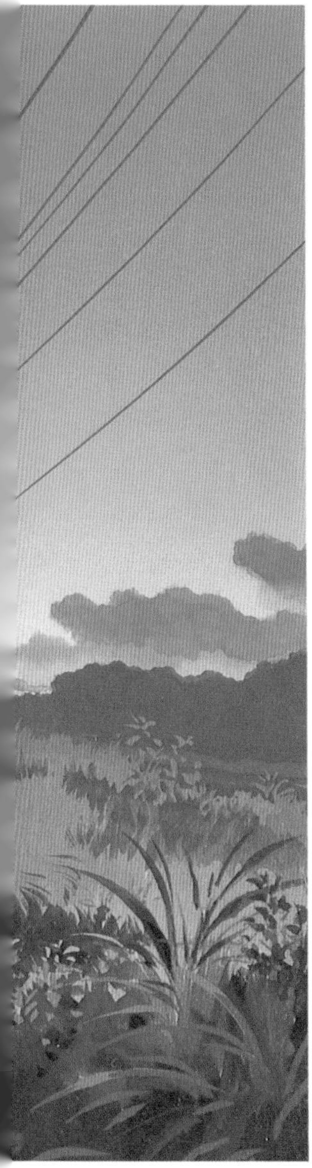

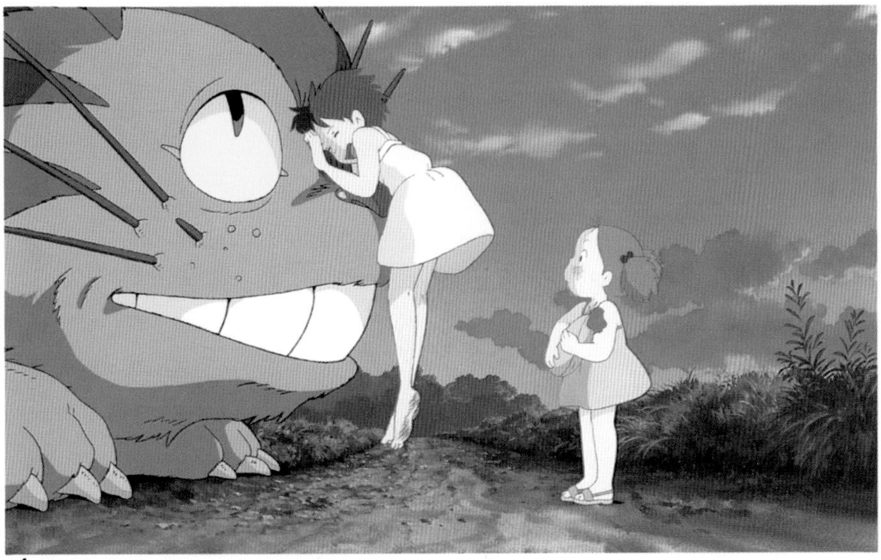

4

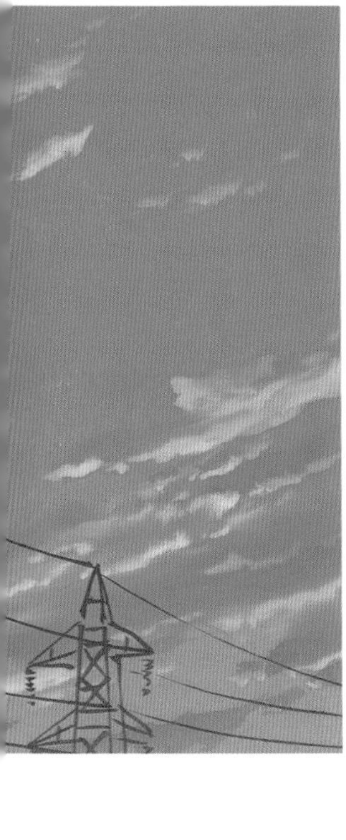

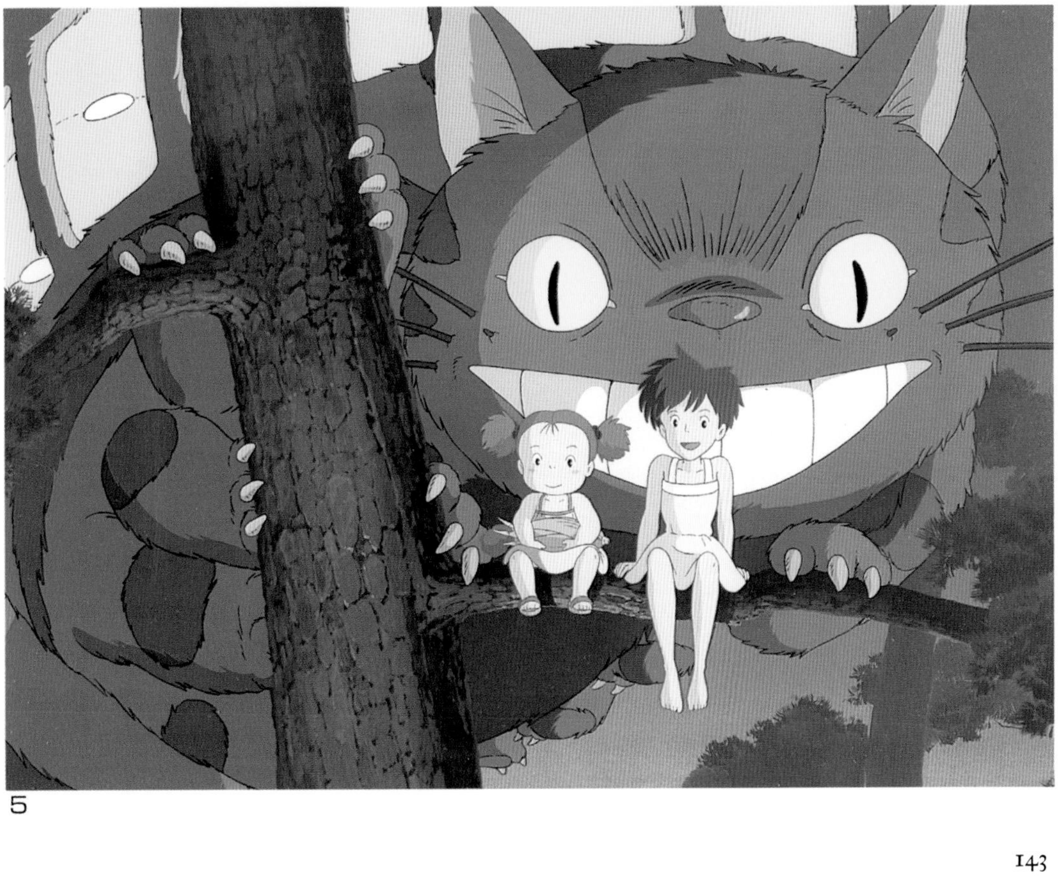

5

1

2

3

4

5

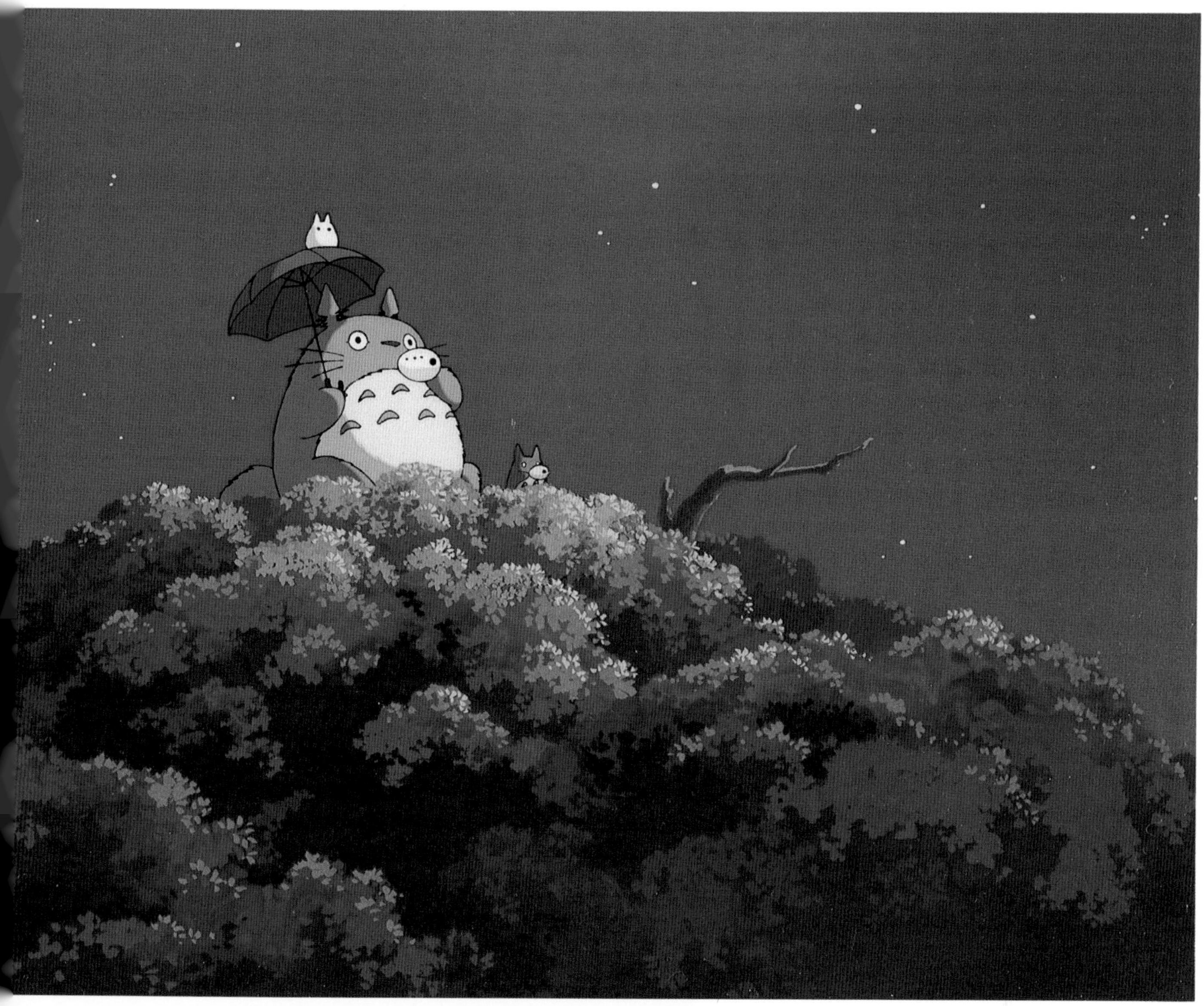

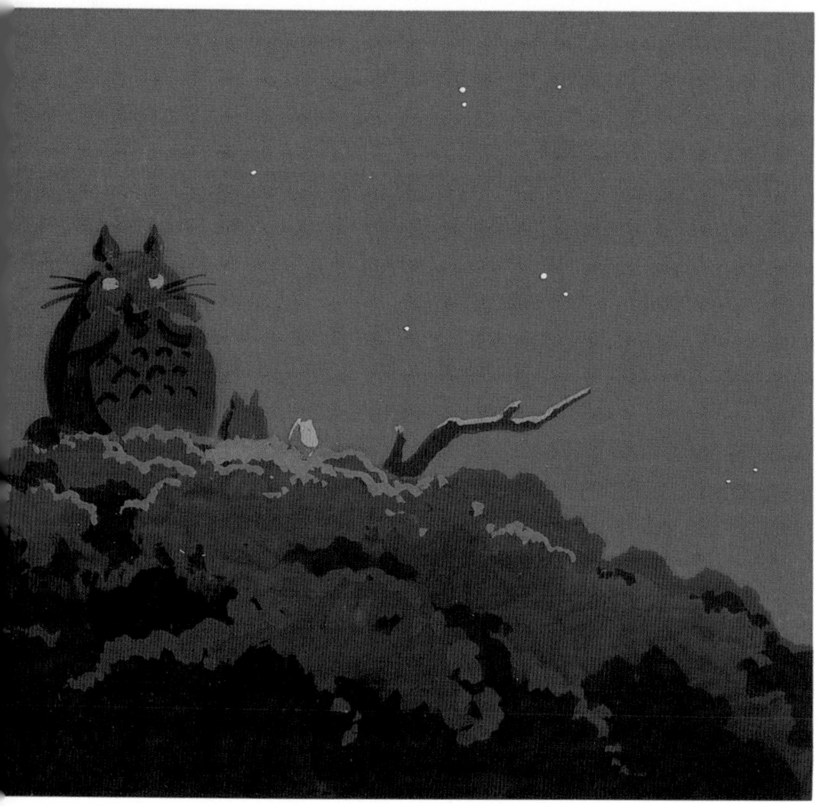

1 On top of the roof the Cat Bus grins. It leaps up into the sky and vanishes. *(concept sketch)*

2 Concept art for 1.

3 Cel art for 1.

4 Totoros blowing on their ocarinas on top of the forest. *(cel art)*

5 Concept art for 4.

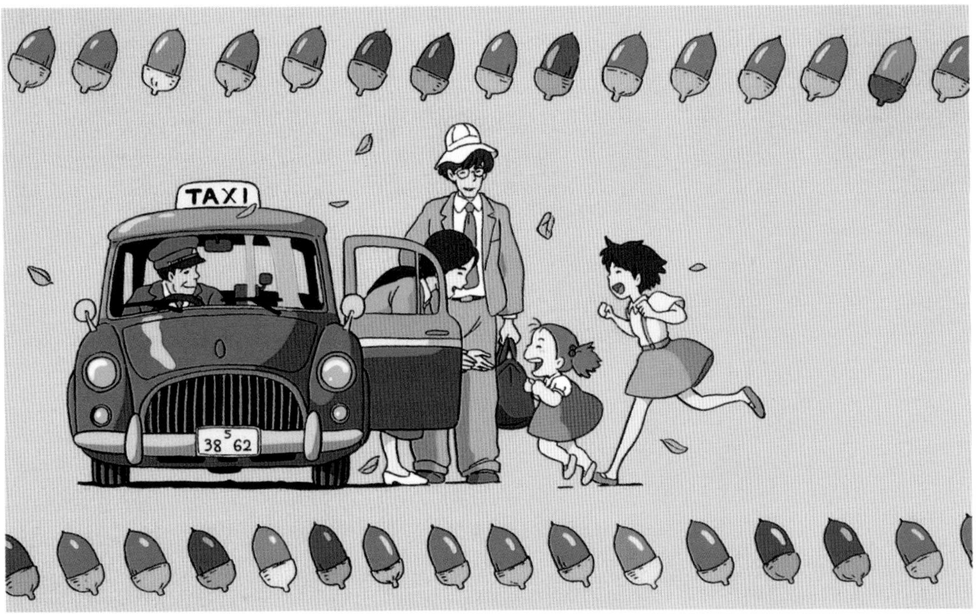
TAXI
38 5 62

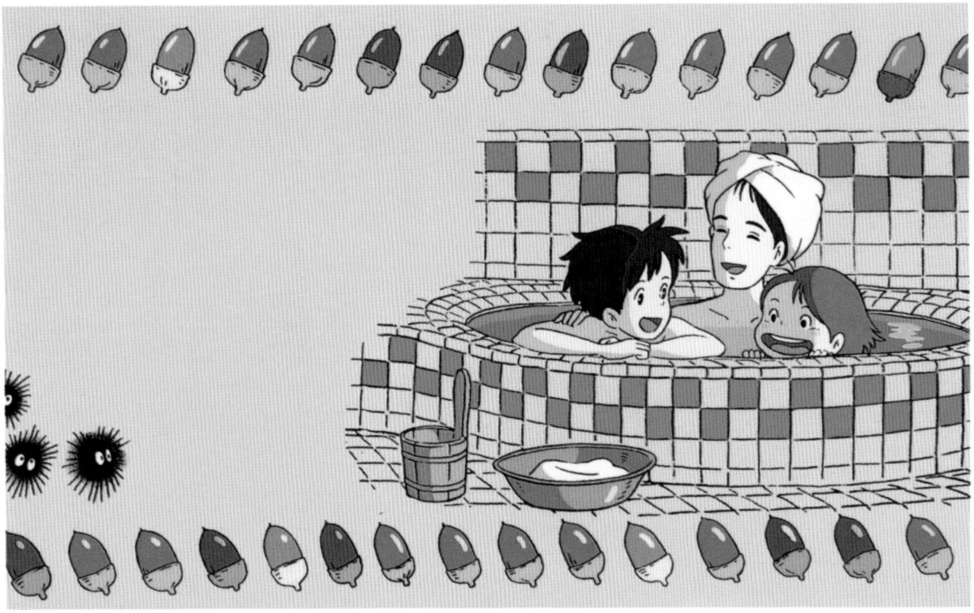

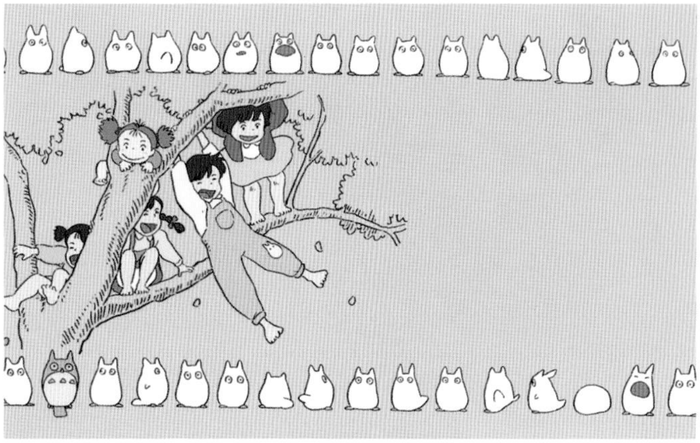
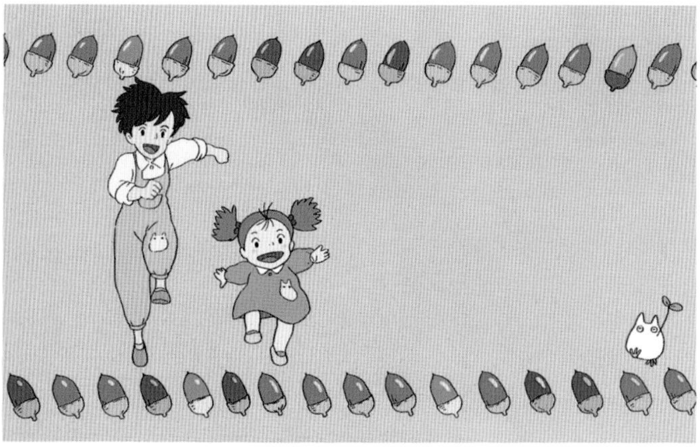
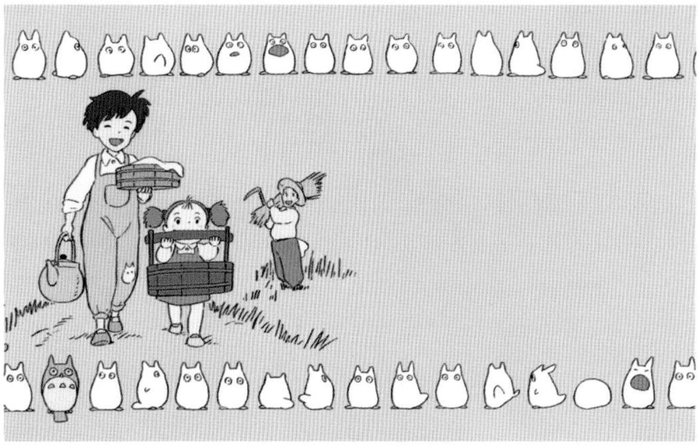
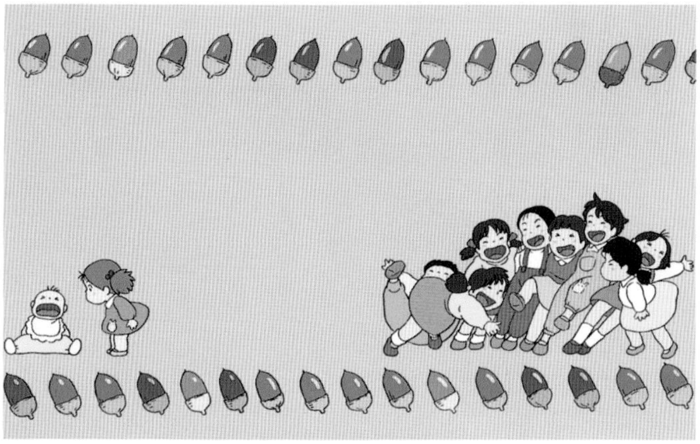
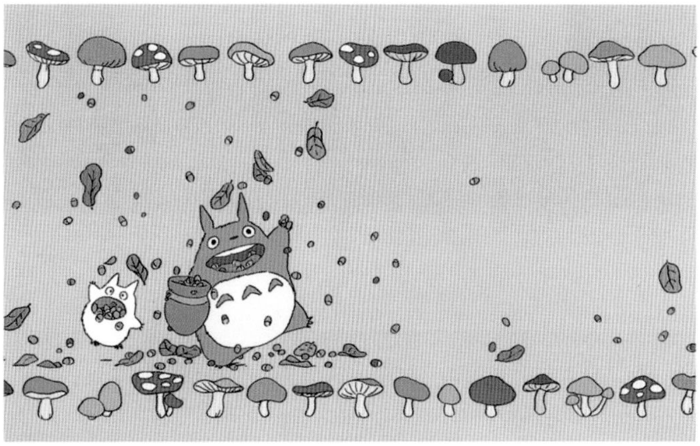
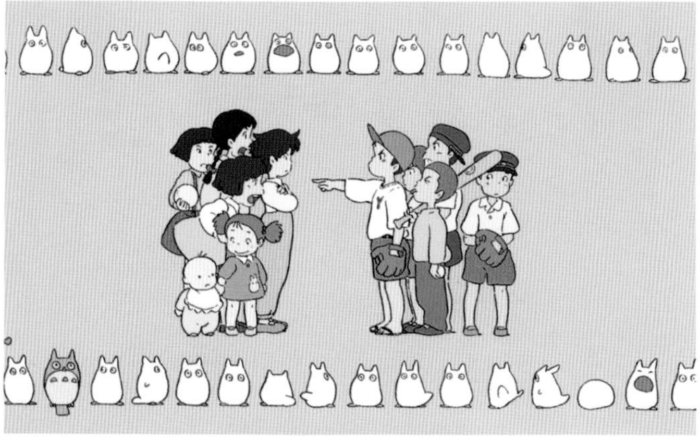
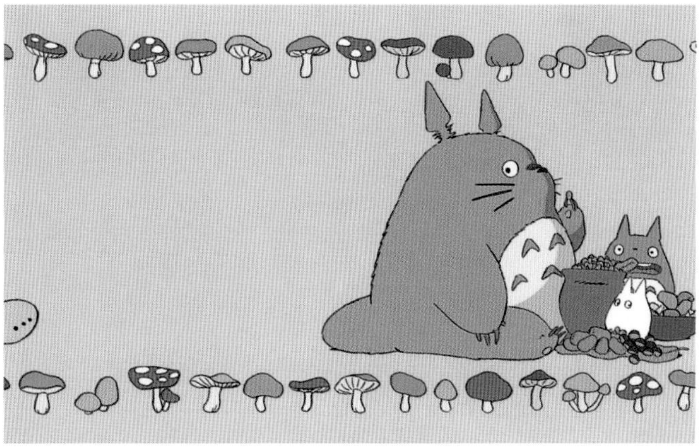
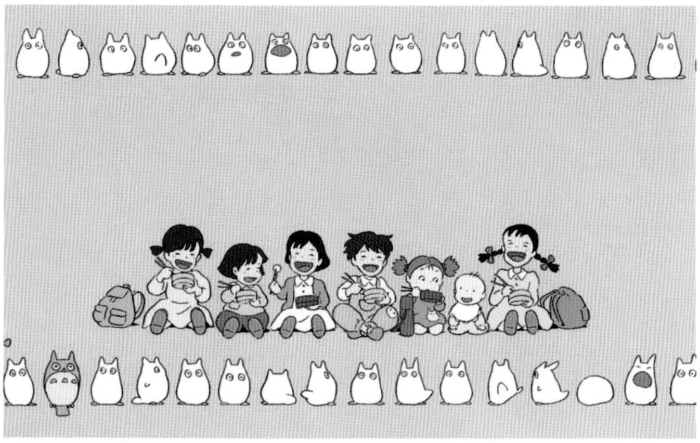

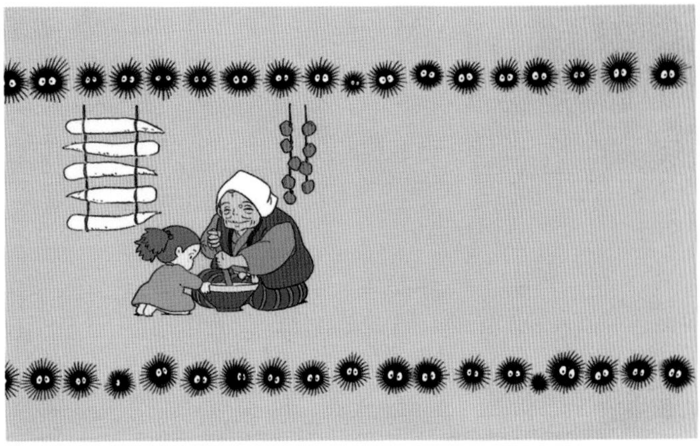
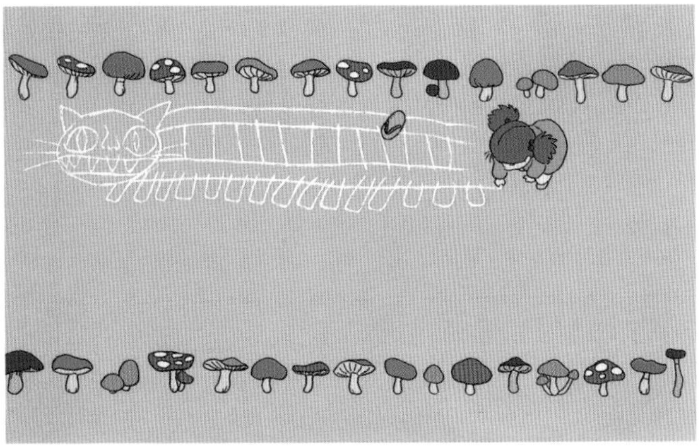
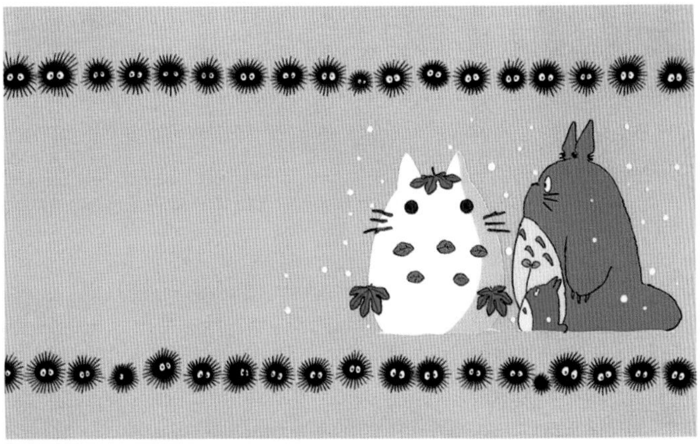
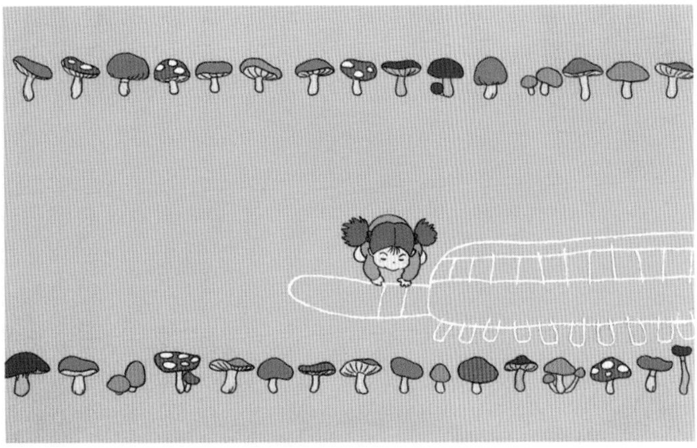
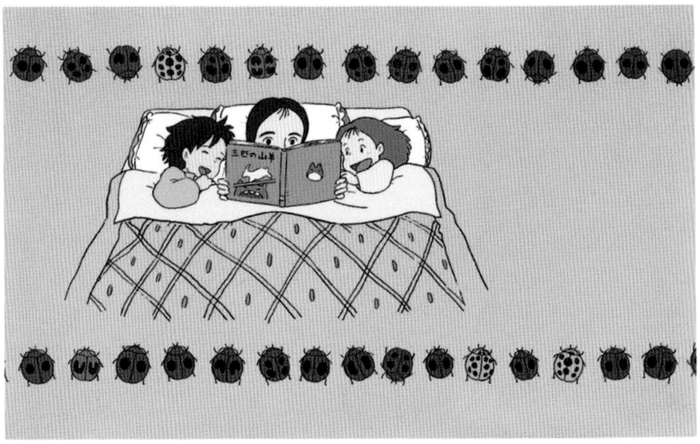
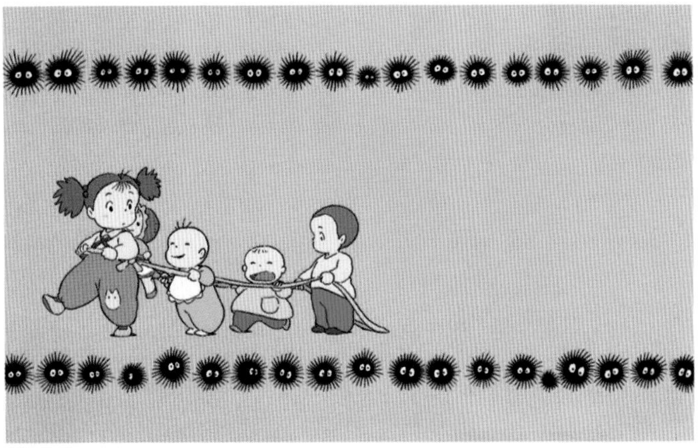
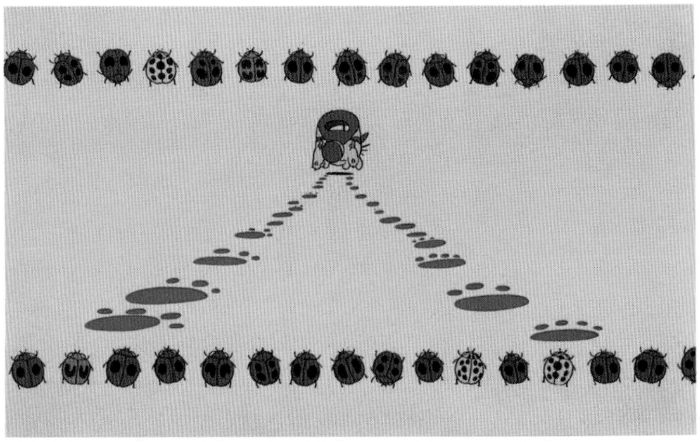
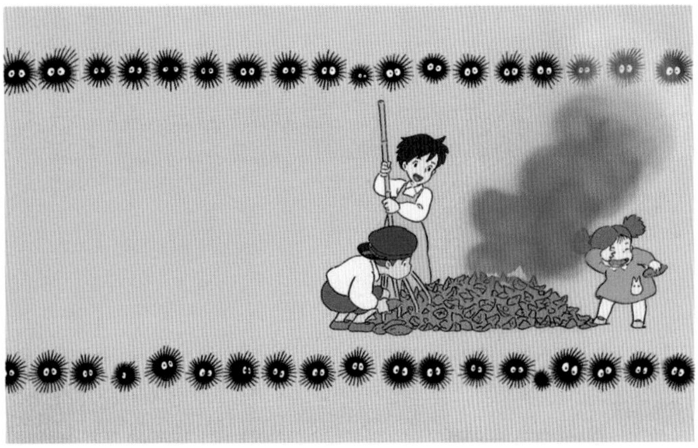

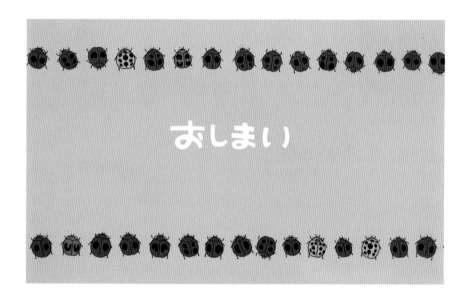

おしまい

The End

"The final cel animation had to depict the mother back at home. There was no need to have her return during the film. We needed to show her taking a bath and going to bed with them. We also had to show that she had recovered—playing outside with them, climbing a tree, and even quarreling with somebody. That way the Totoros could gradually fade away from them, making it seem unlikely that they'll meet again. That's why we didn't have a single image of them playing with the Totoros. The Totoros are eating their acorns. As the acorns fall, they get excited. They gather and feast on the treats in the mountains. That seemed more appropriate." *(Miyazaki)*

忘れものを、届けにきました。

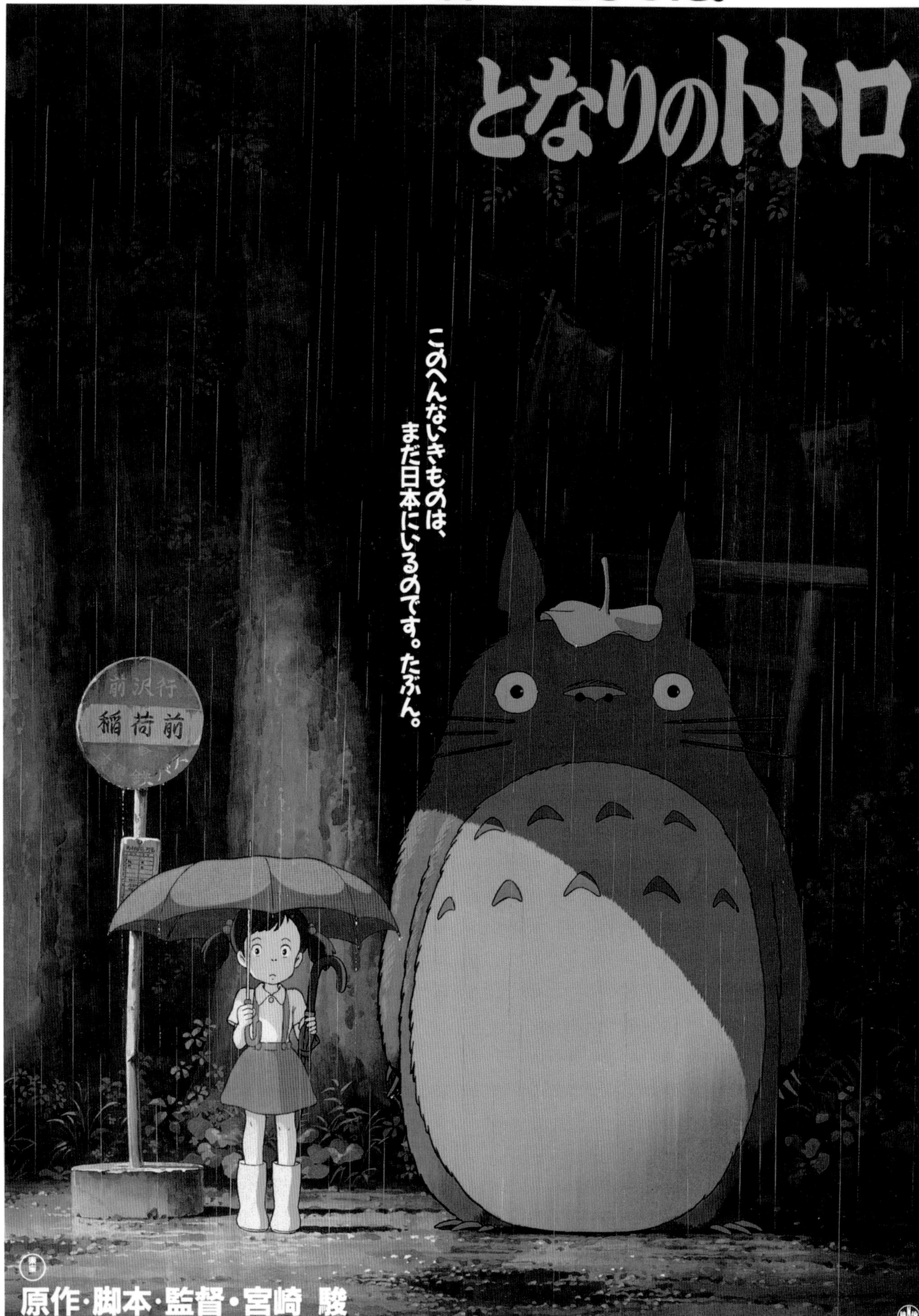
となりのトトロ
このへんないきものは、
まだ日本にいるのです。たぶん。
前沢行
稲荷前
原作・脚本・監督・宮崎 駿
製作●徳間康快/企画●山下辰巳・尾形英夫/作画監督●佐藤好春/美術監督●男鹿和雄/プロデューサー●原 徹/製作●スタジオ・ジブリ/音楽製作●徳間ジャパン
徳間書店作品/配給●東宝
199100-228

# My Neighbor TOTORO

## *Totoro Animation Technique*

Like *Nausicaä of the Valley of the Wind* and *Castle in the Sky*, new animation technology was used in *My Neighbor Totoro*. This chapter will cover the technology developed to depict "Japan's natural scenery" and "everyday life movements" that are so prominent in this film. Tetsuya Endo, a director's assistant, selected and provided commentary on each technique applied in *My Neighbor Totoro*.

# Brown Charcoal

One of the key features of the drawing process of *My Neighbor Totoro* is the use of brown charcoal.
This has been used in the past as well, but this time we developed and utilized a charcoal that would prevent coloration and emphasize the line.

Compared to the average black charcoal, we were able to produce a softer, more elegant image. Furthermore, by adjusting the color designs, we could add color to the characters.

Black Charcoal (alters color)

Brown charcoal (normal color]

Combined with the detailed artistic backgrounds, the images managed to evoke an intimate, warm feel to the world of "Totoro."

However, the brown charcoal can be inappropriate at times. The machines in this film, for example, have all been treated with black charcoal.
One feature of black charcoal is that it gives definition. So we used it to depict objects including the three-wheeler truck, the pump, the windows, and doors.
There were many scenes where the black charcoal objects and the brown charcoal characters had to blend together. These had to be copied onto the cel with each separate charcoal color.

The outline for Big Totoro is basically black charcoal, but brown charcoal was used for his stomach. The animators had to draw these separately, which is a lot of work.

# Special Effects

This group of soot sprites was done with paint and black brush on top.

Miyazaki wanted the soot sprites to be soft, so we had the director's assistants draw them.

At this size, painting, tapping, and brushing highlight were used.

Mei's dirty hands were also tapped.

This was done with paint and tapping, as well as brushing on the back to accentuate their presence.

## Making the Soot Sprites

●First, paint-in the eyes with W (white).
●Then draw-in the body inside the solid lines w/ BL (black).
●Finally, paint with BL inside the dotted lines using the tapping method.

*Tapping is a special effect applied with any number of tools including sponges or cotton swabs.

Here we used cotton swabs.

●First, dilute the cel paint BL in a bowl.
●Apply the paint to the cotton swab. It must be tested first on another spot.
●If the shade is appropriate, tap the cotton swab on the back of the cel to add the effect.

# Brush—Little Totoro Appears

The Totoro has a strange look here because we made it look transparent in the middle by brushing around that spot.

This was also a special effect we achieved by brushing the area. The shadow below was also brushed.

# Tadpoles

These tadpoles were painted using four different colors, so it was really difficult not to make any errors in the key animation process. The animators spent a month on this scene.

The camera supervisor complimented the staff with a phone call, claiming how the tadpoles running away from Mei "looked real." There's some blur applied to muddy up the water slightly.

ひきがえる
色トレス
BL カーボン
BL マリ
動画様
わかりにくくてすみません.
右図を参考にして
トレスして下さい。
こんな角度以外は
まず
しっぽの濃い部分が見えて
それに 半透明（この場合 色トレス）の
部分がついている と考えて下さい。

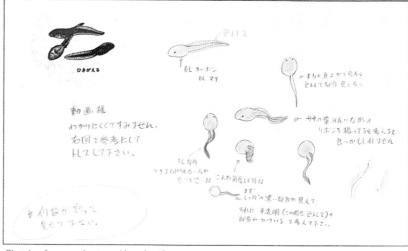

Sketch reference chart used in animation.

# Bathtub steam

Because there's no light in the bath-room, the bath steam in this scene had to be illuminated by the kitchen light. The room is only lit in spots.

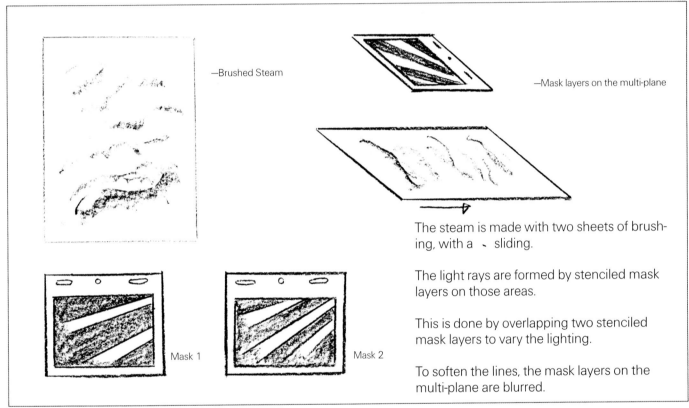

—Brushed Steam

—Mask layers on the multi-plane

The steam is made with two sheets of brushing, with a ⌣ sliding.

The light rays are formed by stenciled mask layers on those areas.

This is done by overlapping two stenciled mask layers to vary the lighting.

To soften the lines, the mask layers on the multi-plane are blurred.

Mask 1

Mask 2

# Negation

Totoro's sketch was filmed in reverse. We started from the bottom and worked our way to the top of the image.

# The Rain

The rain scene is essential in this film.

When it starts to rain, they seek shelter at the Jizo statue. The rain pours heavily until they reach the pond. To achieve the look, we copied the illustrated rain onto the cels with W carbon.

From that point on we scratched in the cels. Depending on the scene, we would superimpose or directly film it, which gave a softer feel to the rain.

Without camera processing the images end up like this.

# Ripple

The ripples are created with two colors of high-lighting and shading.

# Superimposition

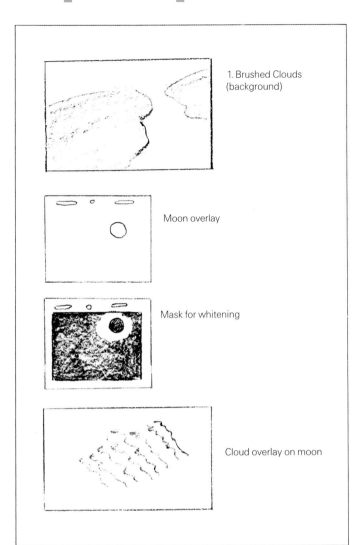

1. Brushed Clouds (background)

Moon overlay

Mask for whitening

Cloud overlay on moon

The moon is visible through the clouds in this scene.
The light glowing around the moon is superimposed by applying a stenciled mask layer.

[bullet]
1, 2, 4 are overlapped and shot with mask 3 and 4 superimposed.

# Spot Superimposition

In this shot, the nighttime darkness was accentuated by obscuring the rain in the dark.

We processed this shot to enable the illuminating lamp to obscure the darker areas.

# Mosquito Net

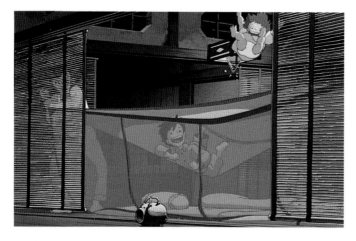

This is a unique shot, where the mosquito net is a combination of paint and superimposition. We came up with this method in order to depict Satsuki and Mei's expressions, as well as the net mesh, in a single long shot.

After this the net was done by cel with animation lines, but we still had to deal with the color. There are all kinds of color carbons including red, white, yellow, and blue, but in this case we traced over the brown carbon with green carbon, combining the two colors to form soft green lines.

Here the dark areas were done with brown + green carbon. The lit areas were drawn with background overlay.

The same process from above was applied for the dark areas of this shot. The lit areas were done with white + green carbon.

# ART

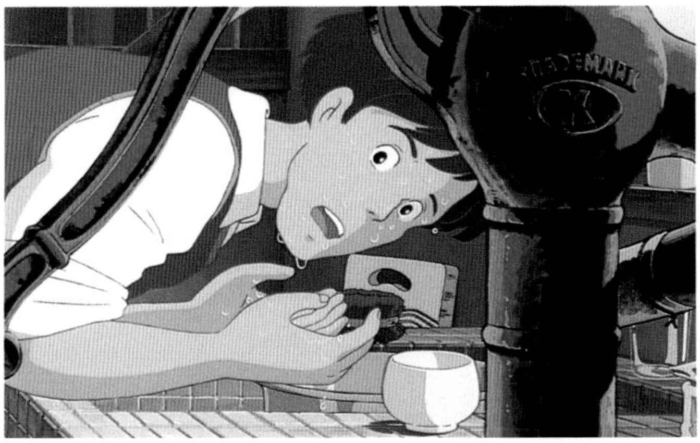

The complete cel art for this pump was processed to add texture.

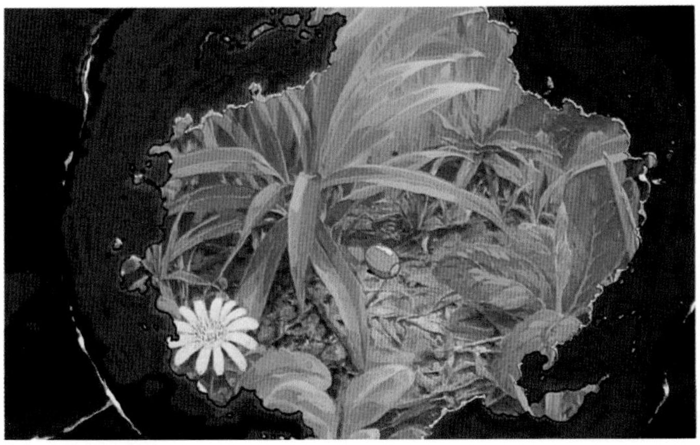

Hole in the bucket.

The art played a crucial role in creating the world of Totoro. The backgrounds are extraordinary, and the images have so much presence. I was really impressed by the mastery of the creator behind this art, Oga, and Miyazaki's careful guidance. Oga also ended up working on tasks normally assigned to the special effects staff. There were countless occasions when he made revisions on each image before submitting the art for shooting. The way he added texture to the cel art, like the pump image for instance, was extraordinary. The following panels illustrate this.

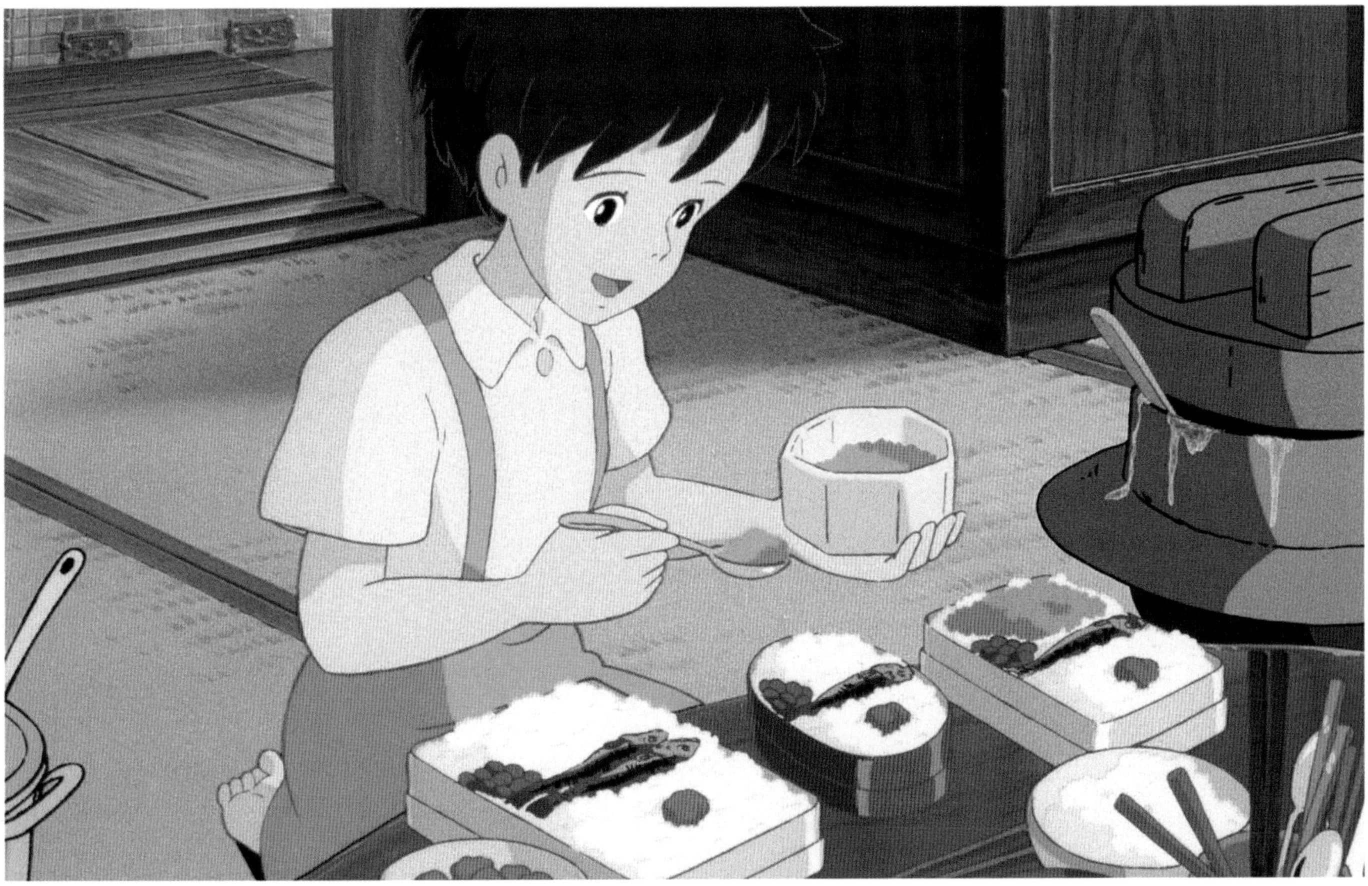

Processing rice goo overflowing from container.

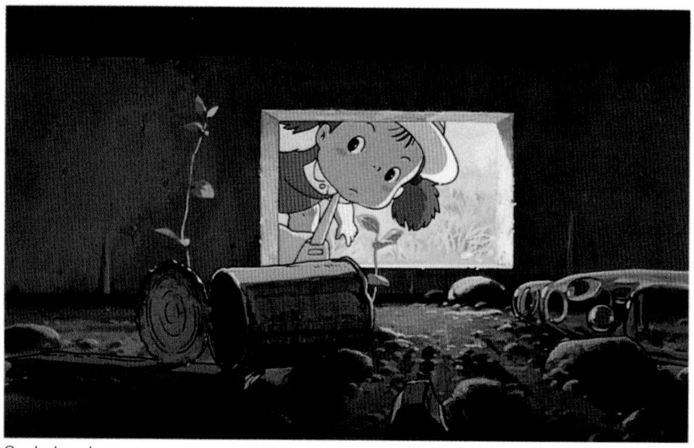

Soda bottle

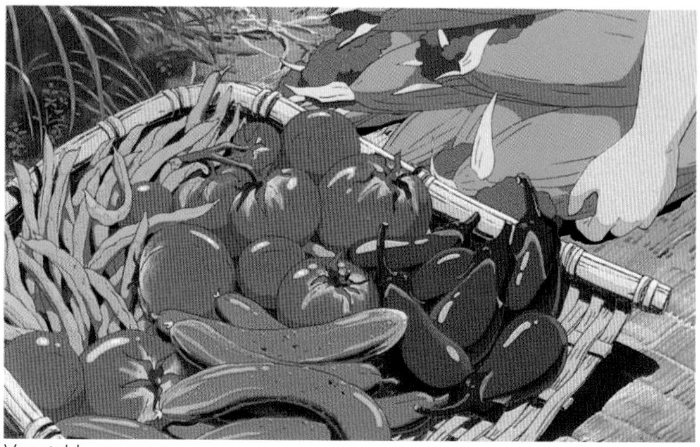

Vegetables

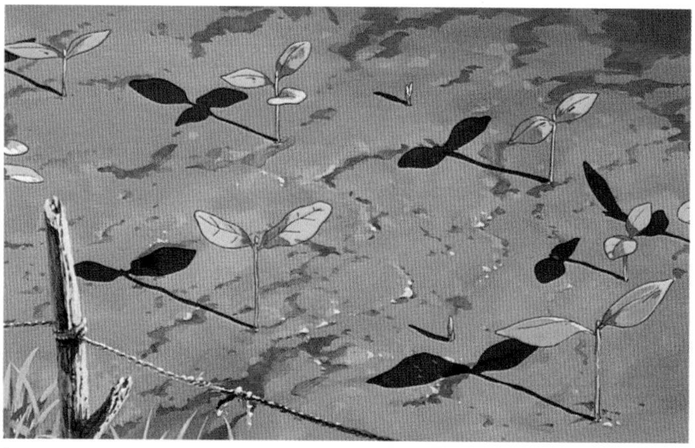

Leaves

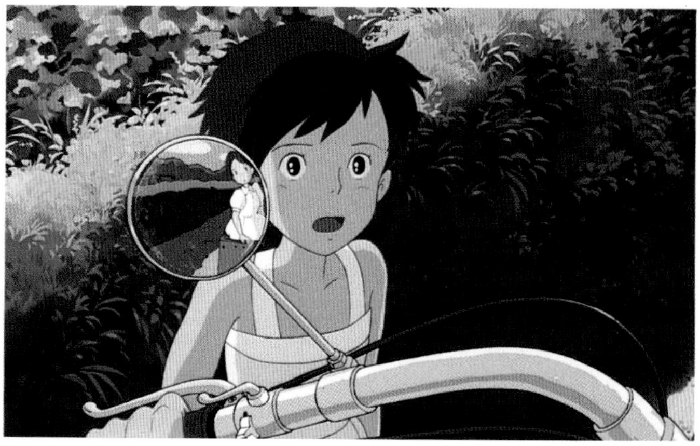

Handle and rearview mirror of the three-wheeler truck

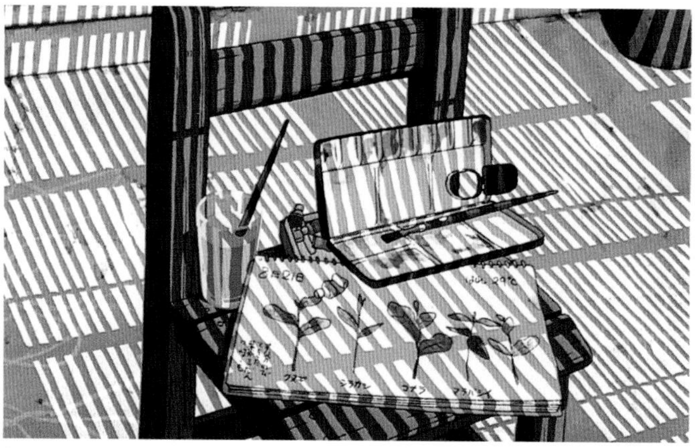

Sketch books and palette

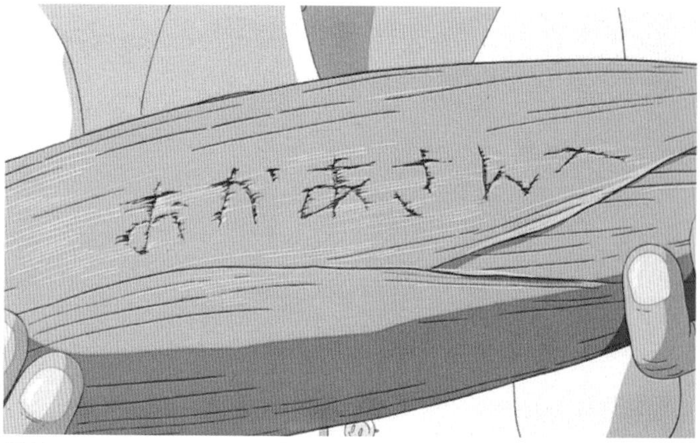
おかあさんへ

Writing on corn

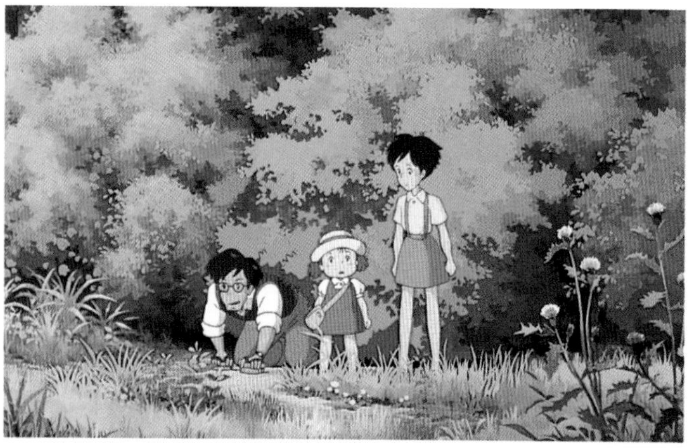

Grass. Overlay processing of the moving art matches up the cel art with the background.

Although I could cite plenty of other examples, I'll have to stop here because of limited space.

# My Neighbor TOTORO

## Totoro Production Report

"Masaaki Nomura's Ghibli Production Report" by film critic Masaaki Nomura was originally serialized in the monthly magazine *Animage* in December 1987. Nomura's on-site report on (animation production company) Studio Ghibli's double feature production of *My Neighbor Totoro* and *Grave of the Fireflies* (directed by Isao Takahata) is a valuable resource on animation production. The original text of this report on *My Neighbor Totoro* has been modified.

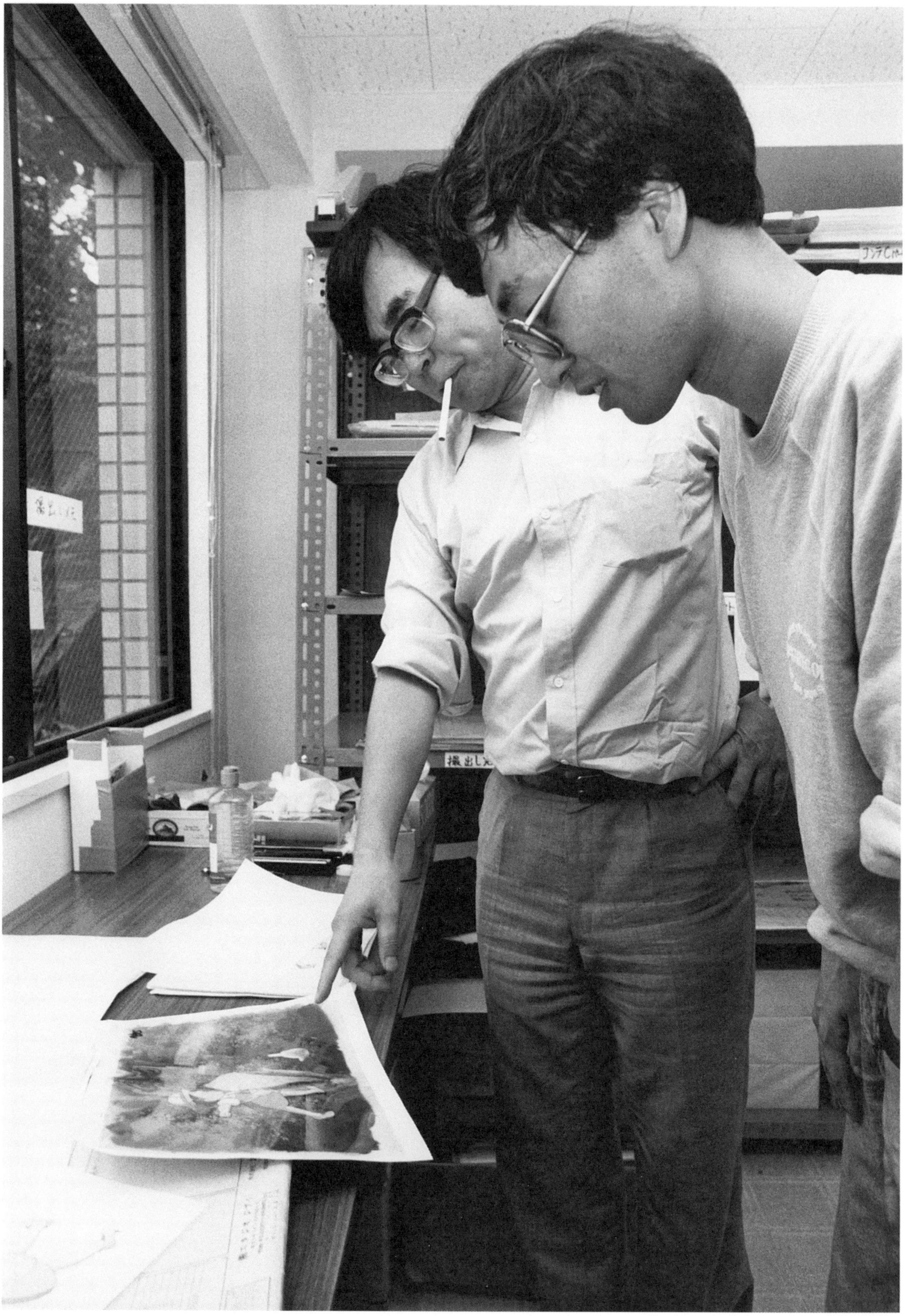

# Masaaki Nomura's Ghibli Production Report

This article is based on the column "Masaaki Nomura's Ghibli Production Report," serialized from December 1987 to May 1988 in *Animage* magazine. At the time, I was also assigned to cover the concurrent production of *Grave of the Fireflies*. This modified version, though, touches on *My Neighbor Totoro*. Rereading it now, I'm not sure my writing captured the essence of the project, but I hope it provides a glimpse into the inner dynamics of the film's production.

## On Hayao Miyazaki

**The cordial atmosphere of Totoro Studio was due in large part to Miyazaki's endearing personality. From the very moment our interview began, Miyazaki shared his thoughtful observations, covering a wide range of topics. I listened with rapt admiration.**

The rain was pouring on the very first day of my coverage. If this were a live-action film, the shooting would have been canceled, of course, but the studio production continues without any interruption. With the exception of films shot in studios (like Naoto Yamakawa's *The New Morning of Billy the Kid*, which was entirely shot in studios), the shooting conditions for live-action films almost entirely depend on weather conditions. As a result, poor scheduling and tense relationships are often weather dependent. "What happens then in the case of animation? Do similar conflicts exist, and if so, how do they get played out? How do they affect the film production?" I pondered these as I arrived at Studio Ghibli in Kichijoji, Tokyo.

When the editorial department proposed the project, I immediately jumped at the opportunity to report on the studio production of *My Neighbor Totoro*. The mere opportunity to get an early viewing of Miyazaki's latest opus excited me. But once I calmed down, I began to realize how difficult this assignment was going to be. When you're reporting on a live-action film, you observe as the director physically directs the actors' movements. You watch and then summarize part of this process into a report. So even a novice can get a sense of the shooting process with each scene. But covering an animation film was going to be a completely different ballgame. It would be hard to relate each specific activity inside the studio to the overall filmmaking process. If I were reporting on the illustration process, all I'd have to do is report on the studio's environment. But I lack that expertise anyway, so I visited the studio with my untrained eye, letting my curiosity guide me.

I once visited Studio Ghibli to interview Miyazaki right before the completion of *Castle in the Sky*. During that time, they had to lease another floor in a new local building to meet expanding production demands due to the concurrent production of Takahata's *Grave of the Fireflies*. Studio Number One was in use for *Grave of the Fireflies*, so the production of *My Neighbor Totoro* was moved to Studio Number Two. The two studios are approximately 100 meters apart, and the two buildings are almost identical. Apparently, both buildings had the same owner—hence, the similar design. While Miyazaki frequents Studio Number One to discuss production—bantering with the on-site staff—Takahata plants himself there, without ever visiting the Totoro Studio. This contrast illustrates (in a good way I might add) the two directors' contrasting temperaments.

So I'm introduced to the production assistants, Mr. Kihara and Mr. Tanaka. They were very helpful later in showing me around the studio. I also met Miyazaki, who informs them that I am a familiar acquaintance. It felt good knowing he remembered me. The environment at the Totoro studio was serene and friendly. Instead of being divided by duties and responsibilities, the desks for staff supervisors of key animation and in-between animation are carefully combined. Apparently, the layout was based on their personal data, including blood type (a colored diagram was pasted on the wall). Handmade Totoro characters are placed in designated spots. It was such an endearing sight. Examining the sketches on the walls, I acquainted myself with the characters Satsuki and Mei. The country house I'd envisioned from the rough draft of the screenplay turned out to be more modern looking and brightly lit than I'd expected.

And while the figure lines for the previous animation films were drawn in black, I was struck by how they were brown for *My Neighbor Totoro* and *Grave of the Fireflies*. The blend between the characters and the backgrounds seemed all the more natural because of the brown. I was curious to find out how they would appear in action. I could see Satsuki and Mei puffing up their cheeks, running

[Original Story·Screenplay·Director] Hayao Miyazaki was born in 1941 in Tokyo. Miyazaki worked at Toei-Doga as an animator for films such as *The Adventures of Hols, Prince of the Sun* and *Puss in Boots*. He has directed *Lupin III: Castle of Cagliostro, Nausicaä of the Valley of the Wind* and *Castle in the Sky*, which were all awarded the Ofuji Noburo Prize.

around, and giggling.

I interviewed Miyazaki in the downstairs cafe. He began by discussing how both *My Neighbor Totoro* and *Grave of the Fireflies*, originally intended as medium-length films for a double-feature project, turned into feature-length films.

**Miyazaki (1):** The projected length of 70 minutes became 85 minutes. It was supposed to be a medium-length film, so I'd planned on using one girl as the protagonist. She would have to carry the story forward. But while we were depicting her everyday life, we realized the story required further configuration. So, for the sake of structure, we needed the girl to be quite naive but strong, yet dependable enough to endure a divided family. However, one side of her proved to be too immature, so we split this dichotomy into two characters. The story structure mandated that decision, but that's what also made the film run longer.

This may be good news to fans, but I'm sure it was no easy feat for the production staff.

**Miyazaki (2):** I knew the film right after *Castle in the Sky* had to be *My Neighbor Totoro*. I thought it was the perfect time. You go through transformations even in filmmaking. So in the context of my art, rather than film action scenes with laser beam attacks, I yearned to work on an animation with girls playing in the fields. And I wasn't the only one who felt this way. Apparently, the animators also felt "a little tired of doing action scenes." Everyone was contemplating what they should be working on instead. If the staff were focused, consistently coming up with good projects, then the animation industry would be in much better shape. Trouble was, there wasn't an abundance of good proposals.

After this rallying call to encourage younger artists, he discussed how the world of *My Neighbor Totoro* was set 30 years ago.

**Miyazaki (3):** While working on this film, I realized that details I normally wouldn't care about if the setting was either foreign or in an alternate world suddenly became quite important to me. For instance, you know how Japanese houses generally face south. If you stood in the garden, your shadow's direction would be set. Let's say it's May and the morning light pours into the house. In animation it's tough to determine accurate lighting. It was a challenge, and in some areas, we were lax [*laughs*]. During the summer the light will come in, but it wouldn't reach the veranda of most houses

because of the eaves, right? They're built to block off that hot sunray. As long as the house directly faces south and juts out a little to the west, the bright west sunlight before sunset won't enter the room. If the west sunlight did enter, you could lower the reed screen. There is a lot of wisdom to one's lifestyle. The west sunlight might be glaring on the street while you're standing in a dark room. That's the perfect image of a Japanese summer. There's no sense of season and cultural custom in Japanese films anymore partially because this kind of detail is almost entirely absent. Our cameraman Miyakawa made a similar observation, claiming, "They don't do this in TV dramas." In other words, the lighting is completely fluorescent. You can capture on film the type of season and time of day in a Japanese house without any exterior shots. By that, I mean you can express the season by taking into account detailed factors such as the length of light coming in and the contrast in light between the interiors and immediate exteriors of the house. It's important to depict this setting accurately because everyone shares this sense of season as a cultural custom, which can be communicated. In some ways we altered a few things, but in other ways, as we did here, I took pains to keep the artistic reality intact. Realistic lighting in film has been marred by the use of fluorescent lighting. Now this lighting is everywhere—inside the house, on the street, you can't escape it.

The interiors for the girls' house that I was shown at the studio faithfully depicted this kind of dark lighting. *My Neighbor Totoro* takes place 30 years ago, and this depiction has nostalgic overtones for viewers in the present [1988]. Given how faithfully *My Neighbor Totoro* represents that era, I hope its earnest warmth will touch the audience. Heated topics of discussion included Spielberg and Daiei's historical films. If *My Neighbor Totoro* becomes a masterpiece, then it will only be an inevitable result of the filmmakers' commitment to follow in the footsteps of their predecessors, and to stay true to the proper techniques that are no longer used in the art of film. Having observed various shooting locations for feature films, I have to say that this level of dedication is very rare with filmmakers (with the exception of a handful of young film directors).

Visiting their studios this time, I got the impression that an animation's shooting location occurs in the minds of the filmmakers. I felt as if I'd caught a glimpse of their intense struggle as they proceeded to express their original ideas (through trial and error) along with ones that actually went beyond the conceptual stage. The entire staff for

[Producer]
Toru Hara was born in 1935 in northern Kyushu. He was involved in production at Toei-Doga. In 1972, he founded Top Craft for joint film productions. Its first domestic theatrical film was *Nausicaä of the Valley of the Wind*. He has since produced other Ghibli films including *Castle in the Sky*, and the upcoming *My Neighbor Totoro* and *Grave of the Fireflies*.

*My Neighbor Totoro* had to face this challenge.

Surpassing each one's limits, each staff member rose to the occasion to realize his or her full potential. It's the environment here and talent sitting at each desk that will determine the effect these drawings will have on the real world.

There was a whirlwind of activity at the studio. Miyazaki made many thought-provoking observations other than the ones I've mentioned here. I also managed to interview other staff members. I wanted to see how this environment would evolve as the film neared its completion. It's not often that you get the chance to report on the making of a film such as *My Neighbor Totoro*.

**Staff Interview I**

Getting the busy staff to sit down for an interview in this tense studio environment was no easy task, but the key members graciously interrupted their work to answer my questions. As I viewed the completed film later, I recalled every single one of them.

---

### Year's Vacation Schedule

Let's work hard up until New Year's. Here is our upcoming schedule.
● This year ends Dec. 30.
● Resume work Jan. 4.

Studio Ghibli

P.S. Director Miyazaki will only be absent on New Year's Day, so his assistants must accompany him on all other days.

---

I found this notice posted on a door at Studio Ghibli's Studio Number Two in mid-December, during my coverage on the making of *My Neighbor Totoro*. I stared at the notice, once again realizing how dedicated they were to their art. It didn't matter that the New Year's holiday was approaching. *My Neighbor Totoro* comes straight from the hearts of the staff so dedicated they've given up their New Year's holiday. I was visiting the studio to interview them.

First I met with producer Toru Hara who has worked with Miyazaki ever since the Toei-Doga film *The Adventures of Hols, Prince of the Sun*. I asked him to comment on the film's origins and its crew.

"When we finished *Castle in the Sky*, we began discussing the next project for Studio Ghibli. All kinds of proposals were considered, but in the end *My Neighbor Totoro*, which Miya [Miyazaki] had wanted to make over the past 10 years, edged out the others. But initially, it was only supposed to be a 70-minute medium-length film. So we had to come up with a proposal for another film if we were going to make a double feature. I wasn't involved at all in that decision. In the end, Shinchosha offered to produce *Grave of the Fireflies*, which gave way to the double-feature project. They both started out as medium-length films, but as the staff worked on their storyboards the films became feature length. This was great for our viewers, but it was hell for the studio."

Takahata, the director of *Grave of the Fireflies*, and Miyazaki have collaborated together for many years. As a result, they requested the same staff members. As Miyazaki observed at a press conference, they actually had to wrangle over their staff members [*laughs*].

Even Toei-Doga had never released a double feature of two feature films. It wasn't hard to imagine the stress involved in producing both films simultaneously. Mr. Hara grimaced during the interview and took out a bag of prescription medicine, swallowing both pills and powder as if it was a regular treat. The gesture was enough to indicate the amount of stress he has endured since production started.

"Miyazaki's a hands-on manager. He directs the key animation while he draws. You know his tough-sergeant approach to animation? He's the hard-as-nails sergeant barking out orders at the trenches. You couldn't make any progress without a tough sergeant."

"Meanwhile, we had to hire an entirely new crew for *Grave of the Fireflies*. To make matters worse, the animation industry has become even more rigid. Even if there are freelance animators available, they're managed by production companies. You have to work with these various production companies to hire the right crew, which only increases our costs. On top of that, the members aren't familiar with each other, so forming the right staff is a challenge in itself."

Michiyo Yasuda supervises color design for both *My Neighbor Totoro* and *Grave of the Fireflies*. She has worked with Takahata and Miyazaki back when they were at Toei-Doga. She observes, "There were all kinds of people at Toei-Doga, but I was always amazed at Miyazaki's drawings and approach on the one hand, and Takahata's talents as a director on the other. They seemed incredibly unique." The

[Color Design]
Michiyo Yasuda was born on April 28. She began working for Toei-Doga in 1958. After working on *The Adventures of Hols, Prince of the Sun* and *Puss in Boots*, she left and worked on films such as *From the Apennines to the Andes*, *Conan, The Boy in Future*, *Nausicaä of the Valley of the Wind* and *Castle in the Sky*. She is the color design supervisor for Takahata Isao's *Grave of the Fireflies*.

color design supervisor is responsible for all the colors except background colors. Simultaneous supervision of two films must be difficult, but both directors adamantly insisted on her—a clear indication of their respect for her work.

"I do 'color designs according to the director's orders' [*laughs*]. I create colors to add life to the drawings and to communicate the director's intentions as much as possible.

"The work is difficult because Miyazaki is very clear and particular about what he wants. What I really find impressive is how, like when I'm assigning colors to natural objects such as water, he provides material that's tailor made to the right color designs. The color assignment itself may be off [*laughs*], but his drawings allow me to make the right color composition.

"I'm always struck by how positive I feel when I color Miyazaki's drawings. I realize how well the image is composed. Because he's enormously talented as an illustrator, he really takes those elements into account, which is quite extraordinary.

"Without comparing the two directors too much, I might also add that Takahata, the director of *Grave of the Fireflies*, is also very thorough in incorporating various elements. Yoshifumi Kondo's drawings are very creative, so the color designs come naturally. In that sense, I find both directors remarkable."

In order to bring out a soft tone in the overall color, they used brown carbon (the outlines are brown instead of black), and mixed original colors as well. Some of her assistants were only employed as recently as last year, and some even had no experience at all.

"You'll get decent results if you train the staff with a hands-on approach. They can realize their full potential once you share the essentials with them. They may not be great immediately, but they give their best. And even though they may be complaining, 'This is so hard,' I get the impression they really enjoy the work." [*laughs*]

Yasuda's kind and caring personality must have been crucial to the production of these two films, as well as *Nausicaä of the Valley of the Wind* and *Castle in the Sky*.

The suburbs of Tokyo in 1957, where Satsuki and Mei encounter Totoro, were still largely undeveloped. I interviewed the art director, Kazuo Oga (*Harmageddon, The Dagger of Kamui* and *The Time Travelers*) as he talked about his first opportunity to work with Miyazaki.

[Art Direction]
Kazuo Oga was born in 1952 in Akita Prefecture. He was hired by Shichiro Kobayashi's Kobayashi's Pro in 1972, drawing backgrounds and supervising art direction for animation including *Tomorrow's Joe 2, Unico*. He worked as the art director's assistant for films such as *Cobra, Harmageddon,* and *The Dagger of Kamui*. He was the art director of the films *Barefoot Gen, Fantastical Beast City,* and *The Time Travelers*.

"When we were kids we had rivers and forests in our neighborhood, so we'd catch fish or pick mushrooms. That was how we played outdoors. That was what we did for fun after school, so the world of Totoro came very naturally to me. I'm from Akita Prefecture, so even though Miyazaki is 10 years older than me, I don't feel much of a gap when we're trading childhood stories. I bet our childhood experiences overlap because there's about a 10-year gap in culture between Tokyo and Akita [ *laughs*]. The antiquated cultural aspects of Tokyo/Kanto also didn't seem odd at all.

"The background illustrators are having a really tough time—Totoro, the Cat Bus, and the big camphor tree at the top of the forest are all equally important. We're following everyday life without much artifice, so the backgrounds have to be 'as is'—and it's keeping things 'as is' that's so difficult. We're supposed to be experts, but as soon as we have to draw something like this, it's easy to fail. Even when you're just drawing a single leaf, it ends up looking too contrived if you elaborate too much, like deliberating over how it should droop. The essential thing is drawing things 'as is' in the simplest form possible.

"If the backgrounds appear natural, then we increase the chance of more comic images of Totoro and the Cat Bus blending naturally…as if they might really exist. At least that's what I'm hoping for [*laughs*].

"The backgrounds are the most delayed part of Totoro's production," Oga remarked with a grimace. Still, one look at the paintings is enough to see how these beautiful landscapes evoke a warm nostalgia. I wish Oga success in his endeavor to invigorate Totoro and the Cat Bus.

### Staff Interview II

The staff trusts Miyazaki's direction. This may not seem unusual, but I was thrilled to witness this level of commitment, which one rarely finds nowadays in live-action film productions. Although the reputation of *Nausicaä of the Valley of the Wind* and *Castle in the Sky* led to the success of *My Neighbor Totoro*, I believe the staff's dedication was equally crucial. I conducted the following interviews during the final stage of production.

I found several New Year's cards from children posted on a bulletin board by the entrance to Studio Ghibli's Number Two studio. Next to a cute illustration of Totoro, there's a message, "I'm definitely going to see *My Neighbor Totoro*." It's now 1988. The production is in the homestretch.

A handwritten, detailed schedule grid including shot numbers is posted where production assistants Tanaka, Kihara, and Kawabata work. The background/art staff shows up around 10 a.m., and the In Between/Clean Up Animation staff shows up for work around noon. Given how late they work every night (actually into the early morning) they must be exhausted. According to the progress report from last November, the final schedule was now complete with "every task scheduled in." There's an encouraging note: "Let's all work toward completing the film." But now this January's progress report reads: "It all comes down to how hard we work this month," along with "Let's make use of every precious hour and day." It's now a war zone.

I continued my series of interviews with the production staff. First, I interviewed supervising animator Yoshiharu Sato, who was incredibly cordial despite his apparent exhaustion.

—How late did you work yesterday?
**Sato:** Until around 3 a.m., I think. I try to stop around 2 a.m. at the latest, but…[*laughs*].
—Is this the first Miyazaki film you've worked on?
**Sato:** Yes, it is. I'd never met him before, so yes, this is my first time working for him.
—Where were you previously employed?
**Sato:** Nippon Animation. So this is the first time I've worked on a film production.
—Is it the sheer workload that makes the work difficult?
**Sato:** Sure, the volume is daunting, but the upside is realizing how much Miyazaki cares about his characters. Whether it's Satsuki or Mei, you have to make sure you can keep up with him and not get left behind. Once you start losing track, Miyazaki will request another take even if the only issue is a single facial expression.
—Do you feel like you've gotten the hang of things?
**Sato:** No, not at all [*laughs*]. I feel the same. One thing that kept me going with my last job was the thought of children—along with my own— watching my work. That kept my spirits high. I hope a lot of children come see it, and I hope it stays with them.
—How many shots per day are you completing?
**Sato:** Well, it's supposed to be seven, but last night we only got four done [*laughs*]…We're shooting for 40 shots per week, but Miyazaki warned us, "If you don't increase the shot per day ratio, we won't complete this film." Each day I start out thinking, "Hey, I have a feeling we'll get this done."
—I'm sure you have to be positive to get the job done.
**Sato:** If I start feeling negative, then the paintings will suffer too. I mean, I can't be lax about it, and I do think I'm dedicated.

This is also the first Miyazaki film for director's assistant Tetsuya Endo. I began the interview by inquiring about his work as a television anime director's assistant.
**Endo:** I would organize everything necessary for the shooting, making sure there were no mistakes. Once I've gone over every detail, I submit the work to be shot. In addition, once Miyazaki goes over the key frames and corrects the timing sheets, I organize the batch and submit it to the In Between/Clean Up Animation staff. When a problem arises, I contact the production staff or look up resources as well.
—Do you have to correct timing sheets often?
**Endo:** Almost every scene. The key animators are really talented, but Miyazaki has altered the timing of over 80 percent of their work. The storyboards can change, but Miyazaki himself might also redraw the key animation by expanding on it or reducing it. His method of adding and reducing is really astonishing. Also, submitting the animation for shooting is a meticulous process, so that can be really hard.
—Do you find any difference between TV animation and feature films?
**Endo:** A single film production is a huge undertaking. A lot of thought goes into it. Overall, I find that analytical process enjoyable. With a 30-minute TV program, you have to submit what you've got. However, working on this film made me realize how you could rework the material, analyze it, and make decisions along the way.

Endo himself joined this industry to become a film director. "The genre could be science fiction—it doesn't matter as long as I can make a warmhearted, sincere film." As for Miyazaki, he says, "I could never be that strong, both physically and mentally. He's so extraordinary; he's a source of inspiration." I look forward to Endo's work in the future.

During our interview, I realized something about production assistant Hirokazu Kihara. He looks a lot like Miyazaki. In fact, when he first started here many visitors and new employees mistook him for Miyazaki. I even heard he was nearly dispatched as Miyazaki's double for an award reception ceremony. Kihara, who has been a member of Miyazaki's staff ever since *Castle in the Sky*, described Miyazaki's amazing self-discipline.

[Supervising Animator] Yoshiharu Sato was born in 1957 in Kanagawa Prefecture. He was hired by Nippon Animation in 1979 to work on the masterpiece theater series, beginning with *Anne of Green Gables*. In 1986, he became the supervisor for character design/animation for *Tale of Pollyanna, Girl of Love,* whose cheerful heroine became widely popular. This is his first experience working on a feature film production.

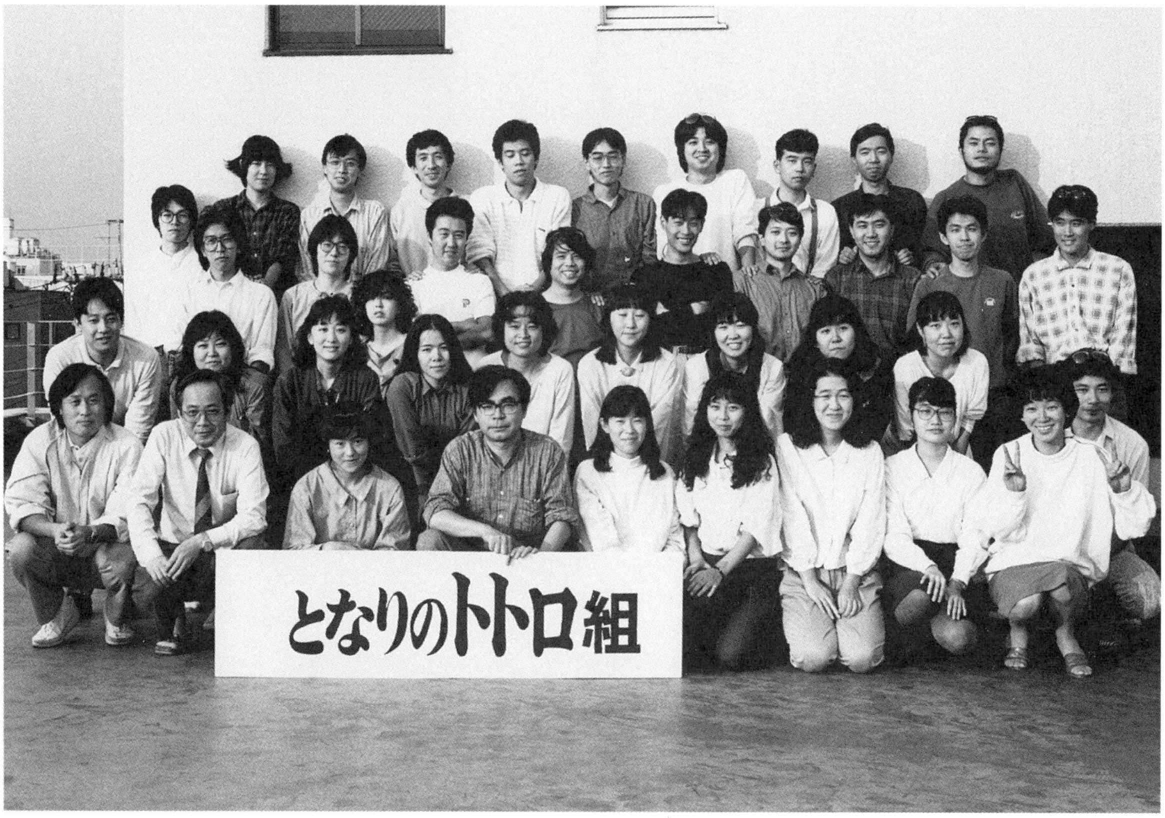
となりのトトロ組

Totoro Staff.

From lower left:
Takeshi Seyama (editing), Toru Hara (producer), Teruyo Tateyama + (ink and paint), Hayao Miyazaki (director), Kiyomi Ota (background), Hitomi Tateno (animation check), Kiyoko Sugawara (background), Hiromi Suzuki (in-betweener), Takayo + Mizutani (in-betweener), Yoshinori Kaneda (key animation)/Hiroshi Adachi (editing assistant), Masako Sakano (in-betweener), Yuka Endo (in-betweener), Makiko Niki (key animation), Kiyoko Makita (in-betweener), Emiko Iwayanagi (in-betweener), Ritsuko Shiina (in-betweener), Kumiko Oya (in-betweener), Shoko + Tejima (in-betweener), Shinji Otsuka (key animation), Toshiyuki Kawabata (production), Riwako Matsui (in-betweener), Nobuko Shinohara (key animation), Masaki Yoshizaki (background), Hirokazu Kihara (production), Katsuya Kondo (key animation), Masaaki Endo (key animation), Makoto Tanaka (key animation), Yoshiharu Sato (animator), Toshio Kawaguchi (key animation)/Yasuko Tachiki (animation check), Shinji Morohashi + (in-betweener), Kazuo Oga (art), Yoji Takeshige (background), Kazuyoshi Ozaki (in-betweener), Tetsuya Endo (director's assistant), Hiromi Yamakawa (key animation), Keiichiro Hattori (in-betweener), Hajime Matsuoka (background).

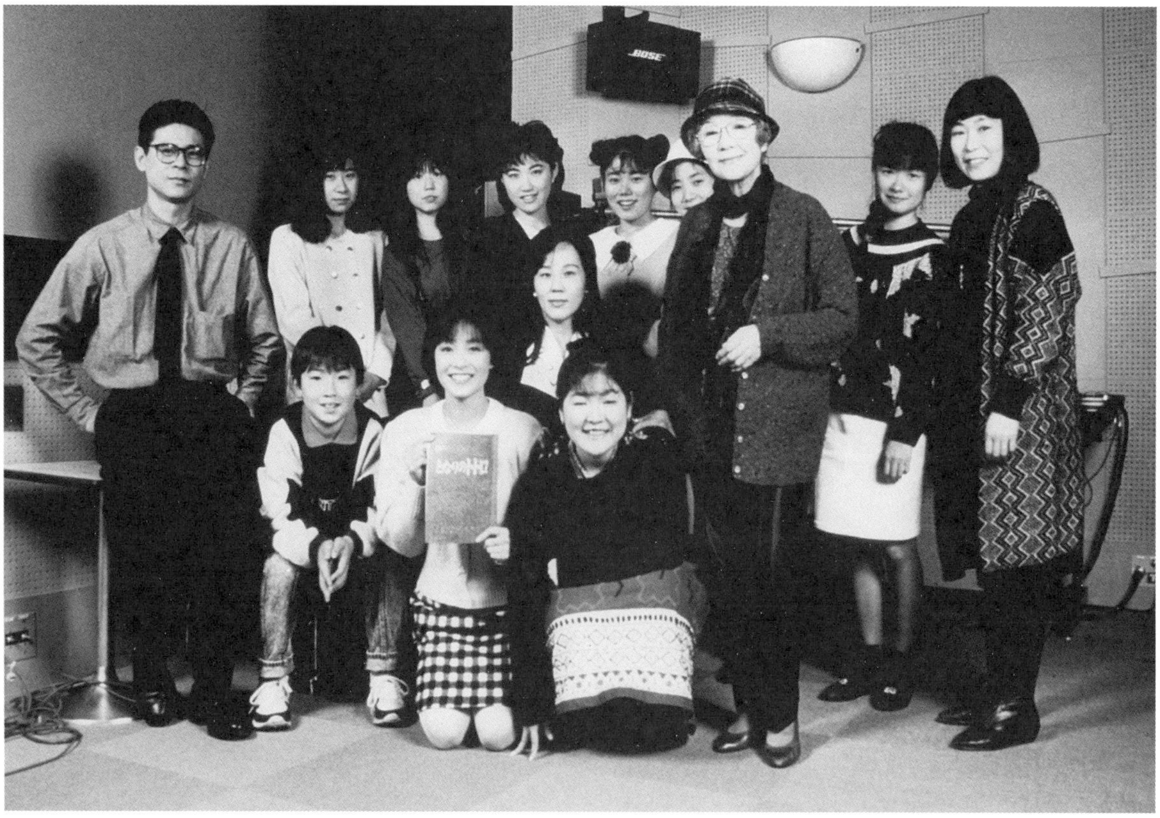
BOSE

Voice actors.

**Kihara:** There must be another Miyazaki inside him. One that says, "This is your daily quota," or "Come on, you have to get up early and go to work." He even applies a dose of human engineering to our work environment—figuring out the ideal lighting from outside, the best flow of work between staff members, and assigning desks according to our personalities. He's so thorough in every aspect. He never does something without a good reason. He's never whimsical. Even if he says something came spontaneously, it's based on some form of intuition or experience.

—That must be instrumental in his filmmaking.
**Kihara:** Yes, I think it is instrumental. He can see right through the barriers. I mean, I feel as if I'm clear as glass when I'm working with him. I even have this impression Miyazaki knows some staff members better than they do themselves. With his solid grasp of each staff member's talents, he can say, "You take care of this task." Some people have this impression that he has to correct everything and get involved with everything, but that's not what's going on. What he's doing is pushing the limits of each person's unique talent, so that if a certain aspect or assignment is even slightly short of perfection, he helps them complete the work—that's what his process is all about.

I also managed to interview color design assistant Nobuko Mizuta. Nobuko Mizuta assisted Michiyo Yasuda as a color design supervisor for *My Neighbor Totoro*. She encountered Yasuda's work in *Nausicaä of the Valley of the Wind*. "I was really struck by Yasuda's defined color designs. I admired her work so much that I told her I would love to have the opportunity to work with her." This request resulted in Mizuta's current position.

Mizuta's works reside next to Yasuda's at Studio Number One, where *Grave of the Fireflies* is currently being produced.

**Mizuta:** First, I assign colors for every scene. Yasuda gives me advice on the particular colors before we enter this stage. I'm still inexperienced, so I lack the expertise in discerning how a certain color will appear on film. So I'm learning about this process throughout the entire ink and paint process.

—What was the most difficult part?
**Mizuta:** The water scene where they're drawing water from the stream—water is transparent, so it's colorless, right? One approach was to have the surrounding colors reflected by the water, but that didn't quite work with Yasuda… I had the most fun working on water, but it also turned out to be the trickiest part.

She first began work on color designs with

*Arion*. "I knew so little, but the staff looked after me." This is the first time she's worked on a Miyazaki film.

**Mizuta:** Miyazaki doesn't like wishy-washy colors. If it's going to be dark, it has to be dark; if it's bright, it has to be bright.

—Could you elaborate on how you're drawn to Miyazaki and Yasuda's work?
**Mizuta:** Their work is so clear and concise. There's no compromise. They stand by their beliefs and work accordingly. It's really incredible. Having the chance to work with her, I really see how extraordinary she is compared to me. I really wish I could attain her level of mastery.

Her admiration is the source of inspiration for Mizuta's work. I can relate to her. I once met an extraordinary person I admired so much I felt like I wanted to pursue his line of work no matter how hard I had to struggle.

### Joe Hisaishi Interview

I interviewed the music director Hisaishi before he began composing his magnificent music for this film. Hisaishi fell ill from his grueling schedule after this interview. The music was incredibly moving, though, without a trace of this setback.

—I heard you were part of an ultra avant-garde contemporary music scene in your teens and 20s?
**Hisaishi:** I began playing minimal music in my teens. Most of my influences came from contemporary composers including Terry Riley, Phillip Glass, Steve Reich, Stockhausen and John Cage. As for Japanese composers, when I was a student, I studied Toru Takemitsu and Akira Miyoshi, analyzing their music scores.

—Is your background in classical music?
**Hisaishi:** Yes. If I were to trace my career back to my very first beginnings, it would be at the age of four when I began playing violin. You can't master classical music quickly. For example, you see how pianists begin their lessons at the age of four or five. The same holds for violinists. And dedication won't necessarily lead to mastery either [*laughs*]. The form requires a lot of time.

—On the other hand, with movie soundtracks, speed seems to be of the essence.
**Hisaishi:** I know what you mean. But I don't accept work that's like fast-food—"fast, cheap, and tasty." I don't take on work that can be finished in a day. I use the Fairlight (a computer sampling keyboard that processes real sounds and vocals) and other devices, so

my work takes a lot of time. Naturally, that translates to expensive, and I have to spend days holed up in the studio. On top of that, I hire a full orchestra in the final stage, so it's really quite involved.

When I was a budding composer in my 20s, I didn't have much work so I'd end up taking on work to the point where I was composing 70 songs in three days. I can compose quickly, but taking on work that's all "fast, cheap, and tasty" isn't good for me. So right now I turn down anyone who can't meet my budget requirement, which requires a production period of several weeks.

—If you include your work on the image album, you must spend a lot of time on Miyazaki's films...
**Hisaishi:** I do. It's...a lot of work [*laughs*]. But his work is so rich and personally compelling, it's very important to me. A Miyazaki film always becomes my top priority. I make room for it in my schedule. Everything else is secondary.

—Your music for the previous film *Castle in the Sky* was inspired by Irish folk songs. What was the music for *My Neighbor Totoro* based on then?

**Hisaishi:** Well...it's hard to say. I actually had a hard time with the music for *Castle in the Sky*. The love, romance, and adventure tale in that story is so foreign to me [*laughs*]. I tend to be more jaded. For example, I'm better at composing mature minor melodies. But it's not that easy to come up with a melody full of imagination, kindness, and warmth. It was quite an ordeal during the production. I was wondering what I should do when all of a sudden the story became even cuter [*laughs*]. I really felt like, "Oh, what do I do now?" On top of that, while I was producing the image album for *My Neighbor Totoro,* I had to work on the music for *ANZUCHI,* which was performed by Kenji Sawada and Koji Yokusho at the Saizon Theater (Ginza, Tokyo). So I had to inhabit this really dark, evil world on the one hand, and a totally innocent world on the other, which drove me a little crazy [*laughs*]. But it turned out to be a good learning experience.

—Have you seen the film rushes?
**Hisaishi:** The other day I saw several unsequenced segments spliced together.

—Did it help?
**Hisaishi:** Yes, it did. I'm sure this is going to be another extraordinary film. By putting emphasis on the melody, I felt like I could come up with something moving. There isn't really a plot-driven storyline.

—That's true. Plot is really crucial in *Nausicaä of the Valley of the Wind* and *Castle in the Sky*.
**Hisaishi:** That's right. There was a clear story. But this time, it's a day in the country. There's a subtle development in the story, so it's not large scale at all, which means I have to change my approach accordingly in contrast to my previous film music. I can't be very specific, but I want to approach it intuitively this time.

—Now that you have worked on three consecutive film projects with Miyazaki, I was wondering if you could share your impressions of him.
**Hisaishi:** His approach to life and his art, expressed through the medium of animation, correspond perfectly. He doesn't make films for the sake of filmmaking, or animation for the sake of animation. Animation—it doesn't even have to be animation because it's such a personal vision—is incorporated into his approach to life. So his approach is very clear. I have a lot of respect for him because of that.

The work can be really hard because there's no room for imperfections. At the same time, I can really grow a lot as a result of the work. The work is a struggle as much as it is a learning process. It also provides an opportunity for me to confirm my own identity, so I really cherish it.

In my profession, we have to produce a lot of material in a year. Some work we take on purely for the money. Others we do for different reasons. But there are several assignments every year to which we are drawn. Of those assignments, composing music for Miyazaki's films is the most important work for me.

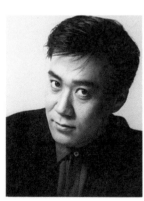

[Music]
Joe Hisaishi was born in 1950. After composing music for *Nausicaä of the Valley of the Wind*, he became an active film soundtrack composer. He has composed animation soundtracks for TV series including *Clever Sarutobi*, *Genesis Climber Mospeada*, and the animation films *Arion* and *Castle in the Sky*. He has also composed film soundtracks for *The Tragedy of W*, *Spring Bell*, *The Time for Lovers*, *The Drifting Classroom*, and *The Story of this Love*.

## Totoro Cries—Voice-Over Recording

I had the chance to observe the voice-over production for two days. I was thrilled as the film came to life with these overdubbed voices. The best part for me, though, was watching Totoro come to life.

"URRR! AHHH URR!" The studio booms with Totoro's voice. Hitoshi Takagi shakes his entire body to emulate the strange creature Totoro. He's become Totoro.

"If I have to get the part down quickly, my entire body has to be into it. Whether it's Totoro being happy or sad, the emotion has to be in the delivery of my voice. I can't say, "mom" or "dad." I can only work with "ahh, ahh." So it's like I'm a baby who can only babble. There's no restraint here, nothing superfluous." (Takagi)

Takagi first worked as a shingeki actor. He appeared in Akira Kurosawa's *Throne of Blood* and

Shohei Imamura's *My Second Brother,* as well as countless plays. He has since become a veteran voice actor, having once played Papa Moomin. Now he's creating Totoro's voice.

"I'm really enjoying this. My voice has to reach beyond words. I have to express the emotions of a porgy fish on a cutting board or a cat on a hot tin roof [*laughs*]. I am honored to play such an important character." (Takagi)

The voice-overs for *My Neighbor Totoro* are being recorded at Tokyo TV Center in Hamamachi, Nihonbashi (Tokyo) at the beginning of March. The voice actors breathe life into the projected film in front of them. I have the opportunity to observe them through the window of the control room. It really feels like the film is approaching completion. The audio director, Shigeharu Shiba, who also worked with Miyazaki on *Nausicaä of the Valley of the Wind* and *Castle in the Sky,* gives detailed instructions for each line. Sometimes he enters the studio room to elucidate the characters' thoughts and emotions for each voice actor. Miyazaki also joins him, explaining, "The intonation here should be like this."

I knew the silent moving images for *My Neighbor Totoro* were extraordinary on their own. It wasn't just because I spent six months observing the production; I was amazed by the intensity of the images. Now once again, without any bias, I was absolutely convinced *My Neighbor Totoro* was going to be a masterpiece.

Noriko Hidaka, the voice actor for Minami in *Touch* plays Satsuki. Chika Sakamoto, the voice actor for Kentaro in *Maison Ikkoku,* plays Mei. This is the first time Hidaka has worked on a Miyazaki film. Sakamoto played the anonymous lookout kid on Prince Asbel's vessel in *Nausicaä of the Valley of the Wind*—you know, the one who says, "Give the password!" During the scene where Satsuki and Mei romp around their new house, the two women played their roles as if they might crash into the screen—it was really an amazing sight.

This is the first time Hidaka has played a child.

"Because the animation is so natural, I don't need to use baby talk to emulate a child's voice. I played the role recalling my own childhood. I had two brothers, and since I was the oldest, I was a bit of a tomboy as a kid. So that was perfect for playing Satsuki. But the boy who played Kanta is a real boy in elementary school, so that was hard [*laughs*]. Every time he spoke, I felt like, "Oh you can act the part without even trying [*laughs*]."

Sakamoto, who plays Mei, observes, "I end up trying to speak with a cute voice because it's a girl's part, but then I'm told my voice should be groggier,

that I should be more of a tomboy." Everyone says I look a lot like Mei, which makes me feel a little funny [*laughs*]."

I looked beyond the control room window as Sakamoto, her hair just like Mei's, breathed life into her character.

The father was played by—wow!—Shigesato Itoi.

"Voice-overs are hard. There's a lot of tension, as if I'm in a batting cage, swinging against a fastball. Also, I couldn't hide my lisp [*laughs*]. Most people can't tell, but I can't pronounce 'ra ri ru re ro.' But there was no way I could hide it with all these instructions and corrections on my delivery."

Itoi was bantering about during his breaks, making everyone feel comfortable in the studio. His caring personality seems to be a perfect match for the character of the girls' father.

Sumi Shimamoto, who plays the mother, is an actor so dear to Miyazaki fans that her performances have moved them to tears.

"The images have a nostalgic feel. They're soothing, perhaps because there aren't any battle scenes as there were in *Nausicaä of the Valley of the Wind*. The film seems warm and light-hearted. I like that." (Shimamoto)

Tanie Kitabayashi, who plays Granny, has been a prominent actor in film and theater. Her enthusiasm was infectious. Her performance was so good everyone just nodded in admiration during the session.

"I have a hard time with noisy animation. When that kind of show appears on TV, I yell 'Shut up!' and turn it off [*laughs*]. When I was offered this role, I read the screenplay by Miyazaki, whose *Nausicaä of the Valley of the Wind* was quite wonderful. I saw how incredibly poetic and imaginative it was. It was a beautiful story. So I gladly agreed to play the role."

With regard to the animation, Kitabayashi states, "I really like the Cheshire cat in *Alice in Wonderland,* but then a cat like that showed up as a bus, which really cracked me up [*laughs*]. I'm sure he was thinking of Cheshire cats when he worked on it. The film had all these poetic aspects. The idea for the film itself was very cute. I'm certain it will be one of my favorites."

But was the Cat Bus really based on a Cheshire cat?!

## Finishing the Report

It was July 7 of last year that I received a phone call from the editorial department's Funano offering me the assignment of Studio Ghibli's production of *My Neighbor Totoro* and *Grave of the Fireflies*. I also met with the chief editor Suzuki to discuss the project. How could I forget that day?

[Audio Director]
Shigeharu Shiba was born in 1934. He first worked in live theater and then moved onto overdubbing foreign films, eventually becoming an audio director for animation. He has worked on other Miyazaki films, including *Nausicaä of the Valley of the Wind* and *Castle in the Sky,* as well as Mamoru Oshii's *Uruseiyatsura* and *Angel's Egg*. He also worked on the live action feature film, *Teito Story* .

I gladly accepted the assignment assuming it wouldn't require more than a single visit, but as it turned out the report was serialized for half a year up until the film was released. I had no idea this could happen. I remember feeling as if I were in a dream.

Having been a huge fan of Miyazaki's work ever since *Nausicaä of the Valley of the Wind* and *Castle in the Sky* (or to go back further, Takahata's *The Adventures of Hols, Prince of the Sun,* which included Miyazaki's key animation), I couldn't believe how fortunate I was to be reporting on these two films, which were nearing completion.

I held back my urge to laugh gleefully, pretending the work was grueling as I began working on this serialized report. A reporter basically has to be an observer, but I couldn't just be any observer. I had to be committed, always assuming the perspective of a film buff.

I wrote at the beginning that the task was difficult because there's no real shooting to observe the way there is in live-action film productions. Animation comes from the brush strokes of the staff poring over their desks. So I ended up interviewing as many of them as I could, beginning with director Miyazaki. Each member's concept of the film would come together, synthesized into a concrete work—I wanted to trace that flow, although I'm not sure I entirely succeeded.

One thing I know for sure is that *My Neighbor Totoro* is a sunny story, and its twin feature, *Grave of the Fireflies,* is dark. The double feature provides quite a contrast. The images I got to see during my coverage of both films were very powerful, and my conviction that both films were going to be extraordinary never faltered. I didn't expect that the process of interviewing these people so committed to the creation of a wonderful film would actually end up inspiring me. I would like to thank all the staff members from both films for their cooperation, assistance, and willingness to participate in my interviews in spite of their demanding schedule.

A wonderful film inspires hope and faith in its makers and its audience.

March 28. *My Neighbor Totoro* hasn't been completed yet. I know the story. I've read the script and seen some of the rushes, but my interest hasn't waned at all. If anything, I'm even more excited. Francois Truffaut, who directed *Day For Night* and *The 400 Blows,* once observed, "A magnificent film gives you the impression it's opening a door. It gives you the impression that this is where film itself begins, this is where film is being newly born." I'm certain that's the kind of film *My Neighbor Totoro* will be.

[Writer]
Masaaki Nomura was born in 1954 in Yamaguchi Prefecture. After working in Toei Foreign Films' publicity department, he became a film critic. He has written for magazines such as *Cinema Report, City Road,* and *Playboy.* He is the co-author of *Cinema Album/A Movie Nobuhiko Obayashi* and *Cinema—Film Buff Land.*

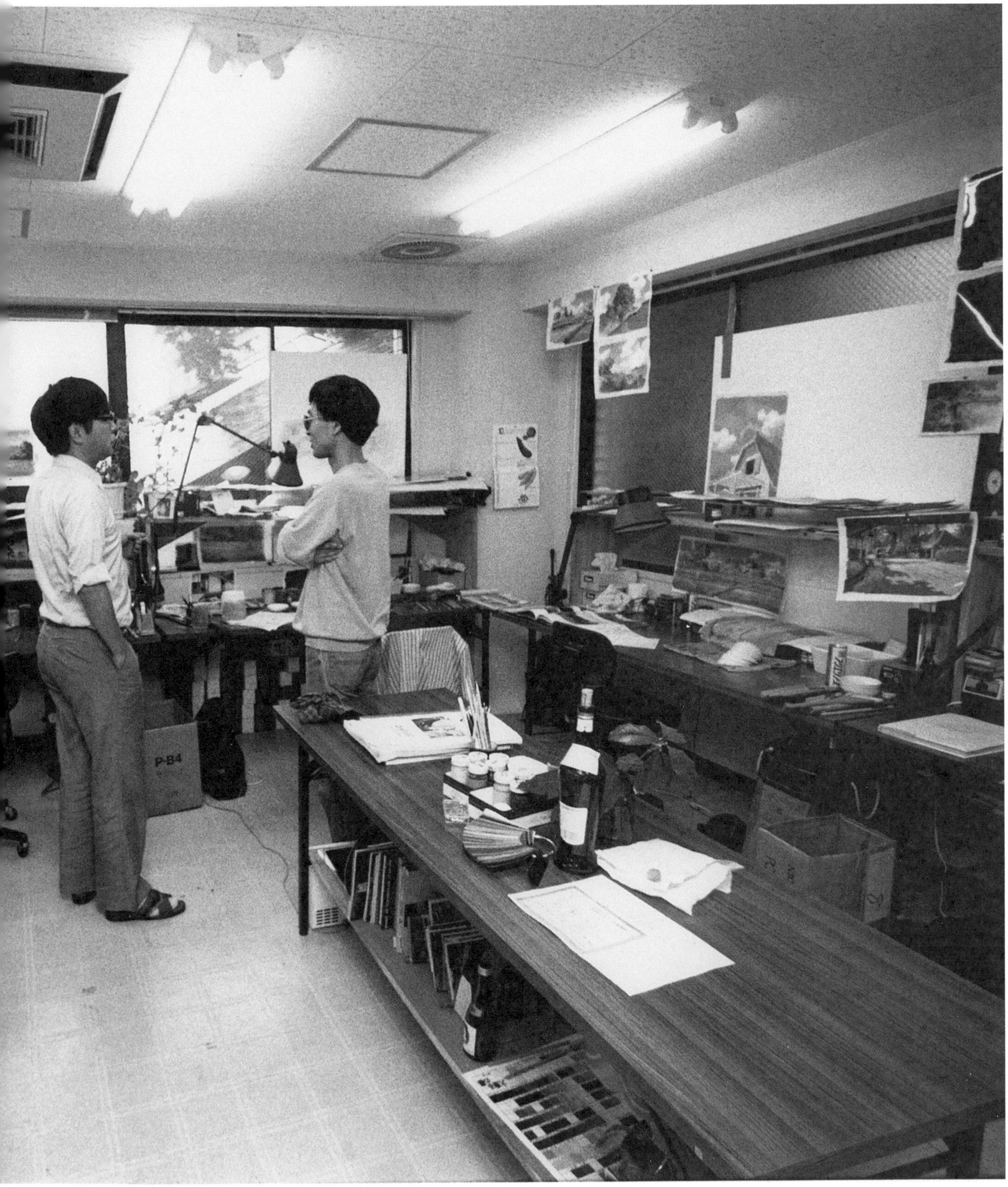
P-B4

# CREDITS

EXECUTIVE PRODUCER
Yasuyoshi Tokuma

ASSOCIATE EXECUTIVE PRODUCERS
Tatsumi Yamashita
Hideo Ogata

SUPERVISING ANIMATOR
Yoshiharu Sato

ART DIRECTION
Kazuo Oga

MUSIC
Joe Hisaishi

KEY ANIMATION
Tsukasa Tannai
Shinji Otsuka
Masako Shinohara
Masaaki Endo
Toshio Kawaguchi
Makoto Tanaka
Yoshinori Kanada
Katsuya Kondo
Makiko Futaki
Hiroomi Yamakawa
Hideko Tagawa

BACKGROUNDS
Hajime Matsuoka
Toshio Nozaki
Kiyomi Ota
Masaki Yoshizaki
Yoji Takeshige
Kiyoko Sugawara

COLOR DESIGN
Michiyo Yasuda

CAMERA SUPERVISOR
Hisao Shirai

EDITING
Takeshi Seyama

ANIMATION CHECK
Yasuko Tachiki
Hitomi Tateno

COLOR DESIGN ASSISTANT
Nobuko Mizuta

INK AND PAINT CHECK
Masae Motohashi

AUDIO DIRECTOR
Shigeharu Shiba

RECORDING AND SOUND MIXING
Shuji Inoue

SOUND EFFECTS
Kazutoshi Sato

PRODUCTION MANAGER
Eiko Tanaka

PRODUCTION DESK
Hirokatsu Kihara
Toshiyuki Kawabata

ASSISTANT TO THE DIRECTOR
Tetsuya Endo

VOICES (Original Japanese version)
Noriko Hidaka
Chika Sakamoto
Shigesato Itoi
Sumi Shimamoto
Tanie Kitabayashi

Hitoshi Takagi
Hiroko Maruyama
Machiko Washio
Reiko Suzuki
Tadashi Hirose
Toshiyuki Amagasa
Shigeru Chiba

Naoki Tatsuta
Tarako
Tomohiro Nishimura
Mitsuko Ishida
Chie Kojiro
Taiju Nakamura
Yuko Mizutani
Akiko Hiramatsu
Ikue Otani

SONGS
"Sampo"
LYRICS by
Rieko Nakagawa
"Tonari no Totoro"
LYRICS by
Hayao Miyazaki
MUSIC COMPOSITION AND ARRANGEMENT
by Joe Hisaishi
PERFORMANCE
Azumi Inoue

KEY ANIMATION SUPPORT
Mad House
Nobumasa Shinkawa
Yutaka Okamura
Masaaki Kudo

INK AND PAINT CHECK
Teruyo Tateyama
Kenji Narita
Miwako Nakamura

SPECIAL EFFECTS
Kaoru Tanifuji

IN-BETWEEN / CLEAN-UP ANIMATION
Masako Sakano
Komasa
Shinji Morohashi
Kumiko Otani
Kiyoko Makita
Ritsuko Tanaka

Riwako Matsui
Keiichiro Hattori
Kiyo Mizutani
Ritsuko Shiina
Yuka Endo
Kazutaka Ozaki
Akiko Teshima
Emiko Iwayanagi
Nagisa Miyazaki
Yukari Maeda
Naoko Takenawa
Kazumi Okabe
Rie Niidome
Masakazu Okada
Aki Yamagata
Kyoko Higurashi
Keiko Watanabe
Kazuko Fukutomi

Studio Fantasia
Hajime Yoshida
Junichi Nagano
Masayuki Ota
Naoki Kitamura
Tsuyoshi Yamamoto

Anime Torotoro
Yukari Yamaura
Koji Ito
Akiko Ishii
Tadateru Kawamura

Dragon Production

INK AND PAINT
Studio Killy
Toshichika Iwakiri
Michiko Nishimaki
Naomi Takahashi
Nobuko Watanabe
Mayumi Watabe
Michiko Ode
Chiyomi Morisawa
Hisako Yoshida
Noriko Yamamura
Naoko Okawa
Yuriko Kudo
Yuki Takagi
Tokuko Harada
Toyoko Kajita
Fujino Komei
Aiko Takahashi
Toki Yanagi
Miyoko Oka
Fumi Yamane
Hatsue Tanaka
Michiko Ota
Junko Adachi
Yoko Fujino
Yoshiko Murata

INK AND PAINT
Studio Step
Yuki Kyono
Tomoko Asahi
Hiromi Hanawa
Yorimi Sawauchi
Reiko Suzuki
Reiko Shibuya
Hiroe Takekura
Studio Runrun
Domusha
Studio Beam
Studio Hibari

Kyoei Production
Reiko Suzuki
Reiko Shibuya
Group Joy
Trans Arts

BACKGROUNDS
Kobayashi Production
Shinji Kimura
Makoto Shiraishi
Nobuhiro Otsuka
Sadahiko Tanaka
Yuko Matsuura

Atelier Bwca
Hidetoshi Kaneko
Keiko Tamura
Tsuyoshi Matsumuro

Akira Yamakawa
Junko Ina

CAMERA
Studio Cosmos
Yoichi Kuroda
Motoaki Ikegami
Katsunori Maehara
Noriko Suzuki
Tetsuo Ofuji
Kiyoshi Saeki
Kazumi Iketani
Hiroshi Noguchi
Hiroshi Ito
Mitsuko Nanba
Tomoko Sugiyama
Katsuji Suzuki
Shinji Ikegami

PRODUCTION ASSISTANTS
Hiroyuki Ito
Takaaki Suzuki

EDITING ASSISTANT
Hiroshi Adachi

TITLES
Takagu Atelier

INK AND PAINT TECHNICAL COOPERATION
Josai Duplo
Mamoru Murao

MEDIA SUPPORT
Tokuma Shoten
"Animage" Editorial Department

SOUND EFFECTS ASSISTANT
Hironori Ono

DIALOGUE EDITING
Akira Ida

ASSISTANT AUDIO DIRECTOR
Naoko Asari

RECORDING STAFF
Makoto Sumiya
Koji Fukushima

Mutsuyoshi Otani

AUDIO RECORDING
Omnibus Promotion

MUSIC PRODUCTION
Mitsunori Miura
Takashi Watanabe
Tokuma Japan Co.

RECORDING STUDIO
Tokyo T.V. Center

FILM DEVELOPING
Tokyo Laboratory

PUBLICITY SUPPORT
Hakuhodo Inc.

TECHNICAL COOPERATION
Continental Far East Inc.
Mikio Mori

"My Neighbor Totoro" PRODUCTION COMMITTEE
Tokuma Shoten
Hiroyuki Kato
Toshio Suzuki
Akira Kaneko
Osamu Kameyama
Masahiro Kasuya
Hikogoro Shiraishi
Minoru Tadokoro
Hisayoshi Odaka
Tsutomu Otsuka
Tomoko Kobayashi
Takao Sasaki
Michio Yokoo
Shigeru Aso
Yoshio Tsuboike
Tetsuhiko Yoshida

PRODUCTION
Studio Ghibli

PRODUCER
Toru Hara

ORIGINAL STORY, SCREENPLAY WRITTEN AND DIRECTED by
Hayao Miyazaki

# THE ART OF My Neighbor TOTORO

BASED ON THE STUDIO GHIBLI FILM

ORIGINAL STORY AND SCREENPLAY WRITTEN AND DIRECTED BY
HAYAO MIYAZAKI

English Adaptation/Yuji Oniki
Design & Layout/Izumi Evers
Editor/Michelle Pangilinan


First published in Japan by Tokuma Shoten Co., Ltd.

This book was originally published in Japan in 1988. The interviews, creator profiles, and other contents of the book are current for that publication date only.



Printed in China

Published by VIZ Media, LLC
P.O. Box 77010
San Francisco, CA 94107

First printing, October 2005
Ninth printing, March 2019

Visit www.viz.com

VIZ media